WITHDRAWN

STUDIES ON VOLTAIRE AND
THE EIGHTEENTH CENTURY

363

Manuscripts (two copies with a brief summary)
should be submitted to the
Voltaire Foundation
99 Banbury Road, Oxford OX2 6JX, U.K.

For further information about *Studies on Voltaire*
and other publications see
http://www.voltaire.ox.ac.uk/

WALTER E. REX

Diderot's counterpoints

The dynamics of contrariety
in his major works

VOLTAIRE FOUNDATION

OXFORD

1998

ISSN 0435-2866
ISBN 0 7294 0620 2

Voltaire Foundation Ltd
99 Banbury Road
Oxford OX2 6JX

A catalogue record for this book is
available from the British Library

Printed in England at The Alden Press, Oxford
Bound at Green Street Bindery, Oxford

In memory of my mentors

Jean Seznec
Herbert Dieckmann

Contents

Illustrations

Acknowledgements

EARLIER versions of three chapters have previously appeared in print as follows: 'Contrariety in the *Supplément au Voyage de Bougainville*', *Diderot studies* 27 (1998), p.149-68; 'The landscape demythologised: from Poussin's serpents to Fénelon's "shades" and Diderot's "ghost"', *Eighteenth-century studies* 30 (1997), p.401-19; 'Diderot contre Greuze', *Recherches sur Diderot et sur l'Encyclopédie* 24 (1998), p.7-25.

The author and publishers are grateful to the following for permission to reproduce paintings and drawings in their possession: © La Réunion des musées nationaux: Louis Michel Van Loo, *Portrait de M. Diderot*; Carl Van Loo, *Portrait de Mme Van Loo*; Nicolas Poussin, *Orphée et Eurydice*; Jean-Baptiste Greuze, *Le Fils ingrat* and *Le Mauvais fils puni*; Watteau de Lille, 'Le Violoneux'. National Gallery of London: Nicolas Poussin, '*Paysage avec un homme tué par'un serpent* (painting). Courtesy of the Editors of *Diderot studies*: Jean-Baptiste Garand, *Portrait de Diderot* (cover). © The Sterling and Francine Clark Art Institute, Williamstown, Mass.: Joseph Vernet, *Clair de lune*.

Preface

DIDEROT'S place in the eighteenth century as the most audacious, intriguing and probably also the most beloved of the *philosophes* is so solidly established one can scarcely believe it was not always so, that most of his reputation dates only from the late 1940s. Before that Diderot was traditionally seen – a tradition reaching in part back to his own century – as an important, in fact a great figure who, paradoxically, had never written anything of lasting significance. In the USA, even at Harvard, later to become a major centre of Diderot studies through the simultaneous presence of Herbert Dieckmann and Jean Seznec, the great encyclopedist never appeared on the reading lists of undergraduate survey courses – prior to the arrival of these scholars. Though students dutifully learned who Diderot was, they did not read him. For that matter, if one lined up all the significant books ever written about Diderot until then, the row occupied just one medium-sized bookshelf – about the same space currently taken up by the books and articles published on him every few years. Certainly it is true that, already in the nineteenth century, some of the greatest creative minds – Baudelaire, Balzac, Stendhal, Nerval, Goethe, Hegel, E. T. A. Hoffmann, Marx, to mention just a few – had enthusiastically recognised Diderot's genius. And in France individual scholars had been devoting their lives to him – but nothing like the number working on Rousseau, or Voltaire. It would take generations for the scholarly world and the serious reading public to catch up.

Diderot's time would come only much later, after the world had become – no doubt through Marx and Freud – more experienced, possibly more sophisticated, sadder, wiser. He would have his day only in the aftermath of World War II, and obviously his popularity happened for all the complicated and innumerable reasons events do when they combine historically to create a moment whose time has come. It is tempting to find connections between the post-war Diderot phenomenon and the politics of the late conflict, for some of the greatest Diderot scholars in France had been prominent anti-Fascists, starting with Franco Venturi, and later one finds among their numbers refugees from the war. One of the prime movers was Herbert Dieckmann, whose inventory of the Diderot manuscripts of the Fonds Vandeul (1951) suggested the possibility of rediscovering Diderot from the ground up, on the basis of new textual understandings. At Columbia University, the founding of *Diderot studies* in 1949 inaugurated an international forum for Diderot specialists. 1955 saw the start of Georges Roth's masterful edition of the *Correspondance*. Jean Seznec's edition of the *Salons*, another heroic enterprise, began publication in 1957 – which was also the date of the first volume of Arthur Wilson's monumental biography, to be entitled *Diderot*, the work of a lifetime, and which would subsume virtually all of the documentary researches that had gone before. Robert Niklaus's collations of the *Pensées philosophiques* appeared in 1950; Roland Mortier's classic *Diderot en Allemagne* was published in 1954; Jacques Proust's great study, *Diderot et l'Encyclopédie*, dates from 1966; after almost twenty years of preparation, R. N. Schwab's seven-volume *Inventory of Diderot's 'Encyclopédie'* was launched in 1972. Thanks to efforts such as these – and of course the above list is the barest sampling of an infinitely richer reality – textually and factually Diderot's future was secure.

If one had to choose a single quality most responsible for this newly found popularity, perhaps, above all, it was the informality of Diderot's genius that made him so appealing to the modern world: that he would sit for his portrait, and write with his pen, in wigless attire and without the literary conventions – Voltaire's indispensable *bienséances*, Rousseau's gestures towards Latin sentence structures, the bourgeois decency of Rousseau's vocabulary – and (apparently) let his thoughts flow unrestrained, almost as if he did not need a persona in order to write. The appeal was also, needless to say, in the freshness of his insights which, sexually, morally, aesthetically and in terms of the dynamics of human thought and behaviour speak to us today with an intensity unlike anyone else's in Diderot's time.

All this, and much more, awaited discovery in 1950. The boundaries of Diderot's thought were still unknown, his political ideas virtually a blank; even his theatrical theories awaited elucidation. And fortunately, in the miraculously favorable seedbed of the post-war era, not only were learned and dedicated individuals waiting to take up the task, but eventually even teams of scholars became cooperatively engaged, so that for almost half a century Diderot's works have been textually revised, analysed and researched. One might have imagined that, by now, the main points had been revealed and agreed upon, and scholars would be turning to other things. But of course such is not the case: the Diderot phenomenon goes right on, as if all questions still remained open and unexplored.

The explanation lies not merely in the indigenous perversity of scholars, but, I believe, in certain uniquely curious qualities in the way Diderot thought and wrote, and that make agreement about him extremely difficult, next to impossible. One of the classic examples in this connection is H. R. Jauss's 1984 article, '*Le Neveu de Rameau*: Dialogique et dialectique (ou, Diderot lecteur de Socrate et Hegel lecteur de Diderot)'.[1] Before supplying his own interpretation, the author lists about ten scholars, including some of the most illustrious ones in France and abroad, who had previously written on this topic, and in extremely skilful résumés he situates their various opinions, revealing the differences between them, and pointing out any weaknesses that occur. He then gives his own interpretation, which supposedly carries the day. And in fact this is one of the most searching and erudite discussions of *Le Neveu de Rameau* ever written; it ranges widely over some of the most important and difficult topics, and proposes ideas from which we can profit, even if we ultimately decide not to concur with them. And in the present context this last is the main point: Professor Jauss has written an excellent, indeed a profound, article that, to various degrees, takes issue with his predecessors. But his own brilliantly paradoxical interpretations are just as debatable as the ten arguments he is refuting, completing or correcting. Indeed some aspects of his main proposals have already been ignored or rejected by the majority of Diderot scholars. Where there had been ten disagreements, Professor Jauss makes it eleven.

No doubt *Le Neveu de Rameau* is a special case, more ambiguously obscure than anything else Diderot wrote, but even so it simply magnifies problems that are inherently found in many other texts – in the *Salons*, in the *Supplément au Voyage de Bougainville* and the *Contes*, in *Jacques le fataliste* and *La Religieuse*, in the *Correspondance*, everywhere perhaps except in the 'scientific' writings: not only is it generally impossible to say the final word about them, sometimes it is even hard to pick out the main theme(s) or to be sure of Diderot's intent in creating them. Except for the *drames*, his writings are apt to do without the objectively given structures that are typical of neo-Classicism and that one might have expected from someone pleased to think of himself as a philosopher, not to say *encyclopédiste*. But particularly in the works that are not intentionally didactic, Diderot's structures have a way of being generated not objectively from without, but subjectively from within. Furthermore, his ideas may evolve in ways that are not rational.

Traditional studies on Diderot have tended to overlook, or even to reject, implicitly or explicitly, the last two points. To locate the generating forces of Diderot's creations scholars have usually appealed to elements located essentially on the outside, rather than to inner workings: they have turned to literary 'sources', or traditions of genre, or personal experiences, or given ideas, or personality traits. They have not seen how much his works may be obeying pressures produced, so to speak, autonomously. Above all, scholars have

---

1. *Revue de métaphysique et morale* 89 (1984), p.143-81.

wanted to believe that Diderot's arguments are coherent: that they move forward in straight lines and 'make sense'; that when Diderot states something passionately, the idea he enunciates will henceforth remain stable and constant; that one can speak of 'his thought' on such and such an issue because his ideas represent certain values that can be ascertained objectively and add up to form a doctrine. The present study will challenge all these notions: only incidentally will it take 'sources' and literary traditions into account, and instead of analysing Diderot's ideas according to an assumption of coherent doctrines, it will propose that his ideas travel via illogic and disjunctions.

If Diderot has provoked so much disagreement, perhaps one of the under-lying causes has been a failure to come to terms with the elements of disunity in his thinking processes; the fault has been the general postulate that ideas are not comprehensible – not to mention philosophically acceptable – unless they are coherent, and that Diderot's writings should be analysed accordingly. My reading of Diderot bypasses such suppositions, and instead brings to the fore the most blatant kind of logical disjunction: the contradiction – or contrariety, to put the idea more philosophically. The justification for such a move is simply stated: in Diderot, the positive enunciation of a concept frequently (though by no means always) leads to the denial of that concept. The mere proposal with approval may bring Diderot to see, in counterpoint, the other side of the argument, the negative, which can then become the main element of his discourse – often without even the slightest warning to the reader that he has reversed himself or turned things upside down. The process is a dynamic one, in which enunciations, or occasionally whole modes of discourse, assume their character and shape by pushing against, and even denying, what precedes them, somewhat the way voices in musical counterpoint may be conceived as doing. This phenomenon in Diderot is frequent and important, sometimes dominating the way his ideas, or modes of thought, are linked together, to the point that they may form several chains of reactions. This is why I will claim in a number of instances that his structures are generated from within: they are generated from within by contrariety.

Much else relating to the contrapuntal structure of Diderot's discourse is implied in this hypothesis, no doubt; and Diderot texts do not all proceed via a series of reversals: many kinds of contrapuntal responses are discernible in Diderot's writings. But the following chapters will explore the most dramatic and interesting of them, and do so in considerable detail – by necessity. For it is not possible to give a simple overview of such diverse shiftings as will be recorded in these texts. Moreover, these intricate and immediate impulses which trigger the conception of Diderot's ideas – whether by affirmation or negation – are among the most precious qualities of Diderot's art as a writer, since they are, in the most literal and essential sense, the vitality of the text.

In 1948, Leo Spitzer, another notable refugee from Fascism, published in English translation one of the most influential articles on Diderot ever written.[2] He pointed out something about Diderot's style which no one had noticed, or at least ever written about, before: that Diderot's manner of writing is exceptional among the *philosophes* in that his words and rhythms mimic the objects they describe or the experiences they relate; in other words, that Diderot's style is uniquely onomatopoeic. Spitzer's famous demonstration revealed how the erotic rhythms of Diderot's text fittingly orchestrate the *Encyclopédie* article 'Jouissance'. Not only did his insight open the way for unexpected comparisons with Rabelais and even Joyce, it altered fundamentally the way everyone read Diderot. Once the reader was alerted to the aural and rhythmic dimension Spitzer had suggested, Diderot's texts would never be the same again. An awareness of the dynamics of contrariety in Diderot's writing processes may have a similar effect: it can alter essentially the way we define him.

The following pages propose radically new readings of most of Diderot's major works,[3] readings that take into account unexplored tensions and pressures in the texts, and which also reflect my own enjoyment as I rediscovered the hidden energies of Diderot's dynamics. I am not aware of anyone else who has focused specifically on contrariety as a general approach to Diderot. As the footnotes suggest, however, in recent years enough scholars have been studying various sorts of disjunction in his works to signify an authentic trend in the direction of the method I will employ.

Diderot's mental operations appear to be, in respect to contrariety, unique among the *philosophes*: no one else thought the way he did. Nevertheless, one encounters other authors in both the seventeenth and eighteenth centuries whose literary creations were informed by a sort of contrariety – albeit in a manner distinct from Diderot. The following Introduction will study this phenomenon in well-known texts by three of Diderot's most illustrious predecessors (one being an overlapping contemporary): La Fontaine (I), Molière (II) and Voltaire (III). The point is not to reveal the literary 'sources' of Diderot's method, but rather to supply examples of the modes in which contrariety could operate during the Classical period. These texts, when

---

2. 'The style of Diderot', *Linguistics and literary history: essays in stylistics* (Princeton 1948), p.135-91.

3. *La Religieuse* is omitted from consideration because I have already analysed it from the perspective of contrariety in my previous volume, *The Attaction of the contrary: essays on the literature of the French Enlightenment* (Cambridge 1987).

arranged in roughly chronological order, and according to the temperament of each author, can be imagined as reflecting stages in a development leading to Diderot as the final outcome – even though in reality his own peculiar movement of thought happened for reasons of its own. In order to prove that point *inter alia*, section IV of the Introduction will analyse a particularly revealing short text by Diderot, one totally informed by Diderot's own brand of contrariety, as a test case to validate the argument of subsequent chapters.

Although the present study will be confined to Diderot's writings, more broadly speaking 'contrariety' is but one example of a phenomenon modern critics refer to as 'symbolic negativity', and which can express itself in a variety of literary forms: in the creation of diverse sorts of carnival figures and topsy-turvy worlds, for example, or in utopias of several species (some radical, some not), or in high style as escape from vulgarity, or in vulgarity as escape from high style, etc., etc., and sometimes also in painting and opera. Readers desirous of perceiving the present discussion in that larger context are referred to my previous volume, *The Attraction of the contrary: essays on the literature of the French Enlightenment* (Cambridge 1987).

Walter E. Rex
University of California, Berkeley,
September 1998

Introduction
The dynamics of Classical contrarieties

I

AMID the confusions and disarray of today's approaches to literature it may be hard to remember, or even conceive of, the purposeful excitement of French literary studies in the late 1940s and 50s. It was not only Diderot who was at that moment being rediscovered and reassessed, even as new textual data on him were being brought to light, but in every sphere traditional literary studies were being radically rethought and revised. 'Modern' painting, music, theatre and 'modern' literature too had challenged aesthetic and philosophical perceptions, resulting in a whole generation of younger scholars eager to explore fresh approaches. More exacting critical standards had revealed deficiencies even in standard editions of literary works. The need for wide-ranging textual revisions was evident. The recent war, too, seemed to have confirmed scholarly respect for the role of history as a vital force in literature, not to mention the importance of documents as its basis. René Jasinski, speaking in the early 1950s as he surveyed contemporary literary scholarship on the age of Louis XIV, declared that the whole field gave him the impression of 'un immense chantier, où tout reste à faire'. Not only in the seventeenth century, but in many periods, scholars felt the same, and so did the critics: everything remained to be done.

Among those most restively anxious to set literature on a different footing was the Communist lyric poet Paul Eluard who, in 1951, published a *Première anthologie vivante de la poésie* [française] *du passé*.[1] The cutting edge of the title was of course the adjective *vivante*, insinuating, not without sarcasm, that all preceding anthologies were as good as *mortes*. No doubt Eluard exaggerated the defects of his forebears, as well as the novelty of his own enterprise; yet his collection remains in fact a lively and original one, and it features a number of poets from the Renaissance and Baroque eras who still looked rather obscure when Eluard collected them, and some of whom, like Sponde and Chassignet, later turned into major figures. But in this anthology the omissions are just as telling as the inclusions, and left out entirely are two of the finest French poetical playwrights, two of the giants of Classicism: Eluard dared to ignore

1. Paris 1951.

entirely the dramatic poems of Corneille and Racine. He also omitted *in toto* the Fables of La Fontaine.

As his preface makes clear, the main motive behind the banishments was not poetical, but social and political; indeed Eluard grudgingly conceded that, in individual lines [*sic*!], Racine occasionally rose to greatness. But he also maintained that these isolated instances did not outweigh the essential fact that Racine's art, like that of Corneille, was dedicated to an aesthetics of false 'grandeur', part and parcel of the idealisation of a social regime Eluard found intolerable – even in the abstract context of an anthology: 'Et c'est parce que je me suis, sans baragouiner, voulu sincère, qu'on ne trouvera pas ici d'extraits de tragédies de Jean Racine, de Pierre Corneille, ni de fables de La Fontaine' (i.11).

Sincère? Eluard's statement implies that one cannot be a purveyor of propaganda for monarchy, as these poets were, and at the same time speak truth from the depth of the soul. The sycophancy is inherent; hence the mere presence of these authors would poison the integrity of the anthology. But given the seventeeth-century context of Eluard's remarks one is inevitably hearing as well an echo of Alceste's famous line from *Le Misanthrope*, 'Je veux qu'on soit sincère', which in the context of Molière's play means *inter alia* someone willing to tell others of their defects, render 'honest' judgements and denounce abuses – or at least such was the role Alceste had claimed for himself. This is also the role being assumed by Eluard in this anthology as he shuts out the accepters, glorifiers and embellishers of an evil social order. Had they been 'sincere' they would have stood against the tide, as he and Alceste strove to do.

Eluard sees La Fontaine also as playing a false game, feigning simplicity and ignorance, alleging as natural good sense what was actually cynical propaganda for a society based on privilege. La Fontaine deliberately blinded himself, Eluard claims, to the human implications of an ethics based on 'might is right' (i.12): 'La Fontaine plaide, dans ses fables, pour le droit du plus fort; il en fait une morale et, pour prouver, il joue très habilement de son ignorance, de son faux bon sens. Il refuse cyniquement à voir plus loin que la perfection de l'ombre animale. Eloignons-le des rives de l'espérance humaine.'

How much Eluard's posture belongs to his era – to the aftermath of the second world war, the political and moral disarray (I remember it well) of a France haunted by the compromises and collaborations of the recent disaster. Yet Eluard's adaptation of Virgil's famous line concerning the 'shores of light' certainly bespeaks a form of idealism also. Naturally, he was not the only writer to interpret these 'shores' as designating the realm of literature. But, Marxist that he was, Eluard also saw them as representing both literature and social progress inseparably combined, *les rives de l'espérance humaine.*

Viewed in a more contemporary perspective, Eluard's attitude towards Racine, Corneille and La Fontaine seems not only exaggerated, but fanatical, perhaps even repugnantly so. It reminds us of other Procrustean eliminations by Marxists of the 1950s – Stalin's time – and of the ruthless narrowness apparently indigenous to certain forms of Communism. And yet, in one sense, his reaction has a salutary lesson to teach, because it suggests the possibility of viewing the past, the literary past, not as a dead irrelevance, but as a factor of extreme pertinence to our own sense of identity and to the values one needs to serve. In the 1950s, for many an era of *engagement* if ever there was one, as Eluard went about collecting France's poetical past into an anthology, perforce this poet gave himself a political definition in the process. Nor, of course, was his gesture in this respect without its ambiguities: surely his uncompromising decree of banishment exiling Corneille, Racine and the Fables of La Fontaine was testimony, homage even, to the power of the poetry he felt bound to outlaw.

Eluard was right too in sensing the extraordinary presence of the social and the political in these authors. Particularly in Corneille and Racine, the least line of their high-minded, politically positioned tragedies exudes acceptance of moral and political norms that are being taken for granted, sometimes idealised, just as Eluard stated. Perhaps this political presence may strike us as less noticeable in Racine's poetry than it would become in the following century in the tragedies of Voltaire, or in the *drames* of Sedaine, where axe-grinding political and social messages impinge relentlessly on our consciousness. But the difference is partly an illusion: though Voltaire's political message is certainly perceived as more forceful, this is due to the fact that he was – albeit in limited ways – striking out *against* the prevailing order. The heat comes from the abrasion of contradiction which sets the disagreements in the clearest possible relief. In Racine obviously there is virtually no friction, nothing that will not be smoothed away by a seamless acceptance of an order that is a foregone conclusion. The machine is so well oiled, so silent, that in reading Racine one may indeed have the illusion, of which Auerbach, Thierry Maulnier and others of that generation had written, of experiencing pure subjectivity in a setting that is timeless. It takes the hostile alienation of an Eluard to bring out the notion that Racine's invisible propaganda, pro rather than contra, is just as potent and pervasive as it would be in the Age of Reason.

It remains to be seen whether the other poet, La Fontaine, belongs properly with the first two, and whether he truly was preaching 'le droit du plus fort' in his Fables, as Eluard argued. Actually, there may be no simple way to decide the issue, since La Fontaine usually manages astutely to avoid taking sides, and in any case his poetical universe contains many disparate elements. But surely the best way to approach a settlement would be to consider the

3

fable which formulates in so many words the dictum claimed by Eluard to be the basis of La Fontaine's ethics: might is right. Is it still possible to take a fresh look at a poem learned by heart so long ago, and familiar anyway in so many other versions, as 'Le Loup et l'Agneau'?

> La raison du plus fort est toujours la meilleure:
> Nous l'allons montrer tout à l'heure.
>
>
> Un Agneau se désaltérait
> Dans le courant d'une onde pure;
> Un Loup survient à jeun, qui cherchait aventure,
> Et que la faim en ces lieux attirait.
> Qui te rend si hardi de troubler mon breuvage?
> Dit cet animal plein de rage:
> Tu sera châtié de ta témérité.
> – Sire, répond l'Agneau, que Votre Majesté
> Ne se mette pas en colère;
> Mais plutôt qu'elle considère
> Que je me vas désaltérant
> Dans le courant
> Plus de vingt pas au-dessous d'Elle;
> Et que par conséquent, en aucune façon,
> Je ne puis troubler sa boisson.
> – Tu la troubles, reprit cette bête cruelle;
> Et je sais que de moi tu médis l'an passé.
> – Comment l'aurais-je fais si je n'étais pas né?
> Reprit l'Agneau, je tette encor ma mère.
> – Si ce n'est toi, c'est donc ton frère.
> Je n'en ai point.–C'est donc quelqu'un des tiens;
> Car vous ne m'épargnez guère,
> Vous, vos bergers et vos chiens.
> On me l'a dit: il faut que je me venge.
> Là-dessus, au fond des forêts
> Le Loup l'emporte, et puis le mange,
> Sans autre forme de procès.

La Fontaine drew heavily on classical models for his fable; yet neither the version ascribed to Aesop nor the one attributed to Phaedrus began with a *moralité*, much less with a paradox, as this one does.[2] This beginning was La Fontaine's own genial invention, and, according to one of the manuscript

---

2. In both the classical models, the *moralité* comes at the end. The fable attributed to Aesop ends with words to the effect that any excuse will serve a tyrant; Phaedrus (*Fables*, Paris 1924, p.2) avers that 'cette fable vise certains gens qui, sous de faux prétextes, accablent les innocents' (Haec propter illos scripta est homines fabula, / Qui fictis causis innocentes opprimunt). Thus both Classical versions of the *moralité* draw rather obvious conclusions after the fact; they do not awaken (false) expectations, and are innocent of the ironies and duplicities of La Fontaine.

variants,[3] it came as an afterthought: the poem had originally been created entire as the fable proper. Yet the liminary preface, by adding an extra layer of irony, rather radically affects the impact of the poem; in fact it sets everything in a very different perspective.

The message of the preface is a paradox of the most basic kind: it goes directly counter to what civilised humanity has always known to be incontrovertibly true. Surely, no one with any moral sense would seriously maintain that might was, by nature, right, or that the argument of the strongest was automatically the best. The inherent falseness of the proposition, obvious in any age, must have been especially evident in seventeenth-century French society, when on all sides the injustices of power and privilege were on such ample display.

Even as the paradox is stated in the extreme ('toujours la meilleure'), so, too, the terms of the demonstration, the animals, are formulated as stylised types, just as Eluard saw ('l'ombre animale'). Their simple attributes characterise each one unmistakably, and – daring stroke on the part of the author – until the very end their behaviour seems to imply they are working against, rather than for, the message of the preface; that is to say, each word spoken by the animals seems to tend towards a conclusion going directly counter to the maxim stated in the *moralité*. The first part of the demonstration rests on the Lamb, who is, naturally, innocent, weak and vulnerable; whose soul is as pure as the crystal stream he drinks from; whose whole life has been spent downstream, not making waves or doing harm to others; whose politeness and tact, as he addresses his interlocutor, are exquisite enough for a king's court; whose existence has been so brief he has not had time to be corrupted by the ways of the world; and whose replies to his accuser radiate truth, purity and innocence simply because they reflect his own life and soul – surely all these traits combine to prove beyond a shadow of a doubt that, even though the Lamb is physically the weak one, his arguments are in fact the strongest and best.

The verdict would be foregone even if one heard only this side of the story. But in addition, there is the Wolf, and his every word, every gesture and every motive reinforce the same conclusion – contrary to the opening paradox. If the Lamb is innocent and young, the Wolf is fully grown and worldly-wise. If the Lamb is weak and vulnerable, the Wolf is strong and rapacious. If the soul of one is pure as crystal, the other's is cloudy with the murk of his misdeeds; his life has been spent doing harm, and as he comes prowling now, looking for prey, his speech is abrupt, familiar and rude. Naturally his accusations are

3. I use the Pléiade edition, ed. René Gros (Paris 1954), p.674, n.2.

filled with patently false inconsistencies, they are only self-serving lies anyway, and eventually the Wolf doesn't even bother to cover up their deceptiveness. If there is any justice in the world his arguments will be judged not only false and deceptive but wanting in logical cogency... At which point the Wolf settles the issue by running offstage with the Lamb and, preserving all the *bienséances* of respectable tragedies, devours his victim in the wings.

Only at the conclusion does the reader perceive that he/she has been tricked, for, contrary to the expectations seemingly raised in the preface, the author never intended that 'la meilleure' have its normal moral and/or forensic sense, but only a practical one that sidesteps ethics and legality entirely: the reason of the strongest always *wins out*. The world has always known that, too, ever since Aesop and Phaedrus. And so the Wolf vanishes from sight, while the Lamb makes a double disappearance inside his devourer as well as in the wings, and the poem abruptly ends, thus making the poet vanish, too, into a sibylline silence which the reader is left to interpret however he/she wishes.

The particular perfection of this poem depends of course on many elements: on the special loveliness of the two opening lines of the fable proper, for example, and also on the contrasts in the essentially two-part rhythm of the action, which starts with a slow series of delays as the Lamb tries to keep the Wolf at bay with politeness and reasoned argument, while the tempo increases along with the Wolf's impatience, until the Lamb's replies, growing shorter and shorter, are abruptly halted by the precipitous lunge of the conclusion, whose inexorable finality suggests the springing shut of a trap, or jaws clamping down. The action has been so engrossing, the reader finds he/she is quite unprepared for the revelation of the end, when at just the moment the Wolf, Lamb and Author all disappear, it becomes clear that the reader too has been an innocent victim of the poem's misleading strategy, but that it is now – even as it is for the vanished Lamb – much too late to argue, protest or even ask questions. In the Fables (just as in the 'Mais ...' of Voltaire's *Zadig*), protests have a way of coming too late.

This duplicitous, hoodwinking quality was La Fontaine's speciality. The classical versions do not have it, although otherwise they are quite similar: they feature the same animals engaged in essentially the same conversation, the Lamb having logic and veracity on his side, the Wolf having brute strength and ravenous appetite on his. Predictably, the strong devours the weak, a truth which the reader instantly recognises as belonging to the natural order of things everywhere. Though the classical animals have been endowed with the faculty of speech, one senses in their presentation a familiarity with real wolves and real sheep which is not nearly so strong in the seventeenth-century French version. The authors we call Aesop and Phaedrus were closer to the barnyard.

By the same token, La Fontaine's animals are indeed more stylised, and in this fable the two caricatures have been constructed so as to form opposites, or reversed images, of each other – another aspect which is not exploited nearly to the same extent in the classical models. But in La Fontaine's fable, every single feature of the Lamb has its counterpart, reversed, in the Wolf, as if the Lamb were simply a non- or un-Wolf; the Wolf, an un-Lamb. In other words, they were created to belong together in a quasi-philosophical way: not only can they not be separated, but each might be said to argue the existence of the other, the way a shadow argues the existence of light.

Need one point out that such a paradigm of poetical confrontation through the principle of contrariety is a hallmark of many of La Fontaine's fables – at least of the most familiar poems, the ones everyone learns by heart as a schoolchild?[4] Of course it was fated that the Grasshopper, useless, pleasure-loving, heedlessly living in the present, would find her way to the practical, busy, economical, petty-bourgeois Ant, whose present life has been nothing but a preparing for the future: one called for the other, if only because the Ant was such a perfect denial of all the Grasshopper's indulgences, and the Grasshopper such a perfect indulgence of all the Ant's denials. Through the same principle it was fated that the soft-spoken, low-lying, endlessly bending Reed would turn up in the shadow of the toweringly rigid, deeply rooted, pompous Oak so full of his grandeur. The qualities of one dictated, created, the qualities of the other, just as surely as the steady, slow-plodding, single-minded tortoise gave birth (so to speak) to its opposite in poetry, the fleet and slightly flaky hare – and vice versa.

As was suggested earlier, these contrarieties become distinctly more apparent in La Fontaine than they had been in the originals, as if there were an added willingness in the age of Descartes to build upon formal principles that were absolute. On the other hand, the Fables being products of the greatest moment of French Classicism, not to mention being also the creation of a poet of genius, the extra degree of formality in no way dulls the sharpness of the dialogues or hampers the liveliness of the characterisations. On the contrary it contributes to their perfection. It would not be until much later, in the age of Diderot, that certain authors began to perceive a discrepancy between creative, or emotional, impulses and their ordering according to formal principles, as though one were a sort of control imposed upon the other, and as if literary

---

4. Actually, I am not aware of any other scholar who has pointed out such a pattern of contrariety in the familiar fables. In a general way I have learned much from Marcel Gutwirth, *Un merveilleux sans éclat: La Fontaine, ou, la poésie exilée* (Geneva 1987), which also provides a copious bibliography.

expression had lost the perfect harmony and equilibrium that in the age of Mme de La Fayette and Pascal had been taken for granted.

La Fontaine claimed that the 'ample comedy' of his fables was universal in scope, and it is true that, as scholars pointed out long ago, the Fables contain a whole world of experience: every class of society from court to barnyard, every human situation imaginable, every age of life (except very young children), a whole gamut of emotions – everything except the genuinely tragic ones. In so far as contrariety is involved, at least in the most familiar fables, the poems show things that do not work together; in fact, one of the useful ways to read such fables (and here again I simply repeat what scholars have known for a long time) is to see them as recording the frictions of a whole society. It is obvious, too, that in many of the contrarieties, economics is a central issue, even as the emptiness of the Grasshopper's cupboards drives her to the plentiful larder of the Ant, or as hunger brings the lean Wolf to the tender young Lamb. Likewise, class differences are frequently stirred into the mixture, as when the pointedly bourgeois mentality of the Ant is played off against that of a Grasshopper who is as heedlessly squandering, and short of funds, as any aristocrat might have been.

Finally, the contrarieties operate psychologically in a broad sense, through the principle of perversity: one of the unwritten laws of social intercourse is that people seek out others who possess the qualities they themselves lack. Opposites attract. In our time this law has become slightly obscure because of another law – this one more favoured by psychologists – which declares that, in human society, like attracts like. Though contradictory, both laws are equally true, and although in the fables one can find some spectacular examples of the second law, as in *Les Deux pigeons*, it is the first law – opposites attract – that is given freest play. *Le Chêne et le roseau* is not only a tale of how even the Fouquets of the world may incur royal disfavour and fall crashing into disgrace, it brings together these two species of plants because obviously in real life pompous oaks need humble reeds so that they may feel superior to them (the conclusion of the fable suggests that the reverse is equally true). In real life, it often occurs that economical Ants and spendthrift Grasshoppers gravitate together, if only to exchange reproaches – a familiar feature of one type of poor marriage, and one which has provided innumerable authors with plots, from Molière's *Médecin malgré lui* to Chekov's haunting story, actually entitled *La Cigale*. The world is equally full of vain crows who are just asking for some clever fox to steal their cheese. In Freud's scheme, there is even a separate species of innocent Lamb who psychologically needs the Wolf who devours him or her.

In La Fontaine's world there are no psychiatrist's couches, no ameliorations possible, and the author, as Eluard correctly saw, never stays to fight. Even in his most politically daring fable, *Les Animaux malades de la peste*, in which the crime-laden, animal-devouring Lion gets off scot-free, while the poor grass-cropping Donkey is sentenced to death, one should not forget that the animal chosen to be the victim of the fable is not a lamb this time, but quite literally an ass. Even though the daring message of the poem does unmistakably declare that the social hierarchy spares the highly born, no matter how guilty they be, and punishes the lowly born innocent in their stead, the message is heavily counterbalanced and held in suspense by the particular rank and character of the players. A double contrariety and a double irony are at work in this fable, not only in the situation of guilt being declared innocent and innocence declared guilty, but also in the translation of these terms into the proudest and noblest of beasts versus the silliest and least consequential. These contrarieties do not cancel each other out (tensions are never resolved in La Fontaine); instead they serve as checks to keep the poem within its own bounds: they prevent the issues raised from spilling out into anything transitive like social indignation, or its opposite, totalitarianism. In other words, the inherent silliness of the Ass stops our indignation at least somewhat short, while at the same time his innocence forestalls any possibility of enthusiasm for the guilty Lion who saw him condemned.

Not only do the contrarieties dramatised in the most famous Fables imply an unwillingness to take sides, they make commitment impossible. How can one take a stand on one side of an issue when the opposite opinion is displayed as equally compelling, or at least having equal weight? It has long been obvious that serious commitment to a 'cause' almost necessarily entails blindness. Commitment implies Eluard shutting his eyes to Corneille and Racine, and declaring that La Fontaine favours the ethics of might is right, despite the obvious ambivalences and equivocations. It *is* true, to be sure, that La Fontaine's wide-eyed presentation of values is paralysing, stranding one morally and politically in a limbo of inaction where any sort of *engagement* is out of reach. The situation would be intolerable had not the poet played many of the dramas on the level of animality rather than humanity, and even so the stylisation of the animal fictions may eventually bring on a sense of claustrophobia. Who can read the familiar animal Fables of La Fontaine indefinitely?

II

Meanwhile, the pleasures of Molière endure forever. And this is true even though his plays swarm with contrarieties, although admittedly not exactly of the animal kind. Even so, just as in a fable by La Fontaine, the cruelly egotistical avarice of calculating old Harpagon plays off perfectly against the warmth and spontaneous feelings of the young lovers; the reasonably humane religion of Cléante forms a satisfyingly total contrast with Tartuffe's fanatical inhumanity – and so on. Equally obvious, however, are the differences dividing the two authors, the main one being that Molière so often takes sides and stays to fight. Nor is it unusual to find that Molière's contrarieties function as a punishment mechanism, with one side – often the fanatical or irrational side – being held up for ridicule and disapproval (obviously both *Le Tartuffe* and *L'Avare* provide examples of this). In other words, reading at least some of Molière's comedies one discovers that the result of the clash of contrariety is by no means a stasis, nor is one permitted to feel stranded in a limbo of inaction: Molière's aim is frequently *engagement* on the side of reason, love and humanity against the forces of folly and self-delusion. In a word, while La Fontaine's contrarieties (at least in the famous *Fables*) usually have a static outcome, Molière's tend towards the dynamic, and occasionally the good side of the contrariety is allowed, at least in appearance, to triumph over the bad – with full approval by the audience and the author.

The plots themselves also contribute to the dynamic impression: at the end of *Le Médecin malgré lui*, the drunken woodcutter actually ascends to wealth and incipient fame as a doctor; he breaks out of his social class. In *L'Ecole des femmes*, one thinks one sees the instinctual feelings embodied in the young lovers actually triumphing over Arnolphe's selfish egotism and unnatural constraints. The sensible strategies of Dorine apparently stand a real chance of succeeding against the wiles of odious Tartuffe, who in fact at the end of the play gets hauled off to jail. Likewise Scapin's brilliant improvisations give the doltish old fathers an excellent run for their money in *Les Fourberies de Scapin*. One has the impression that in Molière a jay may indeed turn into a peacock; that the protests of lambs may not be in vain; and that the social order with all its injustices may not always prevail.

This element of apparent dynamism is what in Molière serves to permit, and in fact provoke, laughter, as distinct from the smiles of La Fontaine. The difference is critical, since laughter is designed to purge tensions, to let the air out, whereas smiles are signs that the tensions are still bottled up, only momentarily rendered tolerable under the guise of pleasure. In the case of the Fables, this means that the conflicts depicted have been miniaturised, thus allegedly diminishing their painful components, distanced from the real human condition by being attributed to animals or mere types of human beings, and theatricalised, that is, taken as pretexts for little dramas, for the aesthetic pleasures of art. Certainly the smile at the end of the fable signifies a recognition of the truth of the lesson, but it also signifies an awareness of our helplessness to change an order that never allows exceptions to the rules ordained by the world's hierarchies. The smile is a resignation, an agreement that such is life.[5]

What a contrast with the finale of *Le Bourgeois gentilhomme*, where, the plot having been 'resolved', with the lovers united, and M. Jourdain permanently ascended into his Turkish folly, the whole play is then blown away by the six Entrées of the *Ballet des nations*, which have nothing whatsoever to do with the action that has preceded them. After each nation singly has had its turn on the stage, at the very end the dancers of all three nations (Spain, Italy, France) join in together, with everyone onstage clapping hands and – to the glorious music of Lully – singing about how such pleasures are fit for the gods themselves. Amid all the noise and gaiety it must have been difficult for the audience even to recall what the comedy proper had been about, much less concern themselves with the lessons of some *moralité*.

To be sure, this is only one side of the coin, for certainly not all, in fact very few, of Molière's major comedies reach such joyously mind-blowing conclusions. And even with the gayest of them, at the end there remain shadows and problems which convey, upon reflection at least, emotions that are quite different from the cloudless, reasonless enjoyments of the *Ballet des nations*. Although at the end of *Le Tartuffe* the problems that formed the 'knot' of the action appear resolved, with the foolish father finally brought to his senses, the family saved from financial disaster, the lovers united, and the villain fittingly punished and out of harm's way, nevertheless this resolution was made possible only through a very unlikely (albeit flattering to the Sun King) *deus ex machina*, coming from without, rather than from within, the dramatic situation, as though the grim problems the play enacts were actually insoluble in terms of the real elements of the plot. *L'Ecole des femmes* is only brought to a happy conclusion thanks to a cluster of coincidental unlikelihoods, another sort of *deus ex machina*, and whose implications are equally disturbing: the painful truth they suggest is that according to the normal order of things and the rules laid down by real society, the Agnèses of the world can never

---

5. Naturally, La Fontaine gave a rather different slant to this idea in his famous statement about 'gaieté': 'Je n'appelle pas gaieté ce qui excite le rire, mais un certain charme, un air agréable qu'on peut donner à toutes sortes de sujets, même les plus sérieux' (quoted in P. Clarac, *La Fontaine*, Paris 1969, p.54).

find their way to love and marriage with the Horaces. The cards are all stacked in favour of Arnolphe, and to make things otherwise would require a series of coincidences so preposterous it just makes us laugh to hear them. The same lesson is implicit in the lucky coincidences that form the conclusion of *Les Fourberies de Scapin*: their obvious unlikelihood intimates that in real society nothing would have favoured those charming young couples, no matter what prodigies of invention Scapin achieved. *L'Avare* follows a similar pattern: though the young couples have got free and obtained permission to marry, this happy ending too depends on coincidences that are patently unbelievable; furthermore the young people's strategy rests in part on a blackmailing ploy whose effectiveness is temporary and incidental. If for the moment Harpagon is deprived of his prey, he and his mania remain just as potent and dangerous to society as ever.

Some scholars have assumed that the final swarm of unlikelihoods which tie up the loose ends of these conclusions are evidence of Molière's limitations as a playwright since he was incapable of unifying all the elements of his plots; others have suggested that the unlikelihoods should be taken as flights from reality, fairy-tales, the real world melting into pleasant fantasy at the end. Perhaps indeed their immediate effect does resemble that of a fairy-tale: they charm and enchant because they suggest a universe magically obedient to the dictates of true love, a providential system ready and eager to serve the desires not only of the young lovers but of the audience which hopes to see them happily united as well. But even so, in the longer run – upon reflection – their effect is, I believe, exactly the opposite: they function, backhandedly, as reminders of a world governed strictly by cause and effect, and since their contrived nature is so obviously played up, they actually, in the long run, bring home the unhappy truths they seemed designed to evade.

In other words, even though Molière's contrarieties sometimes seem to have a dynamism that would be unthinkable in the world of La Fontaine's fables, and furthermore though his social attitude in such cases apparently moves us measurably forward towards the Enlightenment, I am also suggesting that some of the alleged differences between Molière and La Fontaine are in important ways an illusion – that, for example, hidden behind the appearance that love can win out and the forces of irrationality be kept at bay is the realisation that the social order prevails and the wolves always get their prey, that jays are probably fated to remain just what their species determines them to be, that in real life there is no viable solution to men's follies and blindness. Critics have long been aware that Molière's laughter is the purest and most genial sleight of hand.

Of the great comedies, only one eschews all fairy-tale coincidences and unlikelihoods at the conclusion. Furthermore the particular brand of comedy of this play generally provokes inconclusive smiles rather than laughter, and the ending is explicitly not a resolution of anything; all the tensions remain just as before. This is *Le Misanthrope*, and esthetically it is the closest of all Molière's plays to the Fables of La Fontaine.

One grants the Eluards of the world, to be sure, that La Fontaine would never have invented a main character such as Alceste, whose essential role (at least as Alceste saw it) was to perceive, denounce and oppose moral abuses, someone whose function (again, such was Alceste's own view) was to stand and fight. Furthermore his spirited protests (however severe their practical limitations) endow the play with exactly the sort of freshness and vitality the familiar fables seldom, if ever, attain.

And yet, this play, just like the best-known Fables, is structured throughout by the perverse magnetism of contrariety; as Jacques Guicharnaud perceived many years ago, ironic confrontations of opposite personalities are almost everywhere.[6] Furthermore, as in a fable, no one changes during the course of the action, and at the end the characters (along with the author) all disappear, leaving the stage empty and the page as blank as it had been at the conclusion of *Le Loup et l'Agneau* – at the very moment an interpretation is most desired.

The structure of *Le Misanthrope* seems to grow out of the nature of the characters, even as the characters seem to grow out of each other. Pliant Philinte came into being as a reversal of unyielding Alceste, as surely as – for other reasons – the bending Reed took its place beside the rigid Oak. And how marvellously the proximity of one contrariety allows us to perceive the qualities of the other: not only does Philinte's easy-going, complacent view of society serve as a perfect foil to enlarge all the stubborn negativity of Alceste's rejections – and vice versa – but in so far as every perception philosophically requires an awareness of its opposite in order to achieve completeness, these two contrary characters actually serve to define each other.

Since both of them are comic exaggerations, extremes, to follow either Alceste or Philinte would mean renouncing a large part of what one normally calls human nature (for want of a better term). No matter how believable and powerfully individual they seem, or how much their self-satisfaction may

6. *Molière: une aventure théâtrale* (Paris 1963), esp. p.347-517. Of all Molière critics, Guicharnaud's approach is probably the closest to my own. He does not, however, explore the implications of the opposing elements in Molière's comedies as I do; in fact the dynamics of his basic term 'repoussoir' are very different from what I understand by the tensions of 'contrariety'. A number of my points about *Le Misanthrope* have been anticipated by Roger Ikor, *Molière double* (Paris 1977), esp. p.140-47. In a general way, my greatest debt is due to Judd Hubert, *Molière and the comedy of the intellect* (Berkeley 1962).

obscure the fact, each is only a half-person, or a half-truth. Equally incomplete, each of them possesses exactly the traits, the plenum, corresponding to the vacuum in the other. There may be a positive side to this mutual need, for indeed Alceste seems to require the compromises of society's Philintes to keep his indignation boiling, and Philinte's compliancy apparently needs Alceste's rigidity as well, as something to act upon. But in the long run the main support for the action of the play is the perverse irony that Philinte is constantly asking Alceste to display the very qualities Alceste has deliberately eliminated, in fact the qualities that make him the non-Philinte who is Alceste – and vice versa. Later generations would come to resent the perverse incompatibility inherent in the relationship and seek some way out of the impasse, some middle ground where Philinte might stop slipping and sliding long enough to take an occasional moral stand, and where Alceste would soften just a bit – enough to sound reasonable rather than ridiculous. But of course in the seventeenth-century context the characters could never be inconsistent with their essential identity, and naturally their dialogue is fated to be an almost puppet-like jockeying back and forth between polarities, the two characters being caught in the impossibility of ever partaking meaningfully of each other. Inevitably, too, the end of the play turns out to be almost an exact replica of the opening, with Alceste angrily stalking off, determined to flee the vices of humankind, while Philinte follows after soothingly to urge compromise. One might think that nothing at all had happened during the preceding five acts; the plot has barely moved an inch, while psychologically the two characters remain exactly the same – only perhaps a little more so. On the other hand, viewing the matter from an ideal position, perhaps perched high above on some epicycle of Mercury, and drawing a line between the two poles represented by the intractability of Alceste and the compliancy of Philinte, one discovers that the space in between implies an extraordinary variety of possible social behaviours and attitudes, which is to say that the conflict between these two characters involves the entire range of one aspect of human experience.

Thus far the contrarieties of Molière's *Misanthrope* have been seen as composed of mutually exclusive elements, 'repoussoirs', to use Guicharnaud's term. But there is a second requirement for a contrariety to be operational, which is, paradoxically, that there be some bond of agreement that ties the poles together. Despite the appearances, all is not contrast in the familiar Fables of La Fontaine: the fact that the allegedly humble Reed remains so unimpressed by the blustery Oak's posturing suggests he may have just as much *amour-propre* as the other, though in a different form. Even in the fable of the Lamb and the Wolf, which goes as far towards total opposition as any fable can, both animals share at least one attribute, deriving from their common animality, which is hunger or appetite: the Lamb comes to the stream to drink, just as the Wolf comes to the Lamb to eat. Nor do Alceste and Philinte disagree about everything; on the contrary they both see society as full of hypocrites and persons doing harm. Their disagreement concerns how to react.

By the same token, in the second ironic confrontation between incompatibles of *Le Misanthrope*, the 'sonnet' scene between Alceste and Oronte, the two characters have in common a willingness to accept the medium of poetry, at least for purposes of conflict and debate, and this common ground allows their contrariety to take wing, the coyly ornate, sighing indirection of Oronte's poetic conceits playing perfectly against the egotistical, self-centred directness of Alceste's unadorned verses, their opposition suggestively hinting at a masculine-feminine contrast (in the seventeenth-century sense) as well. If Oronte's embellished sonnet belongs to a world of decorum, seduction and never-ending fore-play, the thrusting bluntness of Alceste's 'chanson' obviates all necessity for preliminaries: it assumes, without even asking her, that the sweetheart of the poem ('ma mie') would rather be appended to someone like Alceste than be mistress of the king of France. Much else is implied sexually and socially in this contrariety. For present purposes, however, the main point is that it anticipates in several ways the central dilemma of the comedy around which everything revolves, the contrariety between Alceste and Célimène.

Just as with Oronte and Alceste, here too an almost invisible bond unites the two characters Alceste and Célimène, who everywhere else are almost stridently in opposition. The bond in common is of course the illusion of love, creating desires so strong that neither wants to resist. But the perverse laws of contrariety are also powerfully at work in their relationship, setting the dynamics into action with a perfection that is positively metaphysical. According to popular conceptions, misanthropes behave as though they hated mankind. Coquettes, on the other hand, behave as though they wanted to love everyone, or at least all the males. True misanthropes are, by definition, impervious to seduction; coquettes have no other function but to seduce. Naturally it was fated that this would-be Misanthrope would fall in love with that Coquette, thereby compromising Alceste's alleged misanthropy in the most fundamental way, to the core. As for Célimène, later moralists spelled out what Molière seems to be implying in this play: a coquette is by definition incapable of feeling true love for anyone. Furthermore, as the play makes clear, Célimène's 'love' is plural: it cannot belong exclusively to anyone in particular. This truth is indicated so many times during the course of the action that one can only conclude that vanity alone prevented her suitors from recognising it long before the final scenes. It is equally clear that Alceste's love is by definition singular, in fact unique. Naturally it excludes everyone but himself, as his ultimate proposal to Célimène makes explicit. Meanwhile, for the audience the compelling interest and pathos of the comedy lies in watching Alceste and Célimène moving towards the dead end, the blank 'fin de non-recevoir', symbolised by the empty stage, as all depart at the conclusion. But the blankness of the final separations is also psychological, since it still has not dawned upon either of the two protagonists that – just as with the pair Philinte-Alceste – each had been demanding of the other the one quality the other did not possess.

Le Misanthrope is also unique in having all the characters (except for Eliante) positioned around the protagonist according to a single principle, namely contrariety to the character traits of Alceste. Perhaps the most useful way to look upon the phenomenon is to think of contrariety as a creative agent, or inspiration, one side of Alceste's character requiring, summoning, its opposite, Philinte, another side calling for Célimène, another bringing forth Oronte, another Arsinoë, and so on.[7] Isolated from each other, he and they would be respectively incomplete, so to speak, because they all serve to define each other, to magnify each other's qualities, and to give each other a target to act upon. Perhaps the singleness of this principle which positions the others around Alceste is the unifying force that endows this particular play with its special quality of flawlessness. Other Molière plots do indeed feature ironic contrarieties, but they lack the completeness of this sort of ordering and simplicity.

Self-containment is the essence of this comedy. For even though one may perceive tremors of potential subversion in Alceste's daring criticisms of society, whatever anti-establishment energies the comedy might have generated are systematically ringed around and blocked by contrarieties, and also – as in La Fontaine – by the irony that Alceste's allegedly noble sincerity is undermined by elements of ridiculousness (in the eyes of society), and egotism as well. Above all, this comedy has no answers to all the worrisome and profound questions it poses; at the end its message remains as blank as the stage the players have left behind them; nor is there any helpful *moralité* at the beginning. Not all the comedies of Molière share this airtight unforthcomingness, nor do contrarieties always inform the entire structure, as they do here. But even so, their frequency makes it clear that contrariety as a literary form of expression was, in various guises, perfectly suited to Classical comedy, and that in particular the La Fontaine species of contrariety was instrumental in producing

---

7. Eliante is in some respects the exception that proves the rule, though she too in her advocacy of love's delusions is presented as a partial contrariety to Alceste.

not only the structure of Molière's greatest play, but its sublimely self-contained densities as well.

One final point about most, though not all, Classical contrarieties: chronological time is of almost no importance in their functioning. The conclusion of *Le Loup et l'Agneau* was implicit from the start, and throughout the fable the Wolf, so to speak, had already been devouring the lamb with words. Time means nothing; it scarcely exists. The two parts of the contrariety are brought together simultaneously, and furthermore there is no character development: at least in the world of the familiar Fables I have discussed, characters cannot change, and therefore time has nothing to act upon psychologically. This is another quality *Le Misanthrope* shares with the familiar Fables: the end is just like the beginning. But even in a more dynamic play such as *Le Tartuffe*, both honest Dorine, with her good sense, and always-reasonable Cléante remain psychologically immutable throughout the action, and, more interestingly, so does the other side of the contrariety, Tartuffe, who is so much the essence of a hypocrite that his exposure at the end simply makes him fall silent, deprived of his right to existence in words. One grants, to be sure, that there are important exceptions to this rule, the most sensational one being the heroine of *L'Ecole des femmes*, whose continual character development – stage by stage from innocent ignorance governed entirely by the instincts of love to the maturity of a woman fully wise to the complexities of her own character and desires and determined to fight for them – forms a perfect contrariety with Arnolphe's myopic rigidity. But despite the exceptions (Orgon would be another) enough of the characters of Molière's contrary pairings do remain prisoners of their own immutable psychology to justify calling this timeless form of contrariety the 'Classical' one, as I will take the liberty of doing henceforth.

III

As Enlightenment gathered impetus in France, inevitably the impact was felt in all literary forms of expression and in many ways – even though, in the present context, only the most obvious and familiar results can be touched upon. But naturally the move to centre stage of the new philosophy, along with its social and political concerns, entailed an overriding of the kind of literature for which the century of Louis XIV was famous, literature whose glory lay less in making daring social statements or in publicising novel scientific ideas than in plumbing the depths of the human soul and the plight of the human condition. More grit came in the mixture, more of a cutting edge, too, as politics, science and religion turned against received opinion. Meanwhile the art of writing lost something of the profundity, resonance and grandeur of the age of Pascal, along with the self-contained poise essential to it. Most significant for present purposes, in the new age there was a general move away from the archetypical kind of contrariety that had flourished so brilliantly in Molière's time. Under pressures from Enlightenment, contrarieties were fated to lose both their purity and the essential stasis that had informed them. They took on a new sort of dynamism that tipped towards the present, even as, in literature generally, the timely so often replaced the timeless. Everyone agrees that Voltaire was incomparably the most eloquent spokesman for the new era, as the *philosophe* who not only reflected the new trends better than anyone else, but actually created them. It has long been clear also that this role as spokesman for the age was established and confirmed above all by the publication of his *Lettres philosophiques* (1734), the work many scholars consider the opening salvo of Enlightenment. Given Voltaire's leadership in the new trends, and the particular significance of this work in the movement, it may seem a paradox that right at the opening of the *Lettres philosophiques* Voltaire stages a contrariety whose balanced perfection and poise seems (at first appearance at least) a throwback to the Classical era, a return to the aesthetics of La Fontaine.

Like most of the letters in this collection, this one, 'Sur les quakers', clearly derives from Voltaire's own personal experiences in England: he had actually known the particular Quaker he describes; the topics discussed are among those that really interested Voltaire at that time. Yet the two figures who appear in the letter, the Quaker and the unnamed narrator, are no closer to reality than the Wolf and the Lamb were to real animals. In fact Voltaire has stylised both personages in order to exploit the dynamics of contrariety in a manner that, at first, very much recalls the strategy of La Fontaine.

Each of Voltaire's personages is everything the other is not: the Quaker is English to the core; the narrator, totally French. In style of life the Quaker is soberly clean-living and exudes middle-class virtue; the narrator displays the decadent manners of an aristocrat, and doubtless something of their vices as well. The Quaker is a 'square': inflexibly upright, he never bows to anyone, nor does he doff his hat, even in polite company. The narrator is all bends and curves, bowing and scraping, hat in hand (it went without saying) just as fashionable custom demanded. The Quaker wears clothes that are entirely plain and unadorned, innocent of pleats or fancy buttons. The narrator's dress, French readers would immediately understand, is elaborately ornate in the French style. The Quaker's speech is simple, moderate, *multum in parvo* and so lacking in formality that he even says 'tu' to an upper-class stranger. The narrator is all 'formules de politesse', excessive verbiage, oaths and self-serving compliments (using 'vous' and 'Monsieur'), exaggerations, fits of pique, bluster, *parvum in multo*.

As for religion, the Quaker's could not be more Protestant: thoroughly grounded in Scripture, entirely unceremonious, his religion stems directly from an inner disposition of mind and heart. The narrator's religion could not be more Catholic (as Voltaire saw it): ignorant of Scripture, completely external, the narrator's Christianity has nothing to do with inner disposition; it is purely a matter of ceremony. ('Eh pour l'amour de Dieu, que je vous baptise, et que je vous fasse chrétien.') The Quaker's characteristics have about them something of eighteenth-century stereotypes of the male, while the narrator's hint at those of the female. Throughout the letter, both in respect to manners and religion, the Quaker is substance personified, and he is played against a narrator who is all hollow appearance.

If, in this letter, Voltaire chose to present the contrast between French and English as a contrariety, one of the advantages of this dynamic was obviously comedy: since each was so very unlike the other, each acted as a foil that enlarged the other's traits, and thus increased their comic potentialities, almost to the point of caricature. Given eighteenth-century French prejudices, the Quaker was inherently the ridiculous one: the unconventional style of dress, the deliberate ignoring of good manners, the grotesquely familiar mode of speech, everything made him obviously the odd man out. In contrast, the narrator's respectability in costume and manners really did not lend itself to ridicule at all. And yet, by genially clever sleight of hand, Voltaire reverses these values, not only deflecting ridicule from the Quaker, but schooling the reader to recognise in him a person of respect, honour, and even true nobility. The narrator, for all his high-class manners, turns into a laughing stock.

To be sure, Voltaire manages to have his cake and eat it too. When the Quaker first appears, hat on head, greeting the narrator by calling him 'tu', the outlandish audaciousness of his affront to convention automatically makes him the droll one. And there is drollery, too, when this bizarre person is repeatedly called upon to bring the supposedly respectable narrator to order for his intemperate swearing ('Mon fils [...] ne jure point'). Even after the Quaker's moral elevation has begun, something of the comedy of his hat-on-head plainness remains.

Contrarywise, the danger for the narrator (from Voltaire's point of view) was that he *not* be thought ridiculous. Perhaps the reader would be impressed by all his courtly flourishes. As an antidote, Voltaire borrows a device earlier perfected by Fontenelle, by which the description itself lays bare the constituent parts and literal causal functions lying behind the thing described, deliberately destroying any aura of grandeur tradition may have ascribed to it. Thus the action of bowing is so broken up into pieces and processes in Voltaire's celebrated description of it that it turns into an almost grotesque combination of mechanical movements that seem an affront to good sense. At the end the narrator is left foolishly holding the bag, with a hat in his hand, instead of on his head, as good sense demanded. Furthermore, thanks to the contrast with the Quaker, the gestures are revealed as having no relation whatsoever to the sentiment they purport to convey.

In order to counteract the Quaker's inherent ridiculousness, the narrator lards his descriptions with little tip-offs that train the reader to look beyond ordinary stereotypes and recognise a different set of values. These tip-offs propose radically new criteria for judging social behaviour in which the rules of courtly etiquette are superseded by values that are purely moral. What counts in this Quaker is not his flaunting of the code of etiquette, but the openness and humane qualities one sees in his face. All of these factors are brought into play as the Quaker is introduced: 'Il me reçut avec son chapeau sur la tête, et s'avança vers moi sans faire la moindre inclination de corps; mais il y avait plus de politesse dans l'air ouvert et humain de son visage qu'il n'y en a dans l'usage de tirer une jambe derrière l'autre, et de porter à la main ce qui est fait pour couvrir la tête.' The analytical way in which Voltaire describes the narrator's own bow reinforces the same effect: ' – Monsieur, lui dis-je, en me courbant le corps et en glissant un pied vers lui, selon notre coutume, je me flatte que ma juste curiosité ne vous déplaira pas.'

In the masterful manipulations of Voltaire's prose, the mysteries of social grace, and above all, courtly manners, disintegrate and turn ridiculous under the cold light of reason. More significant, this elevation of the unbending Quaker at the expense of the bowing narrator aims as well at the ceremonial act, the ritual, of paying homage, which was – needless to say – an indispensable ingredient, perhaps even the *sine qua non*, of a society based on rank and privilege. Obviously in the religious domain, as the simple Quaker repeatedly shows up the ignorance of the Catholic narrator concerning his principal articles of belief, one realises that there are large spiritual issues at stake in this letter. But the social issues were equally momentous. And uncannily, Voltaire has put his finger on matters that would remain crucial for the rest of the century: such ceremonial bowing and scraping as he describes here would be explicitly forbidden when the Revolution came, and all Citizens would be required to address each other by saying 'tu', out of exactly the same egalitarian spirit stipulated by the Quaker: 'nous tutoyons également les rois et les save-tiers'.

But the most astonishing innovation is saved for the end. The Quaker has been explaining various features of his sect: their deliberately different style of dress, the reasons why they always shun 'assemblées de plaisir', the theatre and gambling, their objections to swearing oaths in the name of God. He comes finally to their refusal ever to go to war (this rule being given in the absolute, allowing for no exceptions), a daringly radical concept that the Quaker justifies eloquently by reasons of humanity, and Christianity. His logic appears unassailable as he points out the flagrant contradiction between the merciful lessons of the Gospel and the murderous purpose of war, and he destroys any aura of mystery conscription may have had by again breaking the thing down into its constituent parts, each of which (whether the silly little sticks or the tightly stretched ass's skin of the drum roll) reveals with pitiless clarity the emptiness and absurdity of the whole process. At the end Voltaire rises to an intensity of eloquence he would seldom again equal. He describes the great city of London ablaze with celebrations of victory – one can almost feel the pounding rhythms of the rejoicings in the rhythms of his sentence–and then, poignant counterpoint, the little band, the tiny few, alone in their grief and distress:

Et lorsque, après des batailles gagnées, tout Londres brille d'illuminations, que le ciel est enflammé de fusées, que l'air retentit du bruit des actions de grâces, des cloches, des orgues, des canons, nous gémissons en silence sur ces meurtres qui causent la publique allégresse.

This, the last sentence of the letter, dispenses with any final salutation, and above all dispenses with any rejoinder from the lightweight narrator, who has disappeared from sight, apparently blown away to nothingness by the sheer force of the Quaker's moral conviction. In sum, if at the beginning the narrator, simply through the multitude of class, national and religious prejudices in his favour, was the presumed winner, at the end he is the loser, just the way the whole populace of London, despite their frenzy and fireworks, finally lose out – in the reader's mind at least – to the awesome strength of the Quakers' moral truth that is even more impressive because it is silent and ignored. This time the Lamb has won.

The narrator wears several hats during the course of this letter: he represents not only the unjustified snobbery of the French and the ignorance of Catholics, but aristocratic weaknesses as well. Though the fact is not actually specified in the letter, it went without saying that war was the principal function of the aristocracy, *la noblesse d'épée*. After abundantly demonstrating the emptiness of their religious beliefs and their code of politeness, this last passage gives a *coup de grâce* that takes away their chief, perhaps their only, title of glory: prowess at war. That too is presumably part of the Quaker's victory.

In sum, although Voltaire's letter starts by juxtaposing two totally different characters whose qualities counterbalance one another in a dynamic relationship reminiscent of Classical contrarieties, at the end there is no ironic stasis of self-containment, such as was found in La Fontaine and in Molière's *Misanthrope*; instead the impetus tips over into a resolution irresistibly favouring one side. Nor is this situation comparable to the victory of the Lion over the Ass; in this text Voltaire, after weighing the merits of each position, calls upon the reader to make a judgement in favour of one of them. There is no irony at the end, no hints that in the long run values might be different; there is not even comedy, and the reader is swept into agreement by the torrent of Voltaire's eloquence and the urgency of his social concern. The social dynamism of this text far outstrips anything by Molière. Perhaps even the difficult Eluard might have approved.

Anti-Catholic and anti-aristocratic themes would be heard again in subsequent letters, sometimes with telling force. The celebrated instance is the balancing (lettre x) of the well-powdered French aristocrat, uselessly doing nothing with his life but pay homage and dance attendance, against the infinitely useful *négociant*, whose occupations enrich his country, and contribute to the well-being of the entire world. Again the confrontation tips compellingly against the French aristocracy, and in favour of the English middle class. In the religious discussions, too, one usually finds a pattern by which the Catholics come out on the short end of the stick. Nor is there any need to point out the multitude of ways in which, through comparisons both explicit and implied, England defeats France in this work: the phenomenon is obvious, and frequent.

Oddly, though the Quakers are discussed in three other letters, their pacifism is never singled out for praise again, and only mentioned in passing. Nor is this sect always shown in a favourable light; in several letters the ridiculousness of their trembling and pretended inspirations from on high seem momentarily to outweigh their merits – even though Voltaire's final assessment is generally favourable. After lettre IV the Quakers disappear, forgotten, while the author turns to other, more numerous religious sects, to questions of government, and in lettre x with its famous jibe against aristocrats, to one of the great themes of these letters: commerce.

Voltaire is at pains to explain that, while England is rather lacking in natural resources, her commerce has made her rich, and also powerful – in the military sense. He tells how, in 1723, England was able simultaneously to send out three fleets to the extremities of the world: one before Gibraltar, which Voltaire describes as 'conquise et conservée par ses armes', a second to Porto-Bello to prevent the King of Spain from enjoying the treasure of the Indies, and the third to the Baltic Sea to prevent the Northern Powers from fighting. He also relates how, when Turin was threatened by the armies of Louis XIV, and Prince Eugène needed a large sum of money in order to rescue the duke of Savoy and save the city, English merchants arranged the loan in a mere half-hour. The prince and his troops arrived, the French were beaten, and the prince wrote to the English merchants as follows: 'Messieurs, j'ai reçu votre argent, et je me flatte de l'avoir employé à votre satisfaction.' Voltaire remarks that 'tout cela' gives a just pride to an English Merchant.

No doubt it did; perhaps there were even rejoicings in London over the three-fleets episode – fireworks, organs, canons, *actions de grâces*, and so on. On the other hand, this kind of military pride and bravura was quintessentially what the Quakers stood against; nor was there any doubt about that point in Voltaire's mind: the eloquent ending of lettre I had made it unmistakable. The least one can say is that this new attitude approving English military success was prompted by sentiments that were exactly contrary to those expressed earlier. Nor do I think – given that the Quaker's pacifism was proposed as an absolute position, brooking no exceptions[8] – that this contradiction can be resolved in favour of a single position. The point is that the Quaker's eloquence is so overwhelming, while at the same time the narrator is made to seem so foolish, that one forgets that lettre I is actually part of a dialogue, a mere stage in the author's thinking. The narrator may seem to be blown away at the end, but obviously, in Voltaire's mind, there was still another side to the question, ready to turn up at the appropriate moment, which it does in lettre X.

The same is true of the treatment of Quaker austerities in lettre I: there can be no doubt that Voltaire found something admirable in the simplicity of the Quaker's dress, the absence of pleats and fancy buttons, the plain speech, and so on; perhaps he also respected the Quaker way of shunning all idle entertainments out of religious principle – their refusal to indulge in 'assemblées de plaisir', theatre (NB) and gambling. Yet in the long run, these 'virtues' had little or nothing to do with Voltaire's own character or way of life, accomplished playwright and frequenter of aristocracy that he was. How instructive, in this connection, to compare Voltaire's literary portrait of the Quaker with the real portrait of Voltaire himself, painted by Largillière in 1716 – admittedly a number of years prior to the English excursion. Perhaps indeed Voltaire's style of dress had sobered down somewhat by the time he wrote the *Lettres philosophiques*, but even so, the young Voltaire one sees in Largillière's portrait, with his jaunty wig, laces, heavily embroidered vest, velvet coat, above all the prominently displayed large gold buttons, bespeaks

8. On the general theme of Voltaire's pacifism see Henry Meyer, *Voltaire on war and peace*, Studies on Voltaire 144 (1976), *passim*.

a personality and a sense of values that could hardly be more different from the Quaker's buttonless simplicity. The letter on the Quaker reflected just one aspect of the question.

Furthermore, even though the Quaker's sober restraints on the pleasures of the senses seem to win out in lettre I, at the end of the collection (lettre XXV, 'Sur les *Pensées* de M. Pascal'), the easygoing, pleasure-loving side of Voltaire is brought back into action. In fact one is supposed to believe that Pascal's bleak austerities simply succumb to the pleasantly optimistic views being put forward by Voltaire. Theologically, the key issue here is the narrator's total rejection of the doctrine of original sin, which of course, for Christians, was the root of the whole notion of penance, mortification and the other austerities, and which was for Pascal in particular the indispensable key that unlocked the mystery of the miseries of the human condition. Voltaire is bent on denying both original sin and the miseries, and even though Voltaire's answers are not nearly so handily conclusive as he expects one to believe they are – in fact we sense potential seeds of the deepest sort of pessimism hidden in a number of his arguments – nevertheless, this time the austerities are said to lose out, giving the palm to the narrator, for all his pleasure-loving, sensual indulgences. No doubt significant differences separated the austerities of Quakerism from those of Jansenism, so significant that Voltaire could be at least momentarily beguiled into accepting one, even while rejecting the other. Nevertheless, in so far as Voltaire's position in the final letter is indulgently self-centred and pleasure-loving, it does indeed represent a reversal of the moral values of the first letter, and in that sense forms a contrariety with it.

Scholars have frequently wondered why, in a collection of allegedly English letters, the final letter, the longest of all, should be exclusively devoted to a writer who was French. There is no simple answer to the question, especially in view of Voltaire's diverse statements in response to the various *Pensées*. A partial solution may have to do with the influence of Pope, whose persuasive answers to Pascal in the *Essay on man* may have inspired Voltaire's own efforts. Another partial answer may be the one I have been suggesting: that Voltaire, seduced by the warmth and humanity of Quaker views, especially their pacifism, and seeing the possibility of turning these virtues into weapons against Catholicism and French aristocracy, had been willing to go along with Quaker austerities as well – for the sake of argument. But before the letters could end, the other truth, and the other real Voltaire, had to come out and redress the balance.

Certainly one finds strong, un-Classical elements of reform in this work: smallpox vaccination, Locke's sensualist philosophy, Newton's discoveries in physics, the call for a better system of taxation and of justice, for religious toleration, pacifism. All these campaigns are indeed part of this daring work, which Lanson, for better or worse, declared to be 'the first bomb hurled against the *ancien régime*'. But if one redresses the balance as Voltaire does in the final letter, one perceives – despite the daringly new ideas – at least a suggestion of a stasis, of the kind of stability that characterised the traditional Classical contrariety. This mixture of innovative and conservative confirms what scholars have been aware of in other contexts, that Voltaire remained in many ways tied to the traditions of Classicism and, for that matter, to the *ancien régime* he was attacking,[9] no matter how many contradictions such ambivalence entailed.

My assumption in treating the *Lettres philosophiques* has been that the work makes most sense when not taken as a treatise might be, that is, built upon immutable principles, constants that always behave in the same way and bestow on the text a sort of Newtonian order and coherence. Instead I see the work as changing as it evolves – as laudatory respect for Christian austerities yield to pleasure-loving self-indulgence, and the fervour of pacifism is replaced by military belligerence and admiration for martial bravura – even though the author himself paid no attention to the contradictions, and in fact must have been unaware of them. No doubt other segments of the text display more consistency than the parts I have chosen, which were distinctly 'moral' rather than 'scientific' (to use the terminology of today). But even so, the changes and inconsistencies one encounters in this text are exceptional in Voltaire: one never finds them to this degree in his works of maturity. Perhaps they reveal a sort of moment-by-moment impetuousness and impatience that is part of a younger perspective, or perhaps it simply manifests a new sense of relativity that belonged to the new era. But for present purposes only two points are essential: first, that these contrarieties, far from weakening the force of Voltaire's ideas, widen the text, increasing its scope and even, in the free play of contrasts, endowing it with a sort of liveliness and intensity that are unique in this work, part of its perfection. Secondly, that in so far as this text can in fact be analysed discursively, incrementally, in terms of stages and even contrary impulses, Voltaire anticipates – by pure coincidence – his younger contemporary who is to be the object of this study, the man he would come to call 'Frère Platon', in other words, Denis Diderot, the most brilliantly contradictory thinker of his age – as it will be the task of this study to prove.

9. This point is abundantly demonstrated in the recent five-volume biography of Voltaire edited by René Pomeau, *Voltaire en son temps* (Oxford 1985-1993). In a more controversial vein see Robert Ellrich, 'The cultural meaning of the anti-Rousseau question: a hypothesis', *Romance quarterly* 38 (1991), p.309-18, esp. p.315f.

IV

The Van Loo portrait

Of course the preceding remarks are not intended to imply that the transition from Voltaire – even from the early, more experimental Voltaire – to the mature Diderot is an easy one, or to suggest that it can be accomplished without a jolt. Indeed, especially if one concentrates on the texts by Diderot which were not intended immediately for the public at large, it would be difficult to find two writers from the same century and allegedly from the same philosophic team, who thought and wrote so diversely.

I have long suspected that, for Diderot, these differences might, at least to some small degree, be intentional: that Diderot may have taken special pleasure in cultivating a style that seemed privately personal, intimate, spontaneous and almost carelessly unconstrained because these qualities (allegedly) bespoke a writing personality quite unlike that of Voltaire, whose style seemed more calculated in its cleverness, and who, even in his supposedly intimate communications, never for a moment lost sight of the wider audience he was playing to. No doubt there were other, more consequential reasons for Diderot to cultivate a 'private' mode of discourse, including the oft-cited difficulties he had encoutered in his public roles as dramatist and *encyclopédiste*. Furthermore, there was a 'catch' to Diderot's allegedly intimate mode, namely, the understanding that off in the future, or far-away in some distant land, strangers would not only be allowed to listen in to his words, but might even supply an admiration and applause that was out of reach in the here and now. Thus, while bowing-out of any sort of immediate confrontation with the Patriarch's famous style, the author opened the door to other, later eventualities that would be left in the hands of posterity.

Whether by design or by chance, the text in question[10] – to be analysed after a few preliminaries – exemplifies virtues that are totally un-Voltairean. In style and in substance, it is everything Voltaire never was, and never wanted to be. Written as a letter to a close friend and sent abroad to strangers, not only is its tone intimate and personal, but it is explicitly an attempt to establish

---

10. This familiar text is readily available in Diderot, *Œuvres esthétiques*, ed. P. Vernière (Paris 1965), p.509-14 and in Jean Seznec's edition of the *Salons*, vol. iii (Oxford 1963; 2nd ed. 1983), p.66-68. The text of the DPV edition, vol.xvi (1990), p.81-84, based on the autograph, is seriously defective in that the variants omit what was undoubtedly the original ending of the article, with no warning to the reader of the omission. (The Seznec edition puts the ending in the notes; the Vernière edition puts it in the main text.) Gérard Gauthier, 'Diderot et son propre portrait', *Recherches sur Diderot et l'Encyclopédie* 21 (1996), p.15-21, unfortunately shows no awareness of this omission or of the other variants in his remarks on the merits of the autograph text.

the author's own 'true' character, something the Patriarch, for his part, would never have sought to reveal. The text probably contains more contrarieties per square inch than any other writing by Diderot. Nor is it surprising that such a radically structured piece should come, as this one does, from Diderot's *Salons* on art: rather the way odours were to do for Baudelaire, or the way dreams may do for ordinary mortals, visual images for Diderot often energised his thinking in a special way, as if his immersion in things visual turned off the usual controls that govern rational thought, freeing it for more extraordinary possibilities.

The particular *Salon* in which the text appears is the greatest one, the *Salon de 1767*. And yet, at the outset of the *Salon* the author goes to astonishing lengths to undermine any expectations the reader might have regarding the interest of the text to come, in fact to make sure everyone realises his inadequacies for the task ahead:[11] Diderot's very first words are a warning to Grimm not to expect any of the richness, variety, wisdom, folly or fecundity he may have displayed in the preceding *Salons*. And Diderot was well supplied with explanations and excuses to justify the alleged inferiority of the work at hand: his ideas have become worn out, with no new source to enliven them; his friend Falconet, on whom he might rely for help, is no longer available, nor was Diderot able to make some exciting trip to Italy to gain fresh material and points of comparison; if only some way could be found to give him intimate knowledge of the French and Flemish schools, and have sketches made to accompany his descriptions – all of which forms the deceptive prelude to the longest and most fecund *Salon* of them all, not to mention the most original, the liveliest, the richest, the most full of wisdom and folly, the most everything that Diderot had sworn it would not be. I leave to others to determine how much of this was clever calculation on Diderot's part, that is, a deliberate effort to capture the reader's benevolence and sympathy all the more surely by admitting to weaknesses he knew were non-existent, and how much represented Diderot's genuine apprehension concerning his handling of the task before him.

When at last, after all the disclaimers, and also after a lengthy theoretical discussion of *la belle nature* and related matters, Diderot finally plunges into the *Salon* itself, the first painter to come under his scrutiny is Louis-Michel Van Loo, who had submitted a substantial number of portraits, and also some allegories, to the *Salon*. The discussion is wide-ranging and given partly in dialogue as Diderot dramatises the objections he imagines to his own statements. One after another Van Loo's paintings come up for consideration, and,

11. As Seznec points out: *Salons*, iii.vii.

rather informally, Diderot either approves or blames, or both, employing a variety of approaches along the way. This almost helter-skelter presentation in no way prepares us for the surprise when one of the pictures Diderot is about to evaluate suddenly turns out to be, not the allegory of Sculpture or Painting, or the portrait of Cardinal de Choiseul, or the one of Abbé de Breteuil, or some other distant personage, but the portrait of himself, Monsieur Diderot (Figure 1). Abruptly, the movement from picture to picture comes to a halt. Diderot will give this portrait his undivided attention, in detail and at length – and so will this present discussion.

To find, as one does in this review,[12] a great writer pondering the details of a painted image of himself is a privileged event, *rarissime* in eighteenth-century France. Curiously, the only other comparable text from this period is the famous letter by Voltaire telling how Pigalle set about sculpting the Patriarch's own ancient body, stripped naked, right down to its skin and bone, just as Diderot himself had insisted. As might be expected, these two texts are completely diverse in content and style. Yet in each case something rather unique is disclosed about the author, and naturally such revelations make us yearn for other texts like them. But apparently philosophers such as Montesquieu or Buffon had no inclination towards similar reflections, nor would the idea have occurred to abbé Prévost or Laclos; even Rousseau did not need the stimulus of a visual image to indulge in intimate ruminations about himself. To be sure, the Enlightenment was better off in this respect than the preceding century, when there were no such texts at all – as if writers' images, even images of philosophers, had not yet attained sufficient importance to be worthy of comment.[13] There may even be vestiges of this earlier disparaging attitude lingering in this precious commentary by Diderot, and also in the one by Voltaire, in their ironies and self-depreciations. There is also a hint of Montaigne.

It would be easy to interpret Diderot's *compte rendu* of Louis-Michel Van Loo's portrait of him the way Sir Kenneth Clark did, as an angry put-down

12. Much of the material of this part of the present discussion has been published, in different form, in *Ici et ailleurs: le dix-huitième siècle au présent. Mélanges offerts à Jacques Proust* (Tokyo 1996), p.111-21. My analyis, though independently conceived, coincides on a number of points with that of Julie C. Hayes, 'Diderot's elusive self: the portrait by Van Loo in the *Salon de 1767*', *Kentucky language quarterly* 31 (1984), p.251-58. Cf. Daniel Brewer, *The Discourse of Enlightenment in eighteenth-century France* (Cambridge 1993), p.255-56.

13. There were also fewer portraits of authors painted by famous artists, the exceptions being Molière, painted repeatedly by his friend Mignard, and La Fontaine, likewise a friend of Mignard, and whose portrait was painted by De Troy, Rigaud and Largillière (according to Antoine Adam), and also by Le Brun.

or dismissal. Certainly Diderot is anxious to distance himself from Van Loo's rendering; in fact in this passage he lets loose several outbursts demanding that the reader, or Diderot's imagined posterity, side with him in making a negative judgement of the portrait. And yet, at the same time, other statements go directly counter to this position, so much so that the passage might be interpreted as a dialogue in which several sides pull against one another as they advance the discussion to further stages. Nor do these constant contrarieties interfere with the text's proceeding positively via associations of ideas; thus the progress of these reflections involves a complex and multi-faceted growing process in which each statement seems to bring the next one into being, if only as an answer to it. The ensuing discussion will keep track of how this occurs.

The first sentence, the dramatically singular word 'Moi', puts both the painting and the problem of Diderot's true appearance before the reader in one stroke. The word is 'hieroglyphic' in Diderot's sense of the term, and all the rest of the first half of the text will be devoted to unlocking its meanings, both hidden and obvious. The question having been opened, Diderot proceeds to stake out his first position with a strong statement, resonant with classical[14] overtones, declaring that, though he loves the painter dearly, he loves truth more. The implication is certainly that he intends to speak against the portrait despite his friendship for the artist, and the commanding opening position of this negative implication will cause this expectation to weigh powerfully throughout the text. Yet, surprisingly, the following phrases do not carry on the same attitude; instead they do an abrupt about-face, asserting a position that runs counter to the expectation just established: they declare that in fact the portrait looks rather like him ('assez ressemblant'), and that if people do not think so, it is just because they have never seen him without a wig. Diderot adds, likewise in a favourable vein, that the portrait is lively ('très vivant') and, injecting at least a semblance of objectivity by speaking of himself in the third person singular, that it combines his gentle qualities ('douceur') with his vivacity. Thanks to this unexpected turn of events a new, favourable point of view is on the upswing; one may say that so far so good; in fact, excellent.

But now another voice is heard, coming from the opposite corner, and which will momentarily drown out these positive implications. A miracle of historical luck has preserved the document that identifies the original behind this other voice: it was none other than the author's wife, Mme Diderot, never known for pleasantness or generosity of disposition, and who had declared,

14. The idea is frequently attributed to Aristotle, though usually given in Latin: 'Amicus Plato, sed magis amica veritas.'

seeing her husband's portrait just after it had been publicly displayed in the Louvre, that it gave him 'l'air d'une vieille coquette qui fait le petit bec et qui a encore des prétentions'.[15] This is the tone that now slides in with the disjunctive 'mais', and, as if gathering energy and sarcasm as it proceeds, goes from the relatively innocuous complaint 'trop jeune', to the more serious 'tête trop petite', the adjective 'petite' leading to the main issue: 'joli comme une femme', whose disparagement is immediately reinforced by three bisyllabic modifiers snapping abruptly in its wake ('lorgnant, souriant, mignard'), and that clear the way for a direct quotation from Mme Diderot which comes popping nastily in a cluster of labials and fricatives ('faisant le petit bec'), and whose unpleasantness then infects Diderot's own ironical addition, even though the sounds of its closed, back-in-the-throat vowels are almost voluptuously contrasting: 'la bouche en cœur'.

Mme Diderot's attitude of disapproval, so artfully orchestrated by Diderot to bring out all the irony of the caricature, also seems to linger on in Diderot's judgement of the portrait's colouration, now apparently criticised for having nothing of the 'sagesse' (balance? moderation?) of one of Van Loo's other portraits, and it even echos on in the humorous complaint that, given the extravagant luxuriousness of the clothes he displays in the picture, if the tax collector ever decided to make his assessment on the basis of that dressing gown, Diderot would be a ruined man. Looking back, through Diderot's wittily exaggerated description, at this overdressed old coquette, plying her winsome glances, with her unwise colours and Cupid's-bow mouth, one already senses here the overtones of whorishness that will always make themselves felt each time the theme reappears.[16]

Mme Diderot's intervention having momentarily spent itself, Diderot

15. 'A Sophie Volland' (11 octobre 1767), *Correspondance*, ed. Georges Roth, t.vii (Paris 1962), p.174. Diderot comments, 'Il y a bien quelque chose de vrai dans cette critique. Quoi qu'il en soit, c'est une marque d'amitié de la part d'un excellent homme, qui doit m'être et qui me sera toujours précieuse' (p.174-75).

16. In his caricature, Diderot is rejecting and holding up to mockery the feminine or androgynous side of his personality. As I was reminded by Anthony Strugnell at the 1995 International Congress on the Enlightenment held in Münster (panel discussion on Diderot, Roland Mortier presiding), Diderot did not always take this negative attitude towards this aspect of himself in his writings; in fact there were contexts in which he was quite willing to accept the emotionality of his own temperament as being feminine. One remembers as well Mlle de Lespinasse's famous suggestion in *Le Rêve de d'Alembert* that biologically man might be the 'monstre' of woman, and vice versa, the word 'monstre' being exquisitely, genially two-faced. Such gender ambiguities are fascinating and important in Diderot; I have written about some of them in the past, and do so occasionally in the present study. The main task at hand, however, is the humbler one of simply establishing that, in this revealing text in which he seeks to propose an acceptable visual identity, Diderot's thought processes work via contrarieties, and hence to suggest the importance of looking for them elsewhere.

switches back to the favourable assessment and exactly the same pattern repeats itself. First he finds all manner of things to praise – the accessories, the colour, the effect up close and from afar, the fine hands, and so on; Diderot notes too that he is depicted from the front, bareheaded (wiglessness also being a favourable trait for Diderot) ... whereupon the familiar voice of Mme Diderot is heard again, instantly turning the approving tone into one of mocking disgust: the grey toupet combined with his 'mignardise' give him, to quote Mme Diderot's very words, 'l'air d'une vieille coquette qui fait encore l'aimable'. In an instant, all the merits Diderot had just praised so warmly are forgotten. And just as before, Mme Diderot's criticism brings another in its wake, for Diderot takes the occasion to complain that his pose in the portrait is that of a secretary of state, not of a philosopher, as it should have been.

Until this moment one has assumed that the painter himself was guilty of all these faults; indeed Diderot had as much as said so at the opening. But now, unexpectedly, the ground shifts and the blame for everything is put on Mme Van Loo (not the wife of Louis-Michel, but his aunt), who had come to chatter foolishly in the doorway while he was being painted; it was she who gave him that look, Diderot declares, and that was what spoiled everything. ('C'est [...] Madame Van Loo [...] qui lui a donné cet air-là, et qui a tout gâté.') What did Mme Van Loo look like as she stood in the doorway? Fortunately her husband, the famous painter Carl Van Loo, drew her portrait, and if one places it beside the portrait of Diderot by the nephew Louis-Michel, one discovers a very curious relation between them (Figure 2): Diderot's expression seems actually to have taken on something of the look of Mme Van Loo, in fact he looks more like her here than in any other portrait of him. No doubt part of the resemblance can be explained in stylistic terms by the fact that Louis-Michel may have been schooled in portraiture by his uncle. But, especially in view of Diderot's exceptionally mimetic literary personality, it is very tempting to conclude as well that Mme Van Loo's facial expression had in fact decidedly affected his own, through a kind of sympathetic vibration as he listened to her, thus confirming Diderot's claim that Mme Van Loo was responsible for his expression.

But regardless of who is to 'blame', for present purposes the important point is that Diderot, while holding Mme van Loo accountable, has tacitly conceded – contrary to his earlier positions – that his expression in the portrait is authentic. This concession may be slightly obscured by Diderot's wording: 'La fausseté du premier moment a influé sur tout le reste.' In this context, the only 'falseness' lies in his expression being, in his view, quite 'wrong' for a good portrait of him. This interpretation is confirmed by the ensuing phrases, in which Diderot imagines the kind of expression his face might have displayed

31

Figure 1. Louis Michel Van Loo, *Portrait de M. Diderot*

Figure 2. Carl Van Loo, *Portrait de Mme Van Loo*

if, instead of chattering in the doorway, the divine-voiced Mme Van Loo (praised for her singing in Rousseau's *Confessions*) had sat at her harpsichord and performed some emotion-charged Italian air about the abandonment of Dido. The portrait, says Diderot, would then have been completely different. Thus everything in this part of the text implies that Diderot's expression in the portrait, inspired and spoiled by Mme Van Loo, is a real one.

But of course, even more than the pleasure of listening to Mme Van Loo's singing, Diderot would have preferred a depiction that showed him alone with his meditations, and he proceeds to imagine – in a passage exactly paralleling the explanations accompanying Le Brun's 'Têtes d'expression' in the *planches* of the *Encyclopédie* – the position of his mouth, the look of his eyes and the whole of his face as his intense mental preoccupations make themselves evident. The sentence ends with a wistful sigh about the fine portrait Michel might have painted in such circumstances. 'Mon joli philosophe', he adds, pretending to be complimenting the figure in the painting, but in the demasculinised characterisation one already senses that Mme Diderot cannot be far away.

This time it is not clear just whom Diderot is addressing as he wonders out loud how he will explain to his grandchildren that his sorry writings, 'tristes ouvrages', can possibly have been composed by 'ce riant, mignon, efféminé, vieux coquet-là'. Though the 'coquette' of the earlier intervention has now been given its masculine form ('coquet'), the accompanying adjective 'efféminé' compensates and preserves Mme Diderot's denigrating demasculinisation. One notes too that the adjective 'riant' is patently false, since he is clearly not laughing in the portrait (even the 'souriant' used earlier may be close to stretching the point, since his smile is only modestly suggested). One can only assume that the disparagement of the satirical caricature has got out of hand, that veracity no longer matters. And now Diderot is ready to take the final plunge: he simply declares to his grandchildren that the figure in the portrait is not he, and further that of the hundred expressions worn on his face in a day, not a single one ever looked like this. He surveys in rapid succession all the various kinds of mood his face actually did display – doubtless so the grandchildren can verify for themselves that none of them matches the expression Van Loo has given him. One also suspects that this final step, the denial that the portrait is he, has been on Diderot's mind from the start, from his opening statement that, however much he values the artist's friendship, he loves the truth still more. This is the truth he is determined to declare.

This statement, that the Van Loo portrait is a non-likeness, marks the end of the first half of the *compte rendu*. He will never again mention the portrait directly. And yet Diderot's task is far from ended, for if the Van Loo portrait is not the real picture of Diderot, one naturally wonders what does (or 'did' for the grandchildren of the distant future) represent his true likeness. Diderot first has recourse to verbal description, somewhat disjointedly trying to convey some notion of the breadth of his forehead, the liveliness of the eyes, the rather large features, the head absolutely like that of an ancient orator (Cicero? Demosthenes?), and his almost hopelessly emotional 'bonhomie' that recalls – so he states – the rustic manners of antiquity. Perhaps the obvious incompleteness of this verbal characterisation makes him resort henceforth to images of himself by other artists. In any case, the notion of 'antiquity' is probably what leads him to think next of the engraving after the sketch by Greuze, for Greuze had shown Diderot's head in 'Roman' profile and given him a 'Roman' nose as well. On the other hand, Diderot claims he does not like the way the engraving exaggerated all his features. Abruptly there is a new explanation: his face is a mask, deceptive to the artist – although Diderot cannot decide whether this deceptive quality derives from the unmanageable complexity of the elements the mask melds together or, on the contrary, from the fleeting rapidity, the incessant mobility of the changing emotions it expresses and which renders the artist's task so dauntingly and surprisingly difficult.

Contrary impulses now come thick and fast; virtually every assertion will be immediately denied: the stress placed on the quasi-impossibility of making a true image of his mask brings Diderot to think of an artist, a no-account fellow named Garand, who had done just that, the only one to catch him perfectly, the real Diderot. The forceful emphasis on the uniqueness of Garand's accomplishment leads Diderot to remember other artists who had done 'good portraits' of him. He now recalls having forgotten the fine bust by Mlle Collot, and which had replaced the poor one (another contrariety) by Falconet, an inferiority which the latter artist recognised. The most dramatic moment in Diderot's account comes when Falconet is said to take a hammer and smash his bust, the violence of the hammer blow putting an end both to the sculptor's work of art and to this series of contrarieties in the text. At the same time it introduces the theme of the artefact as revealer of secrets: even as the crumbling statue brings to light Diderot's real ears, until then covered up by an unnatural wig (the wig being an emanation from Mme Geoffrin), so too, prior to its smashing, the expression on the face of the bust reflected the unspoken pain of the soul that 'devoured' Diderot as he sat for the sculptor. And now[17] a final question; how can an artist miss the obvious facial features, and yet divine and faithfully render such secrets hidden in the depths of the soul? Instead of giving an answer Diderot recounts another anecdote proving

17. For the end I follow the text of the five manuscripts cited in the Seznec edition, p.68, line 16; in Vernière, p.514.

that such a thing has happened, this time when La Tour intuitively sensed, and rendered in his drawing, the unspoken, and apparently invisible, fatigue of a friend who, unbeknownst to the artist, had just spent the night at the bedside of an indisposed relative.

What a curious way to end the *compte rendu*! Van Loo has long since vanished, as has, apparently, the question of Diderot's true appearance; even La Tour is left behind as the text moves off with an unspecified friend to sit in an unlocated room while tending to a relative of undeclared closeness who is suffering to an unspecified degree from an unnamed malady. To be sure, the late autograph manuscript version of the text omits these details – suggesting, perhaps, that the author had come to doubt their relevance. And yet, as five other manuscripts attest, Diderot himself originally felt that they formed the right conclusion of his piece, as though they were what gave it completion. And for the modern reader, too, this passage in some mysterious way does convey a feeling of finality and closure. Perhaps this is due in part to the silence of the final night-time 'scene' beside the bed of the sick person. But probably the main ingredient bringing the piece to an end is the fact that the voice of Mme Diderot has finally been stilled: the two last anecdotes take us so far from her in theme and location that they seem doubly to conjure her out of the picture.

Furthermore, it may just be possible that Diderot has given a final answer to her, though hidden in code, in the last lines, a message quite as unspoken as the ones Falconet and La Tour uncovered intuitively in their models, without a word being said, something even belied by formal appearances. Perhaps I should confess that my conviction on this point was formed as I studied the original in its old location in the Louvre, when it had an entire segment of a spacious wall to itself and was lit partly by a daylight that changed from hour to hour, rendering subtleties that are invisible as it is currently displayed, with flat artificial lighting, and crowded tendentiously next to the *Accordée de village*. Remembering the picture as it used to be without the Greuze, it seems obvious that Mme Diderot's nasty little caricature was quite wrong: this is a magnificent depiction, breathtaking even among all the splendours of the Louvre. Diderot and his wife to the contrary notwithstanding, there is nothing whorish about it. But the portrait renders a personality of considerable complexity, not at all the simple sketch of the man meditating caught so well by Garand, and doubtless showing more of Diderot's 'feminine' side than the image of the Roman orator which Diderot claimed he preferred (an idea probably suggested by Mme Therbouche's bare-chested portrait of him at the same Salon). My own suspicion is that Diderot was simply not prepared to recognise officially and out loud the diverse ambiguities of the personality of the portrait, an unwillingness that left him vulnerable to Mme Diderot's satire. And yet, even as the *compte rendu* stands, one has only to ignore her intrusions to find in the first half of the text the makings of a splendidly favourable review, and at the end, confirmation of this assessment in a more covert avowal, tacitly insinuating that, despite the almost raucous protests to the contrary, Van Loo had known the secrets of Diderot's soul.

Looking back over the whole, where have we been? In résumé: Diderot loves truth and the portrait is false. The portrait is essentially true ('assez ressemblant'). It is false because it makes him look like an old coquette. It has true qualities. It is an ageing coquette and false. Actually the expression is true, but Diderot does not like it and Mme Van Loo is to blame. The expression is totally false: he never looked like that. The engraved portrait after Greuze is infinitely better (truer), although all the features are exaggerated (partially false). His face is a mask whose complexity deceives the artist, or perhaps, on the contrary, his expressions are so fleeting that to capture them truly is extremely difficult (thus all portraits of him are likely to be false). Garand captured his expression truly and was the only one to do so. Other artists have done good (true) portraits of him, among them Mlle Collot; even Falconet had divined his secret (true) sorrow, the way artists have been known to do: witness La Tour, who had divined the (true) secret of someone else.

In the first part of the account these shifts in the angle from which the portrait is being viewed (favourable or unfavourable, true or false) cause the portrait too to change its appearance (in the imagination) according to our evaluation of it. In the second part of the passage the shifts persist, but now they are translated into other portraits which succeed and replace each other in Diderot's recollection, and which modern readers too are able to visualise, thanks to photographic reproductions.[18] And if, for oneself, one flicks through these other images – just as Diderot himself ticked them off in his memory – Diderot's mask takes on different expressions with an uncanny, quasi-kineto-scopic effect.

As Diderot's account undulates back and forth between opposing evalu-ations, each calling up the other, in free counterpoint, as though each declara-tion naturally – without even thinking about it – opened the door to contradic-tion, it turns out that Diderot is never pinned down by his statements. Any other writer of the period would have been willing to accept the consequences of such a categorical and unqualified declaration as 'Je n'ai jamais été bien fait que par un pauvre diable appelé Garand': henceforth – for anyone else – Garand's portrait would have sat alone, commanding an otherwise empty

18. See the Seznec edition, plates 5-9.

landscape, his solitary presence bleakly laying to eternal rest the question 'Did anyone ever do a good likeness of Diderot?' But for Diderot the barrenness and lifelessness produced by categorical answers becomes a sort of vacuum in nature, instantly inviting denial: almost before one knows it, Mlle Collot's fine bust makes its recollected appearance, along with other 'good portraits of me' in the plural, and the question has moved to another stage. There had to be a categorical answer, no doubt; but there had to be also its overturning and a renewal of the question, even as, in Diderot's materialistic philosophy, regeneration and life automatically proceed from death and disintegration. The almost incessant production of contrarieties one from another means that Diderot's thought is, at least in a text such as this, in a constant process of rejuvenation, continually liberating itself from itself through denial: the past is so regularly abolished or superseded, with new prospects opening up, that one wonders whether any answer can ever be terminal.

In *Le Rêve de d'Alembert* (1769) during one of Alembert's dream monologues the awesome question arises: 'What is life?' After a short pause marked by *points de suspension* the answer comes in a single succinct phrase: 'Une suite d'actions et de réactions.'[19] But this is exactly the process of the sentences of his *compte rendu*: they are nothing but a series of actions and reactions. In other words, this text – Diderot's quest for a pictorial identity, a search that goes forward impelled by a multitude of contradictions – not only re-creates a thinking process but enacts Diderot's concept of life.

Since the contrarieties of this text are sequential and discursive rather than simultaneous, they are closer to the vagaries of those found in Voltaire than to La Fontaine or Molière. They appear to be unconscious as well, even as Voltaire's sometimes were: one has the impression that Diderot's text simply evolves, one thing leading to another. To be sure, in general unconscious contrariety was less of a creative principle for Voltaire than for Diderot: it crops up far less frequently, even in the *Lettres philosophiques*, and with a strong admixture of Classicism. I think that, in this connection, Diderot's text represents an authentic rupture with the past. Since contrariety emerges here as simply the natural way for Diderot, and for the reader too by sympathetic vibration, to think and react, the process implies a breakdown in the kind of objective control that had always characterised the aesthetics of Classicism. Diderot's contrarieties in this passage – no matter what their Classical ante-

19. On the philosophical background of these terms in Diderot, see the magisterial article by Jean Starobinski, '"Action et réaction" chez Diderot', *Dilemmes du roman: essays in honor of Georges May*, ed. Catherine Lafarge (Saratoga, Calif. 1989), p.73-87.

cedents may have been – actually bespeak a form of anti-Classicism. The spontaneity (real of feigned) that his contrarieties imply, the movement forward that appears to take place via a free association of ideas rather than by following a plotted argument, the seeming openness that occurs when an assertion regularly or irregularly becomes an incitement to denial of itself, the freedom (again whether apparent or real) and the immediacy one feels as the now ancient past is repeatedly abolished by an exhilaratingly new present, all these happenings represent a breaking out of the confines of rules and the aesthetic of 'recul' that went along with them, which had been the glory of Classical art. It might even be tempting to see the text as a declaration of war on the aesthetics of Classicism – in the name of spontaneity, inconsistency and subjectivity.

To find so many contrarieties coming so rapidly in so brief a space is exceptional in Diderot's writings. Elsewhere, the pace can be more moderate; contrarieties can operate singly in the text, and of course there are some texts which lack them entirely (or so it seems). No single rule governs them all. Furthermore the present study has been entitled *Diderot's counterpoints*, in the plural, to allow for at least some awareness of the infinite variety of ways in which Diderot's ideas play against one another. Certainly 'contrariety' will be the main counterpoint to be examined in the following pages, but with the understanding that the creative tensions of Diderot's style push and pull in every direction imaginable, contrariety being just one of them.

To preview the bare bones of the substance of the chapters to come: in the *Supplément au Voyage de Bougainville*, a single powerful enunciation generates the dynamics of a reversal that will dominate much of the rest of the text; but the reversal itself also generates counter-reversals (chapter 1). The contrarieties of the *Lettre sur les sourds et muets* form a web that stretches right across the text from one end to the other, and (the contrarieties themselves being incipient dialogues) dramatises the profound ambiguities of Diderot's reactions to Classicism (chapter 2). The main position taken by Diderot in *Le Paradoxe sur le comédien* is in effect a dramatic about-face that denies the theatrical values he himself had so forcefully put forward in the earlier *Entretiens sur le Fils naturel*; yet the denial itself, so absolutely stated, inevitably brings about other contrarieties within the text (chapters 3 and 4). In the *Salons*, no artist was more highly regarded by Diderot than Poussin. In contrast to Fénelon's Classical analysis, Diderot sees one of Poussin's landscapes as fraught with contrapuntal tensions, some of them tinged with political implications (chapter 5). Elsewhere in the *Salons*, the intense, ambiguous and multilayered fascination exerted by the dense moralism of one kind of painting forms a contrariety with Diderot's equal fascination with the amoral aestheticism of another sort of painting, a dilemma he never succeeds in resolving (chapter 7).

One of the puzzles of Diderot's early philosophical writings has been the simultaneous occurrence of arguments for deism and arguments for atheism in the same work. Naturally scholars have wondered which position most truly reflected Diderot's ideas on religion at that time. One way out of the dilemma is to think of Diderot's atheism as not only an answer to deism, but as forming a contrariety with it. The dynamism of this contrariety can be seen as a major force behind the lyricism of the late *Rêve de d'Alembert* (chapter 6).

While in *Le Rêve de d'Alembert* materialism was the inherently not-very-amusing subject matter, one which the author constantly strove to lighten and enliven by the dialogue form, in *Jacques le fataliste* the essence of the work is not philosophy, but literature seen as reflecting human relationships and experiences, and expressed as story-telling via every imaginable sort of narrative, dialogue and monologue. In such an essentially fictional context, the much-advertised 'fatalism' of the title – and whose absurdity and uselessness in human terms is repeatedly demonstrated – may suggest a sort of *trompe-l'œil*, whose ambiguous effect leaves the reader wondering whether the metaphysical issues involved are intended to be taken seriously, or simply enjoyed as part of the game. At the end, all is fiction (chapter 8).

The culmination of Diderot's artistic life was *Le Neveu de Rameau*, in which multitudes of contrarieties seem to explode into being as, tumultuously and in every direction, they open onto new perceptions of reality. Even so, one may detect a repeated dialectic of contrariety emerging, which gives the dialogue a recognisable dynamic pattern. Furthermore, in one sense at least, these contrarieties represent a return to the earlier Classical form, in which contrariety was not an inadvertent or unconscious phenomenon, but deliberate. There may even be, amid the diverse marvels of this text, reasons to remember Molière and La Fontaine (chapter 9).

Given the essential open-endedness, the ongoing nature, of Diderot's creative processes, the only conclusion such a study can have is really no conclusion. The last word will be Diderot's (Conclusions).

1. Contrariety in the *Supplément au Voyage de Bougainville*

> C'est une nation, dirais-je à Platon, en laquelle il n'y a
> aucune espèce de trafic; nulle connaissance de lettres;
> nulle science de nombres; nul nom de magistrat ni de
> supériorité politique; nul usage de service, de richesse
> ou de pauvreté; nuls contrats; nulles successions; nuls
> partages; nulles occupations qu'oisives [...]
>
> > (Montaigne, 'Des cannibales')

> I'th' commonwealth I would by contraries,
> Execute all things; for no kind of traffic
> Would I admit; no name of magistrate;
> Letters should not be known; riches, poverty,
> Bourne, bound of land, tilth, vineyard, none; [...]
> No occupation, all men idle, all [...]
>
> > (Shakespeare, *The Tempest*, II.i)

I

I AM not the first to see 'contrariety' in Diderot. The original definer of the phenomenon was Herbert Dieckmann, who formulated the conception in response to the astonishing contrast he discerned between Diderot's letter to his daughter Angélique on the occasion of her wedding (13 September 1772),[1] and the *Supplément au Voyage de Bougainville*, which dates from around the same time.[2]

The letter specifies the code of marital behaviour that Diderot expected of

---

1. *Correspondance*, ed. Roth, xii.123-27. The page numbers in the text refer to this edition.

2. Diderot, *Supplément au Voyage de Bougainville*, ed. Herbert Dieckmann (Geneva 1955), Introduction, p.cxvii-cxxxii. Although not using the term 'contrariety', Dieckmann certainly suggests the essentials of the phenomenon when he writes: 'Parmi les écrits dangereux qu'Angélique aurait été obligée de rejeter, le *Supplément* aurait été un des tout premiers. Cependant le contraste n'exclut pas un échange en profondeur, une influence indirecte, opérant, pour ainsi dire, à revers. Au contraire, le contraste joue souvent un rôle décisif dans la formation et la direction de nos sentiments et de nos pensées. Dans la genèse de l'œuvre, les idées que l'auteur refuse au combat, ou même qu'il rejette, en partie inconsciemment, peuvent avoir plus d'influence que celles qu'il accepte. Nous croyons que dans le cas présent il s'agit d'une telle influence par contraste' (p.cxxxi).

his daughter after the wedding.[3] According to this new law, Angélique's whole existence, her every breath, so to speak, was to be fashioned to give pleasure and show obedience to the man she married. The letter explains in exact detail that marriage means that she will now exist solely for her spouse: she should strive in every way to cater to his whims, conform herself to his reasonable tastes, seize every occasion to display her respect for him. Her humour should be 'douce, complaisante et gaie' (p.124), making the home so agreeable her husband will not want to stray elsewhere; and she should make sure to stay in good health, for she cannot perform her duties otherwise, and sickness, while it may temporarily awaken compassion, becomes boring in the long run: her husband may start looking abroad for distractions. Other than what Diderot terms 'l'intérieur de votre maison' (p.124), i.e. the running of the household chores, which is to remain exclusively her concern, there is apparently nothing she can call her own: her reading is to be used to adorn her mind, presumably for her husband's enjoyment, and one assumes that the practice of music is encouraged in part because it will entertain her husband – in addition to providing salutary discipline for herself. Nor are these outward manifestations all that is required, for Diderot stipulates that Angélique's 'soul' too is to be occupied by her husband: 'qu'il soit sans cesse comme au fond de votre âme' (p.123). In other words, Angélique will not even have a soul she can call her own.

This idea is part of a whole programme of thought control: 'Tâchez de ne rien penser que vous ne puissiez lui dire; [...] Ne faites rien dont il ne puisse être témoin. Soyez en tout et toujours comme sous ses yeux' (p.123). And as an extra layer of restriction, to the husband's watchful eye he adds his own: 'si vous vous demandez à vous même: Que mon père penseroit-il de moi s'il me voyoit, s'il m'entendoit, s'il sçavoit, vous ferez toujours bien' (p.125).

As so often in Diderot, sexuality is the central issue in this letter. All the exhortations, menaces and prohibitions ultimately have a single purpose, which is to ensure that his daughter remains the exclusive sexual property of the man her father has chosen for her. Everything is designed to guarantee her conjugal fidelity: to ensure that she does not stray from the straight and narrow path, that she does not engage in flirtations, that she does not tarnish her reputation, that she does not fall. Nor is this simply a matter of observing right principles; for Diderot this is a most personal issue, a question of his own happiness or eternal distress. In other words, on top of the large burden that Angélique is

3. On the details of this wedding, and on Angélique in general, see Arthur Wilson, *Diderot* (New York 1972), p.594-96, 613-17.

already bearing, Diderot loads the additional burden of his love for her (p.124-26):

Je ne vous recommande pas d'avoir des mœurs. Ce soupçon m'accablerait de douleur, vous ôterait mon estime, et me chasseroit de votre maison et de beaucoup d'autres. Après m'être glorifié de vous, je mourrois d'avoir à en rougir. Je suis fait à vous entendre nommer avec éloge. Je ne me ferois jamais à vous entendre nommer avec blâme. Plus vous êtes connue, par vous et par moi, plus votre désordre seroit éclatant. Soyez surtout en garde contre les premiers jours de votre union. Une passion nouvelle entraîne à des indiscrétions qui se remarquent et qui deviennent le germe d'une indécence qui dégénère en habitude [...].

Je vous aime de toute mon âme [...] Malheur à vous, et malheur à moi, si je craignois de passer devant votre porte! Mon enfant, j'ai tant pleuré, tant souffert depuis que je suis au monde. Console moi. Dédommage moi [...].

His final instruction is that she should re-read his letter every month.

This marriage is in no sense a liberation from her father's control, but simply a change in the administration of that control: Diderot's surrogate is now in charge. Diderot states this in so many words at the opening of the letter: 'Ma fille, vous allez quitter la maison de votre père et de votre mère pour entrer dans celle de votre époux et la vôtre. En vous accordant à Caroillon je lui ai résigné toute mon autorité' (p.123).

What an extraordinary document to come from the pen of a materialistic philosopher, someone one is pleased to place at the centre of the movement called 'Enlightenment', and who, elsewhere, seems positively sane in his attitude towards the female sex! Perhaps, *mutatis mutandis*, the vows taken by nuns in Diderot's time were as severe as this programme for Angélique. But actually the closest parallels in the repression of free instincts are to be found in the comedies of Molière. Leaving aside the Christian elements, this is just the sort of programme featured in Arnolphe's 'Maximes de mariage' in the *Ecole des femmes* (iii.2). Diderot's fixation on the all-consuming importance of his daughter's conjugal fidelity is almost as maniacal as Arnolphe's obsession that he not be made 'cocu'. Just as in this letter, Molière's great comedies are full of father figures saying 'Je le veux' to their daughters (or wards) as they marry them off to the men they have chosen for their own reasons. And as Diderot sets about systematically eliminating all the breathing space his daughter might have had, dictating all her activities, suppressing all the freedom of her naturally wandering instincts – especially the sexual ones – installing watchful eyes inside and outside her soul, eliminating every possible avenue of escape from this prison-house of marital fidelity, how one longs for some jovial, good-hearted Dorine to break through all the restrictions: 'Elle? elle n'en fera qu'un sot je vous assure' (*Tartuffe*, ii.2).

1. Contrariety in the 'Supplément au Voyage de Bougainville'

Alas, Diderot's letter is not the world of comedy, but the tyrannical world of the sentimental *drame*, requiring total compliance from the listener. Angélique did not revolt. According to the editor of the Diderot *Correspondance* (xii.122), she carefully preserved the letter, and, judgeing by the tattered condition of its creases, re-read it many times just as Diderot had wished. In the absence of Dorine, perhaps one may be forgiven for recalling at this point that, later on, Diderot's own straightlaced, right-thinking precepts recoiled on him when Angélique and her husband decided to prepare an edition of her father's works which would eliminate everything they thought improper or indecent, and also put his ideas in a more tidily rational order – an aim that occasionally necessitated vast revisions, as certain of the Vandeul manuscripts attest. Fortunately for the peace of Diderot's soul the edition was never published.

The other unexpected happening with which the letter may be associated was the *Supplément au Voyage de Bougainville*.[4] This is to say that at the time when Diderot was locking his daughter into an eternal servitude of conjugal faithfulness, he was not only reading of, but actually creating in his own imagination, a society which had no use for fidelity in this sense, in which new husbands or mates were available for women whenever they wished to procreate with someone else, a society in which no blame was ever attached to a woman for her sexual activities with males, so long as she was in a condition to bear children, and which denounced as illogical and contrary to the laws of nature the very notion of remaining the property of one's spouse. In other words, the *Supplément* was a denial of all the moral assumptions of the letter to Angélique. In some parts of the *Supplément* the moral principles of the letter actually become the main targets for destruction.

I will not even attempt to delve into the motives behind this phenomenon. I will not try to explain, much less justify, Diderot's tyranny over his daughter and his obviously strong and complex (not to say incestuous) feelings about her – even though the parallel with jealous father figures of Molière's comedies makes it extremely tempting to do so. Nor will I dissect the intricacies of the psychological mechanism through which the repressions entailed by these feelings reversed themselves into impulses of liberation in the *Supplément*. It does seem apropos, however, to repeat the generality mentioned earlier that, according to the infinitely curious mode of thinking of this philosopher, a forcefully stated position – especially when accompanied by strong emotions – often brings on a reversal, as if the powerful assertion of some position

4. Wilson, *Diderot*, p.615, points out that Diderot's *Sur les femmes* was also composed at the time of Angélique's wedding.

automatically functioned as a challenge which demanded, and in this case produced, opposition – from the author himself. Secondly, it seems clear that the mechanism of reversal in Diderot was indeliberate, which is to say, unconscious. The *Supplément* is not, or at least not consciously, an effort to sabotage or to take back the precepts of the letter, even though if one runs the two off on the same level one might find that, in effect, parts of the *Supplément* did just that. But Diderot regularly refuses to accept, or even be aware of, the consequences of the contrarieties he creates. In fact his mind regularly operates in separate stages; and even though the initial stage may, through the mechanism of contrariety, produce contradictions with the succeeding one, each becomes walled off from, or invisible to, the other, so that each can operate autonomously.

Dieckmann noted both of these features of Diderot's thought: the relation of contrariety between the letter and the *Supplément*, and the fact that Diderot's thought progressed by stages, which sometimes implied radically discrete changes in his assumed values, and in the direction of his thought as the work progressed.[5] For Dieckmann such notions seem to be particular inferences drawn from his exceptional understanding of various parts of the text. In the following analysis I will apply them somewhat more broadly: I will assume at the outset that in the *Supplément* Diderot's thought grows and changes, and that, in more ways than Dieckmann knew, one of the main governing principles of, and impulses behind, this growth was contrariety.

II

Some of the most dramatic contrasts between the two texts come right in the opening section of the *Supplément* proper,[6] the part entitled 'Les Adieux du vieillard', particularly in the Old Man's description of the lovemaking of a young Tahitian couple (p.470). Everything in the scene is free, open and joyous. The desires of the young woman are paramount in every way: she herself has chosen the young man with whom she makes love, according to

5. See n.2 above.
6. In each of the following chapters, at least one reference is made allowing the reader to locate the text under discussion in Diderot, *Œuvres complètes* (Paris 1975-), ed. Herbert Dieckmann, Jacques Proust and Jean Varloot (henceforward 'DPV'). For the text of the *Supplément au Voyage de Bougainville*, see DPV, xii.365-83, 577-647. In a number of chapters, the DPV edition is used throughout. I take the liberty, however, of using other editions as the basis of my textual analysis whenever there seem valid reasons to do so. Thus in the present chapter, I use Paul Vernière's edition of the *Supplément* (in Diderot, *Œuvres philosophiques*, Paris 1964, p.447-516), on account of the particular relevance of its historical documentation. The page numbers in my text refer to this edition.

the dictates of her heart and the secret voice of her senses. This mating scene is public, and though family members are present, their only role is to form a circle around the couple and, to the sound of flute-playing, look on with happy approval. The young woman takes pride in the sexual excitement she has aroused, not only in the young Tahitian to whose embraces she has abandoned herself, but in other (male) members of the family as well. Thus the female and her desires are the central elements in the tableau; nothing else seems to matter. The male, far from having a determining role in her conduct, is scarcely mentioned. Nor, from all one can tell, has the family made choices for her; one notes particularly the absence of any specified role for the father. Though there are watchful eyes upon the couple, the gazes are obviously not intended to repress or disapprove, as they did in the letter to Angélique, but to admire and enjoy. No social obstacles come between the (mutual) attraction of the couple; in fact society's only function seems to be that of facilitating the young couple's pursuit of their desires. Everything that was private in the letter to his daughter – especially in respect to the woman's expressions of tenderness – is deliberately public here. Apparently no moral proscriptions becloud the pleasures of the senses. Prominently displayed, the words 'innocent', 'instinct', 'bonheur', 'liberté', and 'nature' remind us of the simple, open values being put forward – as opposed to the guilty prohibitions of the letter, and of course the whole point of this depiction of Tahiti is to imagine a situation that can replace civilisation, its repressions and discontents, with the pure, freely exercised instincts of nature – a perfect contrast to the penalty ridden institutionalisation of the letter, just as Dieckmann suggested. My own interpretation of this contrariety, amazing even for Diderot, is that it functions in just the way Dorine had done in Molière's *Tartuffe*, by providing release: having, in the letter, created a sombre, tyrannical prison of perverse, egotistical male oppression, Diderot now puts the female in charge, opens up the sky and lets carefree nature take her own instinctual course.

To return to the context of the *Supplément*, the purity and innocence of this lovemaking scene is being put forward in the Old Man's discourse to make the most vivid possible contrast with the vicious, cruel, diseased values brought to the island by Bougainville's expedition. According to the eloquent, pathetic message of the Old Man's sermon, all this happy, fragile innocence of the natives is menaced, in fact doomed, by the catastrophic evils recently implanted by the Europeans – now on the point of departure, according to the fiction of the *Supplément*. Curiously, the forceful eloquence of this discourse matches Diderot's own in the letter to his daughter, even though the venerable Tahitian is inveighing against exactly the civilised assumptions that underpinned Diderot's sermon to Angélique. Meanwhile, the Old Man puts his case to the maximum degree: the Europeans have brought nothing but false values. Their ideas of property, material wealth and conquest are evil; their concepts of religion and sin pervert and degrade what formerly was innocent (p.466-67). In a great crescendo of a wail ('Malheur à cette île! malheur aux Tahitiens présents, et à tous les Tahitiens à venir', p.469) he rails against the ultimate evil: syphilis, the disease which has poisoned their blood and the blood of their posterity ('Tu as infecté notre sang.'). He woefully predicts that they may have to kill those who have been infected, or countenance the disease being transmitted by their infected children forever. In a last tableau he describes the fearful compound in which the syphilitics have been sequestered, the weapons that formerly served only against enemies now turned against their own children; included in the tableau too are the unfortunate women, companions of the pleasures of the Europeans, now the despair of their families, doomed to die either through disease or by being put to death (p.472).

Syphilis is of course paradigmatic, a potent dramatic device that establishes with the cruellest clarity how the irreversible malady of civilisation invades, seizes hold of, infects and destroys the state of nature. It may also be pertinent to note the existence of an established theological tradition behind the use of venereal disease to dramatise the consequences of original sin.[7] And of course the Old Man's discourse, though secular, has very much the tone of religious eloquence. Its force is achieved partly through the use of an elevated, tragic style and also because of the advanced age, dignity and wisdom of the speaker. It is as though one were hearing a Moses, a Jeremiah or, closer to Diderot, an ancient Troglodyte out of Montesquieu, or even a Fabricius out of Rousseau. For one moment the Old Man, as if hearkening to the angry tones of Rousseau's Roman hero, actually feels an impulse to call on the islanders to rise up and destroy the Europeans before they can depart.

III

If my theory is correct, this position, so emotionally stated through the voice of the Old Man, should now in turn reverse itself via contrariety – precisely because the Old Man's commitment has been stated with such forceful eloquence.

And indeed, in the next dialogue of the 'manuscript' (p.475-92) one finds, not the accomplishment of the Old Man's prophecies of disaster for the natives,

---

7. Jansenists such as Nicole were particularly expert on this theme: see my *Pascal's 'Provincial letters': an introduction* (London 1977), p.11.

but the reverse:[8] civilisation being defeated at the hands of the inhabitants.[9] This is the lesson, in Part III, of the Chaplain's repeatedly succumbing to the sexual enticements of the native women: civilisation is the loser, and the reason is that, time and again, the Chaplain's own sexual instincts – pure nature – prove stronger than all the strictures civilisation has tried to impose on him as his 'condition'. Both the 'victory' of the native women as they arouse his irresistible instincts and the 'defeat' of the Priest's hollow values have philosophical implications, of course, the point being that the natural is both better and stronger than civilisation, whose values, being unnatural and hence inherently false and weak, are doomed to succumb. Good (nature) is now playing the prevailing role which evil (civilisation) played in the Old Man's discourse: nature is the irresistible conqueror.

Religion of course bears the brunt of Diderot's attack in this section, and the blasphemy of the situation could not be more intentional: even as Peter thrice denied his Saviour before dawn, so the Chaplain not only thrice but four times desecrates his Christian vows before sunrise (on successive nights, to be sure). It was the Jesuits – according to Pascal – who claimed that for an act to be counted as a sin the doer must actually be conscious of the evil nature of the act and commit it nevertheless. But even the Jesuits could not have got this Chaplain off the hook, for each time he succumbs (at least on three of the four nights) it is in proffering the words 'Ma religion! Mon Etat!' that he does so, evidence of an extraordinarily clear and present awareness of the forbidden character of his act, and of the vows he is breaking.

If the partisans of nature easily win the fight on the level of the sexual instincts, they also triumph on the level of philosophy and rational argument. The spokesman for the state of nature, Orou, ignorant of formal logic or metaphysics, to be sure, but allegedly made mighty by the natural light of reason, argues like a genius (and not unlike Diderot himself) against Christian precepts. Meanwhile, like d'Alembert in the first part of the *Rêve de d'Alembert* trilogy, the Chaplain is easily trapped into making statements so obviously ridiculous they undermine the beliefs they allegedly advance. And then

8. The scholar who has come closest to my own view of this relationship is Georges Benrekassa, 'Dit et non dit idéologique: à propos du "Supplément au Voyage de Bougainville"', *Dix-huitième siècle* 5 (1973), p.29-40, esp. p.37: 'Le discours d'Orou et le discours du vieillard occupent donc à l'intérieur du *Supplément* des positions symétriques et inverses.' Not being primarily concerned with contrariety, Professor Benrekassa explains these relationships differently, and comes to different conclusions.

9. Again Dieckmann has partly anticipated my conclusion on this point: 'Dans le second chapitre, nous avions sous les yeux la violation et la ruine de l'état de nature; ici la nature affirme et défend ses droits: droits de la vie à naître, et, plus précisément, de la race humaine à se perpétuer' (Introduction, p.xxxiv).

Orou has ready answers for everything: whole discourses that leave no stone unturned, no doubts remaining, nothing that is not perfectly clear. If the Chaplain (civilisation) speaks in sentences, Orou (nature) gets whole paragraphs, sometimes whole pages as the torrent of his reasoning waxes eloquent.

In the early part of Orou's assault (p.480), it is rather surprising to discover that the central point of attack is the very doctrine that Diderot himself put forward so emotionally in his letter to his daughter: the necessity of sexual fidelity in marriage. Orou calls on a dozen irrefutable arguments against what he disparagingly terms 'ces préceptes singuliers', i.e. that in marriage the man and the woman belong exclusively to each other, and that these rules are binding for the couple's entire lives – precisely the pure monogamy Diderot preached so eloquently in the letter to Angélique. One senses a whole philosophical system backing up Orou's refutations, and furthermore the system is founded on the same principles as Diderot's own materialism: that the marriage pact, which gives one person into the ownership of another, is contrary to the changeability of will inherent in the character of a human being; that such a pact is contrary to the general law of beings: nothing in the universe is immutable, nor should marriage laws be; that such a pact implies moral laws which are in the worst sense arbitrary since they have no relation to the good of the individual or to the general good; that, as a result, people are forced either to become hypocrites, or unhappy wretches, instruments of their own misery. This is obviously a far-reaching indictment. If the doctrine of the Old Man could be said to resemble that of Rousseau, here the liberal sexual attitude is pure Diderot.

The Old Man's discourse marked the emotional high point of the dialogues; Orou's arguments form the rational climax, being a philosophical demonstration in favour of the doctrine of the work's subtitle, 'sur l'inconvénient d'attacher des idées morales à certaines actions physiques qui n'en comportent pas'. This is perhaps the best-known part of the work and there is no need to review again the details of Orou's attack on the very notion that marital infidelity (whether on the part of a man or a woman) is a crime, or that there is anything at all evil in incest (p.495-97). Perhaps it is obvious as well that Diderot's letter to Angélique was intended to inculcate a doctrine exactly contrary to this one: to make her realise how much her sexual actions were freighted with moral consequences, consequences so serious that any infringement of the rule would be sufficient to make her father wish to die of shame. The exactness of the opposition between this section of the *Supplément* and the letter to Angélique is what leads me to conclude that at least this section of the *Supplément* was in fact 'inspired' by the repressive morality of the letter – as an answer to it, or an imaginary release from it. Historically, to be sure, Orou's arguments are based on false data – wishful thinking on Diderot's part: Orou claims that the natives were innocent of the notion of God and all religious precepts, in other words, that they were atheists, whereas the historical reality described in Bougainville's account made it clear that they were already engaged in a host of religious superstitions on their own.

I suggested earlier that by predicting so eloquently the approaching disaster of the Tahitians, the Old Man, may actually, via contrary motion, have been calling forth a different vision of their fate, one that was quite opposite to his own. Another aspect of the Old Man's discourse whose eloquence might be calling for a reversal was his depiction of the guileless spontaneity, liberty and innocence of the Tahitians which he set in contrast to the wily corruption and diseases of the tyrannical, conquest-hungry Europeans. One remembers too in this connection that not only were the Tahitians alleged to be superior in physical strength, but the Old Man stressed the perpetual good health of this carefree people: before the arrival of the Europeans, the only malady they had ever experienced was simply the infirmity of old age, he declared (p.468-69). Nor, finally, did the Tahitians previously have any concept of ownership – of 'thine' and 'mine'; ownership was another evil import of the Europeans (p.466-67). But now one reaches a new stage of Diderot's creation, and, in Orou's discourses to the Chaplain, the innocent, spontaneous guilelessness of the Tahitians evaporates, as does their liberty, as does their pre-Bougainvillian pristine good health, as does their ignorance of property. All these attributes will be replaced by other values.

Scholars concerned with utopias have remarked how often the effort to create a perfect society actually results – perhaps simply through the process of schematising all the rules – in a police state where everything is regulated and no one is free. Something similar occurs in this section of Diderot's *Supplément* (p.498f.), although via a curious double movement that renders this development singularly complex. We now move into a new stage in which one perceives a new set of motives: everything becomes part of a large scheme to increase and improve the population, everything has this utilitarian goal. Women have a commodity they must produce – children – in order to augment the 'wealth' of the state; men are part of the same plan, and their offspring are indeed treated as 'property' in that they belong to one or both of the parents. Parental authority assumes new importance as the father and mother designate the young prospective mates from which their offspring must choose, once they reach a suitable age. An elaborate code dictates the standards a couple must meet in order to be thought physically suitable for one another.

As the entire society turns into a children-producing machine, the new utilitarian perspective produces a new sexual code with the far-reaching restrictions according to which sex is licit only for procreation. Otherwise, so the code declares, sex is not only forbidden but 'blamed' when infringement of the rule occurs, and sometimes there are extraordinarily cruel punishments for disobedience – confinement, exile, even slavery – that sound as bigoted as anything civilisation had produced (p.494-95, 498). In other words Orou's stern blast against Christian morality, which appeared so liberating, actually tends, as it evolves, to substitute new duties and strictures for the old ones. Most ironically, as Dieckmann pointed out, Orou's concept of sex as being licit only for purposes of procreation coincides perfectly with the limitations enforced for centuries by Catholic Christianity.[10] In other words, though Christian morality began as the enemy, a secularised portion of Catholic sexual doctrine now turns out to coincide with the one Diderot's personage puts forward as the norm. Predictably, under the new regulations not a woman's beauty, but her fecundity now becomes the critical element, and in some cases ugliness – according to Diderot/Orou's fantasy – may even be an advantage: 'Je suis laide, mais je fais de beaux enfants, et c'est moi que les hommes préfèrent,' says the native woman (p.489). According to such terms copulation has been taken out of the sphere of enjoyment, where one was earlier encouraged to assume it was included: population increase is the only factor taken into consideration. Perhaps it is not totally inappropriate to recall at this point that St Augustine, who struggled so arduously and so long with his guilty awareness of the pleasures of sexuality, finally invented an imaginary state of innocence in which the sexual act was no more pleasurable than raising one's arm ...

In short, contrary to earlier appearances, the former paradise of free instincts is turning out to be run by pure calculation, with everything being required to fit into a grand, perhaps even totalitarian, design. In his eloquent discourse the Old Man claimed that the Tahitians had no problems at all before the arrival of the Europeans: there were no diseases and everyone was free and happy because living according to nature. Now one learns that they have a host of problems – some of them arising because the programme of population increase implies conditions to be met and quotas to fulfil. In any case, Orou speaks of vast acreages lying unploughed, the need to restore populations that have been diminished by 'epidemic calamities', the need for men to fight against neighbouring enemies, the sterility of certain women, the outnumbering of males by females, and finally the necessity of paying an (annual?) quota of men as a tribute to an oppressive neighbour (p.500).

According to Orou's analysis, population increase is the single factor that will provide the solution to all these problems. Furthermore, in each instance

10. Dieckmann, Introduction, p.lxvi, n.1.

of the problems cited, he reveals that the natives have had recourse specifically to the companions of Bougainville to repair the damage (p.500). They have sent their women to have intercourse with the Europeans deliberately, so that additional offspring will increase their numbers; more hands will plough the fields; the populations diminished by epidemics will be augmented; more men will fight in the army; perhaps Bougainville's companions will render the sterile women fertile and create a better balance of males to females. Even if the offspring turn out to be inferior they can help to fill the quota for the tribute of men required by the oppressive neighbour. In the Old Man's view, the Europeans were the problem, in fact the Tahitians' only problem. According to Orou, far from being a problem, the Europeans are the remedy.

Since sexuality is always so important for Diderot, it was almost to be expected that when, in the Old Man's discourse, Diderot wanted to dramatise the infamous consequences of the contamination of nature's innocence by the evils of civilisation, at the climactic moment he used the arresting image of syphilis, the poison of the semen that infected the guileless native women. Naturally, too, the Old Man's final tableau stressed the same theme. Yet, despite the irresistible pathos of his discourse, it must be noted that the historical facts are quite otherwise: according to Bougainville's account (and there seems to be no plausible reason for Diderot to have disbelieved him) he took infinite pains to make sure the Europeans did not infect the natives. Furthermore, historians relate that in reality it was the other way round: the companions of Bougainville caught syphilis from the already infected natives.[11] One may certainly conclude that the Old Man's image is a fictional invention – somewhat in the way that the *droit du seigneur* was to be for Beaumarchais. Perhaps its fictionality in this sense is what facilitated the replacement, as one moves to a later stage of Orou's dialogues, of venereal disease by new and totally contrary values: as Orou's perspective becomes dominant, syphilis miraculously disappears, and the hitherto hateful semen of Bougainville's companions, no longer spoken of as contaminated, is now what the natives seek above all to obtain for themselves. Although no doubt the Europeans believed they were seducing the native women, Orou reveals that actually it was the other way round. For their semen has turned into an abundant remedy to restore and even enhance the population: thanks to it, the intelligence of the Tahitian race may one day actually be improved (p.500).

In the Old Man one hears the voice of doom and saw an innocent population helpless on the verge of an unavoidable disaster. For Orou, the population is

11. See the Vernière edition, p.469, n.1, and Bougainville's account.

neither innocent nor helpless. On the contrary it is full of guile and calculation and it is successfully engaged in controlling and making brighter its own future. At the end of Orou's discourse – contrary to the doleful plaints of the Old Man – the winners everywhere are the Tahitians.

In interpreting the *Supplément* in this way, I am assuming that, like everything else in Diderot's materialistic universe, this work grows and changes as it moves onward. Thus – such is my assumption – one should not expect that the values will remain constant, for each section represents a new stage of his thought (perhaps several new stages), a new situation, something like a moving picture, or like the 'grand rouleau' of *Jacques le fataliste*. My theory is also that contrariety is one of the prime movers in this generation and progress of new ideas. I would distinguish two sets of contrarieties in the parts of the *Supplément* examined thus far. The first functions via an impulse generated outside the work proper: my claim is that the straightlaced repressions that Diderot invented for his daughter's marriage were a principal factor causing him to develop at least one part (and possibly more) of his dream of a society where such repressions would serve no purpose, in which, not society's dictates but the sexual desires of the female – along with the duration of the moon – determined who married whom and for how long, a marriage where faithfulness had no importance, a society in which 'incest' was accepted, and even the evident physical display of the father's sexual attraction to his daughters was thought innocent and natural (p.506). This final point was never suggested by Bougainville, of course: it is pure fantasy on Diderot's part – no doubt, as dreams so often are, wishful thinking. Yet the reality of Bougainville's actual account was indispensable as an inspiration for the *Supplément*, if only because it invited Diderot to have the momentary illusion that his *Supplément* depicted a world totally unconnected to the one to which Diderot belonged – especially unconnected to the immediate circumstance of Angélique's marriage – covering over, masking all the connections by travelling to the other side of the globe, to a land where Diderot had never been and where his fantasies could have free play because they were unrelated to reality. In other words I suspect that Diderot's fascination with Bougainville's true account enabled him to remain blind, unable to see how much the impulses behind the *Supplément* challenged the morality of his prescriptions for Angélique – not to mention what they revealed about the intensity of his feelings towards her.

The other group of contrarieties function within the work proper: first the view of Bougainville and the purposes of his expedition, so favourably looked upon in the opening dialogue of the *Supplément*,[12] sets up, by contrary motion, the Old Man's denunciations of Bougainville, his expedition and the civilised values it represented.[13] Second, the creation of the Old Man's moan, as he saw the natives doomed to be enslaved and destroyed by the European disaster, brought Diderot to invent a contrary vision in which the natives are not doomed or destroyed, but, on the contrary, discover a principle on which to prosper, grow strong and actually win out as they turn the European arrival to their own advantage.

Towards the end of Orou's conversations, Diderot makes a final attack at the barbarism of European civilisation which institutes monks and nuns in order that they – theoretically – do not have sexual experience and do not produce children: 'Vous êtes plus barbares que nous,' Orou declares (p.503), familiarly echoing Ovid, Montaigne and Rousseau, and perhaps, on some subliminal level, helping Diderot to get back at the 'condition' of his own brother, the intolerant priest, who had recently been raising religious objections to Angélique's marriage. The account then concludes by telling how the Chaplain spent his final night sleeping 'par honnêteté' with the wife of his host. Perhaps the finality of this conclusion is not so dramatically marked as the end of the Old Man's speech: there is no organ-swell of emotion followed by empty silence, nor are the themes inherently of a conclusive character, in fact both the barbarism of celibacy and the succumbing of the Chaplain had already been introduced. Yet obviously the author has momentarily said all he wished to say about Orou and the Chaplain, and to the reader as well this section feels as though it has reached the end. My hypothesis is that the sense of closure has been brought about because the theme of the positive advantages of copulating with the Europeans turned the discussion irrevocably 180 degrees away from the Old Man's perspective. The contrariety is now complete. The final scornful dismissal of celibacy and the account of the Chaplain's last 'defeat' simply confirms that on every level, moral and physical, the true victory lies with the Tahitians over their alleged conquerors.

12. In the opening dialogue Bougainville, described by the reliable *B*, represents ideally the Frenchman-explorer of the age of Enlightenment: 'Bougainville est parti avec les lumières nécessaires et les qualités propres à ses vues: de la philosophie, du courage, de la véracité; un coup d'œil prompt qui saisit les choses et abrège le temps des observations; de la circonspection, de la patience; le désir de voir, de s'éclairer et d'instruire; la science du calcul, des mécaniques, de la géométrie, de l'astronomie; et une teinture suffisante d'histoire naturelle' (p.457-58).
13. This point is also made by Benrekassa, 'Dit et non dit idéologique', p.34.

IV

In general, it seems that the negative impulse which is the basis of contrariety, that is to say a desire for liberation – the urge to get away from one state by creating a state that is totally different – seldom, and perhaps never, succeeds, at least not in the sense of achieving a true liberation. Inevitably Diderot's dream of Tahiti, which begins apparently as complete natural freedom, will turn, with its variously coloured veils restricting women's conduct, its puberty chains for men, and its bigoted punishments for infringements of a new sexual code, into something more and more regulated, and finally the society becomes nothing but a baby factory whose functioning permeates all activities. Children have become an essential product on which the economy of the society is said to depend – as other islands depend on sugar or particular spices, or as free trade allegedly did in the theories of European physiocrats. In sum, the impulse to escape from bourgeois repressions in the long run only produced other strictures that eventually came to resemble perpetuations as much as they did liberations, and Diderot's dream of the islanders' victory over the Europeans actually resulted in a system crudely aping European concepts of economic well-being.[14] For the rest Diderot himself suggests an awareness of something like this problem in the final dialogues between *A* and *B*. Though in a different context, *B* makes the most apposite declaration: 'Méfiez-vous de celui qui veut mettre de l'ordre. Ordonner, c'est toujours se rendre le maître des autres en les gênant' (p.512). As order establishes itself more and more in the society Diderot imagines for Tahiti, the individual and individual freedom become increasingly subservient to it, until freedom may seem to vanish entirely.

The final dialogue between *A* and *B* – part v – attempts to reach conclusions that will explain the 'lessons' of Tahiti. And yet, the true genius of this work, it seems to me, lies not in its liberating solutions (it does not really solve anything) but in the way, particularly in this final part, it explores and elucidates various aspects of a problem from various points of view, and in the light of all that has preceded. No one before Freud understood the tension between natural sexual impulses and the impositions of society, as Diderot did. His famous diagnosis of the misery of the modern human condition – 'Il existait un homme naturel; on a introduit au dedans de cet homme un homme artificiel; et il s'est élevé dans la caverne une guerre continuelle qui dure toute la vie' (p.511) – seems a century and a half ahead of his time. I do not know

14. Many of these implications are explored, from a rather different point of view, in Bernard Papin, *Sens et fonction de l'utopie tahitienne dans l'œuvre politique de Diderot*, Studies on Voltaire 251 (1988), *passim*.

of any author before Diderot who realised so clearly that the root of the problem of the modern (eighteenth-century) marriage started with the tyrannical appropriation of the female by the male.[15] Finally, his insight that the sexual act – what he terms 'le frottement voluptueux de deux intestins' (p.510) – was inherently not susceptible to the moral values attributed to it by religion is another of those bold strokes that brings him closer to our era than to his own time. But of course his treatment, in this dialogue between *A* and *B*, of the problem of civilisation versus the natural impulses is deeply ambiguous, fascinatingly so.

If Diderot's letter to his daughter was pure folly, as it seems today, the *Supplément* to which it helped give birth may contain pure wisdom, although I am not so sure of the validity of the *Supplément* when taken as a statement about colonialism or about anthropology. No doubt it does contain a cry of distress from someone who sees the destructiveness of colonisation, of civilising – a distress that we in our time feel we share; and it conveys a sense, too, of at least some appreciation of the infinite preciousness of the 'natural' human values that are being irretrievably lost. One notes also that in other late works by Diderot – his contributions to the *Histoire philosophique des deux Indes* being the famous example – these concerns would take a more radical form. Here they may seem embodiments of the general 'mauvaise conscience' or 'malaise' rather frequently found among *philosophes* of Diderot's generation. The 'malaise' dates at least from Montesquieu and the challenge of the anti-philosophical Rousseau, but obviously it spread widely, as the *philosophes* found it increasingly difficult to ignore (as some had tried to do) the enormity of the damage inflicted on a Third World exploited by the civilisation for which they were allegedly spokesmen.[16] Perhaps Diderot's *Supplément* confronts both issues, colonialism and anthropology, inadequately: it is too filled with fantasy to be a valid scientific account of primitive man, and it hardly begins to come to grips with the disasters of colonial exploitation.

To my mind, the real insights concern what Diderot knew at first hand, in other words, civilisation and its discontents: his realisation (in part v) that because of what modern society makes and demands of people, the primitive cry of distress voiced so poignantly by the Old Man will always be part of

15. *A*: 'Mais comment est-il arrivé qu'un acte dont le but est si solennel, et auquel la nature nous invite par l'attrait le plus puissant [...] soit devenu la source la plus féconde de notre dépravation et de nos maux?' *B*: 'Orou l'a fait entendre dix fois à l'aumonier: écoutez-le donc encore, et tâchez de le retenir. C'est par la tyrannie de l'homme, qui a converti la possession de la femme en une propriété' (p.509). No part of the text forms a more perfect contrariety with Diderot's admonitions to Angélique.

16. See Yves Benot, *Diderot: de l'athéisme à l'anticolonialisme* (Paris 1970), p.156f.

(civilised) human nature; and secondly, through Orou, his sense of the falseness of society's moral values, particularly the sexual ones.

Much has been written comparing Diderot's 'primitivism' to that of Rousseau, particularly to his second *Discourse*.[17] There are of course numerous similarities, but in the present context perhaps the important point is that Rousseau had a moral and political purpose that was, to use the modern term, 'performative': Rousseau's essential aim in his second *Discourse* was to force the reader who had followed him step by step in the understanding of how humanity's ills had come from the process of civilisation, and how moral and political inequality were contrary to nature, to the point where one could share Rousseau's outrage at the intolerable social injustice that was the inevitable consequence of this development. In other words, the ringing statements in the final phrases – the genial paraphrase of Montaigne's *Des cannibales* – are the heart and soul of Rousseau's message: everything that preceded was building towards this explosion of indignation at the end.

In the *Supplément*, tensions are not allowed to accumulate this way: the Old Man's wails, by his own admission, come too late; they simply function as an outlet for tragic sentiments whose hopelessness is reinforced symbolically in the empty beach at the end. Orou's indignation is systematically dissipated through the Chaplain's sexual defeats and victories, and through Orou's own victories in argument.

In the final dialogue (part v) several contrarieties are simply left in suspension. Thus at least two fundamentally diverse attitudes are in contrast in this section. The first is Diderot's willingness to accept the simple opposition of the 'law' of nature – given in the singular and valorised as 'good' – to the evils of civilisation, and to assume that the unhappiness of the modern individual comes from the internal conflict between them. The second attitude is at least as deeply rooted in Diderot's philosophy: it stems from an awareness that (contrary to the earlier position) nature's laws are not singular but plural, and hence that human individuals, while sharing similar needs and pleasures such as eating and sexuality, are really a collection of tendencies that may assume a multitude of diverse forms. Thus on the one hand Diderot is drawn towards the espousal of nature's true law, and to the condemnation of civilisation's artifices (particularly its moral inventions) as false and evil. In fact he explicitly accepts the dichotomy between what is 'naturel' versus what is 'd'institution' (p.507), and furthermore the most pathos-filled moments of the *Supplément* indicted civilisation in the name of 'nature', taken in this sense.

17. Dieckmann's discussion remains one of the most perspicacious: see Introduction, p.lxxv-xciv.

Yet simultaneously, other impulses draw him in the opposite direction, to accept all forms of human conduct as belonging to nature.

Almost as precisely as life produces itself out of the raw matter of the egg described in *Le Rêve de d'Alembert*, in the *Supplément* Diderot's second attitude, his willingness to accept all human conduct as natural, is distinctly 'germinated' in the text by a particularly strong affirmation of the first. *A* comes out forcefully for the 'law of nature', declaring that any other laws which develop, religious or civil, should be the merest copies of that first law: 'il faut que les deux dernières ne soient que des calques rigoureux de la première que nous apportons gravée au fond de nos cœurs, et qui sera toujours la plus forte' (p.505).

This strong affirmation of the singularity and inevitable prevalence of the law of nature opens the way for the development of the contrary argument. *B* replies: 'Cela n'est pas exact. Nous n'apportons en naissant qu'une similitude d'organisation avec d'autres êtres, les mêmes besoins, de l'attrait vers les mêmes plaisirs, une aversion commune pour les mêmes peines: ce qui constitue l'homme ce qu'il est, et doit fonder la morale qui lui convient' (p.505). This line of reasoning tends towards diversity, and eventually leads *B* to the culminating formulation: 'vices et vertus, tout est également dans la nature' (p.507). This implies, of course, that plurality has now replaced singularity, and that a variety of different codes of behaviour will be accepted as belonging to nature.

But as was suggested earlier, both these attitudes, though contradictory, exist side by side in the final dialogue of the *Supplément*. Diderot's unwillingness, or inability, to opt finally for one position or the other in this critical matter was probably the leading factor (there were undoubtedly others) which made the conformism of the ending of the *Supplément* inevitable: be like the Tahitians when in Tahiti, says the ever-reliable *B*; when in Europe, though one may indeed cry out for reform of legal injustice, one should meanwhile obey the laws – even the laws governing monks – since the worst that can happen to any society would be the disruption and chaos caused by disobedience (p.515). The final words of the dialogue, humorously and light-heartedly, imply acceptance, at least for modern European women as individuals, of the conflict between the natural sexual instincts and the rules of civilisation, a conflict that was earlier seen as the main source of mankind's endless distress.

'Vices et vertus, tout est également dans la nature.' Not only 'in nature', but in Diderot as well: one finds everything in this most universal of the *philosophes*. The point is that the insights of Diderot's discourse come from his involvement in the contradictory aspects and implications of the situation which was his concern. If in the *Supplément* he writes so tellingly of the false, artificial nature of the moral order imposed by society, this was the order he himself participated in, up to the hilt in the famous letter to Angélique. The *Supplément*'s evocation of the attractions of natural society are so intensely poignant because he himself had indulged in the other half of the equation.

Perhaps these remarks give the impression that the main interest of the *Supplément* is supposed to be biographical, or that Angélique's marriage somehow explains it all. Actually, my idea is quite different, for I think it clear that Bougainville's voyage evoked a series of radically different and/or contrary responses in Diderot, and led to the diversities which are recorded in the *Supplément*. As for its initial inspiration, of course the work was born out of the infinite complexity of causes – both personal and historical, from within and from without – that any gesture in life would be. But amid this infinite complexity, I do indeed believe that the sexual repressions of Diderot's letter to his daughter was one factor which produced, by contrary motion, the Old Man's unforgettably poignant cry of distress, and furthermore that these merciless repressions are enough to make anyone dream of walking barefoot (at least) on the beach.

2. Evolving experiments
in the *Lettre sur les sourds et muets*

I

No work by Diderot is more formidably confusing[1] than the *Lettre sur les sourds et muets* (1751).[2] Despite the claim of the title, it is not centred on the deaf and dumb; no particular group occupies the central position; no main argument is being put forward – as there would be in *Le Paradoxe sur le comédien*, for example – nor is Diderot's aim to preach the doctrines of a philosophy, as Diderot's friend Condillac had done in his *Essai sur l'origine des connaissances humaines* (1746),[3] and as Diderot himself would do so notably in *Le Rêve de d'Alembert*. Instead the *Lettre* just seems to float along, erratically changing topics, changing assumptions, rendering obscure what has just been made plain, undoing what has just been done. At one stage, discussions of Greek and Latin stylistics become so abstruse that even scholars steeped in classical traditions can do no more than offer postulations as to Diderot's intended meanings. What the reader was led to believe was the main issue at the beginning, i.e. inversions in language, gives every appearance of melting into non-existence as the text progresses through a series of contradictions. Certainly there are brilliant insights along the way, but at the end one may

1. Jacques Chouillet remarks in his introduction to the DPV edition that 'la *Lettre sur les sourds et muets* s'affirme [...] par son caractère explosif et spontané. De là vient sa difficulté. On sent bien la nécessité intérieure qui l'a dictée. On discerne mal son but' (iv.111). Likewise James Creech avers at the start of his analysis of the work that 'Its complexity [...] can be daunting' (Diderot, *Thresholds of representation*, Columbus, Ohio 1986, p.123).

2. The full title is *Lettre sur les sourds et muets, à l'usage de ceux qui entendent et qui parlent; Où l'on traite de l'origine des inversions, de l'harmonie du style, du sublime de situation, de quelques avantages de la langue française sur la plupart des langues anciennes et modernes, et par occasion de l'expression particulière aux beaux-arts.* Page references are to vol.iv of the DPV edition, which includes notes from the still indispensable edition by Paul Hugo Meyer published in *Diderot studies* 7 (1965). I have also used the edition by Norman Rudich published in Diderot, *Premières œuvres*, vol.ii (Paris 1972), p.65-156. For all points of detail not covered by the present discussion, the reader is referred to these editions, and also to Gérard Genette, *Mimologiques: voyage en Cratylie* (Paris 1976). Representing a more theoretical perspective, there is also the lengthy study by Marian Hobson, 'La *Lettre sur les sourds et muets* de Diderot: labyrinthe et language', *Semiotica* 16 (1976), p.291-327. Since the present chapter is constantly concerned with the author's intent and with meaning, other more semiotic critical approaches to this work have not proved as useful.

3. This work will be discussed in the conclusion to this chapter.

feel at a loss to know where one has been or what underlying message Diderot had been hoping to convey.

Diderot's alleged 'sources' are not much help either. Many of the topics, such as 'inversions' or the origin of languages, being very much the order of the day in Diderot's time, scholars have been seeking for generations to relate his work to contemporary linguistic debates. Yet despite the considerable body of research on the topic, the results have been frustratingly inconclusive. One problem has been the ambiguities of Diderot's discourse, which sometimes make it impossible to tell whether he agrees or disagrees with other philosophers of language on a given point. The famous example in this connection is abbé Batteux, the alleged addressee of Diderot's *Lettre* and whose blithely adventuresome proposals on inversion[4] undoubtedly seemed intriguing to some of Diderot's contemporaries, even as they irritated *grammairiens philosophes*. What, one might wonder, was Diderot's own reaction? The answer is difficult to determine. At times, Batteux is treated by Diderot with sarcasm, and an oddly supercilious, patronising tone creeps in, almost as though he were dealing with a rival. This kind of gratuitous arrogance is so untypical of Diderot that one might even wonder whether he was speaking for himself as he wrote the remarks, or whether he might have been prodded into making them by someone else – his nasty friend Grimm, for example. On one occasion (p.182), Diderot criticises Batteux, chiding him for failing to explain himself on a point of major consequence for his doctrines, when in fact Batteux's explanation is both extensive and clear.[5] Apparently, Diderot had not taken the trouble to understand what Batteux had written.[6] On other points Diderot shows partial agreement, and some scholars are convinced that, even when not mentioning him by name, Diderot owed to Batteux some of his most important insights concerning the relationship between the various arts. Lévi-Strauss was convinced that Diderot used his attacks on Batteux to cover up his

4. Since he was – ostensibly – opposed by Diderot (everyone's favourite) and by all the later *grammairiens philosophes*, and because he dared to defend Latin word order, Batteux has generally not received his due from scholars. One of the few willing to appreciate the interest of his ideas is Gérard Genette; see *Mimologiques: voyage en Cratylie* , p.199-203.

5. Batteux's rather lengthy explanation of the principle that is the heart of his theory could hardly have been more clearly designated in his text *Les Beaux-Arts réduits à un même principe*: 'Ce que c'est que la belle nature' (book II, ch.4). One might also note that Diderot repeated his criticism of Batteux in his article 'Beau' in the *Encyclopédie*, an article in which the concept of beauty rests entirely on the idea of 'rapports' – a concept which Diderot deliberately never defines. Curiously, most scholars who have treated this topic have not made it clear how much Diderot was at fault on this point.

6. Cf. the views of Annie Becq, *Genèse de l'esthétique française moderne: de la raison classique à l'imagination créatrice, 1680-1814* (Pisa 1984), i.425-32.

outrageous plunderings of the abbé's ideas.[7] Yet the most learned scholars who have discussed the matter – Franco Venturi,[8] Paul Meyer[9] and Jacques Chouillet,[10] for example, are by no means in agreement on all aspects of their assessments, and the evidence for their conclusions is often circumstantial. Diderot seems to have rethought everything in his own peculiar way, so that Batteux's presentation of ideas seldom serves helpfully to clarify Diderot's own.

More promising in this connection is Condillac's *Essai sur l'origine des connaissances humaines* (1746).[11] Since he and Diderot shared numerous conceptions (some of them, needless to say, derived from Locke), on occasion the *Essai* is indispensable, especially when it spells out with care and precision points that Diderot is content to leave unelucidated, in compressed form. Yet here too the answers are by no means clear: the two men were friends who saw each other frequently, and one cannot always tell who originated what and who influenced whom.[12] Nor did they concur in every instance: the disagreements between them are numerous and significant.[13] But even the areas of accord can be deceptive: they lead us to forget how much the resemblances are counterbalanced and outweighed by deviations in method, direction of argument and polemical intent, so that although the two authors seem to be proposing the same doctrines, they may, in effect, be saying different things.

Assessments of the allegedly minor influences on Diderot's *Lettre*, such as La Mettrie and Du Bos, have been even less helpful or conclusive. In their magisterial critical editions of this work P. H. Meyer and Jacques Chouillet collected a host of parallel passages from other authors, many of whom were undoubtedly in the background of Diderot's thinking; yet the *Lettre sur les sourds et muets* remains as obscure as ever.

The present chapter will take a different tack. I assume at the outset that

---

7. Claude Lévi-Strauss, *Regarder écouter lire* (Paris 1993), p.69.

8. *La Jeunesse de Diderot* (Paris 1939; repr. Geneva 1967), ch.8.

9. See n.2 above.

10. In addition to his introduction to the DPV edition, see Chouillet's *La Formation des idées esthétiques de Diderot* (Paris 1973), p.151f. On the ambiguities of Diderot's attitude towards Batteux, see p.156-57. See also the views of Ulrich Ricken, 'Die Kontroverse Dumarsais und Beauzée gegen Batteux, Condillac und Diderot: ein Kapitel der Auseinandersetzung zwischen Sensualismus und Rationalismus in der Sprachdiskussion der Aufklärung', *History of linguistic thought and contemporary linguistics*, ed. Herman Parret (Berlin, New York 1976), p.460-87.

11. On the main doctrines and historical importance of this text see Hans Aarsleff, *From Locke to Saussure: essays on the study of language and intellectual history* (Minneapolis 1982), esp. ch.3, 'The tradition of Condillac', p.146-84. On Condillac's influence on Diderot, see Chouillet, *La Formation*, esp. p.167-69, and the conclusion of the present chapter.

12. See the Meyer edition, p.15.

13. See Chouillet, DPV, iv.114.

although Diderot does, on a number of important occasions, borrow ideas or respond to opinions coming from the outside, in general his text is responding to pressures from within. Instead of looking for sources and influences, this chapter will study the ways in which Diderot's ideas grow, change and produce other ideas, one thing leading to another, sometimes by positive association, often through the impulse of contrariety. The ideas of Diderot's text have no rational order, and there is no grand design to them. However, at times recognisable stages in his thought emerge, as though he had been working towards a certain concept, which therefore acquires a particular weight or significance when it occurs. What distinguishes such stages is apt to be a shift in the meaning of terms, compared to a previous or later stage. This is to say that in this text Diderot's terms cannot be counted on to remain constant, and, contrary to traditional approaches, no attempt will be made in the present chapter to achieve a consistent interpretation. It will be assumed that the meaning of Diderot's words often evolves from place to place, and that to understand the meaning of the text at any given moment, one must keep track of the shifts of context and direction of argument – in patient detail.

Because so many quicksands lie ahead, it may be useful at the start to propose a few life-saving verities, however humble and homely; just something to cling to when the deeps rise and the ground gives way. For one can indeed detect constants amid the confusions of metamorphosis in this work, indicating that, even though Diderot may not have an unchanging main subject, he does at least have persistent preoccupations. To begin with the most obvious of these, Diderot's abiding concern in the *Lettre sur les sourds et muets* is with *language*, taken in the broadest sense, to mean anything that communicates. Certainly it is clear that all the ideas in this work are connected to this topic. A second preoccupation is *expressivity*: Diderot repeatedly tries to ascertain how language becomes more intense, or more natural, or less artificial; how to make it poetical or oratorical; he wants to decide which languages are inherently better suited for various kinds of expression and so on. Needless to say, this second preoccupation is inseparably a part of the first, being merely its aesthetic dimension. A third preoccupation is with *translation*:[14] how to translate words into gestures, and vice versa; how to translate the essence of poetical expression from one language to another; how music and painting can be translated into other media; and so on. This third concern is likewise implied in the term *language*, for, like many of his contemporaries, Diderot – at least most of the time – assumes that a word, or a gesture, is an *imitation* of a thought, or of

14. Chouillet saw the categories of expressivity and translation as connected to Condillac: see *La Formation*, p.160.

some other movement of the 'soul'. Thus both words and gestures are inherently translations of something else and Diderot's well-known syn-aesthetic interests simply build upon that perception.[15]

The *Lettre* begins with an investigation of the natural order of words versus inversion; towards the end Diderot stages a virtuoso display in which he essays a comparison between three kinds of expression – in poetry, music and painting – of the same subject. Despite incidental disparities, the opening and semi-final texts, and everything in between them, are linked by the preoccupations listed above.

Another concern in this text has to do with polemics, and before proceeding one needs to ponder the immediate motives which may have impelled Diderot to write the *Lettre sur les sourds et muets*. It is clear that, at least in some sense, Diderot intended this work to take its place among the innumerable linguistic debates that crowd their way into mid-eighteenth-century philosophical litera-ture. And yet, at the same time this text is unique among these controversies in that Diderot is not putting forward some cohesive theory of language. He is not even proposing a system of thought, as Batteux had devised in his *Beaux arts réduits à un même principe* or as Condillac had done. Diderot's ideas are not framed as a system, and only incidentally (as in his jibes at Batteux) does he adopt a combative or didactic tone, as though he were, momentarily, jockeying for position or telling the reader what to think. His normal mode was both critical and experimental: he was bringing problems into the open, and trying out ideas.[16] This difference with his contemporaries would seem to indicate that, however much linguistic debates hover in the background of this work, they were not the vital issue for Diderot; his main concern lay elsewhere.

Scholars have already noted that Diderot's opening arguments deal primarily with matters of epistemology; later on epistemology gives way to aesthetics.[17] As the rest of this chapter will attempt to demonstrate, in both of these broad areas Diderot's discussions come most clearly into perspective if one sees them as connected, not to a theory of language per se, but to the dominant language *style* of his age and Diderot's own deeply ambiguous reactions to it. Contrary to the emphasis of all other theorists, the great issue at stake in this work is not a theory of words, but the 'mind-set' and the linguistic *expression* of what one now terms French Classicism, along with the epistemology and the aesthetic values this style implied. In sum, the main direction of the arguments

---

15. For a more detailed discussion see Chouillet, *La Formation*, p.189.

16. I entirely agree with Chouillet on this point: 'C'est tout d'abord que la linguistique est pour [Diderot] un instrument de découverte, mais non une fin en soi' (*La Formation*, p.176).

17. See Chouillet, *La Formation*, p.219.

involves a bringing into question and a trying out of the *literary* language which had reached perfection during the reigns of Louis XIII and Louis XIV (as Diderot himself points out near the beginning of the work proper), and which continued to prevail in Diderot's time.

Nor is the *Lettre sur les sourds et muets* unique among Diderot's works in this respect. Diderot's Classical ambiguities cut deeply into his thinking and, as will be seen in later chapters, they come to the fore in a series of creations, as if Diderot's own character somehow doomed him to demonstrate, indeed to enact repeatedly, how much he was caught in a double bind regarding the high-style literature of the preceding century. Clearly, he could not have denied the extraordinary power of the language of Corneille and Racine: his comments on their achievements are as astute and sympathetic as anyone of his era; but, at the same time, he was equally mindful of the lifelessness and sterility that afflicted, if not all, at least the generality of eighteenth-century contemporary works prolonging these well-worn traditions – especially in the theatre. Furthermore, even though Diderot's Classical misgivings were aesthetic, there are hints as well that they were part of a political disposition: just as Eluard suggested, Classical style powerfully reflected the aristocracy, rank and privilege to which it belonged, not to mention the monarchy under which it flourished; and in at least some 'philosophical' quarters in mid-eighteenth-century Paris where new political attitudes were emerging, the elegances of high-style literature were felt as grating reminders of a way of life whose social defects could no longer be ignored.[18] In short, though often unspecified, politics, one may assume, distinctly coloured Diderot's feelings towards the literature of the *grand siècle* and its eighteenth-century progeny.

The most efficient way to perceive the drama played out in the *Lettre sur les sourds et muets* is to interpret it as Diderot's effort to deal with his ambivalences in this regard. Classical and anti-Classical implications are everywhere: on one side, one finds a searching analysis of the art of Racine, praise of Corneille and other Classical and neo-Classical authors, including Voltaire. There is even a eulogy of the French language in its eighteenth-century state, with all its abstractions and analytically ordered syntax, which Diderot recommends as particularly well suited to philosophical discourse – what he calls the language of truth – even as it is for social intercourse. At the same time, and despite the contradiction, this work (particularly at the opening)

---

18. These trends became especially visible in Diderot's disciple in theatre writing, Louis-Sébastien Mercier. See Rex, *The Attraction of the contrary*, p.162-64,180-83. On Diderot's political persuasions at the time of the *Encyclopédie*, see Jacques Proust, *Diderot et l'Encyclopédie* (Paris 1967), esp. ch.11, 'Diderot réformateur', p.449-502.

dramatically reflects an impulse to break out of the deadening sterility of the Classical language, and explore ways to put life, boldness and energy into the literary – especially poetical – expression of thought and feeling. In other words, Diderot's criticisms are directed towards the very elements in Classicism he is concurrently supporting and admiring, a doubleness that is utterly characteristic. Perhaps it might be more surprising if his attack on Classical traditions had appeared alone, without a complementary defence. The point is that, despite his fulsome *éloge du Classicisme*, questioning of its linguistic basis is essential to this daring work; in fact dissatisfaction in this sense is sometimes the main undertow.

'L'ordre naturel des idées' and 'l'ordre des gestes'

The negative, questioning side of the ambiguity emerges in the opening arguments (p.135-36). It is a matter of deciding whether French is a language of inversions or not. But obviously before inversions can be determined, one has to establish what the natural, uninverted order is. To settle the issue in good eighteenth-century fashion, Diderot goes back to the imaginary origins of language in primitive society (shades of Jean-Jacques), so as to ascertain the order in which humanity invented words – by definition the natural order. Also like Rousseau, Diderot discovered that these primitive beginnings were vastly different from the conditions of language once civilisation had set in. Like Condillac, Diderot finds that in early word development the senses, being the origin of all knowledge, played the dominant role. First, people named objects that combined several 'qualités sensibles'. Next came words that distinguished these qualities one from another, i.e. adjectives. Only in the final stages were abstractions and general terms derived from these qualities: e.g. impenetrability, extent, colour, shape, etc. (Diderot writes of 'noms généraux et métaphysiques', p.135) to which were added almost all the other 'substantifs'.

Though these few sentences have already covered a large part of the history of humankind, the argument does not pause, but hastens with increasing urgency towards the completion of its first stage: people became convinced that the abstractions that they invented actually stood for reality, and that the adjectives were subordinate to them, even though – and Diderot underscores this point by putting it in italics – the belief was totally false: 'et l'on s'est imaginé que l'adjectif était réellement subordonné au substantif, quoique le substantif ne soit proprement rien, et que *l'adjectif soit tout*' (p.135).

Few ideas are stated so forcefully in this work. And even though in substance Diderot simply reiterates a concept already given by Condillac,[19]

19. See Chouillet, *La Formation*, p.168.

the compression and emphasis of his presentation give it a special spin. Particularly when seen in a literary context, the implications are awesomely consequential. For obviously, in the sentence structure of French Classicism, the noun did in fact reign supreme, its initial letter often capitalised to set off its importance. To declare in effect that the French sentence has put a nothingness ('rien') in the seat of authority, while at the same time revealing that all its true power derives from its subordinates, brings into question the most fundamental aspect of Classical expression. This shift in perception may seem to herald a revolution in values, and certainly the movement by which it occurs in this text is an authentically dialectical one. To my mind it anticipates the famous clash in authority between Jacques and his master in *Jacques le fataliste*,[20] which leads to the paradoxical perception that power belongs not to the person who holds the title of 'Master', but to the person allegedly subservient to him, and on whose willing obedience the 'Master's' mastery depends. Diderot sees the abstract noun as having exactly the same sort of relationship to the elements traditionally termed 'accidents' or 'modifiers': the abstraction depends on them entirely for its existence and authority.

This potentially negative evaluation of the Classical word hierarchy is powerfully seconded by the final argument in this stage of the text, an argument no longer based on historical considerations but on sense perceptions, here and now.[21] As a preliminary step, Diderot gives a definition of the word 'body' according to the traditional, Classical word order: 'une substance étendue, impénétrable, figurée, colorée et mobile' (p.136). But against this, he proposes a reordering so that the definition will reflect the natural sequence in which a body is perceived by someone's senses, the actual experience of perception. And, as the dust settles, one discovers that not only an adjective, but the lowliest kind of adjective, the most mindlessly sensual adjective of all, the sort of adjective that Classical authors usually avoided entirely, or employed only under the strictest of controls, has now come into first place: colour. By the same token, the abstract noun, traditionally exalted as a kind of *sine qua non* from which all else flows, now robbed of its prestige, brings up the rear – its

---

20. DPV, xxiii.180-85. This clash will be discussed in greater detail in ch.8 below.

21. Chouillet, *La Formation*, p.166, points out that in reality Diderot's two arguments – language origins and sense impressions – represent two very different, and possibly contrasting, genealogies. And in fact, if one inspects Diderot's first argument closely enough, one finds that the first words uttered by mankind were actually nouns. Diderot avoids the term 'substantif', however, and instead places all the stress on the idea of sense impressions: 'Les objets sensibles ont les premiers frappé les sens, et ceux qui réunissaient plusieurs qualités sensibles à la fois ont été les premiers nommés.' By the slant of this presentation Diderot is attempting to run the two contrary genealogies off on the same level, and treat them both as belonging to the same argument.

position bespeaking its newly recognised subservience. The new ordering reads: *colorée, figurée, étendue, impénétrable, mobile, substance* (p.136).

This insight has a potential that is almost literally boundless, and it might be tempting at this point to note how happily writers of the nineteenth century would carry on in the direction that Diderot appears to suggest, shifting the emphasis from essence to attribute, and laying bare both the hollowness of abstractions and the awesome power of the concrete – exactly the sort of aesthetic perception towards which Diderot seems to be working. Indeed, the writers we are pleased to call realists or naturalists – especially the most famous of them such as Flaubert, the brothers Goncourt and Zola – would discover the infinite advantages of stressing 'accidents' over 'essences' and the particular over the general: of describing chipped crockery, dilapidated furniture and gaunt faces before bothering to set down the word 'misère'; of stringing out Félicité's household duties, one by one, in a long sentence whose concrete details tell far more than any broad category such as 'underpaid', 'overworked', or 'put upon' could ever have done; of letting the 'vulgarity' of Homais rest essentially on his speech and actions rather than on an abstract characterisation. Lowly colour, so often banished or minimised by Classical authors, would come into its own in the novel as early as Chateaubriand, who indeed discovered how to make colour a main attraction that infused his landscape descriptions with unheard-of vibrancy. In view of such future developments, Diderot's insight may appear positively prophetic. Yet, Diderot does not develop his new perception in any of these directions; his dazzling proposal vanishes almost as quickly as it had come, while the notion of inversion starts to capsize into a reversal. And in any case the point is not that Diderot is an incipient Flaubert, but rather that his perception momentarily overthrows the Classical verbal hierarchy along with the epistemology it assumed. Going back to the most primitive beginnings – that is to say, to original sense impressions, or to the origins of mankind (since humankind, too, had arrived at abstract nouns only late in its development) – it hints at an excitingly new way to retrieve the force and energy which words have lost through civilising processes such as inversion,[22] and it hints too at an excitingly new kind of verbal epistemology, an ordering designed to bring sense experience into words, giving first place to that, rather than to intellection. Particularly in view of the whole thrust of this work it seems likely that the motivating force behind this insight is his sense

---

22. For this stage of the discussion I am of course assuming that the order of the senses is the uninverted one.

of the artificiality of Classical verbal constraints – especially the dominance of abstractions – and the urge to tap into the natural energies they stifled.[23]

The gestural language of deaf-mutes

The alleged subject proper of the *Lettre*, communication by those who are deaf and dumb, also represents an effort to get behind, and tap into, the uncivilised sources of energy and emotion that existed prior to verbal language. Diderot himself invites the reader to see a parallel between pre-civilised humankind and those deprived of speech;[24] in fact the reader is asked to imagine the deaf-mutes as stand-ins for primitive man. Diderot does not bother to plot-out the details of the parallel; it is assumed from the start of his experiment, however, that there will be a close connection, perhaps even an identity, between 'l'ordre naturel' of the ideas of primitive man and 'l'ordre

23. Though in the *Encyclopédie* articles were classified according to 'noms métaphysiques et généraux' as given on the 'Système figuré des connaissances humaines', and the articles were theoretically structured in the traditional manner, i.e. giving an abstract definition before going on to more concrete considerations, in an addition to Diderot's *Prospectus*, added when the text was reworked for publication as part of d'Alembert's *Discours préliminaire*, the author (who has every appearance of being Diderot himself) revealed that this traditional pattern was not the one he considered most desirable. Had it been practical to do so, each article would have started by describing the concrete manifestations or applications of the subject of the article, and then worked towards the abstract definition or characterisation, so that the abstraction became intelligible and took on meaning through the concrete, and not the other way round. This kind of thinking is entirely consonant with the opening arguments of the *Lettre sur les sourds et muets*, both texts reflecting an impulse to find alternatives to traditional abstraction-dominated structurings (text of addition in DPV, v.96, n.Z). Certainly, as things turned out, the articles of the *Encyclopédie* are often ordered in the traditional way, so that the *Lettre sur les sourds et muets* represents relief and escape from Diderot's Encyclopedic activities, and the text may even have become more personal, vague, subjective, associative, contradictory and formless as a reaction against the logic and rigour theoretically demanded by his editorship. See Georges May's short article published at the head of the Meyer edition, p.xvi. Something similar might be said of Diderot's relationship to the rigorous discipline of Condillac's thinking, as will be discussed at the end of the present chapter.

24. 'Mais il n'est peut-être pas nécessaire de remonter à la naissance du monde, et à l'origine du langage, pour expliquer comment les inversions se sont introduites et conservées dans les langues. Il suffirait, je crois, de se transporter en idée chez un peuple étranger dont on ignorerait la langue; ou, ce qui revient presque au même, on pourrait employer un homme qui s'interdisant l'usage des sons articulés, tâcherait de l'exprimer par gestes' (p.138). Somewhat further on, speaking of real deaf-mutes (rather than pretended ones), Diderot also explicitly makes the connection: '[un sourd et muet de naissance] est une image très approchée de ces hommes fictifs, qui, n'ayant aucun signe d'institution, peu de perceptions, presque point de mémoire, pourraient passer aisément pour des animaux à deux pieds ou à quatre' (p.142). His use of the adjective 'fictifs', however, has caused some doubt among commentators. Probably the key to Diderot's adjective lies in the fact that those who had been, or were at this time, concerned with pre-civilised mankind – Montesquieu, Condillac, d'Alembert and Rousseau, for example – always stipulated that their descriptions and conclusions were purely hypothetical.

des gestes' of deaf-mutes, indeed this assumption is the pretext for all his explorations of gestural language.

The adoption of a gestural orientation – which Diderot does gradually, easing back into the world of deaf-mutes in two stages[25] – has anti-Classical, or at least un-Classical, implications: particularly in relation to the art of communication, putting words out of the picture amounts to abolishing the key piece in the Classical aesthetic, a point that is especially evident in the pre-eminent Classical genre, the theatre, whose 'tirades' and 'récits' made a point of verbalising every nuance of feeling and description, as if everything could be said in words alone. One need hardly mention, in this connection, that the uniquely French theatrical emphasis on words – played up to the point of reducing costumes, scenery and staging largely to conventions – is one of the main features setting the French theatre apart from the theatrical traditions of other nationalities, particularly the English theatre, throughout much of the seventeenth and eighteenth centuries.

In the first part of the *Lettre sur les sourds et muets* in particular, the 'sacred' word is challenged time and again by other modes of expression.[26] Perhaps this is why, in this text, words regularly appear to be tipping out of themselves – back into the sensations and/or historical situation that was their origin; or tipping out into musical sounds or colours and into representations in painting, into the reactions they were designed to cause outside of verbal discourse; tipping into inarticulate voice sounds; above all tipping into gestures which occasionally become in the theatre so intensely, sublimely powerful – one

25. Diderot first tries out a charade in which imaginary players pretend that they have lost the power of speech (p.138-41). Then, claiming to realise that such pretence cannot reproduce the kind of innocence of verbal language which he seeks to recover, Diderot turns to 'real' deaf and dumb persons (p.142f.). The effect of the 'mistake' of the charade – whose defects are so obvious that the reader immediately falls in with Diderot's dissatisfaction – is rather like that of the Nephew's deliberate mistakes in his pretended performance of an Italian harpsichord sonata in *Le Neveu de Rameau*: in both cases the mistakes seem to guarantee the authenticity of the performance. The charade prepares the reader to accept as reality the – doubtless imaginary – deaf-mute Diderot so artfully describes. (I entirely agree with Jacques Chouilet on this point: see *La Formation*, p.182-85.) This two-stage strategy also serves to dramatise Diderot's unexpected idea that the key to an understanding of verbal language resides in those who are deprived of verbal language, even as the properties of sight can best be explored by studying persons who are blind – as amply demonstrated in the *Lettre sur les aveugles*: see Jacques Scherer, *Le Cardinal et l'orang-outang* (Paris 1972), p.217-18.

26. Discussing Diderot's later theories of the theatre, Scott Bryson writes: 'Spoken language is no longer privileged as the sole means of communication [...] The neoclassical defence of the primacy of language (d'Aubignac: 'Parler, c'est agir') is countered by Diderot's theories of pantomime and tableau, which must be seen as attempts to increase communication [...] through more direct, primal language based on gesture, movement, intonation, inarticulate cries and even silence. What spoken language cannot express, these alternative languages can' (*The Chastized stage*, Saratoga, Calif. 1991, p.66).

famous example being Lady Macbeth – that no verbal discourse can approach them (p.142-44). The tipping may also go in the other direction, towards words: gestures are seen as incipient texts, paintings as mute conversations, and so on. No doubt this strategy manifests a dynamism that is typical of Diderot: he always shows things as part of a relation, as tending somewhere. It also manifests his acute sense of the interchangeability of the senses, i.e. synaesthesia. Meanwhile in this discussion of mutes, real and simulated, Diderot produces some of his most memorable and entertaining moments: his weirdly surrealistic discriminations between the senses ('le goût [était] le plus superstitieux et le plus inconstant, le toucher le plus profond et le plus philosophe', p.140); the dazzling hypothesis of a society composed of five persons, each with only one sense, yet finding in geometry one way to communicate (p.140); the scene with the supposedly real deaf-mute playing dead to signify that Diderot has lost the chess game, and then managing to act out a whole familiar proverb (p.144-45) which one is led to assume he invented on his own; and finally, the tableau in which the reader imagines the deaf-mute lost in wonder as he contemplates le père Castel's harpsichord, playing coloured ribbons when the keys are touched (p.146). These imaginative descriptions of pantomimes and demonstrations of interconnections have often been discussed elsewhere. For present purposes the important point is that this playful strategy of tipping into diverse languages forces the mind open to new, more varied and sometimes stronger and more energetic modes of expression than was possible within the confines of Classical verbalism.

'L'ordre d'institution' and 'l'ordre scientifique'

All the above discussion treats only one side of the story, and it goes without saying that in Diderot's text such a strongly un-Classical undertow was automatically, simultaneously accompanied by a pull in the opposite direction. No sooner had Diderot proposed his challenge to the epistemological basis of Classical word order than he immediately made a leap out of the primitive perspective into the modern one. Contrary to his first position, he fell in with the Classical mind-set with its analytically oriented abstract nouns and its word order placing substantives out in front. He characterised 'modern' French word order thus: 'nos constructions sont pour la plupart uniformes; [...] le substantif y est toujours ou presque toujours placé devant l'adjectif, et le verbe entre deux' (p.136).

From such a perspective, Classical French word order seemed normal and uninverted, while primitive order now became the inverted one. Thus everything is relative to one's point of view. For indeed, Diderot insists, if one examines in itself the question of whether the adjective precedes the noun, one finds that we moderns often invert the natural order – as the previous example (i.e. the definition of 'corps' starting with colour) demonstrated. He goes on to codify the distinction between the two perspectives using the term 'l'ordre naturel des idées' for the first, and 'l'ordre d'institution' or 'l'ordre scientifique' to designate the second. And he insists again on the natural order being specifically the order of the senses (p.137):

> Les adjectifs, représentant pour l'ordinaire les qualités sensibles, sont les premiers dans l'ordre naturel des idées; mais pour un philosophe, ou plutôt pour bien des philosophes qui se sont accoutumés à regarder les substantifs abstraits comme des êtres réels, ces substantifs marchent les premiers dans l'ordre scientifique, étant, selon leur façon de parler, le support ou le soutien des adjectifs. Ainsi des deux définitions du corps que nous avons données, la première suit l'ordre scientifique ou d'institution; la seconde l'ordre naturel.

In so far as Diderot is defining the 'ordre scientifique' in these passages, his terminology (p.136-37) would immediately have been understood by his contemporaries as fitting with one of the main schools of grammar theory of the day, the theories of the *grammairiens philosophes*.[27] In fact Diderot is not creating, but borrowing, ideas to form this side of his argument. Scholars have long been aware of this point, and there would be no object in reviewing the relevant doctrines once more, except that, as I hope to show, these theories also – in addition to putting Diderot's 'ordre scientifique' in perspective – provide the key to some of the most baffling passages in the text, to be discussed further on.

It is well known that the origins of the theories of the *grammairiens philosophes* go back to seventeenth-century rationalism, and particularly to the *Grammaire de Port-Royal* of 1660. Around the mid-eighteenth century, the movement was gathering steam, thanks partly to the publication of the *Encyclopédie*, whose grammar articles were being written by the leading spokesman of the school, Dumarsais[28] – author also of the first article of Diderot's great enterprise, the article 'A', and, anonymously, of the famous and controversial article 'Philosophe'.[29] The influence of these theories on Diderot's text is indisputable and has been well charted by scholars, who have long been

27. On this whole question, in addition to the indispensable notes and commentaries to the Meyer edition, see Nicholas H. Bakalar, 'Language and logic: Diderot and the *grammairiens-philosophes*', *Studies on Voltaire* 132 (1975), p.113-35.

28. The standard work on this figure remains, despite its deplorable hostility towards Dumarsais's theories, Gunvor Sahlin, *César Chesneau Du Marsais et son rôle dans l'évolution de la grammaire générale* (Paris 1928).

29. On this attibution, see A. W. Fairbairn, 'Dumarsais and *Le Philosophe*', *Studies on Voltaire* 87 (1972), p.375-92.

aware that, for example, when Diderot describes French as having a uniform construction, with the noun in front, the adjectives usually coming afterwards, and so on, as he does above, he is rendering quite exactly the view of French propagated by these theorists.[30] Even his idea that when one wishes to identify inverted order, one must first ascertain what the uninverted or natural order might be was a view that they too put forward.[31] In other words, starting with Diderot's earliest statements concerning the 'ordre d'institution' the theories of the *grammairiens philosophes* are a presence in this text.

In the eighteenth century no theory could be counted as complete unless it dealt with origins, and naturally the *grammairiens philosophes* were ready with carefully thought out notions of how languages began and the reasons for their development. They held that the human 'soul' was essentially undivided, and therefore human thought in its original state had no parts of speech or grammar. Grammar and syntax were developed as a means of communicating thoughts to others via words:[32] indeed they believed that without a logical structure such as is provided by syntax, words could not communicate whole thoughts. This is why all languages embodied this analytical syntax in one way or another; it was a universal grammar, and French was considered to have a special perfection in this regard, because its syntax was instantly clear from its word order: the noun came in front because it was, logically at least, the main element. The modifying words (Diderot often refers to them as 'adjectifs') should normally come after because they made sense only when one knew what they were modifying, in other words they needed the noun as something

30. See Chouillet, DPV, iv.136, n.18.
31. 'Toute *inversion* suppose un ordre primitif & fondamental; & nul arrangement ne peut être appellé *inversion* que par rapport à cet ordre primitif' (Beauzée, art. 'Inversion', *Encyclopédie*, viii.852A).
32. Dumarsais's explanation of this process is so thorough and systematic that he seems to leave nothing to chance: 'La pensée, tant qu'elle n'est que dans notre esprit, sans aucun égard à l'énonciation, n'a besoin ni de bouche, ni de langue, ni du son des syllabes; elle n'est ni hébraïque, ni greque, ni latine, ni barbare, elle n'est qu'à nous [...] Mais dès qu'il s'agit de faire connoître aux autres les affections ou pensées singulières, & pour ainsi dire, individuelles de l'intelligence, nous ne pouvons produire cet effet qu'en faisant en détail des impressions, ou sur l'organe de l'ouïe par des sons dont les autres hommes connoissent comme nous la destination, ou sur l'organe de la vûe, en exposant à leurs yeux par l'écriture, les signes convenus de ces mêmes impressions; or pour exciter ces impressions, nous sommes contraints de donner à notre pensée de l'étendue, pour ainsi dire, et des parties, afin de la faire passer dans l'esprit des autres, où elle ne peut s'introduire que par leurs sens. Ces parties [...] deviennent ensuite l'original des signes dont nous nous servons dans l'usage de la parole; ainsi nous divisons, nous analysons, comme par instinct, notre pensée; nous en ressemblons toutes les parties selon l'ordre de leurs rapports: nous lions ces parties à des signes, ce sont les mots dont nous nous servons ensuite pour en affecter les sens de ceux à qui nous voulons communiquer notre pensée: ainsi les mots sont en même temps, l'instrument & le signe de la division de la pensée' (art. 'Construction', *Encyclopédie*, iv.73A-74A)

to sustain them, a function that Diderot terms 'le support ou le soutien' (p.137). This analytic syntactic function of French word order is what Diderot terms 'l'ordre scientifique'.

But how, one might wonder, could these theoreticians maintain that all languages participated in this universal grammar, when, for example, Latin word order often did not observe this syntax? In Latin the adjectives could be sprinkled in far ahead of the noun they modified; they could be inserted long after the noun; the subject-noun could come last, or in the middle, or anywhere. The question was a good one, especially in a cultural era when classical languages were automatically a part of the language question, and the answer provided by the *grammairiens philosophes* was ingenious: they granted that the order of words in Latin or Greek was not strictly regulated in the way that French order was; yet they claimed that such languages were nevertheless informed by the same sort of structure, embodied in the inflectional endings of words, that enabled us to piece together by intellection the relationships which French actually spelled out sequentially. Thus, though Cicero's word order might read 'Long silence [...] the end this day marks', the inflectional endings of the words, beginning in the genitive, enabled the listener to understand that despite its up-front position 'long silence' was not the subject proper, and decipher the text correctly to read 'Of my long silence this day marks the end.' French syntax being more analytic, the French version would normally not invert and would put the subject of the sentence first: 'Ce jour doit marquer la fin de mon long silence.'

This example from the opening of Cicero's *Oration for Marcellus*, famous among grammarians, is actually quoted by Diderot some fifteen pages further on in the *Lettre sur les sourds et muets* (p.154), a place in the text that I designate the 'Cicero stage'. For even though it is sometimes risky to shuffle the order of Diderot's ideas, I will borrow a few points from this later discussion in order to understand the complexities of an obscure passage in his early arguments – being careful, needless to say, to keep the intervening changes in the meaning of Diderot's terms out of sight. In the later text (p.154-56), i.e. the Cicero stage, Diderot settles comfortably into the theories of the '*grammairiens philosophes*, explaining in some detail his version of the theories outlined above. He argues that Cicero was indeed making an inversion in the opening of the *Oration for Marcellus* when he declared that 'Of my long silence this day marks the end'. Diderot adds, however, that Cicero did so purely out of linguistic habit. Diderot surmises that there was probably not a single Greek or Latin author who was aware of what he terms 'this defect', i.e. inverting without realising it. Indeed, Diderot goes on, there was not a single author who was not convinced that the order of his words ('son discours') followed exactly the order of his thought processes ('[l'ordre] des vues de son esprit'), even though this belief was entirely false ('cependant il est évident qu'il n'en était rien').

This later discussion from the Cicero stage', while vividly revealing how much Diderot subscribed to the theories of the *grammairiens philosophes*, also clarifies somewhat an especially muddy part of the earlier discussion about the 'ordre scientifique ou d'institution'.[33] The subject in the early text is the absence of inversions in French, and Diderot postulates (p.137) that this quasi-total disappearance of inversions was caused by the reign of neo-Aristotelian philosophy, which treated general and metaphysical beings as though they were real. And now the passage daunting for its obscurity: Diderot points out that in (Greek and Roman) antiquity people studied nature in its specificity (rather, one presumes, than studying it according to the general, abstract categories brought to the fore by neo-Aristotelianism), and that their language had 'une marche' that was less monotonous (the point of comparison being, presumably, the uniformity of French, with the implication that the word order of ancient languages had greater variety and more inversions). He concludes that, to persons of antiquity, the very concept of 'inversion' would have seemed strange and foreign: 'eût-il été fort étrange pour eux.'

Of course, the key to this final point is the theory, developed in the Cicero stage, that in antiquity people constantly inverted the normal word order, without being aware of it, everyone – wrongly – assuming that their words simply followed the sequence of their ideas. Thus the notion that they were inverting would indeed have come as a surprise ('eût-il été fort étrange pour eux').

Even with the explanations I have offered in parentheses, one must confess that this part of the text is a struggle, and without them, the best one can say is that it is incomprehensible. Although one may deduce, as I have done, that Diderot was mainly concerned with Greek and Latin in this part of the text, Diderot himself does not specify to which 'langues anciennes' he is referring, and even leads one momentarily to wonder whether the term may not include the language of 'nos auteurs gaulois'. Nor can one understand why these 'ancients' would have found inversions so strange, without the explanation Diderot gives fifteen pages later. Certainly there may be particular reasons why Diderot does not spell out this point in the earlier context, as I will suggest when discussing the context of the Cicero stage.

A final note: in the muddy earlier discussion, Diderot uses the terms 'd'institution' and 'scientifique' as though they might be synonymous (p.137).

33. See the confusions recorded in the Rudich edition, p.97, n.1-2.

Yet Franco Venturi[34] pointed out long ago that, although overlapping, they do not mean the same thing: 'd'institution' simply implies that the word order has become recognised by society and instituted as the rule. Diderot also insists that this happened only when languages had had time to become fully developed. On the other hand, 'scientifique' indicates the kind of order it is, and Diderot also makes it clear that this term refers specifically to the analytic syntax of French. Even though the point may appear obvious, in view of future changes it is worthwhile stressing that here, at this early stage in the text, French word order ('l'ordre scientifique') is called an 'ordre d'institution', and not a natural order. Later on Diderot will see the matter differently.

The trend away from gestures

After so much enthusiastic exploration of non-verbal, and particularly gestural, language in the early part of the *Lettre*, it may seem peculiar that Diderot would turn away from gestures, to the point of abandoning them entirely. But this indeed becomes the trend. A number of factors probably brought on this shift in attitude: one of these may have been his own enthusiasm for gestures, which eventually led to a reaction against them. Another was probably the prestige he attributes to the logical perspective of the *grammairiens philosophes*, which by comparison began to make gestures seem less precise, less clearly ordered, less versatile and less efficient. One might also speculate that the partial misfiring of a bizarre experiment may have somehow been involved in Diderot's change of mind. This event occurs in the text just after Diderot's zestful account (p.148-49) of his habit of going to the theatre, sitting far from the stage and stopping his ears in order to judge the quality of the acting solely through gestures – 'me boucher les oreilles pour mieux entendre', he claimed to have facetiously explained to the startled onlookers.[35] Diderot added that the efficacy of his method was confirmed by the nearly stone-deaf playwright Le Sage, who said he could even assess the quality of his own plays by watching the movements of the actors (p.148-49). Having thus pleasurably installed himself in the universe of gesture – where some values are discerned so much more clearly than in the world of words – Diderot carefully sets up an experiment with a deaf-mute, an experiment designed to answer the problem that the deaf-mute had been invented to solve: what is the word order

---

34. *La Jeunesse de Diderot*, p.253.
35. All commentators have assumed that Diderot's story is not a fabrication, and that it can be safely used to document his early interest in the theatre and gesture. My own view is rather more sceptical, allowing as a likely possibility that at least parts of the story may be Diderot's witty invention.

corresponding to the gestures of someone who cannot speak? In other words, what is 'l'ordre des gestes'?

Unexpectedly, Diderot does not begin with an observation of behaviour, but with a general law that he claims to have derived from 'quelque étude' (p.149) of gestural language. Stranger still, this law turns out to fit perfectly with the theories of the *grammairiens philosophes*, in fact it reformulates their concept of French word order. Going counter to his previous definitions, Diderot now attributes to the language of gesture the distinguishing marks of the language he had always assumed previously to be situated archetypically at the opposite pole (p.149-50):

Sur quelque étude du langage par gestes, il m'a donc paru que la bonne construction exigeait qu'on présentât d'abord l'idée principale: parce que cette idée manifestée répandait du jour sur les autres, en indiquant à quoi les gestes devaient être rapportés. Quand le sujet d'une proposition oratoire ou gesticulée n'est pas annoncé, l'application des autres signes reste suspendue. C'est ce qui arrive à tout moment dans les phrases grecques et latines; et jamais dans les phrases gesticulées, lorsqu'elles sont bien construites.

In the limpid clarity of this text, 'la bonne construction' corresponds exactly to the analytic syntax put forward by the *grammairiens philosophes* as the mark of excellence of French, the feature that made it superior to Greek and Latin. Diderot himself will later (p.165) repeat the criticism of ancient languages that he voices here – that they make one wait so long before one can understand the meaning – but then the point of contrast will be specifically the French language.[36] Likewise at the end of this passage 'bien construites' means *logically* constructed, with the subject, typically a noun, coming first, because, as the *grammairiens philosophes* had long maintained, one cannot understand the modifiers until one knows what they are modifying.[37] Diderot seems to be revoking all his previous assumptions concerning the word order corresponding to gestural languages. Mixing together the categories that he had so insistently differentiated, he is declaring in effect that well-constructed communications in gesture will by necessity follow the analytic order of modern French. Although it may be significant, in view of subsequent developments,[38] that Diderot is already attempting here to link analytic order with the naturalness associated with gestures, later on he will not accept the apparent consequences of this experiment: he will not assume henceforth that the order of gestures is

36. A little later in this discussion, as will be seen, Diderot actually uses the expression 'l'ordre naturel des idées' when referring to the analytic order (p.166).

37. Diderot employs the word 'logique' when writing of the unchangeable position of the first gesture: 'Il n'y a qu'un muet sans logique qui puisse le déplacer' (p.150).

38. See below p.79-80.

the same as analytic word order. The experiment is simply one stage in the development of his ideas, and, as events will turn out, an abortive one.[39]

Meanwhile, Diderot amuses himself with a general discussion of the problem of avoiding ambiguities in complex sentences, and notes that good constructions may be the sign of a good mind, whereas the vice of bad construction may be so incorrigible that the only remedy would be to replace the writer's head with a new one. Because of the jocular tone one scarcely notices that the deaf-mute has been abandoned entirely, disappearing forever from the text. One should recall also that the language of gestures was earlier linked to the order of the senses, so that, in effect, the abortive experiment which tried to move gestures into an order of logic has been detrimental to that aspect of Diderot's original scheme as well. The order of the senses too has vanished, never to be mentioned affirmatively again.[40]

Shortly after this point,[41] Diderot begins a general downgrading of gestures, as if the rationality and analytical logic of the *grammairiens philosophes* somehow casts a pall over this other, more primitive kind of expression. As the negative trend sets in, Diderot stresses the limitations of deaf-mutes: they generally cannot cope with abstractions, he claims, nor can one be sure that they understand the different tenses of verbs (p.152). Applying this lesson to primitive mankind, Diderot concludes that for whole centuries humanity had

39. It is hard to tell whether the actual demonstration with the deaf-mute – Diderot describes him asking his servant, in gesture, to pour Diderot a drink – actually bears out the law he has just enunciated. The only conclusion that Diderot himself draws is that the order of the deaf-mute's first gesture – getting the servant's attention – is fixed: it must come first. On the other hand, the order of the other two gestures can be changed according to many different criteria: taste, fantasy, 'convenance', 'harmonie', 'agrément' and style – criteria which, while appropriate for discussions of Latin word order, seem rather overdone and even inappropriate for the cut-and-dried matter of pouring a drink. It is as though Diderot has lost sight of the original purpose of the experiment. Diderot's insistence on the priority of the deaf-mute's first gesture may have been vaguely influenced by, or somehow rearranged from, the theories of Batteux. See his manner of prioritising in the famous 'Serpentem fuge', quoted in Jacques Chouillet, *La Formation*, p.175.

40. In fact, its epistemological relevance will be denied: see below, p.85-86.

41. Meanwhile, Diderot notes that since French is so simple and uniform (code words for having no inversions and being analytically ordered), even if French were to die out, as classical languages have done, it would be an easy matter to learn to speak and write it correctly, whereas when trying to use classical languages, with all their inversions, one can never be sure which structures might have been permissible and which would actually have grated on the ears of a Cicero or a Demosthenes (p.151). Once again Diderot is assuming that French word order is the uninverted rule, other word orders the inversions. His assumption that French is uninverted then leads him, by contrary motion, to remember that French uses inversions such as 'blanc bonnet' and 'méchant auteur', and to speculate with complacent irony on the foolish mistakes in inversion which later generations might make after the imagined demise and revival of French – mistakes at least as foolish as the ones people make in Diderot's time, imagining they are writing correctly in Greek and Latin.

no verb tense other than the present indicative and the infinitive. He holds the order of gestures responsible for having perpetrated the defective verb tenses of Greek and Hebrew, especially the Greek custom of using the same tense to mean two different things (p.153-54). With a tone of satisfied superiority, he adopts civilised rationality as the dominant mode, at the expense of the primitive, now associated with imperfection and also with childhood in its pejorative sense. From this new perspective he comes to espouse the values and associations prized by Fontenelle and Voltaire, and against which Rousseau staged his revolt: 'Je regarde ces bizarreries des *temps* comme des restes de l'imperfection originelle des langues, des traces de leur enfance, contre lesquelles le bon sens qui ne permet pas à la même expression de rendre des idées différentes, eût vainement réclamé ses droits. Le pli était pris, et l'usage aurait fait taire le bon sens' (p.154).

The Cicero stage

Such is the context for the discussion of the opening of Cicero's *Oration for Marcellus*, in which Diderot claims that Cicero was indeed inverting, but was unaware of the fact (p.154-55). Diderot points to the wide discrepancy between Cicero's word order and the one implied in his inflected endings, a gap proving that there was in Cicero's mind a *pre-existing* order, which was 'tout contraire' (p.155) to the order of the words he spoke. The use of the term 'préexistant' (p.154-55) is another clue that Diderot is accepting the views of the *grammairiens philosophes*, for this was exactly their idea of the priority of universal grammar.[42] Furthermore, Diderot has now come to assume, even as they did, that analytic syntax is part of *natural* thought processes:[43] it embodies the way in which people naturally think when they wish to communicate – communication being the main function of language in the first place.[44] Though

42. See Dumarsais, art. 'Construction', p.75A.

43. This view dates from the seventeenth century: see Bouhours, *Entretiens d'Ariste et d'Eugène*: 'la langue française est peut-être la seule, qui suive exactement l'ordre naturel, et qui exprime les pensées en la manière qu'elles naissent dans l'esprit. [...] Les Grecs et les Latins ont un tour irrégulier; pour trouver le nombre et la cadence, qu'ils cherchent avec tant de soin, ils renversent l'ordre dans lequel nous imaginons les choses [...] Les Italiens et les Espagnols font à peu près de même: l'élégance de ces langues consiste en partie dans un arrangement bizarre; ou plutôt, dans ce désordre, et cette transposition étrange des mots. Il n'y a que la langue française qui suive la nature pas à pas, pour parler ainsi; et elle n'a qu'à la suivre fidèlement, pour retrouver le nombre et l'harmonie que les autres langues ne rencontrent que dans le renversement de l'ordre naturel' (1708 edition, p.62-64; quoted in Wladyslaw Folkierski, *Entre le Classicisme et le Romantisme: étude sur l'esthétique et les esthéticiens du XVIIIe siècle*, Paris 1925, p.217).

44. The classic explanation of this theory is in Beauzée: 'L'objet principal de la parole est donc l'énonciation de la pensée. Or en quelque langue que ce puisse être, les mots ne peuvent exciter de sens dans l'esprit de celui qui lit ou qui écoute, s'ils ne sont assortis d'une manière qui rende sensibles leurs rapports mutuels, qui sont l'image des relations qui se trouvent entre les idées

he uses the term 'préexistant' or 'l'ordre des vues de [l]'esprit' here, he later refers to the analytic order by actually using the term 'l'ordre naturel des idées' (p.166).

Looking back to the dichotomies of the opening of Diderot's *Lettre*, one can see that, since the beginning, all the main terms have changed meaning. Originally, the natural order was the order of sensations – which has now disappeared. Analytic syntax, then termed 'l'ordre scientifique', was specifically designated as an 'ordre d'institution', whereas it is now seen as pre-existing or natural – the very opposite of an 'ordre d'institution'. Meanwhile, the only order that qualifies as an 'ordre d'institution' would be the inversions of Greek and Latin, now seen as an instituted social practice,[45] although earlier linked to the natural order.[46] In sum, although Diderot remained blind to the fact,

mêmes que les mots expriment. Car quoique la pensée, opération purement spirituelle, soit par-là même indivisible, la Logique par le secours de l'abstraction, comme je l'ai dit ailleurs, vient pourtant à bout de l'analyser en quelque sorte, en considérant séparément les idées différentes qui en sont l'objet, & les relations que l'esprit apperçoit entr'elles. C'est cette analyse qui est l'objet immédiat de la parole; ce n'est que de cette analyse que la parole est l'image: & la succession analytique des idées est en conséquence le prototype qui décide toutes les lois de la syntaxe dans toutes les langues imaginables. Anéantissez l'ordre analytique, les règles de la syntaxe sont par-tout sans raison, sans appui, & bien-tôt elles seront sans consistance, sans autorité, sans effet: les mots sans relation entr'eux ne formeront plus de sens, & la parole ne sera plus qu'un vain bruit.

Mais cet ordre est immuable, & son influence sur les langues est irrésistible, parce que le principe en est indépendant des conventions capricieuses des hommes & leur mutabilité: il est fondé sur la nature même de la pensée, & sur les procédés de l'esprit humain qui sont les mêmes dans tous les individus de tous les lieux & de tous les tems, parce que l'intelligence est dans tous une émanation de la raison immuable & souveraine, de cette lumière véritable qui éclaire tout homme venant en ce monde, *lux vera quae illuminat omnem hominem venientem in hunc mundum. Joan.I.9'* (art. 'Inversion', p.853A).

45. The following text spells out this point: '[Il n'y a pas un seul écrivain grec ou latin] qui n'ait imaginé que son discours *ou l'ordre d'institution de ses signes*, suivait exactement celui des vues de son esprit; cependant il est évident qu'il n'en est rien' (p.154, emphasis mine). Rudich has pointed out Diderot's two contradictory uses of the term 'vues de l'esprit' (see his edition, p.115, n.1), although he does not consider Diderot's return to his original categories as a further switch, as I do; nor does he see the contrariety as indicating different stages of thought.

46. One sees the relationship between the old and the new perspective in a revealing sentence in which Diderot looks back to his earlier ideas: 'J'ai pensé que les inversions s'étaient introduites et conservées dans le langage, parce que les signes oratoires avaient été *institués* selon l'ordre des gestes, et qu'il était naturel qu'ils gardassent dans la phrase le rang que le droit d'aînesse leur avait assigné' (p.153, emphasis mine). As the rest of the passage makes clear, inversions are now being thought of as imperfections. They are also seen as forming a contrast with the analytic order of French ('le bon sens'). Cf. the views of Jacques Chouillet, DPV,iv.153, n.59, and P. H. Meyer in his edition, p.142, n. for p.56, line 26. In sum, inversions began as a reflection of the order of gestures, and as such could be imagined as embodying the directness and intensity Diderot found in gestures. As inversions came into the spoken word, however, they became 'instituted' in the language and habitual, to the point that people were not even aware they were using them. Thus inversions came to lose the qualities that had made them an 'ordre naturel', and evolved into an 'ordre d'institution'. Meanwhile – a corollary stage in his thinking – Diderot

the devaluation of gesture and the privileging of rationality have brought on a dramatic mutation in his two key concepts, 'ordre naturel' and 'ordre d'insti-tution', which have finally exchanged meanings. I suspect that this exchange is why Diderot did not give more details, in the famously obscure early passage, as to the reason why peoples of antiquity would have been surprised at the idea that they were inverting: the surprise depends on concepts of language usage that had no place in the earlier context.

Just to add to the confusion, at the end of this part of the discussion of Cicero's inversion Diderot congratulates himself (p.155) on having earlier distinguished between 'l'ordre naturel des idées et des signes' and 'l'ordre scientifique et d'institution', with no awareness of the black-to-white turnabout in meaning which has occurred in the interim, nor does he realise that the 'ordre scientifique' is no longer being thought of as an 'ordre d'institution'. But despite Diderot's blindness to them, the changes in meaning are indispens-able for an understanding of the later text. We may even feel a certain irony when, having taken account of the shifts, one looks back to Diderot's opening dichotomies: he has presented these first principles with aplomb and assurance as if their fixed categories were designed to last forever. One would never suspect that in reality they were extremely unstable and bore within them latent possibilities that would eventually capsize them into their opposites.

A brief contrariety

Diderot now starts to turn the discussion in a somewhat different direction. Before leaving the Cicero stage, however, one might well pause to note an especially well-defined contrariety taking place in the text: Diderot has so clearly enunciated his view that Cicero was blind to his inversion that one could almost have anticipated the reversal which occurs in the next paragraph (p.155-56). After reprimanding Batteux for not reflecting sufficiently on the aspects of inversion that he is about to discuss, Diderot proposes that during the opening of his *Oration for Marcellus* Cicero was entirely conscious that he was inverting, and that he deliberately inverted so that *to his audience* his word order would seem the natural, uninverted one.[47] These statements completely overturn his earlier position, which depends on Cicero *not* being aware of his

became conscious of the fact that the 'ordre scientifique', which had only come to prevail in French during the seventeenth century, and had therefore originally been termed an 'ordre d'institution', actually embodied natural thought processes, which made it an 'ordre naturel'. In all of these points, I am using the word 'inversion', as Diderot does in this part of the text, to indicate a sequence of words that is non-syntactical.

47. Despite this chiding, Batteux's ideas certainly lie in the background of Diderot's relativistic concepts of inversion: see Jacques Chouillet's analysis, *La Formation*, p.173.

inversion: Diderot's whole point was that Cicero, like his contemporaries, was a creature of linguistic habit: there was no calculation involved. He used an inverted order 'sans s'en apercevoir, subjugué par la longue habitude de transposer'. Nor – of course – was there any suggestion that his order might have been calculated to appear natural from the perspective of his listeners. For Diderot to overturn his position so dramatically in so short a space – not even a whole paragraph separates the two statements – certainly argues for a sort of intellectual myopia on Diderot's part: each segment of this argument is replacing and even abolishing the preceding one, with no recognition by the author of the shift. The example shows with particular clarity that Diderot's movements of thought, particularly contrariety, can be an unconscious pheno-menon – at least as unconscious as Cicero's inversions were originally thought to be, and perhaps even habitual as well. The undertow through which Diderot thinks in reversals often goes unperceived, and, given the traditional prejudice of philosophers against contradiction, one may assume that such a movement of thought would not have been allowed to proceed if Diderot had taken cognisance of it.

The seeming undermining of inversions

Meanwhile, Diderot's discourse about inversions becomes increasingly domin-ated by relativity. Apropos of the Latin sentence 'Serpentem fuge' – an example famous among grammarians – he concludes that there is no objective way to decide whether the 'first' idea is 'serpent' or 'flees', both answers being conceivably legitimate depending on individual reactions (p.155). In other words, in the case of 'Serpentem fuge' one cannot determine objectively and absolutely whether there is inversion or not. But Diderot is not content to analyse such questions subjectively according to point of view: he deliberately goes a critical step further ('Mais allons plus loin', p.156) in order to consider the undifferentiated mass of reactions within the soul, that is, the soul in the preliminary stage, before ideas became words. He discovers that from this perspective whole complexes of reactions can occur either instantaneously or so rapidly that no order can be discerned (p.157f.). Given that words can be emitted only one at a time, many words in sequence may be required to convey just one of these complex reactions on the part of the soul. Diderot goes to elaborate lengths to prove that in a group of phrases such as 'Le beau fruit! J'ai faim: je mangerais volontiers icelui', the final pronoun indicates a 'return' of the thought process to an object that had already previously been held in mind, and that the three phrases string out in sequence what was in reality a single sensation: 'la sensation n'a point dans l'âme ce développement successif du discours' (p.158). He speculates that twenty mouths capable of speaking at once might have conveyed instantaneously the complexity of the soul's re-actions, or perhaps le père Castel's ribbon-playing harpsichord could deal with such simultaneity, provided each colour signified an individual word element. Since by nature words follow after, and even drag behind, the soul's reactions, he wonders, reversing the situation, what might happen if language were full of energetic expressions capable of saying a great deal in a single word: would the mind then find itself obliged to break into a run in order to keep up with the words? By another backward motion, he also remembers that Greek and Latin teem with just such 'energetic' expressions that convey many perceptions at once, and he concludes that even though French has fewer of them, the fact that they exist at all proves the quasi-simultaneous multiplicity of perceptions.[48]

This entire discussion gives the appearance of challenging fundamentally the notion of inversions: not content with making the concept so relative that it no longer has any stable, objective status, Diderot now appears determined to break down the indispensable underpinning – the very concept of natural order – without which inversion cannot exist.

The interlude of the walking clock

Having reached this brink, a point seemingly of no return, the hitherto ceaseless evolution of ideas in the text jolts to a halt while Diderot conjures up and painstakingly describes his famous allegorical automaton, the 'horloge ambulante', a device which supposedly pictures, diagrams and gives dimension to the workings of human consciousness in all its thoughts, memories and reactions.[49] Admittedly the invention is intriguing: its heart is a spring that works along with the other appropriate pieces of clock machinery in the chest; its head is a bell, fitted with little hammers pulled by strings that go off to all parts of the clock case. He also imagines a small figure sitting on top of the bell, its ear cocked as though listening to tell whether everything was in tune. Was there ever such an ingenious device? Or such a complex situation it was invented to describe?

48. On the historical background of the theory of simultaneousness, see Chouillet, *La Formation*, p.195-97.

49. P.159-60. Aram Vartanian has made an interesting *rapprochement* between Diderot's text and a passage from La Mettrie's, *Histoire naturelle de l'âme*, which he believes to be Diderot's 'source': see 'La Mettrie and Diderot revisited: an intertextual encounter', *Diderot studies* 21 (1983), p.174f. Cf. also Chouillet, *La Formation*, p.199f. Thomas Christensen, *Rameau and musical thought in the Enlightenment* (Cambridge 1993), p.133-68, 216-17, suggests to me that Rameau's theory of 'le corps sonore' may provide the main key to Diderot's conception, in so far as it concerns music.

As he brings his automaton into action, the first sounds that Diderot imagines are the constant ones, which, like our feeling of existence, or our awareness of our body, are so unceasing that one forgets they are there: only some disruption brings them into our consciousness. Thus typically, after completing an imaginary mechanical device centred on a bell whose function is to ring, Diderot's first thought is of the noises it makes which are in effect silent.[50] Diderot is of course unique in his time for his sense of the subconscious, so marvellously indicated here in the discussion of unheard sounds, and when he essays a comparison – 'comme nous ne nous sommes assurés du bruit qui se fait le jour à Paris que par le silence de la nuit, il y aura en nous des sensations qui nous échapperont souvent par leur continuité', uncannily, it is as though one were reading a distant but powerfully suggestive forerunner of an image used by Proust to express his sense of memory and his vocation as an artist: the church bells, silent by day amid the noises of the city, but which start to ring out in the stillness of evening.[51] Nor is this the only instance in which Diderot's idea of memory and consciousness anticipates the great novelist.[52]

Musical analogies with the formation of chords and progressions are invoked to convey the concept of mental operations, the discussion being particularly suggestive because of Diderot's awareness of how much the process is permeated by memory. At the same time, thanks to the ever-listening figure on top, judgement plays a major role in Diderot's conception, not only in deciding between consonance and dissonance but in the formation of chords, whose succession is described as a 'discours'. Diderot's applications become increasingly playful and fanciful, leading further and further away from his allegory, which eventually he comes to deprecate and dismiss as proper only for the restless minds of children (p.161). However pleasantly diverting the episode may be, the imaging of consciousness would have to wait until the composition of *Le Rêve de d'Alembert* to come fully into its own.[53] The walking clock falls short of providing a true synthesis, and remains no more than an intriguing stage in Diderot's thinking.

50. I do not agree with the emphasis of Christensen's interpretation of this part of the text in *Rameau and musical thought*, p.216.

51. *A la recherche du temps perdu*, Pléiade edition (Paris 1987), i.36-37.

52. The celebrated example is Diderot's article 'Mémoire' from the *Eléments de physiologie*.

53. See Jacques Proust, 'Variations sur un thème de l'*Entretien avec d'Alembert*', *Revue des sciences humaines* 28 (1963), p.453-70; Françoise Dion-Sigoda, 'L'homme-clavecin: évolution d'une image', *Eclectisme et cohérences: mélanges offerts à Jean Ehrard*, ed. Jean-Louis Jan (Paris 1992), p.221-28.

The simultaneity of reactions

Diderot has claimed that words string out in sequence the thoughts and reactions which in the soul are actually plural and simultaneous. Such is the context for the best known sentence in this work: 'Notre âme est un tableau mouvant d'après lequel nous peignons sans cesse: nous employons bien du temps à le rendre avec fidélité, mais il existe en entier et tout à la fois: l'esprit ne va pas à pas comptés comme l'expression' (p.161), an idea which brings him, by contrary motion (p.162), to recall for the second time that Greek and Latin can in fact express a swarm of reactions in a single word and, going backwards in another direction, to exclaim to Batteux over how much our 'entendement' is modified by (linguistic) signs, so that even the liveliest diction is but a cold copy of what goes on in the soul. As an extreme example he cites Racine's 'Les ronces dégouttantes / Portent de ses chevaux les dépouilles sanglantes' from the 'récit de Théramène', which, however famously pictorial, does not even come close to the vividness of the scene in his imagination.

The last example is different from the others, because it is taken not from real-life sense reactions, but from fiction: so far as one can tell from Diderot's account, the brambles dripping with the blood of Hippolyte's horses had their origin in no other source than Racine's own verbal expression, so that in effect Diderot is declaring that in his imagination these words created images that far surpassed these words – at which point he exhorts Batteux to please ponder these things if he wants to understand how complicated the question of inversions is! Diderot also confesses that he is more interested in creating 'des nuages' (p.162) than in dissipating them and prefers to suspend judgements rather than judge. This denial of interest in making judgements leads by contrary motion to the addition of more proofs that the soul can have several thoughts at once, and indeed must do so in order to reason, in other words to make judgements (he actually uses the term a few lines later, p.163). One of the examples given of simultaneous sensations is that of the colour and shape of a body, now said to be perceived simultaneously (p.163), whereas earlier Diderot pointedly gave them as sequential.

The apparent demise, and rebirth, of inversions

Diderot concludes ('Une conséquence de ce qui précède', p.163) that in the mind ('l'esprit') there are not and perhaps cannot be inversions, especially if the object of contemplation is abstract and metaphysical. This statement might seem to settle the question once and for all: since natural order does not exist, one cannot tell an inversion from a non-inversion. But in this work Diderot's statements seldom lead to the expected conclusions; and here, after a semicolon (p.164), the sentence goes on using quotations in Greek, Latin and French to show why, in one sense at least, French is actually uninverted! The topic that was dead as a doornail only an instant before has revived for a comeback. Brushing aside all recent trends in the discussion, Diderot apparently reverts to one of his earliest positions: he distinguishes between French word order, on the one hand, and the 'ordre d'invention des mots' or the 'langage des gestes', on the other. (Significantly, he does not mention the order of sense perceptions.) Explaining himself through a reference to Batteux, Diderot denies that he holds generally that Latin does not invert, whereas French does. He simply means that if one compares French sentence construction to the order in which words were invented, i.e. to the order of gestures, then French seems to be the most inverted of languages, whereas if the point of comparison becomes the perceptions of a mind disciplined by Greek or Latin syntax ('[l]es vues de l'esprit assujetti par la syntaxe grecque ou latine', p.164),[54] then French is the least inverted of languages. This last perspective, making French appear uninverted, now seems the endpoint of the preceding development. Inversions and non-inversions, restored to life and ready to function as counterpoints, are henceforth available as a solid basis for discussion. Gone, momentarily, is all hint of speculative playfulness or postulation. Didacticism surges to the fore and the confident arguments deployed launch the text into a spirited defence of the French language, to the detriment of Greek and Latin.

Grammairiens philosophes *and the revival of inversions*

But how did the miracle occur? What brought inversions back to life? The preceding analysis has played along with Diderot's game of appearing to undermine them, and certainly Diderot makes a great show of obscuring the question, revealing its baffling complexities and taking poor Batteux to task for being unaware of the difficulties. Furthermore, by implication he has destroyed one of the basic elements of his original position, namely the assumption that human perceptions could be analysed according to the order of sensations, an order exemplified in his second definition of the word 'corps', starting with 'couleur'. But it now turns out that perceptions are not ordered in that way: sense impressions and judgements occur simultaneously, or quasi-simultaneously, in the soul – as Diderot demonstrates repeatedly with a whole battery of proofs and examples, as though he were determined to render his

54. For a brief moment this term means the morphosyntax implied in the inflected word-endings.

earlier position beyond recovery. Sensationalism, in the earlier sense, has been obliterated from the text. As for inversions themselves, however, Diderot has always held a trump card in reserve that would survive any obfuscation or problematising, namely the linguistic theory of the *grammairiens philosophes* which was designed on the assumption that the reactions of the soul itself were originally undivided and undifferentiated, and that languages were invented simply for purposes of communication.[55] Since in Diderot's view French syntax emerged out of the amorphousness of sensations and reactions via a logical process, Diderot insists not only that French is uninverted, but that its word order is the natural one (p.164): 'Nous disons les choses en français comme l'esprit est forcé de les considérér en quelque langue qu'on écrive. Cicéron a pour ainsi dire suivi la syntaxe française, avant que d'obéir à la syntaxe latine.'

The *grammairiens philosophes* had always held that because French word order represented the natural order of logic it was superior. Diderot is now committed to the superiority of French over other languages, a relationship presented as a dichotomy that gradually hardens into an antithesis. This is a set piece, a *morceau d'éloquence* that gathers energy as it proceeds (p.164-65):

D'où il s'ensuit, ce me semble, que la communication de la pensée étant l'objet principal du langage, notre langue est de toutes les langues la plus châtiée, la plus exacte et la plus estimable; celle en un mot qui a retenu le moins de ces négligences que j'appellerais volontiers des restes de la *balbutie* des premiers âges.

Before continuing the quotation, one may note that by implication Diderot has turned a half circle from at least some of the arguments characterising the perspective of the opening of the *Lettre*. In dismissing the original primitive order of language as 'balbutie' and 'négligences' Diderot clears the path for the refinements of civilisation, which now take pride of place, and provide the criteria according to which the French language is judged 'la plus estimable'. For the moment, Diderot starts to sound like Rivarol (p.165):

Ou pour continuer le parallèle sans partialité, je dirais que nous avons gagné à n'avoir point d'inversions, de la netteté, de la clarté, de la précision, qualités essentielles au discours; et que nous y avons perdu de la chaleur, de l'éloquence et de l'énergie. J'ajouterais volontiers que la marche didactique et réglée à laquelle notre langue est assujettie, la rend plus propre aux sciences; et que par les tours et les inversions que le grec, le latin, l'italien, l'anglais, se permettent, ces langues sont plus avantageuses pour les lettres.

55. Although many have recognised the *grammairiens philosophes* as the source of the following quotations, I am not aware of any other scholar who has appealed to their theories in order to explain this apparently anti-inversion stage in Diderot's thinking.

The argument derives so inexorably from what preceded that Diderot leaves no room for doubt. The only question allowed to occur in the mind at this stage is whether characterising French as a language of precision and the 'sciences' may not be a disparagement. And, through the rhetoric of antithesis and the slanting of terminology, Diderot is attempting to constrain the reader to agree that, although French had to renounce certain attributes, the result has been – when weighed judiciously in the balance as he is doing – worth the sacrifice (p.165):

Que nous pouvons mieux qu'aucun autre peuple faire parler l'esprit, et que le bon sens choisirait la langue française; mais que l'imagination et les passions donneraient la préférence aux langues anciennes et à celles de nos voisins. Qu'il faut parler français dans la société et dans les écoles de philosophie; et grec, latin, anglais dans les chaires et sur les théâtres: que notre langue sera celle de la vérité, si jamais elle revient sur la terre; et que la grecque, la latine, et les autres seront les langues de la fable et du mensonge. Le français est fait pour instruire, éclairer et convaincre; le grec, le latin, l'italien, l'anglais pour persuader, émouvoir et tromper; parlez grec, latin, italien au peuple, mais parlez français au sage.

One could hardly imagine a more unexpected situation for Diderot to put himself in. If it came to a choice, one would have thought that he would side with warmth, eloquence and energy, rather than teaming up with 'le bon sens' and 'les écoles de philosophie'. Once the eloquence gathers momentum, there is no time even to protest against his statement that Latin, being properly a language of imagination and emotions, is not the appropriate language for schools of philosophy (so much for several centuries of experience in European academies), and that the common people should be addressed in (classical) Greek! No doubt it is slightly unfair to take this rhetorical flourish so literally, but the fact that Diderot could be trapped into writing anything so dubious as 'parlez grec au peuple' is a sure sign that his rhetoric has got out of hand, and perhaps also that his French in this instance, far from exemplifying 'clarté', 'netteté', and 'précision', has become one of those deceptive literary languages of emotion and the imagination. Finally, the rhetorical force with which Diderot enunciates his antithesis may also provide a hint that this argument is becoming a marked target for eventual reversal – which in fact is the case, as will be seen.

II

Harmony

Meanwhile a new subject of preoccupation is ushered into the text and, to mark its importance, Diderot returns once more to the origins of humanity (p.166), this time so as to discover the stage at which humankind became concerned with *harmony* in language, that is, a desire to please the ear. Because Diderot writes from the perspective of the *grammairiens philosophes*, harmony is first perceived – paradoxically for someone so aurally sensitive – as an element of disruption, one that often interferes with what he terms 'l'ordre naturel des idées', i.e. the kind of word order exemplified in French. He gives two Latin examples in this connection (p.167), both from Cicero, the second of which is 'Mors, terrorque civium ac sociorum Romanorum', his point being that according to natural order, the first two words should have been 'terror morsque', and not 'mors terrorque'. But what is wrong, one might wonder, with the admittedly more sequentially logical 'terror morsque'? The answer apparently is that there is nothing the matter except the sound: the ugly and difficult to pronounce jamming together of 'ror mor' in the middle, an effect which would have been intolerable to the expertly sensitive ears of Diderot, and which Cicero avoided as a matter of course.[56]

In the other Cicero example, Diderot actually reorders the Latin words of the opening of the *Oration for Marcellus*, familiar through previous discussion, so as to put the words in 'natural' order. Comparing this revised version with the harmonious original, one again discovers that sound and rhythm are the key issues, and that Diderot's deliberately unharmonious rearrangement, for all its logical syntax, creates a 'dissonant' series of 'o' sounds in succession and breaks the rhythm of the clauses with an abruptness that makes them almost impossible to read out loud.[57]

Hieroglyphics: French examples

During this ample discussion, the logical criteria of the *grammairiens philosophes* gradually fade from sight, and one becomes increasingly conscious of how much for Diderot words on the page were, in his own peculiar sense, sounds on the page; and it is in the context of his concern for aural values that Diderot

---

56. It is even possible that Diderot's inadvertent mistranscription of the passage may be related to the same sort of aesthetic consideration: Cicero had actually written 'Mors, terrorque sociorum ac civium Romanorum.' Diderot's rearrangement diminishes the prominent repetition of 'or'.

57. The ensuing discussion of poetical examples in Latin is notoriously obscure (p.168, line 5f.). The only way it makes any sense is to assume that for just one short paragraph the word 'harmonie' has somehow come to include, or be compatible with, 'ordre naturel'. Thus Diderot is saying that for special dramatic effect the 'harmonie' and natural order of words may be altered – which is what a number of examples such as 'Nec brachia longo / Margine terrarum porrexerat Amphitrite' and 'Longo sed proximus intervallo' seem to imply. Admittedly the text thus construed creates a bizarre contradiction with the succeeding paragraph, which flatly declares that taking licence with word order is never permitted except for the *benefit* ('en faveur de') of stylistic harmony.

moves into the most famous and densely meaningful proposals in the work, concerning the 'hieroglyphics' of poetry.[58] These texts are so familiar that there is no need to examine again the passages about the undefinable 'spirit that moves and vivifies the syllables', causing everything to be 'said and imitated' ('représentées') at once, and so on (p.169). The uniqueness of Diderot's poetical insights in these texts has been duly admired, and the kind of simultaneity they advocate sufficiently defined.[59] It does, however, seem worthwhile to stress, and develop further, a point suggested long ago by James Doolittle:[60] that in Diderot's mind the mimicry of sound and rhythm in the words of poetry could be classified as 'painting', even when no visual images are involved. Thus apropos of the familiar line from Boileau: 'Soupire, étend les bras, ferme l'œil et s'endort' (p.169), Diderot remarks that only rarely will people realise 'combien il est heureux pour un poète qui a le *soupir* à *peindre*, d'avoir dans sa langue un mot dont la première syllabe est sourde, la seconde tenue, et la dernière muette' (p.170; second emphasis mine).

Diderot's comment is genially perceptive of course. One may note, to be sure, that nothing is actually *painted* by the word 'soupire', which is entirely auditory; however, in Diderot's manner of thinking such sounds are in fact a kind of painting, and Doolittle's remarks are entirely pertinent in linking this phenomenon to Diderot's concept of hieroglyphic and emblem, terms which are specifically visual in implication. Diderot's readiness to use the verb 'peindre' to describe a purely aural phenomenon may also have a musical dimension, for in the eighteenth century music's imitative function was commonly described as 'painting' in sound.[61]

Painting via sound may also provide the key to Diderot's fascinating, and baffling, exegesis of another poetical text in French which he quotes as an example of poetical hieroglyphics, this time from Voltaire (p.169).

> Et des fleuves français les eaux ensanglantées
> Ne portaient que des morts aux mers épouvantées.

Diderot claims that, however incapable most people may be of grasping such implications, the first syllable of the verb 'portaient' contains a vision of waters clogged as if suspended by the heaping mass of corpses, while at the second

---

58. Thanks to Genette, *Mimologiques, passim*, it is possible to place this phenomenon in Diderot in its broad historical context.

59. Most eloquently in Jacques Chouillet, *Diderot poète de l'énergie* (Paris 1984), p.39-43.

60. 'Hieroglyph and emblem in Diderot's *Lettre sur les sourds et muets*', *Diderot studies* 2 (1952), p.148-55.

61. See the extreme example from *Le Neveu de Rameau* cited in Rex, *The Attraction of the contrary*, p.117-22. There are also some curious correspondences between Diderot's mimetic vocabulary and Charles de Brosses: see Genette, *Mimologiques*, p.86-89, 108-109.

syllable ('taient') these sink down on their way out to sea. Not only does the word 'épouvantées' imply 'fright', but also, at the same time, Diderot finds in the rhetorical emphasis of the pronunciation of the third syllable ('van') an image of the ocean's vast expanse.

Such a seriously detailed and aesthetically oriented commentary on vernacular poetry is unique of its kind in this period in France. Particularly for those who tend to find Voltaire's 'heroic' verses insipid, it would have been helpful had Diderot gone on with this extraordinary discussion, telling us exactly what he saw in his imagination as he perused, syllable by syllable, Voltaire's now famously unread epic *La Henriade*. Perhaps one might be somewhat closer to realising why so many persons of wit and judgement in the eighteenth century considered this work worthy of Virgil. Diderot's commentary on these two lines is particularly revealing in terms of his own peculiar brand of epistemology: it not only shows the ways in which for him the various senses were interconnected (even as they were bound to the intelligence), and thus why synaesthesia was for him a quasi-automatic process, but it almost joltingly reminds us of Diderot's keen sense of the auditory: the moment when the mind comprehended the meaning of the letters, the ear instantly caused the intelligence to retranslate not just the words, but even the individual syllable sounds, into visions for the eye.

But how, one may wonder, does the syllable 'por' in 'portaient'[62] convey Diderot's vision of 'les eaux gonflées de cadavres, et le cours des fleuves comme suspendu par cette digue' (admittedly a rather large message for such a brief syllable).[63] It is clear that 'por' does not mean anything in itself; nor, in this case, does it achieve meaning by etymology, rhymes or homonyms. One can only conclude that this vision depends somehow on the pronounced sound of the syllable, which in some way imitates the movements described. Diderot himself will later suggest this kind of aesthetic possibility when he describes the function of 'l'hiéroglyphe syllabique' as 'l'imitation syllabique des mouvements et des bruits physiques' (p.177), or again, 'le rapport que les éléments [des] mots pouvaient avoir [...] *par leurs sons*, avec les qualités physiques des êtres qu'ils devaient désigner' (p.177, emphasis mine). Thus, in this hieroglyphic context, one should expect that the syllabic sounds will imitate the movements and physical qualities of the objects designated. But if sound must be all, then – no matter how far-fetched the interpretation may seem in our

62. I assume that Diderot used a system of syllabification similar to the one given for 'perte' in Gabriel Girard, *Les Vrais principes de la langue françoise* (Paris 1747), i.11.

63. Cf. the analyses of Genette, *Mimologiques*, p.205; James Creech, *Diderot: thresholds of representation*, p.132-34; and Pierre Seguin, *Diderot, le discours et les choses: essai de description du style d'un philosophe en 1750* (Paris 1978), p.198-99.

own aurally insensitive age – in the first syllable, 'por', Diderot was probably reacting to the pronunciation of the closed syllable, in which the vowel sound 'o' becomes clogged at its end – even as the rivers are said to do – by the sound of the consonant 'r'; whereas, he seems to have noted, nothing impedes the vowel sound of 'taient', an open syllable whose course in effect runs free and unblocked to the end of the word, even as the blockage of the river sank away and opened to the sea in Diderot's interpretation. Through the principle of aural mimesis, Diderot has converted the sound of these two syllables into two distinct sound-pictures.

It is less clear why the 'van' in 'épouvantées' should be pronounced as Diderot says it should, and therefore conjure up, in addition to the general notion of fear, a vision of the ocean's vast expanse. The image is slightly less detailed than the other vision, and of course Diderot expected, that only an élite would be able to share his insights (p.170), this being one of the reasons why he chose an expression implying mysteries or secrets: 'les hiéroglyphes'.

This expression also had more outwardly dynamic implications. For certainly in this passage Diderot has been unlocking – almost as if he were the poet responsible for the text – the hidden creative energy latent in a single, tiny syllable, expanding its potential into an eloquent and complex vision – grasped only by the initiate. Though less hidden, the opening section of the *Lettre sur les sourds et muets* may likewise be seen as an effort to release eloquence and energy, this time imprisoned in abstractions. In that earlier context, the process meant going behind the abstract noun to discover the sense perceptions which are the source of its power; it also implied exploring alternative means of expression, and in effect turning away from the word-centred aesthetic of Classicism. But now in the later text Diderot's thinking has moved to a more advanced stage in which all the valences have changed. His analysis implies unquestioning approval of Voltaire's Classicism, for this couplet – to Diderot so densely expressive – is a perfect example of that sort of high-style poetry. One need hardly mention that some of the essential hallmarks of Classical language are to be found in the two quoted lines: the continually elevated level of abstraction, created and sustained by all the nouns being given in the plural; the fact that each word is taken from the most widely recognised Classical vocabulary, indeed Voltaire's 'mers épouvantées' veers almost uncomfortably close to Bossuet's famous 'Océan étonné' in the funeral oration for Henriette de France (both authors having drawn on antiquity, of course). In short, high-style poetry, mannered and artificial in expression, rife with abstractions and using a choice vocabulary selected from only the most respectable authors, has come into its own in this commentary, thanks to Diderot's power to unlock its secret eloquence. Diderot appears so contented with his singular visions that one might be lulled into believing that Diderot's dialectic had reached a final resting place. But as usual in this text, the discussion, as if self-propelled, is destined to move restlessly forward.

Hieroglyphics: Greek and Latin examples

Constantly stressing the mimetic relation between sound and meaning, Diderot goes on to deal with texts in Latin and Greek, giving more of his remarkable and sometimes quirky explications, and stressing forcefully the near impossibility of translating such complexities as verbal hieroglyphics from one language to another (p.171-74). Related topics intervene: he undertakes to refute an interpretation of several Homeric lines on which Longinus, Boileau and La Motte all agreed, and whose opinion Diderot proves to be quite mistaken, a point he makes in detail and at length, claiming, to be sure, that he takes no pleasure at all in besting three such giants at a stroke, but only in rallying to Homer's defence (p.174-76).[64] He also decides on the period of language development in which 'l'hiéroglyphe syllabique' became a factor in languages (p.176-77). For the moment Diderot's *Lettre* takes on the aspect of the traditional *Pensées diverses*, miscellaneous thoughts, an unpredictable bundle of disparate ideas, to be enjoyed partly on account of its arbitrariness. Meanwhile, the discussion lacks a strong sense of direction.

Pro and contra Racine

Whereupon part of the *récit de Théramène* comes sailing into the discussion (p.178), the lines describing Hippolyte's horses during the ride towards Mycena, which were said to have been cited by the abbé de Bernis to accuse Racine of lacking good taste. Just as he had done with Longinus, Boileau and La Motte, Diderot easily bests the alleged opinion of Bernis, claiming it as further proof of the difficulty of knowing how to read poetry. Though leaving room for the possibility of a certain 'hors de propos' in Racine's description (p.179), he shows how perfectly the quoted lines render Hippolyte's feelings of 'abattement' and 'chagrin', how right the poet was to have written 'Sa main sur *les* chevaux' rather than 'ses chevaux', how the evocation of the former state of these 'superbes coursiers' sets off by contrast the image of what they have now become, and he especially approves the suggestion of the swaying gait of the horses ('la nutation') in the rhythm of 'L'œil morne maintenant et la tête baissée', a perfect example of a hieroglyphic reading. Though he wishes the poet had not treated as a mere figure of speech the horses' sympathising

---

64. See Raymond Trousson, 'Diderot et Homère', *Diderot studies* 8 (1966), p.190-91.

with Hippolyte's sad mood – since it is so clearly established that animals do in fact fall in with the emotions of their masters – he approves in essence this part of the *récit* as well. And he concludes resoundingly in favour of the passage: 'La description de Racine est donc fondée dans la nature: elle est noble; c'est un tableau poétique qu'un peintre imiterait avec succès. La poésie, la peinture, le bon goût et la vérité, concourent donc à venger Racine de la critique de M. l'abbé de Bernis' (p.179-80).

With any other writer, such sustained, solidly argued approval would have settled the question. With Diderot, such a series of powerful positives almost inherently imply negatives, which come as though spoken by someone else's voice:[65] allegedly quoting Porée's commentaries delivered to students at the Collège Louis-Le-Grand,[66] Diderot–Porée points out that however many beautiful traits might be found in the passage, they are distinctly misplaced in this situation. Thésée would have been quite right to halt the description in mid-air, and demand that the speaker get to the point, namely, the son who has been killed: 'eh! laissez là le char et les chevaux de mon fils, et parlez-moi de lui' (p.180).

Even as previously Diderot had struck a series of blows in favour of Racine, he strikes a major, perhaps overwhelming blow against him. For obviously, if Théramène were to follow Diderot–Thésée's advice and skip to the end, the whole structure of the *récit* would go to pieces. It is also clear that Thésée's emotional interjection, 'Parlez-moi de lui', emanates from a Thésée significantly different from the character invented by Racine, the many-sided, darkly hued complexity of his roles in the tragedy having been reduced and simplified to a single one: 'Père', with a capital 'P'. In fact the voice one hears in Diderot's imagined interjection is exactly that of some 'père de famille', with accents prophetically suggestive of Diderot's own sort of *drame*. Clearly no down-to-earth emotional tonality such as this could have found a suitable place in the sophisticated psychological universe created by Racine, especially not in this play. This dismissal of the *récit* in favour of 'true' feelings and 'family' emotions implies that Diderot has now turned against the dramatic conventions that were the essence of Racine's art, and perhaps also that simpler, bourgeois values are replacing Racine's lofty aristocratic ones. Meanwhile, in order to bring out Racine's inferiority by comparison, Diderot cites the great

65. On this procedure in Diderot, see Jean Starobinski, 'Diderot et la parole des autres', *Critique* 28 (1972), p.3-22.

66. Some scholars have believed that Diderot's contacts with Porée may have been real. There is also a strong possibility, however, that this passage is a fiction inspired by Voltaire's well-publicised veneration for Porée's 'leçons': see Voltaire's fulsome praises in his *Lettre de Monsieur de Voltaire au R. P. de La Tour, principal du Collège de Louis le Grand* (Paris 1746).

moment of the *Iliad* when Achilles hears of the death of Patroclus. He notes that everything is said in just two lines, yet – 'Il y a plus de sublime dans ces deux vers d'Homère, que dans toute la pompeuse déclamation de Racine' (p.180).

The least one can conclude is that Racine would have done better to say everything in a few good lines. And now, it is as though Diderot's own former praises of the *récit*, still lingering on in the mind, were determining – by backward motion – what he should criticise. Previously, Diderot claimed that Racine's description was founded in nature, and that, among other qualities, it combined good taste and truth. He also mentioned the 'beauties' the passage contained. Now black turns white, as the text continues: 'Lorsqu'un morceau pèche contre le décent et le vrai, il n'est beau ni dans la tragédie ni dans le poème épique. Les détails de celui de Racine ne convenaient que dans la bouche d'un poète parlant en son nom, et décrivant la mort d'un de ses héros' (p.180).

As a conclusion (p.181) Diderot returns to Bernis, whose speech criticising Racine Diderot claims not to have heard in person. He wonders about the truth of the reports of the abbé's criticisms, and again attributes to Père Porée the idea that Racine's description was 'déplacée'. At the end, he deliberately refuses to declare whether he believes Racine to be guilty of 'mauvais goût'.

In the whole of this part of the discussion, Diderot – even while launching his attack on the *récit* – is making visible efforts to cover his tracks and leave himself a way out: he deliberately gives the reader the option of not taking his criticisms seriously, or at least shifting the blame for them onto someone else, in case the reader does. The possibility that Bernis never made the alleged criticisms in the first place could reduce everything to a point of no practical importance. Diderot's insistence that not he but someone else long ago – Diderot stipulates thirty to forty years – originated his ideas elevates them to time-consecrated status. Thus, instead of voicing his own outrageous opinions, Diderot is simply restating the venerable thoughts of the infinitely respectable Porée – a Jesuit into the bargain. Perhaps Diderot is using the words 'déplacé' and 'hors de propos' in their mildest sense, implying that Racine's *récit*, far from being pompous, wordy or in poor taste, could really have been quite splendid spoken at another moment, or by another person, or in another play, or considered as pure poetry; if so, the issues can be thought minor, even trivial.

From this fairly sizeable cluster of subterfuges and red herrings I conclude that there were indeed vital matters at stake in this text and that Diderot was almost nervously aware of the far-reaching import of his criticisms, and furthermore that the impulse he felt to throw out all Racine's artificial pomposities, replacing them with the fresh air of simple, human, paternal emotions, ran deep within him. His efforts to take cover behind the unassailable respectability of Porée also reveals his awareness that his dismissal of the *récit de Théramène* attacks the most sacred of the sacred cows of Classicism, the jewel of French tragedy. To be sure, this particular *récit* was frequently debated and criticised by eighteenth-century critics and philosophers. Many, both before and after Diderot, argued the merits and defects of the text.[67] Yet no one before Diderot dreamed of converting everything into the kind of speech he had asked for – 'eh! laissez là le char et les chevaux de mon fils, et parlez-moi de lui'.

When dealing with the Voltaire passage, Diderot had found ways to unlock the dramatic secrets hidden in the sounds emanating from words that were high-style abstractions. Here, on the contrary, after giving careful and admiring consideration to Racine's high-style syllables, Diderot adopts another perspective which turns him against them. His alternative puts forward simple, almost primitive emotions, as opposed to the sophisticated complexities of Racine's text, and perhaps something like the familiar dichotomy between the primitive and the civilised may again be at work in this part of Diderot's text, even as it was, *mutatis mutandis*, at the opening.

But then, what is one to make of his repeated insinuations that his criticisms do not have to be taken seriously, and that someone else should take responsibility for them? My own answer is that one should give just as much weight to these denials as to the criticisms that they deny. Diderot's seeming duplicities simply reflect, once again, his own unresolvable ambiguities concerning Classical verbal expression. His exegesis of the lines from the *récit* bears witness to the extraordinary degree to which he himself was in sympathy with Racine's art,[68] to the point of revealing, admiring and vindicating against attack the least nuances of the text; nor could this sympathy outweigh the impulses and criteria coming from the opposite direction which made him question the art that he had just defended, indeed to find other principles that ultimately rejected it. In between – naturally enough – come the red herrings.

Synaesthetic experiment: 'une femme mourante'

Since not merely poetry, but all arts of imitation – music and painting included – are susceptible of hieroglyphic expression, Diderot – having chided Batteux for ignoring such matters, essential to his subject though they were –

67. See Rex, *The Attraction of the contrary*, p.241, n.6, especially the commentary by Marmontel, which appears to be inspired by Diderot.

68. One recalls his later remark to Sophie Volland apropos of *Iphigénie*: 'Je le crois bien, que Racine vous fait plaisir. C'est peut-être le plus grand poëte qui ait jamais existé' (novembre 1760; *Correspondance*, iii.237).

sets up an elaborate experiment that would compare the ways in which these three different kinds of hieroglyphics function in the diverse arts (p.183f.). His far-reaching criticisms of Batteux lead us to expect some extraordinary happening in the text, once Diderot sets about filling in the abbé's lacunae, as though – however casual and offhand his tone – Diderot were conceiving of his experiment as a performance to crown all that precedes. Diderot first chooses a common subject, 'une femme mourante', and then selects some Latin poetry, some music and a 'painting' (actually an engraving), all allegedly depicting a dying woman.

Everything about the experiment is a little odd.[69] The two selections of Latin poetry, which Diderot gives as equivalent options – this one or that one – do not really fit together: the famously pathetic text of Virgil on the death of Dido does not really belong with the two lines from Lucretius, lines that coldly, impersonally and hypothetically depict the way 'all life also would be dissolved out of all our sinews and bones' were we not nourished by food and water. No doubt the second selection is particularly pertinent to Diderot's philosophy of death, but of course it totally lacks the emotional and psychological interest of Virgil. Nor is its subject specifically 'une femme mourante', as required.

Diderot does not discuss these texts in themselves; he supplies a detailed commentary, however, on an anonymous musical example (p.184-85), whose score he reproduces,[70] and which he treats as their setting. Thus there is a sort of exegesis, but given through the music – which is even stranger than the poems.

The provenance of the music of the engraved score is unknown.[71] Only the six concluding measures of the piece are provided, scored for soprano, figured bass and some treble instrument, probably the violin. The character supposedly singing the soprano part is not identified, but the words make up a French alexandrine: 'Je me meurs; à mes yeux le jour cesse de luire.' Meanwhile, as mentioned above, despite the presence of the French text, Diderot treats the music as though it were a setting of Virgil's Latin, with the Lucretian lines brought in at the end for good measure. It is as though Diderot were giving the composer instructions, or a recipe, as to how to imitate musically the

---

69. To my knowledge no one has noticed these oddities except Marian Hobson, 'La *Lettre sur les sourds et muets* de Diderot: labyrinthe et langage', *Semiotica* 16 (1976), p.322.

70. Cf. the analysis of Béatrice Didier, 'Le Texte et la musique', *Interpréter Diderot aujourd'hui*, ed. E. de Fontenay and J. Proust, Actes du Colloque de Cerisy (Paris 1984), p.294-97.

71. See P. H. Meyer's suggestion in his edition, p.188, note for p.84, line 1. Bruce Alan Brown has pointed out to me that, among other oddities of voice-leading in the musical selection, there is a prominent series of normally forbidden – not to say ugly – parallel fifths.

movements the poet describes.[72] Thus, Diderot suggests that in order to render Dido's vain efforts to look upwards (as in Virgil) the composer will create a descending semi-tone in the first measure, just as shown in the printed score; the series of rising melodic intervals – a diminished fifth followed, after a rest, by the 'still more painful' tritone – being given as devices to mirror Dido's repeated efforts to raise herself. The little rising semi-tone which follows is the last ray of light she sees, her final effort, after which there is nothing but descent, step by step, going conjunctively downward. Changing authors, Diderot then explains that she is to expire at the last semi-tone, the final cadence coming at the end of Lucretius' 'exsolvatur', and giving a striking imitation of the vacillating movement of a light going out. Later on (p.185-86), Diderot indicates in still greater detail the ways in which the accompanying harmonies and intervals will be appropriate for the mood of the Latin texts.

Without knowing the origin of the musical quotation it may be risky to draw inferences about Diderot's procedure in this passage. Accepting the situation at face value – that is, assuming that Diderot is adapting music originally composed for a French text for use as a setting of the movements and moods of some Latin poetry, in fact pretending that the composer is simply following the mimetic implications that Diderot finds in Virgil and Lucretius – the least one can conclude is that Diderot is creatively, and on his own, reading into the music interpretations which the composer could never have intended. Such a creative posture seems to have been essential, in Diderot's mind, to his experiment. He might have chosen an easier and more obvious route: to take both words and music from an opera scene or some secular cantata, for example, where words and music were literally made for one another. But clearly he preferred words and music that had been composed independently, presumably so that he could reimagine the music as mimesis of the poetry, as though he were recomposing the piece to render the hieroglyphics of the words he had chosen. According to Diderot's pretence, not the composer but the listener, Diderot, is deciding what the music will express, and how it will do so, what hieroglyphical images it will evoke, and what text it will be a setting of.

Only Diderot could have invented such a bizarre procedure. Of course some sort of mimetic impulse urging the listener to interpret creatively the music being heard – especially instrumental music – was a natural by-product of an age accustomed to believe that music had little interest in itself, that music

72. Even the Latin poetry is presented as a command performance, Virgil's words being prefaced by 'le poète dira' (p.183), and the use of the future tense possibly looking back to the tone of Horace's counsels in the *Ars poetica*.

ought to imitate something. People wanted, and expected, music to go beyond mere notes and rhythms, and even the plainest instrumental music could set the imagination to work, searching to discover pictures or plots in the sounds, whether or not intended by the composer. In one of his most entertaining letters to Sophie Volland, Diderot describes how he and Mme d'Holbach fancied a whole little 'comédie' about a lovers' quarrel, words and all, in the wordless and programmeless mandore playing of a certain Monsieur Schistre:

Voilà Monsieur Schistre qui prend sa mandore. Le voilà qui joue. Quelle musique! Quelle exécution! Tout ce que ses doigts font dire à des cordes! cela est incroyable; et comme Mme d'Holback [*sic*] et moi nous n'en perdions pas un mot! – Le joli courroux! – Que cette plainte est douce! – Il se dépite; il prend son parti. – Je le crois. – Les voilà qui se raccommodent. – Il est vrai. – Le moyen de tenir contre un homme qui sçait s'excuser ainsi! – Il est sûr que nous entendions tout cela.[73]

Thus the main pleasure of this music for the two listeners came from imagining it as personae, emotions and dialogue.[74] Admittedly, the text of the *Lettre sur les sourds et muets* goes much further in this direction, imagining the music to be nothing but an imitation of poetry. In fact Diderot's elaborate discussion of the relation between the musical intervals and the poems, along with the alphabetical keys placed in the engraved score to designate the relevant parts of the text – making it look like some 'planche' in an encyclopaedia – raises the matter above the 'jeu de société' level described in his letter to Sophie Volland, and makes it philosophy. Perhaps the keying also masks the precariousness of the relationship between text and music, disguising, with the look of 'science', what otherwise might have looked fanciful or arbitrary.

At last comes the 'painting' – actually a doctored version of an engraving for an edition of Lucretius. Diderot finds that everything in the figure of the slumping female in the picture – the legs, the left hand, the right arm – illustrates the final word of the lines from *De rerum natura*: 'exsolvatur', life detaching itself from the sinews and bones of the human body. He does not mention Virgil, or the fact that, if the illustration comes from an edition of Lucretius, the dying figure cannot be Queen Dido. Nor does the engraved woman display the wound Dido inflicted upon herself, prominently featured

---

73. 20 octobre 1760; *Correspondance*, ed. Georges Roth, iii.166. Cf. the commentary of Béatrice Didier, *La Musique des Lumières* (Paris 1985), p.148.

74. See also, in the *Salon de 1765*: 'Je fais dire à une symphonie bien faite presque ce qu'il me plaît, et comme je sais mieux que personne la manière de m'affecter par l'expérience que j'ai de mon propre cœur, il est rare que l'expression que je donne aux sons, analogue à ma situation actuelle, sérieuse, tendre ou gaie, ne me touche plus qu'une autre qui serait moins à mon choix' (DPV, xiv.193-94). Béatrice Didier a discuté ce phénomène in Diderot, providing further examples, in 'Les Opéras imaginaires de Diderot', *Diderot, les beaux-arts et la musique*, Actes du Colloque à Aix-en-Provence, décembre 1984 (Aix-en-Provence 1986), p.247.

by Virgil. Indeed, the only trait she shares with Virgil's heroine is that she is dying. On the other hand, perhaps following the tendency to think of all kinds of hieroglyphics as 'painting', Diderot decidedly privileges this depiction over the two other forms of expression, namely poetry and music. For even though the painter is confined to the portrayal of a single moment, and cannot bring in as many 'morbid symptoms' as the poet can, Diderot characterises whatever symptoms are depicted as 'bien plus frappants' (p.185). He further explains – and this would appear to be the key point – that a painter shows 'la chose même',[75] whereas musical and poetical expression 'n'en sont que des hiéroglyphes' (p.185).[76]

Taken at face value, the statement is proposing that music and poetry are mere intimations or suggestions, whereas painting realises the very image the other arts have been striving to evoke. By implication, the ultimate aim of all of the arts is visual, and one might wonder whether Diderot is hinting at the desirability of replacing poems and pieces of music with paintings. If so, large problems loom ahead, for the implied subservience of both poetry and music to pictorial art is to say the least debatable – especially in view of the rather uninteresting engraving that he is claiming to be the very thing that Virgil's glorious poetry was struggling to reveal.[77] Clearly, a position so extreme needs bolstering by explanations. Abruptly, however, the line of the discussion breaks off, while Diderot busies himself adding more details to his already detailed analysis of the musical setting. He gives no general conclusion. He does take time to recognise, however (p.187), that his experiment is incomplete, a mere sketch, which others cleverer than he will doubtless find ways to finish – perhaps Batteux will be the one, since he seems to know so much.

A most unexpected ending! Diderot earlier seemed to promise a summation of his hieroglyphical theories, when he undertook the considerable tasks Batteux had neglected to perform. And yet, once embarked upon, the experiment turns out to be full of yawning gaps, pieces that do not fit and ideas that

75. Although Diderot is re-creating this idea in his own special context, the notion that painting (as distinct from words) is a more direct expression of things goes back to seventeenth-century aesthetics. See Annie Becq, 'Rhétoriques et littérature d'art en France à la fin du XVIIe siècle: le concept de couleur', *Cahiers de l'Association internationale des études françaises* 24 (1972), p.227-28.

76. In the 'Lettre à Mademoiselle' which follows the *Lettre sur les sourds et muets* proper (p.194-208), Diderot reconsiders these ideas and overturns certain of the conceptions stated here. I have discussed this development in *The Attraction of the contrary*, p.123-24.

77. The original illustration by Frans Van Mieris, which has been considerably simplified in Diderot's engraving, is far more dramatic, and furthermore better conveys the sense of the Lucretian philosophy that, one may be sure, was the crucial element making Diderot choose this depiction.

finally tail off – just as arbitrarily as they were invented in the first place. However, if one can forgive Diderot his unjust and unkind thrusts against Batteux (something I myself have trouble doing), there may be a sense in which the ill-fitting clumsiness of the synaesthetic analogies actually creates the unique originality of this part of the text. For, contrary to all the other attempts to define or perceive the relations between the arts of the period, this one has the air of a true experiment: a trying-to-make-things-work in order to reach a conclusion. The fumbling approach that eventually leaves everything dangling and unresolved at least proves that the answers were not known in advance and even suggests that the questions were genuine. For the rest, perhaps the interest of this part of the text lies less in the results achieved than in the larger context of the attempt itself: just as with the 'walking clock', this experiment represents a provocative preliminary move towards directions Diderot will later explore more fully and successfully. In these proleptic concepts of synaesthesia one glimpses the kind of border crossings that will later abound in the dazzling pantomimes of *Le Neveu de Rameau*, and in the exaltation of the graphic, a movement towards the visual emphasis of Diderot's later theatrical ideas, not to mention the building of incipient pressures that will later achieve fulfilment in the *Salons*.

Further criticism of Classical French

Diderot has not yet found his way to a final assessment of the French language, and although within sight of the end of the *Lettre*, a moment when any other writer would be bringing everything into final focus, Diderot still finds room for several more flip-flops on the question. Earlier he declared French the winner for having sacrificed emotion, energy and imagination in favour of exactitude, and praised it as the most polished ('châtié') of languages; one now sees the other side of the coin as, by contrary motion, he launches an attack on the 'noblesse prétendue' and the 'fausse délicatesse' which, he complains, has caused so many 'expressions énergiques' – acceptable in Latin and Greek – to be excluded from French (p.187). He deplores the impoverishment of the language through the efforts at refinement.[78] In the name of authors of strong imagination he expresses regret that people prefer to weaken an idea rather

---

78. Fénelon held similar views: 'Notre langue manque d'un grand nombre de mots et de phrases. Il me semble même qu'on l'a gênée depuis environ cent ans en voulant la purifier. Il est vrai qu'elle était encore un peu informe, et trop verbeuse. Mais le vieux langage se fait regretter, quand nous le retrouvons dans Marot, dans Amiot, dans le Cardinal d'Ossat, dans les ouvrages les plus enjoués, et dans les plus sérieux. Il avait je ne sais quoi de court, de naïf et de passionné' (*Lettre à l'Académie*, quoted in Folkierski, *Entre le Classicisme et le Romantisme*, p.213).

than use a word that is not 'noble', that words excluded from 'le beau style' as too popular were finally rejected by the populace as well, out of their long-standing disposition to ape the great. To Diderot it looked very much as though French, like Chinese, was about to split into two languages, one written, the other spoken.

Needless to say, partisans of 'le beau style', i.e. Classicism, Racine and Voltaire first among them, would never have agreed that the trend towards refinement had spoiled the language, or that purging the vocabulary of so many low-style expressions was a mistake – however 'energetic' the lost words may have been. Furthermore Diderot's text – with its derogatory stress on 'false' delicacy and 'so-called' nobility, and its contempt for the common people for aping the Great – also tends to confirm what was suggested earlier, that Diderot's longing for stylistic energy and directness is not merely aesthetic but part of a social attitude: his hostility towards Classicism relates to feelings of class.

The last appearance of the 'grammairiens philosophes'

Perhaps out of some uneasiness about his shiftings, Diderot reverts, still nearer to the end of the *Lettre*, to his solid-seeming earlier position (p.166), notably in accord with the views of the *grammairiens philosophes*, and declares once again that the advantage of French over other languages is the advantage of the useful over the pleasing: 'Je persiste dans mon sentiment, et je pense toujours que le français a sur le grec, le latin, l'italien, l'anglais, etc. l'avantage de l'utile sur l'agréable' (p.191).

Thanks to this utterly clear affirmation of the dichotomy, in the last paragraph the dichotomy will go to pieces. Now it turns out that French has no monopoly on usefulness: other languages can exhibit exactly that same quality. Furthermore French, admirable as it is in matters of utility, can also be pleasing ('sait se prêter aux choses agréables'). According to this new line of thought, French excels in all the forms of expression in which Diderot formerly declined to recognise its excellence: although he suggested earlier that 'il faut parler grec, latin, anglais dans les chaires et sur les théâtres', he now cites the harmoniousness of Fléchier and the sublimity of Bossuet, surely proving that French has excelled in pulpit oratory; for the theatre he now remembers Corneille and Racine (also Voltaire). Previously he had deplored loss of simplicity and energy in French through the efforts at refinement; he now remembers Brantôme and La Fontaine – and so on: 'La langue [française] est folâtre dans Rabelais, naïve dans la Fontaine et Brantôme, harmonieuse dans Malherbe et Fléchier, sublime dans Corneille et Bossuet: que n'est-elle point dans Boileau, Racine, Voltaire, et une foule d'autres écrivains en vers et en prose? Ne nous plaignons donc pas.'

But if, in addition to these ten authors who are actually specified (all but two from the Classical period), Diderot truly believed in a 'foule' of other writers of equal accomplishment, and if French can succeed in any style, from bantering humour or naïveté to sublimity, then surely his oft-repeated dichotomy is meaningless: French can do, *and has done*, everything.

With any other eighteenth-century philosopher, for the fundamental ground of the main argument to give way in so spectacular a fashion might have indicated an impasse. For Diderot it simply means that the time has come to hop onto another branch – even though such a drastic shift, emerging as it does at the last moment in the last lines of an entire work, must have taken a good deal of cheek on the part of the author. The subject is still the French language (p.191):

Si nous savons nous en servir, nos ouvrages seront aussi précieux pour la postérité, que les ouvrages des Anciens le sont pour nous. Entre les mains d'un homme ordinaire, le grec, le latin, l'anglais, l'italien ne produiront que des choses communes; le français produira des miracles sous la plume d'un homme de génie. En quelque langue que ce soit, l'ouvrage que le génie soutient ne tombe jamais.

At which point the text ends. Here, in the last sentence, before one has time to comprehend the event, much less protest against it, not only the famous dichotomy, but all questions regarding the particularities of language – what the French call 'le génie de la langue' – have evaporated, gone up in smoke, metamorphosed into a different sort of genius, which loftily ignores all linguistic distinctions, 'le génie de l'auteur'.

Conclusions

Diderot himself characterises the movement of his thought in this work as a 'labyrinthe' through whose 'détours' he has guided the reader (p.188). Yet to this reader at least it seems less a labyrinth than a sort of kaleidoscope in which ideas emerge and then change, grow dim or even disappear, as the context alters their meaning, or rules them out entirely. Though, for my own reasons, I have deliberately been trying to hold Diderot accountable for his shifting ideas, actually the 'désinvolture' with which his ideas are presented in this work might be counted among its more ingratiating qualities. Good-humouredly relaxed and disorganised, playfully lacking a main point, the work is at the opposite pole from serious genres such as the *oratio*, the philosophical treatise or, for that matter, many articles of the *Encyclopédie*.

2. Evolving experiments in the 'Lettre sur les sourds et muets'

How instructive in this connection to set Diderot's text beside the work previously mentioned as one of Diderot's probable 'sources', and which shares so many topics in common with Diderot, Condillac's *Essai sur l'origine des connaissances humaines*.[79] However many similarities one may find in contents, the contrasts far outweigh them: theoretically, at least, Condillac never changes his mind about anything; ostensibly, his ground never shifts; he always without fail keeps track of the meaning of the terms he uses and of the direction of his arguments; there is never any question as to where he is going and where he has been; in fact, as he states at the start, his purpose in writing this work is to bring *geometrical* clarity to the propositions he demonstrates in ethics and metaphysics. His epistemology in many ways obviously looks back to Locke, but such a geometrical assertion also suggests the rigour of Descartes. Indeed, the subtitle of the *Essai* promises that everything concerning the 'understanding' will be reduced to a single principle ('ouvrage où l'on réduit à un seul principe tout ce qui concerne l'entendement'). In displaying such disciplined rationalism and strict observance of the rules, Condillac surely belongs to the grand tradition of French philosophy. By comparison Diderot seems as deliberately unprincipled and flighty as the Nightingale in Galiani's wonderful fable – recounted with gusto in Diderot's letter to Sophie Volland – about the heedless songster who, seeking to disparage the method-ridden Cuckoo, proclaimed: 'Je me joue des règles. C'est surtout lorsque je les enfreins qu'on m'admire. Quelle comparaison de sa fastidieuse méthode avec mes heureux écarts.'[80]

In the *Lettre sur les sourds et muets* Diderot was not only freeing himself from the traditional French philosophical method (no doubt with Condillac's pristine example particularly in mind), he was doing away with all the logical constraints that normally tie ideas in place. One can never be sure of what will turn up around the corner in this contentedly disjointed work. Perhaps the truest way to characterise it would be to call it an incipient dialogue: Diderot's wandering ideas are just waiting to be incarnated in fictional personalities who can argue and change their minds whenever they choose – a possibility Diderot would of course fully exploit in his later writings. But then, not just the form, but everything in this work seems to be in a state of incipience: the whole work is a seedbed full of possibilities, Diderot's future *en germe*.

No matter which topics are raised for consideration nothing is treated as

---

79. For an excellent summary of the curious, and still not clearly understood, relations between Diderot and Condillac in the early period see Larry Bongie, 'Diderot, Condillac et le petit frère', *L'Encyclopédie, Diderot, l'esthétique: mélanges offerts à Jacques Chouillet* (Paris 1991), p.81-88.

80. 20 octobre 1760; *Correspondance*, iii.168.

though it were of interest in itself; everything is seen in terms of the effect on (or in) someone, that is to say, everything is given dynamically, in relation. It is in this framework that I see the main movement of ideas, namely, a broad, threefold shift in orientations that begins with the search for primitive and more direct alternatives to the word-expression that was Classicism (while simultaneously sustaining the Classical position, to be sure), and proceeds to the other pole, namely, acceptance of words in the most powerfully Classical sense, the hieroglyphic. Thus Diderot's impulses to turn away from the Classical verbal aesthetic simultaneously and via contrary motion led him to the ultimate kind of tending towards Classicism: a new way of perceiving and releasing the hidden power of the word, in the Classical sense. Nor does his thinking stop there: his own admiration for the art of Racine becomes part of a revolt against Racine's style in the name of the simple, direct, compressed expression of human emotions, a position which recaptures at least something of the original 'ordre des gestes', even as it prefigures Diderot's later aesthetics of the *drame*. Thus, even though Diderot explores many diverse topics in this text, Classicism, pro and contra, functions as the axis around which the main action turns.

Near the end, Diderot attempts a grand synaesthetic synthesis ('une femme mourante') which leads him momentarily to claim priorities for the visual arts. Eventually, however, his experiment collapses and fails to provide the answers he implied it would. As an attempted conclusion he shifts once more to the theories of the *grammairiens philosophes* and reverts to a dichotomy that earlier appeared to show promise, attributing to French the 'scientific' advantages of clarity and precision, and to other languages the advantages of literature and emotions. Evidence to the contrary, however, soon wells up and dissolves his distinction: literary French, especially in authors of the Classical era, wins back a place of honour.

Behind the bravura smokescreen of the last, rather crowd-pleasing rhetorical flourish, one discovers the author clinging to a magically invented at the last moment life-preserver that he calls 'le génie'. Is it too far-fetched to imagine that the final phrase – 'l'ouvrage que le génie soutient ne tombe jamais' – may actually express a rather personal hope that his own arguments – so notably lacking in logic and structural cohesiveness, not to mention buoyant conclusions – will, through some other sort of energy, still stay afloat?

3. The dubious fictions of the *Entretiens sur Le Fils naturel*

IF only because the theatre was never far from Diderot's thinking about language, the meanderings of the *Lettre sur les sourds et muets* (1751) included prominent theatrical examples as a matter of course. Nor is it surprising that some of the experimental ideas of this earlier text – particularly the speculations on gestural and other non-verbal languages, and expressivity – re-emerge and coalesce into a new form in the *Entretiens sur Le Fils naturel* (1757),[1] Diderot's lengthy defence of his own drama entitled *Le Fils naturel*. These *Entretiens* count among the most innovative theoretical writings of the century,[2] and many adventuresome concepts from the earlier work transferred with ease into this later theatrical setting. But at least one feature would, on the face of it, seem to require radical revision before it could pass from the *Lettre* to the *Entretiens*, namely, Diderot's idea of the psychology of language: the *Lettre* assumed that words and gestures, in fact all 'languages', directly reflect an inner state; languages are imitations of the ideas and dispositions of the mind and heart.

The theatre, on the other hand, inherently implies a discrepancy between the inner state and outer appearance, and hence an element of contrivance. The actor is not the individual he pretends to be, in fact his words and gestures are intended to reflect the inner state of a person he is not. Normally, such homely verities as these would be too obvious even to deserve mention. Special considerations bring them to the fore in the present context however: contrary to expectation, this problem does *not* arise in the *Entretiens*; it is ruled out from the start, abolished as if by magic by Diderot's bizarre proposal that his own play, *Le Fils naturel*, is not fiction at all but simply real life transposed into a staged representation. He asks the reader to believe that the story the

---

1. Although I am not aware of any other scholar who has approached this work in the manner that I do here, my discussion shares a number of points in common with James Creech, *Diderot: thresholds of representation* (Columbus, Ohio 1986), ch.6, and especially with Scott S. Bryson, *The Chastized stage*, p.40f. On the work and its background, see the copious account by Jacques Chouillet, *La Formation des idées esthétiques de Diderot* (Paris 1972), p.418-89, and also the useful brief summary by John Hope Mason, *The Irresistible Diderot* (London 1982), p.126-27. The standard critical edition of the text of the *Entretiens* is now that of Anne-Marie and Jacques Chouillet, DPV, x.3-12, 83-162. The page numbers in my text refer to this edition.

2. See Wilson, *Diderot*, p.271.

play tells – no matter how unlikely – really happened to the performers who stage it (the claim is even made that the neighbourhood is still talking about the events that occurred); the words the actors speak are essentially their own, hence no pretence on their part is required, and Diderot's psychological assumptions can remain unaltered.

This preposterous fiction entailed an elaborate support network of explanations whose involvements would have daunted any writer less audacious. But once Diderot had taken the awesome decision to claim that *Le Fils naturel* was reality he almost brazenly carried through his fiction into the least details. Novelists of Diderot's age sometimes employed a similar strategy, pretending that their novels were not fiction but truth itself, letters from an actual correspondence, an account of real conversations, authentic documents that simply recorded events as they happened. Perhaps Diderot does owe something to these novelistic pretences, yet the fiction of reality he employed was devised for significantly different, and more serious, reasons.

Since the play's hero, Dorval, was claimed to be a real person, he could step out of the play, display a personality quite separate from the one he had shown in the drama itself, and discuss informally with Moi the way in which the events had been presented. Just as in the *Lettre sur les sourds et muets*, one finds in the *Entretiens* that Classicism is a frequent preoccupation, and, once again, that Diderot's attitude towards it is deeply ambiguous. On the one hand, as Lessing and others in Germany rightly inferred, Diderot's insistence on the play as reality stands against some of the basic principles of French Classicism, and among the more striking implications, it simply abolishes the aesthetic distance and the aesthetics of grandeur essential to Classical representations. By the same token, Diderot intends that, instead of kings and queens from ancient or foreign lands, distinctly more ordinary people should take the stage and speak and behave in ways unthinkable in Classicism.[3] Yet at the same time, despite such anti-Classical traits, vestiges of Classicism subsist almost everywhere both in the *Entretiens* and in the play proper: the very fact that the rules of the unities are observed is one of the strongest proofs of this remaining attachment to values that Diderot is in other ways rejecting. The ideal of 'virtue' which becomes a main source of dramatic concern for the main characters of Diderot's play is probably another such vestige; indeed the moral conflict of this drama, however different its tonality, is at least within sight of the Classical 'love' versus 'duty' conflict that one attributes to Corneille. Finally, one sees the pressures of Classical traditions in Diderot's timidity in

3. On the consequences of these reforms, see Rex, *The Attraction of the contrary*, p.176f.

some of his 'innovations': though his title might imply a play centred on the unmentionable topic of bastardy, as the plot evolves the bastard son turns into a legitimate heir, an outcome which looks very much like a concession to Classical *bienséance*; though the spirit of the play is quintessentially middle class, if one inspects the text with a strong enough magnifying glass, some of the main characters turn out to be at least petty nobility – no doubt a partial condescension to traditional class distinctions, not to say snobbery.

Clearly, a main function of these *Entretiens* was to show how Diderot's bizarre (and patently false) fiction might be thought of as true: how a printed play, divided into scenes and acts as plays usually are, and which also observes the traditional dramatic unities of time, place and action, can actually be seen as, not fiction, but reality itself transposed into dramatic form. Dorval goes to particular pains to explain that a series of events taking place on several locations, on different days and with many irrelevant incidents intervening can still remain 'true' ('rendre les choses comme elles s'étaient passées') even though they are staged on a single spot as if in a single day, and without any extraneous incidents (p.85). Dorval–Diderot's revealing justification, one of the century's most ardent and convincing defences of the unities, is based on both practical and aesthetic considerations. He simply points out that a play would gain nothing by preserving the confusions and scatterings one finds in real life, that the rules of the unities, though difficult to observe, make sense, and that the theatre – as opposed to the novel – inherently requires this sort of simplification and unification to facilitate the concentrated and undivided attention of the spectator (p.85-86).

Following the doctrines of Aristotle himself, theorists of the Classical theatre always placed particular stress on the doctrine of *vraisemblance* as the key to successful playwriting, and naturally this is one of Diderot's major preoccupations in the ensuing discussion. It becomes clear that he uses the term *vraisemblance* in the most common eighteenth-century sense, implying first of all that throughout the play one event leads to the next with a convincing theatrical appearance of inevitability.[4] At the same time, to be sure, it was understood that there were large differences between what might be accepted as a 'likely' sequence of events at the theatre and what is likely in real life ('Celui qui agit et celui qui regarde sont deux êtres très différents', p.86).[5] This point is worth stressing, for as the discussion proceeds the idea of

4. *Entretiens*, p.125. On the implications of *vraisemblance* see Marian Hobson, *The Object of art: theory of illusion in eighteenth-century France* (Cambridge 1982), *passim*.

5. All the significant eighteenth-century critics agreed with Diderot concerning this distinction. See Rex, *The Attraction of the contrary*, p.222-23, n.2-3.

theatricality moves further and further away from the starting point, i.e. the events that allegedly happened in reality: the hypothetical raw material of this alleged reality is being converted, bit by bit and quite painlessly, into theatrical convention.

Another tenet of the doctrine of *vraisemblance*, closely tied in to the first, was the requirement that each phrase spoken by a given character be entirely appropriate for the kind of person uttering the words and the circumstances in which they are said. Finally, there was also the often unspoken conviction of eighteenth-century playwrights that if they could produce a play which truly observed all the rules of *vraisemblance*, including the unities, the audience would have no choice but to sacrifice their disbelief and accept the 'truth' of the dramatic illusion.[6] This is one of the reasons why one finds them defending their dramatic productions with such ferocity against charges that their play offends one or another of the unities or that a given scene or tirade is not 'vraisemblable'. This is also, I believe, the reason why one finds Diderot defending individually, against the objections of Moi, each and every syllable of his play on the basis that in all cases the sentiment expressed is perfectly appropriate for the speaker and for the dramatic circumstance.

In other words, I am claiming not only that Dorval–Diderot's arguments in defence of *Le Fils naturel* belong to a well-established tradition of theatricality, but also that his apparent defences are really attacks intended to destroy systematically every excuse anyone might have had for not showing total adherence to the unlikely fiction he is proposing. In his arguments about *vraisemblance* and the unities, Dorval–Diderot is subverting the reader's will to disbelieve, and if he succeeds the result will be the equivalent of inducing the reader to accept as true Diderot's daring, and obviously false, claim that his characters are 'real', that their story took place essentially in the way that the play pretends. In the discussions of Dorval and Moi it is a question almost literally of the life of his play.

Another weapon (closely related to the others) in Diderot's campaign to make his play irresistibly believable to the reader is his appeal to a special kind of setting: throughout the text of the *Entretiens*, Dorval–Diderot claims to have written his drama not for any stage with an audience, but for the strict privacy of a salon, where no audience exists. Even Moi, who claims to have watched a performance of the play, pretends that he was secretly admitted and hidden out of sight of the players, who were ignorant of his presence. In other words,

6. See my demonstration of this point on the basis of an analysis of Le Sage's *Crispin rival de son maître*, in *The Attraction of the contrary*, p.76f.

contrary to the fashionable traditions of the 'théâtre de société', those elegant theatricals expensively put on for the benefit of a select audience, Diderot's play is allegedly a 'performance' only in the sense that a ceremonial or a sacrament would be; it was neither written nor staged for any outsider's benefit, but solely for the spiritual comfort of the participants (p.89-90):

'Mais ce ton est bien extraordinaire au théâtre!...'
'Et laissez là les tréteaux. Rentrez dans le salon, et convenez que le discours de Constance ne vous offensa pas quand vous l'entendîtes là.'
'Non.'
'C'est assez.'

Only because this play was supposedly not 'theatre' did Dorval–Diderot allow a domestic to have an important role (p.88), and tea – no doubt unthinkable at the Comédie-Française – to be served (p.90), and Dorval to weep on Clairville's breast (p.92). Furthermore these features are all seen as connected with particularities of character or circumstance. Thus the 'discours de Constance' referred to in the quotation above is justified on the basis of Constance's exceptional elevation of character. It is likewise understood that the realistic intimacy of the scene between Dorval and Clairville relates to peculiarities of circumstance (p.92), and that the long and pathetic scene with the simple but faithful servant, André, reflects a whole complex of factors which brought it into being (p.107-10). The tea is explained by Dorval's long voyages in Holland and his frequenting of foreigners, an explanation that hardly seems sufficient to Moi (p.90):

'Mais au théâtre!'
'Ce n'est pas là. C'est dans le salon qu'il faut juger mon ouvrage ...'

The call for this sort of 'reality' – here embodied in the salon – is what brought Diderot to all the daring theories that set his ideas so far apart from the neo-Classical stagings of his time, and so deeply marked the history of the theatre: the demand for more realistic scenery, for less stylised acting, and for less propriety; the emphasis on gestures and tableaux, on the use of inarticulate sounds and silence, the playing down of the hitherto indispensable and ubiquitous tirade, the hypothetical abolition of the proscenium arch; and so on. In Diderot's mind all these un-Classical innovations were elements that brought the play closer to ordinary experience, and ordinariness was, he assumes, another way to make the drama more 'vraisemblable', and hence compel one irresistibly to believe in it.

Just as in *Jacques le fataliste*, where Diderot takes an almost perverse pleasure in toying with the reader's credulity, in these *Entretiens*, once Diderot can assume the reader is 'hooked' by his fiction, he goes out of his way to strain our credulity beyond any reasonable limit. We see this when an obvious discrepancy crops up in the text of the play – a female character uses an expression whose mannerism is clearly not appropriate for her given personality – whereupon Dorval–Diderot claims the discrepancy was due to a revision by the actor-participant herself, and not by the author, Dorval–Diderot.[7] In fact one is told that this sort of revision has occurred a number of times as the whole cast revised the script in order to make themselves appear more delicate, more passionate or whatever than they 'actually' had been. In other words, one is supposed to believe that after the author's text had created fictional characters who miraculously turned into real beings, these no-longer-fictional creatures took charge and revised the text according to their individual whims and vanities, despite the better judgement of the author! For the rest, these bizarre happenings imply that 'reality', supposed ally of *vraisemblance*, is now, however incidentally, working against *vraisemblance*: Rosalie's inappropriately fancy expression, 'chimère de perfection' (p.94), obviously jars with her personality, and makes it more difficult to believe in the truth of her character. Though this is a particularly outlandish example, this phenomenon of stretching the reader's or spectator's credulity is by no means unique in Diderot's text.

A more consequential sort of contrariety introduces itself as a reaction against Diderot's salon of reality, into which Diderot strives to lock the supposedly restive reader, symbolised by Moi. Dorval–Diderot has been insistent that Moi should confine his thinking about *Le Fils naturel* to the salon, and not let his mind wander elsewhere. Meanwhile Dorval–Diderot has been giving the closest possible consideration to the details of his drama, explaining all the features of character and the minutiae of circumstance that justify this or that word or gesture in terms of *vraisemblance*. The climax of this sort of inward-looking, salon-confined analysis comes in the debate over whether the long scene with the servant André is, or is not, too long. As proof that it is not too lengthy, Dorval reviews the scene, adding the complaints which André made over the cuts in the actual performance, and restoring many of the words and sounds of the action as it 'truly' happened. The scene, already sentimental to the point of mawkishness in the final version, is made almost intolerable as more of the same is poured on, analysed, appreciated and exclaimed over, for several pages (p.106-10). For this reader at least, too much time has been spent indoors in that salon; claustrophobia sets in; the air is unbreathable. Then suddenly Dorval–Diderot is no longer writing about the

7. According to James Creech, Rosalie's expression may have a more significant connection to Diderot's dramatic theories than Dorval–Diderot cares to admit. See Creech, *Diderot*, p.85-86.

details of his drama, he is speaking of the reasons why his play would be so difficult to stage successfully in a Parisian theatre, which leads to a grand fantasy about the new theatre at Lyon, that might, he claims, inspire authors to give birth to all manner of marvellous new theatrical productions. Then, after some incomplete ruminations on the necessary qualities required of a critic, and a pregnant moment of silence, a new vision comes – in a burst (p.111):

Je ne demanderais pour changer la face du genre dramatique, qu'un théâtre très étendu, où l'on montrât, quand le sujet d'une pièce l'exigerait, une grande place avec les édifices adjacents, tels que le péristile d'un palais, l'entrée d'un temple, différents endroits distribués de manière que le spectateur vît toute l'action, et qu'il y en eût une partie de cachée pour les acteurs.

These imaginary settings emanate from a vision that is exactly contrary to the one represented by the salon. If the salon was small, enclosed, private, exclusive, domestic and real, here in this imagining of a great square, a palace peristile, a temple entrance, all is huge, open, public, inclusive, in fact institutional, and artificial. If here the spectators are said to see everything, while the actors have a place in which to remain hidden (presumably to relax or change costumes between scenes), in the alleged 'salon' where *Le Fils naturel* took place it was just the reverse: not the actors but solely the spectator is hidden and not recognised as seeing the performance; meanwhile the participants of the salon naturally have no onstage space in which to 'hide' because they can never cease to be what they are; no relaxation from their roles is possible, nor can they change costume or character. Presumably, the salon performance would not have proceeded had the participants known of the presence of an observer (thus Moi had to be hidden from their sight); here, on the contrary, it is assumed that the drama is nothing but a spectacle created for an audience, who see everything.

The pleasure of this passage is the pleasure of a seemingly systematic escape and release from the oppressive doctrines Diderot has been inculcating so forcefully in his analyses of his play, doctrines that continually insist on unity and reality – in the limited and confining sense in which Diderot has chosen to define them. The salon and all the values that it represented have not only vanished, they have been creatively renewed by being turned into opposites.

In the next part of Diderot's powerful vision, his imagination summons up one of the most dramatic scenes in the entire *Oresteia*, and again it is everything *Le Fils naturel* was not. On one side of the stage Orestes is seen imploring the goddess for aid; on another, the Furies in their frenzy for blood discover his traces, pursue and surround him, crying out, shaking with rage, brandishing their torches. Here Diderot pauses to exclaim over this extraordinary moment of terror and pity, the moment when the audience hears the prayer and groans of Orestes rising above the cries of the Furies and sees their fearsome movements. As *Le Fils naturel* never could have been, this powerful action is the embodiment of the timeless legendary roots of a culture, a play in which the identity of the main character is a given, rather than the invention of an author, in which the action is known in advance and proceeds in a grand sweep, rather than proceeding *ex nihilo* from minute and unforeseeable inter-locking causes, a scene that is pregnant with violence, blood and ferocious physical cruelty, and whose grandeur and diversity could never have been contained in the tight singularity of Dorval's salon, but requires a multiplicity of spaces. To my mind this is the most enthralling moment in the whole *Entretiens*, this unhoped-for liberation when, like Proust's cup of tea, Diderot's essentially middle-class, claustrophobic, virtue-ridden, improbably plotted drama produces and brings to life, by contrary motion, this magnificent scene from antiquity.

Inevitably, to be sure, this kind of escape proves to be a false illusion, for to imagine a theatre based on principles that contradict so totally those expounded in the rest of the *Entretiens* implies that the two sets of principles are still inseparably bound together, as two sides of the same coin. Indeed my point is that the stifling confinements of the private salon were, negatively, the efficient cause of the grandiose, open-air, public setting, and of course this dynamic kind of negative relationship is the hallmark of a true contrariety.

Diderot was aware that this scene, especially because of its two simultaneous scenes in action at the same time (the Furies on one side; Orestes on the other), had nothing to do with ordinary Parisian stage plays (it was actually closer to eighteenth-century opera), in fact for various reasons it was inherently unplayable. He therefore tried (p.113) to find something like an equivalent in contemporary terms, a domestic scene that employed a split stage and that would capture something of the same powerful emotions and, I presume, sense of inexorable fate. Inevitably Diderot's solution turned out to be purest melodrama (in the modern sense). At night a father divines from the conduct of a distraught and despairing servant that a disaster has occurred to someone in his family, and although the servant's grief is so intense that he cannot speak the words, the father realises that his only son is dead (he has been killed in a duel), and falls into despair. In another room of the same house, the mother hears the same terrible news, clutches her crucifix, kisses it and waters it with her tears. ('Voilà le tableau de la femme pieuse.') Meanwhile the body of the son has been brought into the father's room, where another scene of despair ensues. And now the climax: the mother, guided by the servant, advances towards her husband's apartment, and sees... her husband, the father, lying outstretched over the dead son's body. She throws herself backwards, falls fainting into the servant's arms. Soon, Diderot adds, her mouth will be filled with sobs, and then he quotes from Horace, 'Tum verae voces'.

This plot can indeed be identified as 'melodrama' (in the modern sense) because the emotions it creates belong to a general situation, and are virtually unrelated to any particularity. It does not matter who this father or who this mother is, it suffices that they are parents who have lost their only son – whose identity does not matter either. I presume that Diderot considered this general sort of identity – mother, father, son – the modern equivalent of identities that are given in advance by myth – Orestes, the Furies.

But for present purposes the main point of interest is the essentially non-verbal aspect of the scene – the most powerful one that Diderot can imagine, a scene to rival antiquity. But the servant never pronounces the name of the dead son: his tears and his silence at the father's question, 'C'est donc mon fils?', speak more tellingly than a word could have done. Nor, apparently, does the father speak from then on. The emotional effect of the rest derives from the pathetic movements that join the scene of the mother with the scene of the father, the gestures and attitudes of pantomime, the tableaux that were to Dorval–Diderot so effective, along with sounds of weeping and grief. Diderot's point seems to be that the despair of these scenes exceeds the power of words: what words Diderot does allow (p.114) are mainly fragments – monosyllables, exclamations, occasional beginnings of sentences – as if no verbal discourse, no matter how elaborate, could ever capture fully the depth of the experience, but only hint at what is inherently inexpressible. Naturally, Diderot recommends that in such scenes the author should only rarely allow words to form a sequence of thought, no matter how brief: 'Il se permettra rarement un discours suivi, quelque court qu'il soit' (p.114). In short, the emotional impact of the pain felt by these parents is not declared in words at all, it is suggestively evoked by pantomime, inarticulate sounds, and verbal fragments. One need hardly mention that this aesthetic is at the opposite pole from such grandly articulate displays as the 'tirade' of Classical tragedy, in which every nuance of sentiment was verbalised. It is also clear that Diderot's explorations of the possibilities of pre-verbal expression in the *Lettre sur les sourds et muets* reach an imaginary fulfilment in the invention of this scene, whose power comes precisely from resources other than words. Finally, this direct, essentially non-verbal staging of the moment of parental grief was the kind of scene that Diderot could have had in mind when he impatiently brushed aside the chariot and the horses of the *récit de Théramène*: 'eh! laissez là le char et les chevaux de mon fils, et parlez-moi de lui.' In Diderot's imaginary tableau, the grief of the father and the mother receive exactly the sort of expression he considered most appropriate.

I have already mentioned the often tacit conviction of eighteenth-century playwrights that if one could satisfy all the requirements of *vraisemblance*, the audience would have no choice but to accept the playwright's representation as true. Obviously Diderot is substituting various more primitive forms of expression for words in these scenes, but his conviction remains the same: if the author can invent the right inarticulate sounds, gestures, tableaux and so on, the scenes will infallibly seem true to the spectator, for whom in fact the sorrow of the parents will come into being as real. At an earlier point in his discussion (p.112), Diderot suggests that if modern playwrights can combine scenes simultaneously as the ancients did (and as he was about to do in his scenario), the emotions felt by the spectators would be so overwhelming they would literally tremble to attend the performance – to which they would nevertheless find themselves irresistibly drawn.

Nothing preoccupied Diderot more than the magical power of various sorts of signs to induce a given conviction or reaction in someone exposed to them: the preoccupation is basic to all of Diderot's fiction; the whole of *Jacques le fataliste* plays on it. And if in the *Entretiens* he was mainly concerned with the positive aspects of signs, he was also intrigued by the negative or ambiguous possibilities: the situations when the signs producing the conviction may be doubtful or misleading, when the signs are only signs without substance. At one point in the *Entretiens* Moi remarks that it is not a lover's verbal protestation, 'Je vous aime', which triumphs over the scruples of a prude, over the designs of a coquette, over the virtue of a tender-hearted woman, it is the trembling voice with which the phrase is said, the tears, the looks that go along with it (p.103). These accoutrements sound very much as though they belonged to a calculated strategy on the man's part, a design to give the appearance of substance to words that are only words. And perhaps this fascination with the power of appearances – no matter how false – to induce strong convictions may be the explanation of the curious anecdote that crops up in the text at the insistence of Moi (p.120), about his provincial, libertine friend wanted by the police, whom Moi takes to the theatre: seeing all the (uniformed) guards everywhere, and the hole closed by an iron grille (for ticket sales), the young man thought his friend had lured him into a 'maison de force' and that he was about to be locked up. So strong was his conviction that he actually put his hand on his sword and addressed Moi with scorn and fury. Diderot never explains the point of the anecdote, and one can only conjecture that it was simply a curious example of an extremely forceful conviction brought about by signs whose apparent meaning was completely false.

In this connection one might recall the incident in *Jacques le fataliste*[8] in which the two travellers encounter a funeral train bearing a draped coffin that has every outward appearance of containing the body of Jacques's deceased master. The signs are so numerous and their meaning is so clear that it is impossible not to believe them, and yet – Diderot takes malign pleasure in suggesting – the whole display may be a fake: the coffin may be empty, or the body someone else's. Nor have critics failed to note how easily Diderot's extraordinary awareness of the problematics of signs fits into certain twentieth-century theories of semiotics. For words too have a sense in which they are all funeral trains that may not contain the corpses one thinks they do.[9] And it is in fact a testimony to Diderot's genius that in the empire of signs, too, as in so many other ways, he uncannily anticipates twentieth-century modes of thinking.

Of course one must also add that, upon closer inspection, these semiotic similarities turn out to be a demi-mirage. If Diderot so frequently enjoyed playing with the problematics of signs, and if he occasionally shows an uncanny awareness of the hollowness of words, or of the lag between the thought or emotion registered by the 'soul' and its verbal expression, this is simply the other side of a coin that also held the contrary to be true. For Diderot also held that words could be direct and immediate emanations of emotion and thought, and few writers have had a keener sense of this directness. Few writers as well have had such a positive awareness of the impact of words as they conjure up thoughts and emotions in those who hear them. Even in the case of *Jacques le fataliste* – after all of Diderot's mockery of the reader's gullibility, after forcing the reader a hundred times over to realise that this fiction is only a false invention, that the story never happened and that the words on the page are totally empty – paradoxically, the final impression left by the novel is of the reality of the protagonists, of their adventures, and of the stories they tell and hear, not of emptiness. By some backwards quirk of fate which I am very tempted to call 'contrariety', all that the doubting deconstruction of the fiction's authenticity has accomplished is to confirm its reality, to make it more real than ever.

8. Recounted, with several interruptions, in DPV, xxiii.65f.

9. See the interpretation by Daniel Brewer, *The Discourse of enlightenment in eighteenth-century France* (Cambridge 1993), p.221-22. Other doubtless inadvertent parallels to Diderot's conception may appear (as Ann Smock has kindly brought to my attention) in Maurice Blanchot, *The Space of literature*, trans. Ann Smock (Lincoln, Nebr. 1982), p.43, p.194-96, and *The Work of fire*, trans. Charlotte Mandell (Stanford, Calif. 1995), p.322-27.

Diderot's outlandish fiction, that *Le Fils naturel* is true and that the characters are playing out their own lives, renders unnecessary any consideration of 'acting' in relation to this play. Yet he does briefly make some remarks on the question, and not surprisingly it turns out that he regards acting as an entirely intuitive and spontaneous activity, requiring little judgement or reflection, although demanding great sensitivity. Indeed it would almost seem as if the rational side of the brain would only interfere with the acting process such as he conceives of it: he points out that one could never describe analytically all the complex qualities that inform the famous tirades from *Phèdre* (and then proceeds to describe them perfectly), but fortunately acting does not seem to depend on that sort of thinking: 'Heureusement une actrice d'un jugement borné, d'une pénétration commune, mais d'une grande sensibilité, saisit sans peine une situation d'âme, et trouve, sans y penser, l'accent qui convient à plusieurs sentiments différents qui se fondent ensemble, et qui constituent cette situation que toute la sagacité du philosophe n'analyserait pas' (p.104). Diderot goes on to lump together poets, actors, musicians, painters, great singers and dancers, tender lovers, and the truly devout as composing the troupe for whom feeling is the main thing, rather than reflection: 'qui sent vivement et réfléchit peu' (p.104).

This approach has the advantage of fitting rather easily with the general scheme of the *Entretiens* by reducing the element of calculation on the part of the actor to an absolute minimum: even as the original players in the performance of *Le Fils naturel* could say their lines with the spontaneous authenticity of real experience, so too professional actors – according to the theory that Diderot advances – play their parts by intuition and spontaneity, rather than by calculation and conscious artifice. Everywhere in the *Entretiens* one senses an effort to eliminate artifice from the concept of theatricality.

This intent is particularly striking in the account of the alleged performance of the final scene of *Le Fils naturel*: one is supposed to believe that the beloved 'Father' of the play has died before this ceremonial enactment could take place, and so for the performance another person was called upon to act his part. Not only do all the other performers break down weeping the moment that this actor appears onstage, but their emotion is so great the performance cannot continue and the play is abandoned. No doubt the absence of the real father is significant in this work on several levels and for a number of reasons.[10] But for present purposes the importance of these spontaneous paroxysms of grief on the part of the performers lies not only in the intensity of their alleged feelings about the death of the 'Father', but also in restricting this action

10. See Creech, *Diderot*, p.94-95.

exclusively to true people experiencing true feelings and saying true words. Naturally the presence of an actor, a personage by definition implying falseness and deception, is intolerable. Thus while the replacement of the 'Father' does indeed signify his death, at the same time it underscores the impossibility in this context of replacing the true by the false. In sum, the culminating affirmation in this work, dramatised by uncontrollable weeping and disarray, proclaims this stage as uniquely the locus of the sincere and the true. Given Diderot's curious mode of thinking, the teary-eyed intensity with which this idea is orchestrated is a sure sign that it will become, if not sooner then at least later, a target for destruction.

4. Stages of paradox in
Le Paradoxe sur le comédien

A DOZEN years elapsed between the publication of the *Entretiens* (1757) and its contrariety, *Le Paradoxe sur le comédien*, whose first version dates from 1769 (though not 'published' in the manuscripts of the *Correspondance littéraire* until 1770).[1] Diderot, typically, never took cognisance of the contrary relationship between the two. Instead the *Paradoxe* uses as its point of departure the refutation of a traditional theory of acting which assumed that, in order to perform well, an actor should both identify with the person he is playing and draw upon his own 'sensibilité naturelle'. The speaker called Le Premier gives the famous reply that, on the contrary, the secret of great acting lies in never identifying with the person of one's role and never drawing upon one's own natural feelings.[2] According to this argument great acting is pure calculation, an imitation in which the actor never forgets that he is playing someone he is not, and deliberately contrives to simulate emotions he knows he does not feel. Thus 'sensibilité naturelle' is the enemy of great acting. Since the actor must be equally adept at playing all sorts of characters, he should display no personal distinctiveness: the only visible identity is to be the illusory appearance he gives on the stage. Pushed to the extreme this theory postulates a rather complicated displacement in which the actor's natural self is blanked out, *not* in order that he become, or identify with, the person he is playing, but so that he can create in the *spectator* the illusion that he has become that person.[3]

1. On the way towards the composition of the *Paradoxe* came the *Discours sur la poésie dramatique* (1758), which Anthony Strugnell has suggestively explored as a midpoint between the points of view presented in the two other works: see 'Diderot, Garrick, and the maturity of the artist', *British journal for eighteenth-century studies* 10 (1987), p.13-25. For matters of publication see Diderot, *Paradoxe sur le comédien*, ed. Ernest Dupuy (Paris 1902) ('Cette édition comprend 1. Le texte inédit du manuscrit de Naigeon. 2. Le Texte des *Observations sur l'art du comédien* extrait du *Correspondance littéraire*. 3. Le texte du manuscrit de Saint-Pétersbourg'). Occasionally I use the punctuation of the Naigeon text. Because of its excellent documentation and accessibility, the page numbers in the text refer to *Œuvres esthétiques*, ed.Vernière (Paris 1965), p.289-381. There is a more recent critical edition by Stéphane Lojkine (Paris 1992). The most meticulously complete critical text, that of the DPV edition, xx.43-132, ed. Jane Marsh Dieckmann (Paris 1995), was unfortunately received too late for use as the basis of the present discussion. On account of the exceptional clarity of its presentation of the variants, however, it is referred to occasionally later on.

2. *Le Paradoxe*, p.306f.

3. Marian Hobson, 'Déictique, dialectique dans *Le Neveu de Rameau*', *Cahiers textuel* 11 (1992), puts a slightly different emphasis on these elements: 'L'acteur se cache derrière l'objet

4. Stages of paradox in 'Le Paradoxe sur le comédien'

Although many since Diderot have doubted whether this conception tells the whole truth about the psychology of acting, it surely reveals at least a part of that truth, and, no matter how often this topic has been treated by other writers, its significance is conveyed in this work with a vigour and insight that are uniquely Diderot's. If one follows the theory through to its consequences, as Diderot presents them, the vocation of a great actor strangely resembles a religious vocation: it involves an almost abject and total sacrifice of the 'self' and normal relations with the world for the greater good of the dramatic illusion. Naturally, nothing in this vocation implies virtue in the religious sense. On the contrary, Diderot finds that in real life, actors – with only rare exceptions – are cold, not given to sympathy or compassion, given to self-interest; they have almost no morals ('peu de mœurs', p.349), and no friends at all ('point d'amis', p.349), no character of their own ('point de caractère', p.350); they do not even have 'souls' in the sense of emotional depth ('point d'âme', p.351). Such sacrifices or deficiencies are the price they must pay in becoming actors, i.e. persons who can create in others the illusion that they are the poetic 'fantômes' (p.315) of persons they are not. The key concept in this connection is the 'modèle idéal', the idealised conception of their role – at one point in the text hints fleetingly that it may be something like 'la belle nature' in painting[4] – deriving from the dramatic poem, and after which actors must fashion their behaviour on the stage.[5]

Such actors participate in an imaginary order of beings said to be larger than anything in normal experience. Diderot draws on several images to describe this phenomenon: he speaks of a great mannequin surrounding the actor, making him bigger than life-size; twice he compares the effect of acting to children playing ghosts in a cemetery and dangling either their own clothes or a large sheet on the end of a pole above their heads, beneath whose funereal form lugubrious sounds emerge (p.309, p.376); or again he compares it to a dream in which one seems to feel one's head reaching up to the clouds, and

imaginaire qu'est son mannequin, son rôle, et de pâture pour le regard, se mue en celui qui dose ses effets et exploite la sensibilité du spectateur' (p.17).

4. 'Niez-vous qu[e sur la toile le peintre] n'embellisse la nature? N'avez-vous jamais loué une femme en disant qu'elle était belle comme une *Vierge* de Raphaël? A la vue d'un beau paysage, ne vous êtes-vous pas écrié qu'il était romanesque?' (p.319). Cf., however, the objections of Marc Buffat, 'Le *Paradoxe* et le travail de rupture', *Cahiers textuel* 11 (1992), p.79.

5. 'Qu'est-ce donc le vrai de la scène? C'est la conformité des actions, des discours, de la figure, de la voix, du mouvement, du geste, avec un modèle idéal imaginé par le poète, et souvent exagéré par le comédien. Voilà le merveilleux. Ce modèle n'influe pas seulement sur le ton; il modifie jusqu'à la démarche, jusqu'au maintien. De là vient que le comédien dans la rue ou sur la scène sont deux personnages si différents, qu'on a peine à les reconnaître. La première fois que je vis Mlle Clairon chez elle, je m'écriai tout naturellement: *Ah! mademoiselle, je vous croyais de toute la tête plus grande*' (p.317).

one's hands stretching out towards the confines of the horizon (p.308). But Dide ɔt most persuasively captures the potential grandeur of this conception in a small sketch of the great actress Mlle Clairon, imagining her nonchalantly stretched out on her chaise longue, arms crossed, eyes closed, immobile, while, in her memory-dream, hearing, seeing, and judging herself (playing a role on the stage), and judging too the impressions she will arouse. 'Dans ce moment elle est double: la petite Clairon et la grande Agrippine' (p.309). Later, Diderot comes to use a bizarrely intense and poetical metaphor taken from antiquity: 'elle avait trouvé ce qu'Eschine récitant une oraison de Démosthène ne put jamais rendre, le mugissement de la bête "...*bestiam mugientem*"[.] Le poète avait engendré l'animal terrible, la Clairon le faisait mugir' (p.343).

Reading such passages it is hard to doubt the sincerity of Diderot's enthusiasm for his paradox and for the kind of acting that it represents. The text is so eloquently persuasive that it seems almost blasphemous to point out that in so far as the *Paradoxe* is putting forward theories such as these it contradicts the ideas that Diderot himself had sponsored with equal – perhaps even greater – passion a dozen years before in the *Entretiens sur Le Fils naturel*. Again I am not the first to perceive this contrariety: it has already been noted by James Creech, in an elegantly concise discussion in which he remarks that 'the logic of the performance that is described [in the *Entretiens*] diametrically opposes each of the most salient arguments that will be put forth in [...] *Le Paradoxe sur le comédien*'.[6] Creech saw the 'radical disjunction' between the two works as denoting a dynamic relationship, rather than an exception to the rule, as some critics had thought: 'it may make more sense if the two spheres are understood to be bound together – intimately but diacritically – in a term-to-term relationship'.[7] Creech went on to describe several of the opposing features of the two aesthetics that formed the contrariety. But although some of the main points have already been discovered, this matter is worth reviewing in detail, for there are actually several kinds of contradictions between the *Entretiens* and the *Paradoxe*, and far too many of them for the phenomenon to be due to mere chance.

First, the main contrariety noted by Creech: whereas the *Entretiens* strove constantly – relentlessly – to close the gap between the theatre and real life, this effort is reversed in the *Paradoxe* (particularly in the theories just outlined), into an equally vigorous widening of the gap between the two, to the point of no return. To cite just one example: 'Réflechissez un moment sur ce qu'on

6. *Diderot: thresholds of representation* (Columbus, Ohio 1986), p.84.
7. *Diderot: thresholds of representation*, p.93.

appelle au théâtre *être vrai*. Est-ce y montrer les choses comme elles sont en nature? Aucunement' (p.317).

While the *Entretiens* sought continually to turn one's attention away from public theatres and to circumscribe one's view within a purely domestic space (the salon), the *Paradoxe* works in the opposite direction, striving to expand one's attention to take in the demands of the larger public space which theatres are, and make one realise how limited, 'pauvre et faible' (p.314), and even ridiculous salon performances would seem if transported to a real stage. Even when they have audiences, salon performances are dismissed almost scornfully: 'votre petit auditoire de salon' (p.315).

To describe the qualities desirable in an actor, the *Entretiens* invoked the attributes of what popularisers of psychology currently call the 'right brain' – intuition and the emotions – at the expense of the 'left side' – rationality and judgement. In the *Paradoxe* the factors in this predominance are reversed; in the new conception of the actor everything is sacrificed in favour of rational control and judgement, a point that Diderot insists on in his first characterisation of the great actor at virtually the beginning of the work (p.306):

Le Premier

[...] Moi, je lui veux beaucoup de jugement; il me faut dans cet homme un spectateur froid et tranquille, j'en exige, par conséquent, de la pénétration et nulle sensibilité, l'art de tout imiter, ou, ce qui revient au même, une égale aptitude à toutes sortes de caractères et de rôles.

Le Second

Nulle Sensibilité!

Le Premier

Nulle.

In view of the requirement of icy distancing and cold calculation which turns an actor's natural 'sensibilité' into an unwanted factor, to be suppressed or eliminated whenever it is found, the new perspective is in effect declaring war against the most prevalent character trait found in the *Entretiens*. One need hardly mention that in both *Le Fils naturel* and the *Entretiens*, all the actor-participants displayed their 'sensibilité' to the hilt, at every possible moment, as inseparable from their nature. No one lacks it. Perhaps there are moments when, for various motives, characters of *Le Fils naturel* hide their true feelings from one another, but one is never permitted to imagine for an instant that this reticence implies any diminution of their 'sensibilité'. On the contrary the reticence probably bespeaks an excess of feeling, a selfless concern not to hurt someone else.

In the *Paradoxe* one of the most frequently stressed consequences of the doctrine of 'nulle sensibilité' is the requirement that actors themselves should not experience any personal feelings at all, especially not in respect to the parts they are playing. This idea is inseparably linked to the rest of Le Premier–Diderot's paradox, for if nothing on the stage is to be natural, in the sense of being as things are in real life (see the quotation from p.317 above), if the dramatic illusion is created solely by artifice, then the introduction of an actor's own natural feelings can only be a hindrance. Later on, Diderot calls as witness the example of Mme Riccoboni, whose exquisite 'sensibilité' prevented her from ever acting well, and Mlle Gaussin, doomed by her 'sensibilité naturelle' to remain all her life in the category of those actresses whom Diderot calls 'maniérées, faibles, monotones' (p.370). According to this basic argument, natural feelings are supposed to be insufficiently adaptable for all the parts actors must play (p.371), and they are notoriously impulsive and unreliable; calculation alone has the advantage of reproducing the appropriate illusion of emotions at the right moment, doing so repeatedly in performances, and in any role: 'J'insiste donc, et je dis: 'C'est l'extrême sensibilité qui fait les acteurs médiocres; c'est la sensibilité médiocre qui fait la multitude des mauvais acteurs; et c'est le manque absolu de sensibilité qui prépare les acteurs sublimes.' Les larmes du comédien descendent de son cerveau; [...] il pleure comme un prêtre incrédule prêche la passion' (p.313).

In the paroxysm of weeping that ended the performance of *Le Fils naturel*, the one thing of which one can be sure is that the tears were not supposed to have emanated from anyone's brain: they came straight from the heart, and that provenance was the reason why they proved so overwhelming, by sympathetic vibration, to the one-man audience. Indeed, the argument here forms a perfect contrariety with the earlier text.[8]

In the ultimate outpost, logically speaking, of the new war against 'sensibilité' Diderot became so caught up in his argument that he actually started to list the alleged disadvantages of this quality not merely on the stage, but in real life. To add fuel to the flames he recounted anecdotes from his own experience proving that 'sensibilité' resulted in defeat and humiliation, while cold calculation led to resounding success. His conclusion was that nine hundred and

8. My argument may be seen as forming in turn another perfect contrariety with the view of Andrea Calzolari: 'L'image récurrente du mannequin qui magnétise les spectateurs, comme un masque peut épouvanter les enfants, pousse à l'extrême le programme énoncé dans les *Entretiens*' ('Les interprétations du paradoxe et les paradoxes de l'interprétation', *Interpréter Diderot aujourd'hui: Colloque de Cerisy*, Paris 1984, p.119-20). The classic statement of the traditional view of the *Paradoxe*, contrary to my own, remains that of Yvon Belaval, *L'Esthétique sans paradoxe de Diderot* (Paris 1950), p.165f. On the larger issue of how this work fits into Diderot's 'project of sincerity', see Carol Blum, *Diderot: the virtues of a philosopher* (New York 1974), p.86-107.

ninety-nine times out of a thousand, 'sensibilité' will be just as harmful ('nuisible') in society as it is on the stage (p.334).

Meanwhile, to give dramatic illustrations of how unfeeling great performers are, Le Premier–Diderot cites parts of several scenes from Classical plays (and also a moment in an opera), to which he adds, in counterpoint, the utterly mundane, and even scabrous, remarks that the actors were muttering to each other under their breath during the performance. Some of the best anecdotes come near the end of the series: the famous soprano Sophie Arnould, in a pathetic moment from one of the greatest operas by Rameau, whispering to her stage partner, 'Ah! Pillot, que tu pues!' Or Mlle Gaussin, giving every appearance of swooning with distress in a touching scene from *Zaïre*, but meanwhile spotting in one of the boxes some elderly 'procureur' whose grimaces of grief over her performance were too comical for words, secretly muttering to her 'confidante' beneath her stage-moan, 'Regarde donc un peu là-haut la bonne figure que voilà' (p.374).

For present purposes the important implication of this suppression of 'sensibilité' and its replacement by an aesthetic of calculation – that is to say, moving from the private salon to the public stage, and from true emotions to heartlessly feigned simulations – is that it entails complete and unquestioning acceptance of the conventions of French Classicism in the theatre: Diderot preaches calculation and self-sacrifice because he assumes actors will require these qualities in order to declaim measured verses in the role of Agamemnon or Mérope, characters who are not only larger than life, but never had any 'real' existence at all, save in the imagination of the poet. Naturally, the quotations and references for this line of thought all come from authors such as Corneille, Racine, La Motte, Voltaire and Crébillon, and, for comedy, Molière. Classicism is the issue here, and not – so long as Diderot is carrying on his main argument at least – the *drame*.

After such a clear and forceful enunciation of his position, it may seem incredible that in Diderot's mind there might be another side to the argument. But indeed there is – not only in the preceding *Entretiens*, where the *drame* was explicitly Diderot's main concern, but even in the text of the *Paradoxe* proper. Diderot is unable to silence entirely his own suspicion that if so much suppression of natural feeling, and so much unnatural exaggeration, were required to produce Classical tragedies, the fault might lie with Classical tragedies, and not with naturalness in acting. Although the logic of his theory forced him to conclude that 'sensibilité' was the inevitable path to mediocrity, one also senses an urge to declare the reverse: that mediocrity is induced by coldness and calculation, while true emotion can lead to greatness.

These contradictory voices are heard quite distinctly beneath the main theme of the *Paradoxe*, and curiously the first occurrence comes just after the start of the debate proper. Le Premier has launched into his explanation of the various qualities and activities that contribute to the formation of the best sort of actor, all of them designed to fit the anti-'sensibilité' perspective of the paradox to come. At which point, with no break and no warning, the dialogue swerves into the following curious turn (p.303-304):

> Le Premier
>
> [...] Le comédien imitateur peut arriver au point de rendre tout passablement; il n'y rien ni à louer, ni à reprendre dans son jeu.
>
> Le Second
>
> Ou tout est à reprendre.
>
> Le Premier
>
> Comme vous voudrez.[9] Le comédien de nature est souvent détestable, quelquefois excellent. En quelque genre que ce soit, méfiez-vous d'une médiocrité soutenue.

However bizarre it may seem, the values and assumptions being put forward by Le Premier are almost the exact reverse of those of his own paradox – the argument he had just started to enunciate. Here he is declaring that, contrary to everything he 'intended' to say, the actor who imitates never rises above mediocrity (which I assume is the implication of the words 'rendre tout passablement; il n'y rien ni à louer, ni à reprendre dans son jeu'), that the 'natural' actor, though often detestable, is sometimes excellent, and that in all genres one must be wary of sustained mediocrity. Thus the 'comédien de nature' – a code formula implying both 'sensibilité' and spontaneous acting – is being allowed at least an occasional excellence that is denied the 'comédien imitateur', against whose consistent mediocrity one is put on guard, not merely in acting but in all genres. Momentarily, the argument has swung into reverse and come out upside down. Nor can this occurrence be attributed to some misprint or inadvertence, for the essentials of this reversal had already appeared in the earliest extant version of the text in the *Correspondance littéraire*. To Diderot this curious contrary belonged somehow to the start of his argument.

For the rest, the values of the reversal, especially the concession to the temporary excellence of 'comédiens de nature', are reaffirmed in later parts of the dialogue, and these echoes occur not merely in the protests of Le Second (as one would expect), but also in the discourses of Le Premier. In other words, the dialogues are not merely a debate between two opposing discussants; there is another debate going on, or at least a kind of back and forth, a

---

9. The position of the two dialogists vividly recalls the Nephew's criticisms of Mlle Clairon near the opening of *Le Neveu de Rameau*.

counterpoint, even in the proposals of the main arguer for Diderot's paradox. This phenomenon occurs in a variety of ways, as though Diderot, uncomfortable with the consequences of his inflexible theory, were exploring alternatives, but not quite sure where to seek the right remedy. The most frequent counterargument is the one already suggested in the quoted passage, the admission that 'comédiens de nature' are not always mediocre (despite an explicit earlier claim to the contrary), but a mixture of the excellent and the terrible (p.307). As to the manner in which the mixture occurs, Le Premier–Diderot seems to have trouble finding a single answer: sometimes he writes as if the mixture occurred within a given role – good moments and bad ones (p.372); elsewhere, whole performances are seen as either good or bad (p.306); or again, as if the good were simultaneously present with the bad; or again actors with natural feelings are seen as having potentially excellent qualities (good) that are never actually realised (bad).[10] In any case, thanks to such diverse concessions allowing the 'comédien de nature' to have at least aspects of excellence (for example p.318), the natural in acting, pushed out the front door by the logical thrust of Diderot's paradox, contrives to get at least one leg in through the back window – in the arguments of Le Premier, as well as in those of Le Second.

Diderot's own temperament (for obvious reasons) was no doubt responsible for this relaxation of the austerity of his theoretical position, but this concept of natural acting as an uneven mixture of good and bad also reflects the influence of another famous example, the rival of the calculating Mlle Clairon, namely, Mlle Dumesnil. Diderot refers to her quite early in the text, just after his lengthy analysis of Mlle Clairon's art of calculation, and he immediately makes it clear that the acting of Mlle Dumesnil is not at all the same thing as that of her rival: 'Il n'en est pas de la Dumesnil ainsi que de la Clairon' (p.309). The text goes on to explain that Mlle Dumesnil appears onstage without knowing what she will be saying (with no calculation), and even when she is speaking her lines, half the time she does not know what she is saying either (again, there is no calculation). But then comes a moment that Diderot does not hesitate to qualify as 'sublime': 'Elle monte sur les planches sans savoir ce qu'elle dira; la moitié du temps elle ne sait ce qu'elle dit, mais il vient un moment sublime' (p.309).

This description fits perfectly with the category that Diderot has termed 'comédien de nature', or 'les acteurs qui jouent d'âme' (p.307), a kind of actor he describes as 'souvent détestable, quelquefois excellent', or again, 'leur jeu

10. This sort of movement of thought that jumps from a smaller frame of reference to wider ones, thereby abruptly shifting the terms of the argument, is also found in the opening discussion of Greuze in the *Salon de 1765*: see DPV, xiv.178.

est alternativement [...] plat et sublime'. It seems a likely possibility that, for the moment at least, the contrast between Mlle Clairon and Mlle Dumesnil exemplified to Diderot this basic sort of polarity between cold calculation and 'sensibilité naturelle'.

Yet – nothing ever being simple in Diderot[11] – immediately after his declaration that Mlle Dumesnil is capable of sublime moments, the text, in an effort to keep abreast of Diderot's diverse reactions towards all the information at hand, goes off into a mode in which the discourse seems to create its values as it proceeds, phrase by phrase and even word by word. Abruptly abandoning Mlle Dumesnil and her sublime moments Diderot turns once again to consider the method that artists use to create their effect: this time he lumps actors together with poets, painters, orators and musicians, and denies that these artists find 'les traits caractéristiques' of their imitations in the fury of the 'premier jet', such traits being found, rather, in moments of cold tranquillity. So far the text seems to have reverted to the theory associated with Mlle Clairon. But then Diderot upsets the uniformity of the argument by adding, after a comma, 'dans des moments tout à fait inattendus'. The text reads thus: 'Ce n'est pas dans la fureur du premier jet que les traits caractéristiques se présentent, c'est dans des moments tranquilles et froids, dans des moments tout à fait inattendus' (p.309).

'Inattendus'? The idea of unexpectedness raises an entirely new point: hitherto cold calculation had not been associated with the unexpected, but with strategies that were planned in advance and with results that were predetermined. Unexpectedness is more easily associated with the uneven, unreliable Mlle Dumesnil than with the dependable Mlle Clairon. The original version of the text, that appeared in the *Correspondance littéraire*, did not pause to give further explanation of this new point. But in the later version Diderot

---

11. This text is one of the least stable that Diderot composed. For example, it is slightly disconcerting to see Mlle Gaussin categorised at the beginning as one of those actresses doomed all her life to mediocrity by her 'sensibilité', only to find her turning up, in the passage mentioned earlier, as an example of cold calculation, putting on a moving performance of *Zaïre*, although so emotionally uninvolved that she can even make a satirical remark to her 'confidante' during her most touching moment. Most curious, the same metamorphosis applies to Mlle Dumesnil, who, though firmly established in the text as belonging to the type 'comédiens de nature', and contrasted with Mlle Clairon's calculations, later (p.370) appears on the same list with Mlle Clairon of actors and actresses who, the text eventually suggests, perform according to the principles of art, rather than natural feeling. In this part of the text Le Premier lists the actresses Le Couvreur, Duclos, de Seine, Balincourt, Clairon and Dumesnil and then comments, concerning a much less experienced actress, Mlle Raucourt, 'elle est trop novice pour ne point sentir, et je vous prédis que, si elle continue de sentir, de rester elle et de préférer l'instinct borné de la nature à l'étude illimitée de l'art, elle ne s'élèvera jamais à la hauteur des actrices que je vous ai nommées'.

seemed to feel the need for at least a little amplification. And as he developed his thought the text seemed to bring Mlle Dumesnil back into the picture, as though Diderot were searching for a way to stretch his theory so as take her sublimities into account. For just two brief phrases (an addition of the later version), the text seems to go over to Mlle Dumesnil's side of the equation: 'On ne sait d'où ces traits viennent; ils tiennent de l'inspiration' (p.309).

'Inspiration' had never been associated with Mlle Clairon; furthermore the idea of inspiration had been noticeably absent from the text of the first version corresponding to this passage. But once introduced it becomes the opening wedge of a compromise that looks like an effort to remain faithful to Mlle Clairon, while at the same time making room for her rival. Throughout this passage, Diderot is often thinking of the actor in images borrowed from painting, and assuming that the actor, like the painter, habitually compiles sketches in notebooks or dossiers, which are then put to use in the finished painting / performance on the stage. But the passage, a palimpsest of overlapping versions and last-minute additions, is worth quoting more fully, to show the links with what precedes:[12]

Ce n'est pas dans la fureur du premier jet que les traits caractéristiques se présentent. C'est dans des moments tranquilles et froids, dans des moments tout à fait inattendus. On ne sait d'où ces traits viennent. Ils tiennent de l'inspiration. C'est lorsque suspendus entre la nature et leur ébauche, ces génies portent alternativement un œil attentif sur l'une et sur l'autre. Les beautés d'inspiration, les traits fortuits qu'ils répandent dans leurs ouvrages et dont l'apparition subite les étonne eux-mêmes sont d'un effet et d'un succès bien autrement assurés que ce qu'ils y ont jetté de boutade. C'est au sens froid à tempérer le délire de l'enthousiasme.

Diderot has deliberately fashioned this argument to be applicable not only to actors, but to all sorts of artists, and, no matter how disjointedly it may occur in the text,[13] this interpretation of the dynamics of 'inspiration' in the

---

12. P.309. I use the punctuation of the Naigeon manuscript because in this instance it gives a slightly clearer idea of the rhythm of Diderot's thought.

13. Cf. the presentation of the variants in DPV, xx.52. In this connection one might note that the third and fourth sentences of the passage ('On ne sait d'où ces traits viennent. Ils tiennent de l'inspiration.') are later additions, and hence they break into the logical sequence of the text surrounding them. In other words the logical structure goes from 'Ce n'est pas dans la fureur' to 'C'est dans des moments tranquilles' to 'C'est lorsque suspendus', so that the two added sentences function almost disconnectedly, rather like an aside. The final sentence ('C'est au sens froid'), given in two manuscript versions of the text as a marginal addition, brings in still another perspective based on different elements – the text immediately preceding does not imply any necessity of tempering a 'délire d'enthousiasme' – which suggests interesting, if unrealised, possibilities, perhaps even a new compromise. Anthony Strugnell sees parallels between Diderot's views in this passage and the reflections on Garrick occasioned by his critique of the acting of Mlle Clairon ('Diderot, Garrick, and the maturity of the artist', p.23).

creative process is one of the most daringly original and even surprising moments of this text – in itself a sort of 'beauté d'inspiration'.[14] Diderot, uniquely in his time, had an awareness of the dividedness of the self in the modern sense, that is to say, he was aware of the personality as being functionally two-sided – both sides being related, but one side working rather in the dark. In this passage he is certainly describing the process of mimesis as a rational one, in other words, a conscious and calculated imitation of nature; but to this he adds the unpredictable factor of beauty that comes fortuitously from nowhere as a mysterious concomitant to the rational process. According to this conception, conscious intellectual effort is indeed required in the creative process, in fact it appears to be indispensable; but inspired beauty comes from somewhere else, and according to factors over which there can be no rational control. The 'je ne sais quoi' of Classical theorists has been left far behind, and, in this suggestion of the link between 'inspiration' and a secret process that is beyond the boundaries of reason, the way seems to be opening towards modern theories of creativity, theories which will at last attempt to give full weight to the significance of the unconscious. In the paragraph which follows the above quotation, Diderot even goes so far as to hint that the whole procedure may take place without the creative artist being aware that it is going on: 'C'est de ces recueils formés en eux, *à leur insu*, que tant de phénomènes rares [first version: 'traits sublimes'] passent dans leurs ouvrages' (p.310, emphasis mine). Until this passage, the 'recueils' had been spoken of as containing notes or sketches that were fashioned deliberately, while the artist was wide awake; but we now pass to a perhaps deeper stage in which the unconscious dominates and even the sketchmaking is absorbed by it. For Voltaire, such a concept would have been incomprehensible. And it seems unlikely that even Rousseau would have appreciated this insight. One has to wait for much later authors. Nor is this the only instance in Diderot's work when one finds him inventing *en germe* a vision of the functioning of the mind of the creative artist which, although distinctly out of kilter with his own era, looks ahead to authors far closer to our own time – to Proust for example.

Well might one wonder how all this fits into the main argument of the paradox, which gave every appearance of being inhospitable to such uncontrollables as 'inspiration' and 'traits fortuits'. Even the famous 'modèle idéal' seemed to be attained by carefully estimated projection rather than being left to fortuitous occurrence.[15] Although this text is full of repetitions of ideas,

14. Baudelaire seems to have been one of those best able to comprehend the complexities of these ideas. See the passage from *Notices sur Edgar A. Poe* quoted by Otis Fellows in '*Jacques le fataliste* revisited', *L'Esprit créateur* 8 (1968), p.52.
15. See the classic article by Philippe Lacoue-Labarthe, 'Diderot, le paradoxe et la mimésis',

occasionally even to the point of monotony, the concept of 'inspiration', after this brief appearance, will never be seen again; it leaves the argument once and for all. My own view is that, master stroke though it is, this idea crept into the argument as a momentary bending towards Mlle Dumesnil, and had no rightful or lasting place in the unsympathetic, almost hostile environment of the paradox proper.

On Mlle Clairon's side of the equation must also be placed the unforgettable example of David Garrick,[16] one of whose pantomimes Diderot describes in the *Paradoxe* from having seen it in person (p.328). Diderot's slightly unclear account leaves in doubt just how completely he thought Garrick himself had been willing to subscribe to this theory of the total disinvolvement required of an actor.[17] But in any case, Diderot's description of Garrick's pantomime indicates how perfectly for Diderot this actor embodied the ideal of acting by pure calculation. These two examples above all, Mlle Clairon and Garrick, both personal acquaintances of Diderot, explain why Diderot returns so frequently to the austerity of his original position, the one that declared 'comédiens de nature' doomed by their nature to mediocrity. For these two actors (Diderot mentions others as well) had achieved greatness through control of every aspect of their deportment; their pristine example justified his theory in a manner that could not be gainsaid.

Nor, however, can one deny Diderot's ambiguities about these issues, which sometimes intrude despite his alleged intentions and produce effects that in the long run undermine the arguments he is allegedly supporting. Seen in this light, even Diderot's witty anecdotes of the actresses' *sotto voce* stage remarks mentionned earlier may work derisively against the main thesis. No doubt, taken at face value, they do indeed testify to the cold calculation behind the apparent warmth of the actresses' emotions. Yet, one has only to shift the emphasis a little for these comic counterpoints to undermine the seriousness of the stageworks in which they are so unsuitably inserted, and glaringly disparage the artificiality of their surroundings. Diderot obviously thought them droll – else he would not have cited so many, and at such length. But if one laughs at them with him, one reason is that they function as comic relief,

---

Poétique 2 (1980), p.267-81, in which Diderot's concept of the ideal is shown to be Aristotelian rather than Platonic.

16. Cf. Strugnell, 'Diderot, Garrick, and the maturity of the artist', which, in addition to giving a more detailed discussion of the influence of Garrick on Diderot than the present chapter, also provides a useful bibliography of this topic.

17. Diderot's tone, and the fact that the conversation allegedly taking place between him and Garrick is recounted elsewhere as having taken place between Garrick and the chevalier de Chastellux, makes one suspect an element of wishful thinking in the relevant passage (p.346-47).

as a salutory glimpse of reality that cuts through all the weighty, lofty, edifying falseness of French Classicism and opera. 'Ah! Pillot, que tu pues!', an instructive example of a great actress's sang-froid no doubt, but also an enjoyable return to an earthiness that counterbalances, indeed thumbs the nose at, the artificial formality of operatic pomp. (Might it be all that pompousness, really, that 'stinks'?)[18] Diderot was aware of the potentially destructive side of these counterpoints, and voices this awareness through the reaction of Le Second, who twice declares that, had he known of these *sotto voce* remarks (what he terms 'ces deux scènes simultanées'), he would never in his life set foot in a theatre again (p.326, p.328). And it is to challenge these strongly negative reactions that Le Premier immediately describes Garrick's virtuoso pantomime, his point being that such masterful control would be impossible without the actor's complete detachment (p.328-29).

But as the argument wends its way it appears increasingly – especially if one knows how divided Diderot himself was about the issues involved – that Le Premier–Diderot is talking over a series of dubieties, the main one being simply the stated preference for the artificial over the natural, which Le Premier applies not merely to the theatre but even to more general situations. Can one really lend credence to Le Premier's doctrinaire declaration – stated as though every syllable he uttered were not highly debatable in Diderot's mind – that if a catastrophe occurred in the street one should prefer a painted or staged version of people's reactions to it over the real scene produced by their 'sensibilité naturelle' (p.320)? Does the author of the *Supplément au Voyage de Bougainville* and various inflammatory contributions to Raynal's *Histoire philosophique des deux Indes* want to be taken seriously when he complacently expects the reader to prefer the artificial rendering of the street catastrophe to the real scene for the same reasons that one prefers an 'assemblage of civilised persons' to a 'horde of savages'? Does it seem likely that the author of the *Entretiens sur Le Fils naturel* would propose that inevitably actors performed their roles 'petitement, mesquinement' whenever they played characters similar to their own (p.337)?

It is as though Diderot were determined to sacrifice his own natural impulses on these issues for the sake of his paradox, and in doing so were trying himself

18. One of the most revealing passages concerning Diderot's attitude in this regard comes from a letter to Sophie Volland, describing his walk around the country property of Sophie's mother, in her company: 'La maman marche comme un lièvre. Elle ne craint ni les ronces, ni les épines, ni le fumier. Tout cela n'arrête point ses pas ni les miens, n'offense point son odorat ni le mien. Allez, pour un nez honnête et qui a conservé son innocence naturelle, ce n'est pas une chèvre, c'est une femme bien musquée, bien ambrée, qui pue. L'expression est dure, mais elle est vraie' (Isle, 17 ou 18 août 1759; *Correspondance*, ed. Georges Roth, ii.229).

to become as selfless and empty of spontaneous reactions as he demanded great actors to be. Meanwhile, the more Le Premier wins out over Le Second with these arguments, the more one senses contrary pressures building from within. And once, in a telling moment of revolt against the prevailing assumptions, the contrary truth is blurted out by Le Second, with an effect as sensational as if some dangerous and carefully guarded secret (some mad nun) had broken out of its usual place of confinement, threatening disorder and disarray: Le Premier had been insisting on how ridiculous, indeed literally laughable, Le Second's emotions would seem if he brought his own weeping to the stage, and by the same token how inappropriate a conversational tone would appear if used in Corneille, Racine, Voltaire or even Shakespeare. Such is the occasion for Le Second to interject the unthinkable thought that strikes not merely at Classical acting but at Classicism itself in the theatre: 'C'est que peut-être Racine et Corneille, tout grands hommes qu'ils étaient, n'ont rien fait qui vaille' (p.315).

Le Premier's reaction in no way denies the possible truth of Le Second's statement, but simply declares it unspeakable and blasphemous: 'Quel blasphème! qui est-ce qui oserait le proférer? Qui est-ce qui oserait y applaudir?' (p.315). Le Premier then switches back to his earlier 'orthodox' line of argument, stressing the distinction between behaviour in the salon and the deportment of actors onstage. And yet, even here, as Le Premier goes on to describe how strange-mannered, grotesquely untrue, unhistorical, illusory and irrelevant to real life those remote kings and queens of the theatre are – all because 'le vieil Eschylle' had given out some formula three thousand years ago – he seems to be sliding dangerously close to a satire of the values he claims to be supporting.

And in fact the issue is by no means settled; rather it is as though a signal had been given tipping off the reader to a whole contrary, anti-Classical level of argument lurking just beneath the surface that will eventually rise up and take over. What finally brings this other perspective fully and operatively into play is, as one might expect, a particularly forceful statement of its opposite. In a masterful exposition Le Premier lays out the whole system of his famous paradox (p.357-58). The logic is so straight and tight, each element leading inevitably to the next, that no room is left for doubt or dissent. Such decisiveness hints that the argument is now ripe for a reversal that will come in two stages.

First, the preparatory build-up surging like a wave, emerging out of its contrary undertows: subversively undermining terms invade and corrode Le Premier's argument allegedly supporting the acting of Classical roles, now described as 'portraits outrés', 'grandes caricatures assujeties à des règles de convention', and 'bouffissure prescrite' (p.357-58), thus destabilising the text.[19] A violent disagreement breaks out between the two dialogists which further heightens the destabilising tensions, and, bizarre touch, Le Second does not appear to have been listening attentively to the ideas of his opponent. His not entirely apposite rejoinder is an indignant rejection on moral grounds of the artificiality of Classical acting traditions, and, by extension, of Classical tragedy itself. He declares that Le Premier's argument, intentionally or not, is a cruel satire of actors and authors and that, contrary to Le Premier's position, greatness of soul should never be prohibited in any circumstance, nor should one forbid the use of a speech and deportment appropriate to that disposition; the image of true greatness can never be ridiculous.

Even though this position has been presented with crystal clarity and simplicity, Le Premier claims that he is baffled, unable to see what Le Second is driving at, a reaction Le Second angrily – and for reasons that are far from clear – rejects as sheer cowardice, calling it the most transparent strategy to force Le Second to undergo himself the inevitable public indignation which Le Premier would have undergone had he proffered the same thoughts. All this fittingly, if confusingly, dramatises the daring of Le Second's assertion when at last it comes. Need one recall that Diderot's entire paradox, exalting the calculated and the artificial at the expense of the natural, and widening the gap between the theatre and real life, had been designed in support of French Classical traditions?:

Le Second

[Que s'ensuit-il de là?] C'est que la vraie tragédie est encore à trouver, et qu'avec tous leurs défauts les anciens en étaient peut-être plus voisins que nous.

---

19. There are also interesting incidental reversals in the text. One of the most curious comes near the end of Le Premier's exposition: 'Qu'est-ce que le vrai talent? Celui de bien connaître les symptomes extérieurs de l'âme d'emprunt, de s'addresser à la sensation de ceux qui *nous* entendent, qui *nous* voient, et de les tromper par l'imitation de ces symptômes, par une imitation qui agrandissent tout dans leurs têtes et qui deviennent la règle de leur jugement; car il est impossible d'apprécier autrement ce qui se passe au dedans de *nous*. Et que *nous* importe en effet qu'ils sentent ou qu'ils ne sentent pas, pourvu que *nous* l'ignorions?' (p.357, emphasis mine). The first three 'nous' clearly designate 'we actors'. In the last sentence, without warning, the perspective shifts and the word goes to the opposite pole to mean 'we the audience'. Furthermore, one finds almost exactly the same shift in the actor–audience polarity earlier in the text: Le Premier declares in one paragraph that 'les hommes [...] sensibles' were onstage, while the watchful genius was in the audience. And then, in the very next paragraph (a later addition to the original version), Le Premier abruptly reverses the polarity, declaring that 'l'homme sensible' should *not* be allowed onstage, but confined to the audience: 'Remplissez la salle de spectacle de ces pleureurs-là, mais ne m'en places aucun sur la scène' (p.310). But no sooner has this change been enunciated than the image reverses itself again: 'toutes les âmes chaudes occupent le théâtre; tous les hommes de génie sont au parterre. Les premiers s'appellent des fous; les seconds, qui s'occupent à copier leurs folies, s'appellent des sages' (p.311). The variants reveal that these

But then, if French Classical traditions do not embody true tragedy, where does this situation leave Diderot's paradox? This time, far from protesting, Le Premier chimes in, giving examples from antiquity that leave no doubt of his agreement.[20] In other words, the interlocutors are no longer – even theoretically – opponents but members of the same team, united in their opinion that French Classicism is wanting in the essentials of true tragedy. All previous values now go into reverse: even as the original paradox had disparaged naturalness in the theatre as laughable, the path to mediocrity, naturalness now becomes all that is desirable, while artificiality becomes the enemy. Far from seeking to widen the gap between the theatre and life Le Premier praises instances when the theatre has closed the gap – such as a certain speech from Sophocles in which an older man warns a young one about the company he keeps. Le Premier declares himself 'enchanté' to hear such words, adding that they are exactly what Le Second would in similar circumstances say to Le Premier's son today, or what Le Premier would say to the son of Le Second. Clearly, what 'enchants' Le Premier in the speech from Sophocles is that, contrary to everything he has been demanding for Classical tragedy, there is no difference between these stage-words and real life; they could not be more 'natural'. And Le Premier continues to insist on this point, taking the lead as he urges Le Second to agree that the speech from the Greek play is indeed beautiful, that its tone is no different from the tone one would use in present-day society, nor would it be ridiculous in such a social setting (in all this there is categorical agreement from Le Second). Le Premier is now glowingly eulogising the very values he had just condemned and held up to ridicule.[21] The former dispute has been transformed into a harmonious duet.

Momentarily, what makes possible such a dramatic about-face on Le Pre-

shifts occurred as a result of revisions by the author; but the final result is a text in which the basic concepts of 'actor' and 'audience' exchange meaning moment by moment.

20. See Raymond Trousson, 'Diderot et la leçon du théâtre antique', *Diderot: colloque international*, ed. A.-M. Chouillet (Paris 1985), p.479-92.

21. The only scholar who to my knowledge has identified and stressed the importance of this contrariety is Benrekassa, 'Diderot, l'absence d'œuvre', p.139, who sees it as a contributory factor, philosophically, to the 'absence d'œuvre', which is the subject of his article. While admiring Benrekassa's brilliantly erudite and eloquent analysis, I note that the end-product of his study of Diderot is emptiness ('l'absence d'œuvre'), a result which I believe inevitably follows the application of logical criteria to a discourse which is essentially extra-logical. According to the more literary (and more myopic) approach I am suggesting, the opposing elements forming the contrarieties of Diderot's thought should not be brought together so that they cancel each other out; rather each side of the contrariety is to be viewed as an active principle whose energy brings on its opposite, thus creating the vitality and forcefulness of the text. The final result might be termed 'la présence d'œuvre' – which I believe more truly reflects the experience of reading Diderot.

mier's part seems to be the fixing of the issue on antiquity: the pretext for his change of argument is his admiration for the ancients,[22] and presumably one is supposed to concentrate positively on this new position, as a return to ancient values, rather than as a rejection of French Classicism. But of course this 'direction de l'intention' does not work: the new position favouring natural speech and simplicity in the theatre does indeed imply a rejection of French Classical traditions, and quite unsurprisingly, as the discussion proceeds, the new position turns into an attack on the greatest authors of Classicism. Coming out for strong actions and simple words, Le Premier starts to treat the legacy of Corneille with derision, terming the traditions of *Le Cid* 'la rodomontade de Madrid' and contrasting it with the heroism of Rome. Le Second chimes in by attacking the ubiquitous verse form of Classical tragedy, the alexandrine, criticising it as 'trop nombreux et trop noble pour le dialogue', to which Le Premier adds his own disapproval of French decasyllables. Contrasting Corneille's Roman plays unfavourably with Cicero's letters, Le Premier exclaims, 'Combien je trouve nos auteurs dramatiques ampoulés!' And, setting the vigorous simplicity of Regulus's *Discourse to the Roman Senate* against the style of French dramatic authors, he goes even further: 'Combien leurs déclamations me sont dégoûtantes!' (p.360).

Naturally, in this frame of mind both dialogists discover much to admire in Horace's ode recounting Romulus's brave words urging courage, and Le Premier demands that Le Second confess how seldom it is – implying almost never – that French dramatic poets achieve the tone suited to a virtue at once so lofty and so intimate ('familière'). By the same token, he asks Le Second to imagine how unthinkable it would be to have Regulus, of Horace's ode, speak in the manner of current acting, either in the tender, exaggeratedly plaintive mode ('nos tendres jérémiades') or in Corneille's blustery one ('nos fanfaronnades à la Corneille'). Earlier Le Premier had accused Le Second of 'blasphème' when he dared to propose that 'Racine et Corneille, tout grands hommes qu'ils étaient, n'ont rien fait qui vaille' (p.315). But now Le Premier himself pleads guilty to blasphemy, at least in the public eye, on account of his denigration of the sacred authors of Classicism: 'Je serais lapidé dans les rues si l'on me savait coupable de ce blasphème' (p.362).

If Le Premier's sarcastic reference to 'nos fanfaronnades à la Corneille' aims at the Cornelian side of the neo-Classical tradition, his phrase 'nos tendres jérémiades' probably aims at the other side, the Racinian tradition (p.362). In fact the image may link up, by association, with a curious earlier passage in which Diderot, possibly taking a lesson from one of Rousseau's stern 'Roman'

22. See Trousson, 'Diderot et la leçon de l'antiquité', p.485.

texts, has recourse to irony as he mocks the weak and shallow delicacy of French society:[23]

Poètes, travaillez-vous pour une nation délicate, vaporeuse et sensible? Renfermez-vous dans les harmonieuses, tendres et touchantes élégies de Racine; elle se sauverait des boucheries de Shakespeare: ces âmes faibles sont incapables de supporter des secousses violentes. Gardez-vous bien de leur présenter des images trop fortes.

In the later discussion of 'true tragedy' as well, the vigorous elevation and simplicity of antique virtue is being set in contrast to the weak, empty artificiality of French tragedy. In sum, at this point in the text (p.362), Le Premier, in his enthusiasm for the naturalness, simplicity and 'realism' of antique tragedy, has united with his alleged opponent, and abandoned all interest in the artifice and distancing from reality on which his paradox was founded. He has also dismissed as 'ampoulé[e]s' or 'dégoûtantes' the plays for which his paradox had been designed and in which his calculating actors would deploy their art. Clearly, the pro-Classical assumptions of the original paradox have now reversed themselves into an anti-Classical paradox, and all the incipient disgruntlements and guardedly satirical thrusts remarked on earlier have crystallised into a full-blown antibody. This movement has just reached its final phase in a celebration of a kind of tragedy that quite unironically brought natural modes of speech and natural emotion to the stage – modes at least analogous to those Diderot himself had earlier tried to recapture in his *drames*.[24] Such simplicity and naturalness would indeed require stage speech entirely different from that normally practised by French tragedians – the very subject of Le Premier's final remark on this topic.

At this juncture the author seems to come partially to his senses: at least he recalls his earlier arguments against 'sensibilité' and remarks that the criticisms he has been making are rather unusual since in fact nature never created a soul more 'sensible' than his own. Even so, the author never recognises the main point, which is that he has been refuting his own position. Instead, the original argument of the paradox now clicks back into place, and the text goes on as though the contrariety had never occurred. But the very fact of referring to his own character as being out of joint with his central argument suggests at least a subliminal awareness of having given voice to his natural instincts – against the original paradox. As usual, Diderot's discourse remains blind to such implications: the text simply proceeds from moment to moment giving

23. P.343, punctuation as in Naigeon.
24. Diderot shows no consciousness of the degree to which the aesthetic of the *drame* was at stake, in fact being denied, in the original paradox.

little sense of hindsight, or foresight either, for that matter. Even the remembrance here of earlier arguments against 'sensibilité' is an unusual occurrence.

For the rest of the dialogue Le Premier makes a show of maintaining his original hardline position – sometimes quite persuasively, as in the section immediately following the reference to his own sensitivity (p.363). But further on a curious weakness and lack of conviction sets in, as if he were running out of steam. He compromises, or sacrifices entirely, articles of his doctrine that he had formerly defended with fervour, as, for example, when he speaks enthusiastically of the performances of *Le Père de famille* in Naples, even though the actors had been chosen for their close resemblance – both physical and personal – to the characters in the play, and displayed the ability to identify completely with their roles – thus, without recognising it, weakening two cardinal points of the old doctrine.[25]

Occasionally Le Premier admits in so many words that he does not care whether his arguments are convincing or not: 'Ce dernier raisonnement vous paraît peu solide? Eh bien, soit; mais je n'en conclurai pas moins de piquer un peu nos ampoules, de rabaisser de quelques crans nos échasses, et de laisser les choses à peu près comme elles sont' (p.378).

The curious weakness and lack of conviction of this compromise is also underscored by the other main event in the final portion of the text. Le Second cites from antiquity the case of the actor Polus,[26] who, performing in Athens, and playing – as custom at that time sanctioned – a woman's role, appeared on stage dressed in Electra's mourning costume, clutching, not the urn of Orestes which the tragedy demanded, but the urn containing the remains of his own son, who had just died. Aulus-Gellius concluded his account (relates Le Second–Diderot) by declaring that the cries and laments which then resounded in the theatre were not at all the shallow kind that ordinary audiences make, but cries and laments of true grief.

Le Premier is not impressed. While conceding that this effect on the stage may have been 'prodigieux', he promptly dismisses the example as inconclusive: Polus was probably nothing but a mediocre actor; besides, his acting was more artificial than Le Second cared to admit; the audience was not weeping at his acting anyway, but at the spectacle of a father mourning for a son. Le Premier

---

25. On the other hand, once Le Premier has installed himself in the original paradox in this section of the text, he stubbornly resists compromise. Le Second makes a final effort to resolve the dispute by persuading Le Premier to grant that at least when playing their greatest dramatic moments actors might temporarily be permitted to cease conscious calculating, lose their heads (so to speak) and draw on their own feelings (p.368-73). Though Le Premier gives some appearance of conceding, ultimately he remains intransigent.

26. Benrekassa, 'Diderot, l'absence d'œuvre', p.139, also mentions this example.

cites a parallel example from antiquity of an actor becoming so caught up in the fury of his role that he killed a passing slave – clearly the action of a madman.

But to modern readers at least, Le Premier's breezy, not to mention contradictory, dismissal of Le Second's example – in which an actor's grief over the death of his son irrupted onstage and overwhelmed the audience – is in no way adequate to counter this extraordinary testimony to the power of real emotion in acting, and whose effect, so damaging to Diderot's paradox, is perhaps even magnified by Le Premier's subsequent chatter. Nor is Le Premier's final statement (just before the allegedly late hour brings on the suggestion that they go out to eat) exactly reassuring: Le Premier compares the skill of a great actor to that of an experienced courtier, and suggests that the latter may be even more accomplished than stage actors are in simulating the whole range of human emotions, which Le Premier proceeds to specify. He implies that, in such a comparison, the winner would be the 'vieux courtisan' – which are the two last words that bring the *Paradoxe* proper to a close, leaving the reader to wonder why Diderot would end his work with this deadly comparison between actors and a species of humanity whose reputation was then, just as it had been among French authors for centuries, so famously despicable. Of course, before one has time to demand further explanation both dialogists disappear on their way to supper, leaving the page and the question incontrovertibly blank, and the reader, too, hungry for answers.

Everyone will continue to read and remember this work for the famous arguments of the paradox. This is by far the most brilliantly argued part, just as the Old Man's farewell is the most unforgettable section of the *Supplément*. In this connection, however, I see two general conclusions. The first concerns the fact that the text of the *Paradoxe* does not present a single, settled argument, since other positions also emerge in the speech of both dialogists. A number of these stages, divergencies and compromises have been noted in the preceding discussion. But if one were to scrutinise the text in even greater detail than has been done in the present chapter, one might discover a whole spectrum of positions that crop up randomly and in passing as the debate proceeds. No doubt one's primary impression is of a single position being argued to the disadvantage of objections against it, but the full reality of the details of the text – as the debate transforms itself and enters new stages, as the debaters jockey for position or explore ideas – might rather suggest a tendency to reveal all aspects of the subject, something like a plenum, composed of every imaginable position, and this tendency towards 'encyclopedic' completeness might be taken as one side of the 'wisdom' of the text.

But at the same time, in so far as one ignores this detail and simply sticks to the most frequent arguments, one discovers not only that the text came into being as a contrariety which denies the main position of the *Entretiens sur Le Fils naturel*, but that as the paradox proceeds, the dramatic interest lies in watching the force and energy of the original argument accumulate to such a degree that it reverses into its opposite. This phenomenon may serve as a reminder of how easily the main thrust of this work might have been totally otherwise, so easily – the text is so saturated with contrariety – that ideas can turn from black to white without anyone, least of all the author, noticing the difference.

5. The landscape demythologised: from Poussin's serpents to Fénelon's 'shades' and Diderot's ghost

I

'NOUS avons eu, s'il est permis de s'exprimer ainsi, des contemporains sous le siècle de Louis XIV.' So Diderot proclaimed in one of his more resounding statements in the *Encyclopédie*,[1] the 'nous' in question being of course persons like him who favoured 'l'esprit philosophique'. As for his alleged seventeenth-century contemporaries, they were thinkers like Bayle (for at least part of his work), Perrault and Fontenelle, whose ideas, originally enunciated during the reign of the Sun King, appeared in retrospect like milestones on the path to Enlightenment. 'Des hommes rares qui ont devancé leur siècle', Diderot called them; today we say 'precursors', even though most of them never foresaw the uses to which their ideas would be put, not to mention the undreamed-of social and political contexts that would surround them. Yet, despite the anachronisms, it is one of the more seductive myths of the Age of Reason that theirs was a stage towards which civilisation, or at least persons of good will, had been striving for many years, as if the triumph of their ideas had behind it the forces of history and the desires of humankind.

No seventeenth-century French artist could appear less relevant to Diderot's ringing pronouncement than Nicolas Poussin. He was certainly not a precursor of Enlightenment in Diderot's sense.[2] Culturally conformist, Poussin's art – ostensibly at least – belonged with no frictions at all to its own era. His usual inspiration was either Catholic or classical, his style being admired by his contemporaries for its orthodoxy and its exceptional learning. It might even

---

1. Art. 'Encyclopédie', *Encyclopédie*, v.636B; reprinted in DPV, vii.184-85.
2. Poussin specialists are by no means in agreement over whether this artist may have been either a secret freethinker or a subtle propagandist for the Jesuits – among other possibilities. However important or intriguing in other contexts, such problems are irrelevant to the present discussion, which is only concerned with Poussin's reputation for orthodoxy among the Church prelates and high born persons who commissioned and bought his paintings, and especially with the generally non-controversial nature of the paintings that Diderot himself singled out for praise in his writing. The case for connections with free thought has been argued recently by Sheila McTighe, 'Nicholas Poussin's representations of storms and *libertinage* in the mid-seventeenth century', *Word and image* 4 (1989), p.333-61. A brief résumé of various scholarly views of these matters is in Alain Mérot, *Nicolas Poussin* (New York 1990), p.13-15.

seem an anomaly that Diderot, progressive and socially engaged as he was, could have praised such a conservative artist with so much fervour. Not only did Diderot write approvingly of several of Poussin's diverse styles, but among seventeenth-century French painters, Poussin occupied a place that was unique in his esteem.[3] In Diderot's *Salons* Poussin functions as a touchstone by which to judge other painters – usually unfavourably,[4] for in Diderot's mind the excellence of Poussin's art represented a sort of absolute, the mere mention of his name being enough to condemn virtually any other artist to a status of inferiority.

Though Diderot may not have been acquainted with it, Poussin's painting entitled *Paysage avec Orphée et Eurydice* (1650),[5] will be the starting point for the present discussion (Figure 3). In concentrated form this painting typifies one significant aspect of Poussin's art and does so in a way that will serve usefully as a point of contrast later on. For the rest, it is exceptionally beautiful, even for Poussin, and in the present context it is notable for the particular way in which it is informed by myth and classical antiquity.

However harmonious and unified the effect of the whole painting may appear, the composition actually divides in two: on the right of the canvas one discovers Orpheus with his lyre, eyes raised to heaven, entirely engrossed in his art as he sings to the enraptured listeners before him. All is serene in this half of the picture; even the insouciant bathers disporting themselves in the background subtly reinforce the general impression of tranquillity. Closer to the viewer and caught by the rays of the setting sun, the intensity of Orpheus's performance makes time seem to stand still for his portion of the universe, in a moment that should last for ever. In contrast, the instant one moves to the left, the ambiance changes entirely. All sense of tranquillity vanishes, while, against a sinister backdrop of smoky plumes rising skyward from the Castel Sant'Angelo, the scene is invaded by fear and danger. Just beyond the central figure who blocks Orpheus's view, Eurydice, invisible to Orpheus, has already had her fatal encounter with the snake, still lurking in the grass near at hand. As we know from the myth, mere moments later the poison of its bite will cost Eurydice her life. As the artist depicts the scene, she is recoiling in terror, her flowers – eternal symbols of the fragility of existence – having dropped

3. According to Jean Seznec, Poussin's *Testament d'Eudamidas* was for Diderot the summit of 'la peinture d'histoire' (*Salons*, ed. Seznec, i.21).

4. See for example Diderot's devastating comparison of Poussin's *Esther évanouie devant Assuérus* with the recent version of the theme by Restout (*Salons*, i.200-201).

5. Now in the Louvre. Illustrated in colour with copious bibliography in Pierre Rosenberg and Louis-Antoine Prat (eds), *Nicolas Poussin, 1594-1665*, catalogue of the exhibition held at the Grand Palais, September 1994–January 1995, (Paris 1995), p.409.

Figure 3. Nicolas Poussin, *Paysage avec Orphée et Eurydice*

from her hand; she may even have screamed, since the startled fisherman on the bank has turned round as if prompted by some sudden commotion.[6] In other words the moment the painter has chosen is a sharply defined tipping point, the very instant of crisis in which the bliss of the celebrated couple suddenly takes the downward turn towards catastrophe. By the same token, this lovely landscape, still gilded by the slanting rays of the late afternoon sun, is at that very moment being transfigured into a scene of horror and grief. The viewer realises too that the deep shadows across the foreground, lengthening and rising, and which even now slant across the lower part of Orpheus's form, are destined to engulf everything, merging finally in a symbolic instant with the darkness of death.

For present purposes, only one, rather simple point matters, namely to note how much one's understanding of this painting depends on prior knowledge of the myth, which is to say, on the ability to recognise the moment depicted as growing out of a known mythological past, a past that is fully remembered even though not depicted, and giving onto a future that should be remembered still more vividly, though not depicted either. For in fact the tragic outcome of the scene, the great drama of the death of Eurydice, has deliberately been withheld from sight, sensed only as an implication, as something that will take place around the corner. And this withholding suggests in turn an aesthetic that allows unseen events to play just as potent a role as the visible ones – because of the all-powerful functioning of the myth. This is the reason why the painter makes no attempt to magnify or place special emphasis on the frightening aspect of the snake.[7] This reptile appears to be normal-sized, nor is it particularly noticeable (not nearly so noticeable, for example, as the brilliant scarlet of Orpheus's cloak). On the other hand, the painter is counting on the viewer's imagination to dramatise the implications of the scene and to supply an awesome awareness of the serpent's terrifyingly lethal potential and of the catastrophe to come, because that is the tragic truth the myth inscribes.

This painting being entirely typical of Poussin's art, and in fact representing his preferred genre, it is evident how much the artist was at home with an aesthetic that depended on the viewer's own store of knowledge, and on implications which had to be deciphered before the drama could be understood. But what would happen, one might wonder, if Poussin decided to change tactics completely and rid his canvas of myth and classical antiquity? What if he invented a composition that told a story on its own terms without demanding

---

6. See the illustrated detail in Rosenberg and Prat, *Poussin*, p.411.

7. Cf. Malcolm Bull, 'Poussin's snakes', in *Cézanne and Poussin*, ed. Richard Kendall (Sheffield 1993), p.41.

Figure 4. Nicolas Poussin, *Paysage avec un homme tué par un serpent* (painting)

the viewer create the drama for himself by remembering what happened before, and imagining what happened next – a scene without a past, and without an undepicted future? Would the painter of the *Paysage avec Orphée et Eurydice* have even been capable of such a liberating gesture?

One answer is Poussin's *Paysage avec un homme tué par un serpent* (1648) (Figure 4),[8] a picture at least as dramatic as the other landscape (dating roughly from the same period), and containing a number of similar elements, but which simply dispenses with myth and antiquity in order to stand entirely on its own.[9] No prior information is required, nothing is going to take place out of sight in the imagination, everything happens before the eye in this painting, which is designed to be self-explanatory – starting with the snake. Even if one had never been told of the potentially lethal danger of reptiles, this enormous one with its monstrous coils still wrapped around the cadaver of the man it has just killed would bring home the truth instantly, as clear as day. Whereas Poussin's paintings in the classical style invariably feature recognisable people with names and known histories, this victim, and everyone else in the painting, is anonymous – they are nobody. Nor has the artist suggested any preliminaries or preparations that led to the catastrophe: it comes out of the blue. Moreover, it has just occurred – the snake being still coiled around the victim, and this extreme recentness joined with the lack of identities means that the past has been made virtually a blank, almost completely abolished. In a daring stroke, Poussin has reversed the traditional classical procedure and turned it backwards. Instead of creating a scene whose strength derives from its continuity with a known past, he has created a painting whose drama derives, first, from a violence that is unprepared and unexpected, and which, second, sets up *aftermaths* that spin out from the main event, resonating across the central figures of the canvas in shock waves. Contrary to the traditions of mythology, the only aspect that matters is a very intense and dangerous present and its immediate consequences. The first words of the legend beneath the engraved version of the painting catches this point perfectly: 'Divers effets d'horreur et de crainte sont ici exprimés.'

In Poussin's œuvre, pictures without myths (either religious or classical) are

8. Now, in the National Gallery, London. Illustrated in colour and with bibliography in Rosenberg and Prat, *Poussin*, p.406-408. See also Mérot's commentary, *Poussin*, p.151-53.

9. See the genial interpretation of this painting by Louis Marin, 'La description de l'image: à propos d'un paysage de Poussin', *Communications* 15 (1970), p.186f. As the title of the article indicates, Marin focused mainly on the possibilities of 'reading' the painting as text, a point of view which coincides only peripherally with my own. Thus, for example, though it is clear that Marin was aware of the absence of mythology in the painting, the point was of no particular interest to him in the framework of textuality. His article usefully includes in its appendix (p.207-209) the relevant texts from Fénelon's *Dialogue des morts* and Félibien's *Entretiens*.

a rarity: excluding the self-portraits, they number less than a dozen in all.[10] Thus it is abundantly clear that Poussin normally preferred to draw on historical and mythological sources, and to work within the most esteemed of the genres, *peinture d'histoire*. And yet, even though this landscape does without the prestige of myth and is innocent of antiquity, it may be counted among the most 'sublime' scenes Poussin ever painted. This is not my inference; it is Diderot's, who went out of his way to describe and comment upon the engraving of Poussin's canvas in the great *Salon de 1767*.[11] Nor was Diderot the only discriminating and adventuresome writer of the *ancien régime* to select this landscape for special praise among Poussin's achievements. Earlier, towards the end of the seventeenth century, the painted version had also been held up for particular admiration by Fénelon, who in fact used it as a test case to prove that French art could hold its own against the Italians. Since this mythless landscape exerted such a fascination and appeal for both of these enlightened minds, the ensuing analysis will explore their comments in some detail.

II

In the second of two *Dialogues des morts* that concern art, Fénelon imagines a conversation in the Champs Elysées between two 'shades' who are Poussin and Leonardo da Vinci.[12] Leonardo is supposed to be irritated by all the attention the French artist has been receiving, and at the beginning of the dialogue the Italian makes no bones about estimating Poussin overrated. Leonardo allegedly has not seen any of Poussin's paintings, and so, as a rebuttal of his prejudices, Poussin agrees to 'put before his eyes' the whole 'ordonnance' of one of them, so that Leonardo will be able to judge for himself (p.433). By 'put before his eyes' Poussin does not mean that he will show the painting itself, or make sketches of it, but that he will delineate a verbal description so lifelike that the words can literally stand in for the object they describe. This assumption that words were, as imitations, entirely adequate vehicles for the expression of the things they designated is typical of the Classical period, as Foucault[13] and others have pointed out. Furthermore, putting a painting into

10. See the classification by Merlot, *Poussin*, p.295-96.
11. Seznec edition, iii.267; DPV, xvi.399. Because the generally (although not always) superior text of the autograph was not accessible to Seznec, the page numbers in my text refer to the DPV edition, vol.xvi, which uses the autograph as its basis.
12. I use the text of the Pléiade edition, ed. Jacques Le Brun (Paris 1983), i.432-36, sect.LIII. The presumed date of the text is *c*.1685.
13. See *Les Mots et les choses* (Paris 1966), p.14.

words as *descriptio* or *ekphrasis* was a device with a venerable past and very familiar usage in Fénelon's time. In view of Fénelon's vivid and colourful style, and especially the emphasis he placed on action, another relevant precedent for this procedure would be the *récit* of Classical tragedy, where the death of the hero, banished by tradition from the stage itself, is retold in words so graphic that the audience can actually experience the scene in the imagination.[14] Poussin–Fénelon will do the same in his treatment of the ordonnance. Fénelon's device also fits particularly well with eighteenth-century aesthetics because it is not an imaginary scene but a painting that is being painted in words, thus implying the conversion of one art of imitation into another, via a process of synaesthesia.

As Poussin proceeds with the description, he only occasionally reminds Leonardo that he is referring to a painted canvas. Most of the time he is pleased to speak of the scene as if it were happening then and there to real people. Thus the description is not merely a documentation of various aspects of the canvas, as in literary *ekphrasis*, or as it sometimes was in Félibien's sort of art criticism, but amounts to a replaying of the action itself. One need hardly mention that this strategy also anticipates Diderot, who continually sought not only to evoke absent paintings so intensely they would resonate as presences for his readers, but to go beyond painting, as if the scene had slipped into reality, even as the characters had sprung to life. This sort of verbal *trompe-l'œil* attains its wittiest and most consummate extreme in Diderot's great 'Promenade Vernet' of the *Salon de 1767*, a text to which we will later return.

As Poussin sets about describing the painting (p.433), Leonardo is first asked to imagine a rock gushing with water from a spring, pure and clear, bubbling as it falls before going off across the landscape. Actually this rock and the spring are not the first objects that one notices in the real painting; one perceives first the grandiose landscape as a whole, and/or the commanding central figures.[15] Even though visually less significant, however, the rock and spring claim a special importance in terms of the 'story' the picture tells, and,

14. See Rex, *The Attraction of the contrary*, p.172-83.

15. I follow the standard theory of composition in the Classical period, according to which paintings were divided into primary and secondary areas. Thus, for example, Gérard de Lairesse distinguishes between the '*principal Figures* conspicuous and elevated upon the fore Ground' and the 'less objects' that must be 'somewhat lower', as are, in the present case, the bubbling stream, the serpent and its victim: see his *The Art of painting* (English translation 1738), quoted in Lawrence Sterne, *Life and opinions of Tristram Shandy*, ed. Melvyn New *et al.* (Gainesville, Fla. 1978-1984), iii.62. My point is that for reasons of narrative Fénelon's description momentarily ignores the inferior placement of the serpent and victim. I refer later to the dramatic reasons why Poussin deliberately arranged his composition in this manner.

traditionalist that he is, Fénelon gives first priority to the narrative, which means that before all else one will understand the plot of the dramatic situation and the reasons for the action supposedly occurring (Diderot will have other priorities). The 'story' is quickly told: a man had come to draw water from a spring where he had been seized by an enormous serpent, which had coiled itself around him, pinning down his arms and legs, crushing his body, stifling his breath, poisoning him with its venom. Poussin–Fénelon notes that the man is already dead, the serpent remaining coiled around his outstretched body, his limbs now heavy and stiff, his flesh livid, and the expression of his face still bespeaking the ghastliness of his end (p.434). At this point Leonardo interjects (presumably with some sarcasm) that unless Poussin adds something new, the picture is going to be 'bien triste'. But Poussin is undeterred, even promising a second 'objet' which will actually augment the sadness.

Again following the narrative order, Fénelon now turns to the most prominent figures. The man on the right had been running, but seeing the ghastly sight has been stopped motionless in his tracks. Fénelon notes that one foot is still raised in the air; one arm is uplifted, while the other falls downward; both hands are open, marking his surprise and horror. At this point in the dialogue Leonardo starts to soften, conceding that this second 'objet', though sad, nevertheless animates the scene and brings to it the kind of pleasure spectators felt watching those ancient tragedies in which everything inspired terror and pity. This is a challengingly dense and elliptical part of the text, usually skipped over by commentators: 'Ce second objet, quoique triste, ne laisse pas d'animer le tableau, et de faire un certain plaisir semblable à ceux que goûtaient les spectateurs de ces anciennes tragédies où tout inspirait la terreur et la pitié' (p.434).

One might well wonder how this can be so: how un-classical elements can combine so as to produce a classical effect. Fénelon does not bother to clarify his point, as if it should already be obvious – which it is far from being today. Perhaps the explanation lies partly in the intensity of the emotion of terror (no doubt pity as well) expressed by the second 'objet', but since Fénelon insists particularly on the connection with ancient *spectacles*, the key may also lie in the direction of theatricality. For the man with the raised foot is himself a spectator of the fearsome (and no doubt pitiable) central event, and thus he embodies perfectly an emotion with which viewers of the painting – spectators also – can empathise, although at one remove. I suspect this is the point: through a distancing which makes the reaction to the serpent and victim *someone else's fear*, the pain of the picture is converted into the viewer's pleasure, even as it had been, in the tragedies of antiquity, by purgation through pity and terror. The emotional effect remains equivalent.

Poussin–Fénelon now turns to the third figure (p.434), the woman at the centre of the painting, who, in her alarm, has dropped whatever she was carrying and raised both arms in the air and seems to be crying out, screaming.[16] Because of her situation on the terrain she cannot see the serpent and victim, so it is solely the terror of the man that inspires her own reaction, as a *contrecoup*. But psychologically the main interest for Fénelon in this figure is the painter's insight in rendering the reaction of the woman who has not actually seen the cadaver, making it still more obvious and emotional than the reaction of the man who has. Poussin–Fénelon entirely approves, pointing out that these two fears are depicted in the very way painful emotions truly are: the greatest are silent, the least are loudest in complaint. Following seventeenth-century gender conceptions, he notes besides that women are wont to give vent to their emotions in this way, holding nothing back, displaying the whole extent of their alarm. Poussin–Fénelon asks Leonardo to agree that these different degrees of fear and surprise 'font une espèce de jeu qui touche et plaît'. Leonardo, won over, concurs, but goes on to wonder about the nature of this depiction. Is it 'une histoire'? He notes that it is unfamiliar to him. So then it must be, as he deftly puts it, 'un caprice' – a conclusion which Poussin–Fénelon immediately confirms: 'C'est un caprice' (p.434).

Since the two terms, 'histoire' and 'caprice', are viewed as alternatives, and probably as opposites, in this passage, and 'histoire' is given as something which Leonardo would have known, one may assume that this term is taken with the usual seventeenth-century implications of *peinture d'histoire*, i.e. the broad category extending from religion, mythology and ancient history down to modern history, and including stories taken from familiar literary works. In other words, 'histoire' can include pure fictions, but, as Leonardo's reaction suggests, these are supposed to belong already to the public domain.

A 'caprice' on the other hand designates a subject that is not public knowledge, whose plot or action is not given in advance by history, literature or mythology. In the seventeenth century, the term often had overtones of frivolousness or unruliness, even as it does today. It also could have a more serious meaning, and in Fénelon's text the word is devoid of any comic or trivial overtones; on the contrary Fénelon finds authentic tragedy in Poussin's caprice, whose tonality for the rest might seem closer to the agonies of Goya than it does to the whimsies of Callot. But the main point of the word here

---

16. Noting that both Fénelon and Félibien in his *Entretiens* describe the elements of this painting in the same order, Thomas Puttfarken, *Roger de Piles' theory of art* (New Haven 1985), suggests that 'the sequence of the snake with the dead body, the fleeing man, and the surprised woman is as irreversible as the sequence of subject-verb-object in the French language' (p.15).

seems to be that this scene, not given by literature, legend or history, and entirely free from the past, is the pure invention of the artist: the snake-encoiled cadaver was his gratuitous creation, as were the improvised aftershocks and all the rest of the landscape as well. At the same time, however, the form of the painting is in no sense incoherent. On the contrary, this scene impresses the viewer as having the deepest and most compelling sense of unity, thanks in part to the masterful use of perspective and symmetry, and also to the harmonious blendings and juxtapositions of colour. Perhaps these are some of the reasons why Poussin–Fénelon went on to defend the legitimacy of the 'caprice' as a genre, provided it be what he terms 'réglé'. The other requirement he stipulates is that a 'caprice' 'ne s'écarte en rien de la vraie nature' (p.434), implying the necessity of cleaving to psychological truth, in addition to giving a faithful physical rendering of the action or scene.

There is something of a cutting, polemical edge to Fénelon's approval of a 'caprice', for this genre had no academic standing at this time, at least not in France: it is not given a rank on the famous and influential list of genres approved by Le Brun and other academics, for example. Nor is this the only instance of Fénelon taking a rather forward-looking stance in this text, as will be seen. In any case, the emergence of the critical word 'caprice' marks a breaking point in Poussin–Fénelon's description: henceforth the character of the landscape will alter completely. No longer will objects of horror and fear fill his description, but objects of beauty, enchantment and peaceful amusement. He points to a deliciously cool grove of trees that make one yearn to take shelter in their midst on a hot summer's day; elsewhere he discovers still, limpid waters reflecting the beauty of the scene; on one side there is the dark green of the trees, on the other the deep azure of the serene sky. Young people are swimming and playing games in the water; fishermen row or pull on their nets; on the banks people intently play games or go strolling on the fresh grass. In Fénelon's conception this whole background of the landscape is designed not merely as a contrast (though it is that), but as a refreshment, even a compensation, that restores the eye and makes up for the terrible events in the foreground: 'Dans cette eau se présentent divers objets qui amusent la vue, pour la délasser de tout ce qu'elle a vu d'affreux. Sur le devant du tableau, les figures sont toutes tragiques. Mais dans ce fond, tout est paisible, doux et riant' (p.434).

As a conclusion, Poussin-Fénelon concedes that this picture is less 'savant' than Poussin's much-admired painting of the landscape with the dead body of Phocion, which was discussed in the previous *Dialogue des morts* (p.426-32), a depiction that was entirely *à l'antique* and designed to be as historically accurate as possible. Poussin–Fénelon admits that the buildings of the present painting with the serpent manifest less 'science d'architecture' (p.436). Most significant, he also concedes that the picture with the serpent displays 'aucune connaissance de l'antiquité'. But as compensation he puts forward, first, the understanding of the passions it displays ('la science d'exprimer les passions y est assez grande') and, second, the grace and tenderness of the landscape, to which the scene with the body of Phocion cannot compare ('tout ce paysage a des grâces et une tendresse que l'autre n'égale point') (p.436).

One might wonder why literary scholars have so often downplayed this text:[17] it represents one of those rare, privileged moments in seventeenth-century art criticism when a wise and informed writer, with infinite subtlety and that special understanding of motives which only a near-contemporary can have, says all he feels there is to say about a great painting. Fénelon spoke Poussin's language in a way later critics never could, because, even at a few years' remove, he still breathed something of the air the artist had breathed. Naturally, he is particularly expert in handling the elements one now associates with Classicism: his sense of the harmony achieved out of discordant elements, and also the logic in his conception of the painting's 'ordonnance', starting with the terrible serpent and its victim, going next to those caught up in the terror, and finally to the healing tranquillity of the surrounding landscape.

At the same time, few texts of this period announce so clearly the shift to the values that would characterise the aesthetics of the eighteenth century, when the venerable criterion of antiquity would be replaced by simple acceptance of the power of the dramatic experience. Fénelon is clearly open to the novelty

17. See the notes to the Pléiade edition. Even the recent study by art historians Elisabeth Cropper and Charles Dempsey, *Nicolas Poussin: friendship and the love of painting* (Princeton, N.J. 1996), p.289-94 – though noting that Fénelon 'sheds sharp light' on Poussin's conception – tends to override, and even undermine, his ideas. Fénelon's concept of 'caprice' and his emphasis on immediate reactions are overridden by allusions of classical 'sources': first, two ancient funeral urns showing, in relief, a man and a woman fleeing in terror from another man encoiled by a serpent and falling head-downwards; second, a simile from Homer describing a man's encounter with a snake, which twice states that the man 'steps back' or 'draws back and away' from the sight of the reptile. Clearly the funeral urns set a precedent for a scene of terror-inspiring death-by-serpent. It is not certain, however, that 'the central narrative episode' in Poussin actually 'derives' from this 'ancient source' (p.291), for the differences from Poussin are numerous and significant. But regardless of whether these urns may have distantly figured in the background of Poussin's inspiration, in any case, if only because the dress of the participants in Poussin's painting does not conform to his idea of Greek or Roman, and because the surrounding towns of the landscape do not display any classical traits – not a single tell-tale column or block of marble – one may assume that Poussin did not intend that the viewer relate his painting to classical mythology. Perhaps one may also conclude that concern with classical 'sources' is beside the point for this particular scene whose drama, as Fénelon knew, is directed towards the present, and essentially psychological. Nor, finally, do the movements of the man in Homer suggest the riveted posture of Poussin's frozen man; who, unlike Homer's, had pointedly been running.

Figure 5. Nicolas Poussin, *Paysage avec un homme tué par un serpent* (engraving)

of this 'caprice', even giving it a slight edge over Poussin's other painting that was wholly *à l'antique*. Nor does one feel any sort of clash or disparity between the old and the new in Fénelon's dialogue: never losing his poise or seeming to depart from a harmoniously Classical outlook, Fénelon effortlessly encompasses both sides at once.

III

After finding so much to praise in this text, dare one also mention that despite all its merits, when one places it beside Diderot's account of the same painting, in the *Salon de 1767*, it begins to look somewhat lacking in energy, slightly limp? No one would deny, to be sure, that Fénelon more than holds his own in his discussion of psychology, in the accuracy of his description, and also in his own way of conveying the beauty of the object he describes. Yet when it comes to imagining the drama and excitement of a work of art, one would be hard put to find other eighteenth-century French critics who compare to Diderot (Figure 5).

A single phrase alerts one that something dire and terrifying is occurring in this country landscape: 'C'est celui-là [Poussin] qui sait aussi, quand il lui plaît, vous jeter du milieu d'une scène champêtre, l'épouvante et l'effroi' (p.399). After that, Diderot's point of departure for describing the scene begins at the other end of the world, at the farthest depths of the painting, a place where the cause of the peril is nowhere to be seen, but where spaces are immense and the landscape noble and majestic, and from which one must traverse a multitude of separate planes before reaching the level of the viewer. Paradoxically, because of the initial warning of danger ahead, even though objects are described as peaceful and unsuspecting the scene takes on a distinctly ominous tinge: those resting travellers, talking together as they sit or sprawl, are, Diderot tells us, in 'perfect security', but it is precisely their unsuspecting innocence that gives them an air of vulnerability. And this is only the first stage: the sense of fear rises to another level as the description passes to the woman in the centre: she has been washing her clothes, Diderot says, but now she stops and listens, the cessation of her washing being given in the rhythm of Diderot's sentence. The reader stops too, listening with her ('Elle écoute'). Nor does the next figure give any reassurance – the man on the left, now getting up from his squatting position, and looking anxiously to the front and left. Again the rhythm stops as we learn, simply, that he has heard ('Il a entendu'). Next, on the far right, towards the front, one sees a man standing upright, frozen with terror, about to flee. Again the rhythm stops. 'Il a vu.' As one sees when all the pieces are put together in sequence, it is the pauses which build the sense of dread (p.399).

Sur un autre plan, [...] c'est une femme qui lave son linge dans une rivière. Elle écoute. Sur un troisième plan, plus vers la gauche, et tout à fait sur le devant, c'était un homme accroupi, mais il commence à se lever, et à jeter ses regards mêlés d'inquiétude et de curiosité, vers la gauche et le devant de la scène. Il a entendu. Tout à fait à droite, et sur le devant, c'est un homme debout, transi de terreur et prêt à s'enfuir. Il a vu.

The passage illustrates perfectly the idea of the sublime as Burke defined it: terror, Burke's single most indispensable element, pervades this landscape and, as both Burke and Diderot realised, no danger is more terrifying than one whose menace remains felt rather than seen, whose cause is kept in the dark.[18] The original readers of Diderot's account, having no illustrations to show the scene, were entirely dependent on Diderot's prose to tell them what was in the picture. Naturally, with his keen dramatic sense, Diderot has been deliberately keeping the serpent and the cadaver out of sight in his text, capitalising on his awareness of the reader's blindness, delaying the suspense, asking questions to increase the sense of dread while making the reader wait almost indecently long for the revelation of the serpent. When the moment comes, the delays give it the fullest impact (p.399-400):

Mais qu'est-ce qui lui imprime cette terreur? Qu'a-t-il vu? Il a vu tout à fait sur la gauche et sur le devant, une femme [*sic*] étendue à terre, enlacée d'un énorme serpent qui la dévore et qui l'entraîne au fond des eaux où ses bras, sa tête et sa chevelure pendent déjà.

A woman! And so, after all the suspense, Diderot comes up with the wrong answer! The cadaver is a man, of course. No doubt various circumstances might explain the mistake: the gender of the victim shown in the engraved version (the one Diderot knew) is conceivably just slightly more ambiguous than in the painting; the famous precedent of Eurydice's snakebite may have dimly influenced the choice of sex; perhaps men generally tend to think of victims as being female. But for present purposes the usefulness of Diderot's error is that it warns the reader not to take anything Diderot states about this picture without question. It is not merely the victim's sex that Diderot got wrong: the hair does not dangle in the water the way he says it does, nor is the victim being devoured; nor is his demise an ongoing process: in Poussin's image the victim's death is already an accomplished fact.

And these mistakes are just the start: backing up, the frozen man has already

18. See Burke, *A philosophical enquiry into the origin of our ideas of the sublime and the beautiful*, ed. James Burke (South Bend, Ind. 1958), esp. p.39-40, p.64-70.

been running, rather than preparing to run, as Diderot claims; the woman at the centre, the one Diderot describes as pausing in her washing in order to listen, is not washing anything – she is in the middle of a road – and far from pausing to listen, is screaming open-mouthed, with violent gesticulations. Diderot's earlier characterisation of one group as lolling travellers is also a fantasy: none of the groups depicted look as if they have been 'en voyage'. But the rising man on the left, the one described as looking about him with worried glances, is Diderot's most spectacular error: he does not exist anywhere. He is Diderot's own creation, an imaginary filling-in of a blank in the engraving for his readers, a verbal ghost.

Why on earth did Diderot invent him? The simple answer is that this personage serves to shore up Diderot's otherwise slightly shaky concept of an inexorable crescendo in the levels of fear, bolstering the sense of relentless increase in degrees of intensity given in Diderot's account, but which in Poussin's engraving does not work in straight lines in the way that Diderot is claiming. Fénelon's account is a far surer guide to the complexities of the action. But at least on paper, Diderot's ghostly rising man keeps the tension up and the drama abuilding, so that it will surge dynamically without a break, never letting up anywhere, to the final revelation and beyond. Even the climax, the sight of the serpent and its victim, is not allowed to be a terminal event, but one whose horror, even as the viewer looks on, is being created, going onward, and getting worse.

Since these modifications all fit the same pattern, it is entirely possible that the desire to increase the dramatic tension is the whole explanation for Diderot's revisions, as if drama in this sense were the only issue at stake. But the possibility also exists of another, extra dividend hidden in this procedure, in terms of the original story implied in the picture. For, just as Fénelon stated, before there was a victim, there was simply a person who had come to get water at the spring. And, if one returns to that beginning, one easily, naturally, even logically imagines that this person, whoever he or she was, began by being unsuspecting, even as Diderot said those lolling travellers were; then paused to listen, just like the washerwoman; then anxiously glanced around, getting ready to flee, like the ghostly rising man; and finally, stood frozen in terror at the sight of the monster. In a word, these fearsome stages which Diderot went out of his way to invent and describe correspond perfectly to those that the victim would have experienced as he met death in that vast landscape, so that Diderot's descriptions of them constitute – in effect – a frame-by-frame replay of the drama, the aftermath shockwaves standing in for the preliminaries. Conceived in this way, their effect is to endow the sudden, out of the blue, coming-from-nowhere death by serpent with something of a past, in fact, in a reversed mirror, with something of the kind of preparation for the catastrophe one associates with Classical art.

Though Diderot got many of the details wrong and simplified the dynamics of the situation, the drama he imagined is aesthetically, in one important way at least, exactly right: when viewing the picture for the first time, Diderot's ordering, which starts with the distant landscape and then follows the figures closer and closer, until at last one sees the catastrophe, is, in its broad lines, a valid one. Indeed, after the landscape, one perceives the figures in the grip of terror, *before* one sees the serpent. Poussin himself determined this order, aesthetically speaking, by putting the grandly gesticulating washerwoman in the dead centre so as to catch the eye inescapably, and in addition he arranged her look and gestures to be directed towards the frozen man, as if to force the viewer to see him, before following his gaze to the serpent, which is not placed in the centre, or even elevated for immediate visibility, but situated off-center to the left, and down beneath the most prominent elements of the landscape. This is to say that Diderot's concept of the horror of the serpent being, not a given factor that is present from the start, but a discovery one makes after being conditioned by a journey through the figures of terror, is genially right, and it captures masterfully one essential aspect of the dramatic tension of the picture.

This interpretation differs totally from Fénelon's account, of course. As a Classicist, Fénelon was not interested in creating tensions, but in resolving them. Naturally, he began with the stream and the snake, thus eliminating from the start any possibility of suspense, and he offset the stark, terrifying drama of the foreground by emotions of peaceful consolation in the background. There may even be the suggestion of a happy ending in the 'paisible, doux et riant' of the final description. In contrast, Diderot goes in the opposite direction, and he proceeds further, increasing the drama to the point of involving the viewer, too, in its horror. The images function performatively. Diderot is explicit on this point: 'Depuis les voyageurs tranquilles du fond, jusqu'à ce dernier spectacle de terreur, quelle étendue immense, et sur cette étendue, quelle suite de passions différentes, jusqu'à vous qui êtes le dernier objet, le terme de la composition' (p.400).

Diderot's previous description had marked off the direction of his interpretation so clearly – going from the tranquillity of the travellers, through the 'suite de passions différentes', to the terror of the serpent's victim, and finally reaching the viewer outside the painting – everything was put so perfectly in place that, given his perverse penchant for contrariety, conditions were now ripe for Diderot to turn the situation around and go backwards. And in fact, after an interlude of berating the landscapist Loutherbourg[19] for being boringly bucolic ('Des pâtres et des animaux, et toujours des pâtres et des animaux', p.398), instead of thrillingly sublime like Poussin, a contrary direction emerges in Diderot's text, which reverses the old order: contradicting all previous indications, the danger is now said to increase proportionately as one draws *away* from it. No longer is the man so close to the serpent that he freezes in horror the one who provides the most dramatic image of danger, but those who are most remote, because they are least suspecting. Though all the elements of this enormous landscape are still seen as connected to the terror, the persons on the outer fringes, according to this new perspective, are more in peril than the others (p.400-401):

Tous les incidents du paysage du Poussin sont liés par une idée commune, quoique isolés, distribués sur différents plans et séparés par de grands intervalles. Les plus exposés au péril, ce sont ceux qui en sont les plus éloignés. Ils ne s'en doutent pas. Ils sont tranquilles. Ils sont heureux. Ils s'entretiennent de leur voyage. Hélas, parmi eux, il y a peut-être un époux que sa femme attend avec impatience et qu'elle ne reverra plus; un fils unique que sa mère a perdu de vue depuis longtemps et dont elle soupire en vain le retour; un père qui brûle du désir de rentrer dans sa famille. Et le monstre terrible qui veille dans la contrée perfide dont le charme les a invités au repos, va peut-être tromper toutes ces espérances.

Earlier in the account the rhythm had stopped successively as Diderot considered each figure or group, moving inward towards the left-central serpent's victim. Now the rhythm stops successively as he moves outward, pausing to say to each figure or group simply 'Fuis' or 'Fuyez': first the rising man; then the washerwoman; lastly the resting travellers. Meanwhile one notes in the passage quoted above that Diderot's fantasies about the lethal activities of the serpent have produced a series of imaginary *drames* with a domestic cast: the roles are stereotypes ('un époux', 'sa femme', 'un fils unique', 'sa mère') just as they were in Diderot's discussions of the dramatic sketches of Greuze. Perhaps the references to the doomed enjoyments of the country people on the fringes of the canvas hint also at the theme 'Et in Arcadia ego', already one of Poussin's most famous scenes, which Diderot mentioned earlier in this same *Salon*.[20]

19. It was Loutherbourg who brought this whole discussion of Poussin into being in the first place, since the terrifying sublimity of Poussin is, according to Diderot, a perfect object lesson, exactly the manner of painting that Loutherbourg should imitate to rise above the boredom of his usual landscapes.

20. In fact, Diderot saw these two paintings as a pair of opposites: 'Voyez comme le Poussin est sublime et touchant, lorsque à côté d'une scène champêtre riante, il attache mes yeux sur un tombeau où je lis Et ego in Arcadia. Voyez comme il est terrible, lorsqu'il me montre dans un autre une femme enveloppée d'un serpent qui l'entraîne au fond des eaux' (*Salon de 1767*, DPV, xvi.253).

5. The landscape demythologised

But whether moving in towards the serpent or backing away from it, Diderot's perspective shows a unique awareness of the contrapuntal workings of this landscape, that is, a sense of the extraordinary dynamics created by the violence of one single element. In this case a relatively small part of the picture, not even occupying the exact centre, is so powerfully menacing it sets up a horrific discord with its surroundings, forcing the objects nearest to it to vibrate in terror, and potentially affecting, either directly or by contrast, even the farthest reaches of the canvas. This understanding of the contrapuntal tension of the scene is one of the great insights into the art of Poussin. Fénelon, for all his sensitivity, was blind to this dimension. And although Diderot does not name any other works by Poussin in this connection, he has enunciated the essential drama of a whole species of pictures that Poussin painted repeatedly and with innumerable variations, involving not only snakes in the grass (of which there is a series)[21] but many other concentrated forms of danger or horror as well.[22] Traditionally, scholars – Blunt, Wright, Mérot and Rosenberg are prominent examples[23] – ignore or deliberately underplay such

21. See Bull, 'Poussin's snakes', p.30-50.
22. Among the more dramatic examples are the following. In *The Martyrdom of St Erasmus* we see first the joyously cruel, eager faces and the energetic gestures of the onlooking torturers, plane after plane of them filling most of the tall, narrow canvas; meanwhile a slender intestinal thread leads the eye downward through the crowd to the small slit in the stomach of the saint, outstretched at the bottom of the canvas, and bravely enduring what we at last realise are the agonies of evisceration. In *St John on the Island of Patmos* the saint is seated in utter serenity on the island, a calm intensified by the enormous whiteness, dull brown and darkish green of the ruined landscape all around him; but in his hands we see a pen and the sheets of parchment on which he writes, even now as the viewer beholds him, his cataclysmic vision of fiery apocalypse. The counterpoint in this scene, though enormously important for an understanding of it, is almost invisible on the canvas – just some tiny, illegible marks on the parchment. Thus the tension is given by implication, and the violence must take place in the viewers' own imagination, even as it is doing for the saint. At the other end of the scale, reversing the proportions, is the *Landscape with Pyramus and Thisbe*, in which – amid dark night, stormy, windswept weather with scurrying clouds, dimly lit by lightning flashes, and the disarray of Thisbe discovering the lifeless body of Pyramus lying in a field, while beyond in the background a lion rampages among cattle and shepherds, killing and maiming as if nothing can stop him – violence has taken over almost all the visible elements. Inexplicably, a large pool of water stretches, limpid and without a ripple, in the centre just above the rampaging lion, and remains unaffected by the violence of nature unleashed in the rest of the scene. Critics have wondered why Poussin placed such a glaring inconsistency (not to say natural impossibility) in this prominent position. Given the dynamics of similar limpid bodies of water in other landscapes by Poussin, one possible explanation may be that it was supposed to function as a counterpoint to all the other elements, a contrariety whose self-contained stillness creatively dramatises the unchecked violence of everything else. For the rest, this interpretation in no way contradicts the canny suggestion of Louis Marin that this body of water symbolises the serenity of the artist's eye: see 'La description du tableau et le sublime en peinture: à propos d'un paysage de Poussin et de son sujet', *Communications* 15 (1981), p.61-84.
23. To this list one might add Cropper and Dempsey, *Nicolas Poussin*.

contrapuntal dynamisms so as to avoid upsetting the decorum that they associate with Classicism, or the stoicism that they find in Poussin's philosophy. It is almost as if they were determined not to realise how violent, strange and disturbing an artist Poussin could be. As for Diderot, even though he got details of his interpretation wrong, in his perception both of the terrors of Poussin's landscape and of the contrapuntal quality of Poussin's dynamism his interpretation still leads the way.

IV

Throughout his account, Diderot has been tacitly assuming that this dangerous serpent is to be taken literally, as real. But surely he must also have had some nagging awareness that serpents of such monstrous dimensions grow only in the deepest jungles of the tropics, or better yet, in mythology. Curiously, even during the *ancien régime* some individuals claimed the scene was based on a real incident: the anonymous legend accompanying Baudet's 1701 engraving of the painting told of the belief that 'le Poussin peignit ce tableau à l'occasion d'un accident semblable qui arriva de son temps aux environs de Rome'. In England, the catalogue of the Robert Strange sale of 1773 alleged as the 'source' of the scene a catastrophe occurring in 1641 in the neighbourhood of the ancient city of Terracina, in the kingdom of Naples.[24] In our own century, Anthony Blunt, anxious to lend credence to the theory but unwilling to accept the identification of the city mentioned in the Strange catalogue, moved the locus to the town of Fondi, not too far away and, in Poussin's time, notorious for its summer infestation of snakes both so numerous and so large that the town was largely deserted. Blunt provided a drawing of Fondi attributed to Brueghel and a modern photograph of its *castello*, both of which were alleged to document his hypothesis.[25]

Actually, nothing in either the Brueghel drawing or in the photograph corresponds in any meaningful way to the painting: the raised situation of the town in Poussin, the location of the body of water, the buildings, the location of the trees, everything is different. Furthermore, neither of the two astute connoisseurs of Poussin's century who discussed the painting, Fénelon and Félibien, even paused for a moment to consider the possibility that the serpent

24. Various classical legends have also been scrutinised as possible sources, despite Fénelon's opinion that the scene was a 'caprice': see the proposals of Malcolm Bull, 'Poussin's snakes', p.30-50.

25. The documents on all of these matters are reproduced in Anthony Blunt, *Nicolas Poussin* (New York 1967), i.286-91.

and its victim had been real. Fénelon's term 'caprice' in fact rules that possibility out. Nor did Diderot – who, as will be noted, was in some sense willing to assume the reality of the scene – appeal to such an anecdote. But in any case, it is clear from the picture itself that the enormous serpent and the correspondingly intense aftermaths of the painting have been enlarged beyond reality.

Given Poussin's proclivities and habits of composition, the most likely 'source' for this particular serpent was not anecdotal anyway; it was almost predictable that his main inspiration would come from classical art. A far more probable candidate than the snake infestations of Fondi is, as Professor Dorothy Johnson suggested to me, the most celebrated sculpted reptile to have come down from antiquity, jewel of the papal collection in Rome, where Poussin himself resided, namely, the huge coiling serpent in the statuary group of *The Laocoön*. And in fact the resemblance between the snakes depicted in the two works is immediately apparent. In the sculpture group, no one could mistake the reptile's fearsome coils – the punishment of an immortal god – for current anecdote. The lethal entwinings of Poussin's monster, too, inspired incidentally by mythology, convey something of the same cosmic dimension.

But if – contrary to Diderot's tacit assumptions – the snake was too large to be taken literally as a real threat, and Diderot did not appeal either to anecdote or mythology, or to any of the standard categories that might relegate this painting to a given genre, then – especially for a philosopher committed to the principle that serious art must have a serious purpose, and preferably one that served the good of humanity – Diderot was very much left with the vexed question of what it all meant. His dramatic interpretation needed a plausible *applicatio* to make the scene relevant; it still needed a moral.

Perhaps this unspoken dilemma was the reason why, without warning, Diderot – even as preachers do when cornered by some intractable passage of Scripture – changed tack, and resorted to allegory. Leaving the reader no time for reflection, his discourse now does likewise, scattering into three allegories, that come, pell-mell, as rapid-fire rhetorical questions, each of them suggesting a moral for the scene, even if the serpent turns out to be pure fiction. The first and third proposals interpret the serpent as symbolising the dangerous passions or vices – rather traditional allegories for the snake, and not particularly significant for present purposes. But in between these two, there comes, in a burst, Diderot's most audacious and original proposal. One notes that it is slightly longer, and distinctly more explicit in its application, than the others (p.401):

Est-ce que les habitants des campagnes, au milieu des occupations qui leur sont propres, n'ont pas [...] leurs fléaux, la grêle qui détruit leurs moissons, et qui les désole; l'impôt qui déménage et vend leurs ustensiles, la corvée qui dispose de leurs bestiaux et les emmène; l'indigence et la loi qui les conduisent dans les prisons?

However briefly stated, this allegory changes everything: looking beyond the Burkean sublime and the problem of vice and the passions, it addresses the precariousness of the lives of country people and their vulnerability to dangers that come from without, and over which they have no control; it declares – incontrovertible verity – that the evils of the social system can poison their existences just as profoundly and pervasively as the dread serpent was supposed to do in Poussin's serene landscape. With its references to the consequences of 'l'impôt', 'la corvée' and so on, this allegory makes the scene 'performative' in a very special sense, infusing the picture with social consciousness, in fact social criticism, and tinging it with a discontent that implicates some of the most famous injustices of the *ancien régime*.

Perhaps one should pause to mention at this point that, in so far as objective judgements can be made about Poussin's scene, nothing in it calls for such a social interpretation. With an artist like Brueghel this kind of reading would be entirely appropriate; with Poussin it has nothing to do with the painter's intentions. But precisely because nothing in Poussin's landscape even remotely implies the concerns Diderot gives voice to in this allegory, it seems safe to conclude that this gratuitous mentioning of social abuses is the part of the account in which Diderot himself is most present and engaged, perhaps even the heart of this article, the moment Diderot hoped one would wait for, even as one did for the sight of the serpent.

It goes without saying that, as the whole project of the *Encyclopédie* attests, the kind of social preoccupation reflected in this passage is entirely typical of Diderot,[26] who, as Elisabeth de Fontenay reminds us, had once even gone so far as to write – no doubt with some exaggeration – 'Imposez-moi silence sur la religion et le gouvernement, et je n'ai rien à dire.'[27]

It is also only fair to point out that neither Fénelon nor Poussin could have dreamed of such an interpretation: this conversion of a study of the effects of fear into social commentary is a purely eighteenth-century invention, and, as

---

26. See Jacques Proust, *Diderot et l'Encyclopédie*, ch.11, 'Diderot réformateur', p.449-502. The social view enunciated in the *Salon* passage may also remind one of Rousseau, who in fact had virtually invented the imagery of this kind of statement, particularly in the second part of the *Discours sur l'origine de l'inégalité*, in his denunciation of the beauties of the smiling countryside, what he termed 'des campagnes riantes', as simply masking the sufferings, poverty and enslavement of those who produced the harvests. To be sure, Rousseau's statement is part of a long crescendo of indignation, whereas Diderot's concern in this text glimmers briefly, before merging with the other allegories. One has to be alert to Diderot's social preoccupations not to miss the particular significance of Allegory II for the message of the text.

27. *Diderot ou le matérialisme enchanté* (Paris 1981), p.36.

it occurs, typically Diderot as well. For the duration of this allegorical instant, Diderot is, willy-nilly, reinventing Poussin as a 'contemporain sous le siècle de Louis XIV', a precursor sharing his own social outlook. Alas, one know today that this daring interpretation was the purest wishful thinking on the author's part, a mirage as unreal as the fiction of the ghostly rising man, or the vision of the devoured woman. In sum, this text, with all its inventive dynamisms and conflicting resonances, might be called, using Fénelon's term, Diderot's 'caprice' – a gravely serious one, no doubt, and enlightened to its core.

6. *Le Rêve de d'Alembert: Deus sive materia?*

Preliminary considerations

GIVEN the mysteriously unpredictable nature of dreams, in a literary creation deliberately put forward as a dream sequence such as *Le Rêve de d'Alembert* one should not be surprised to find shifts in perspective, and this trilogy[1] develops some startling ones, of Diderot's own special concoction.[2] The most dramatic instance occurs between the first dialogue and the second, when wide-awake d'Alembert, allegedly Diderot's philosophical opponent, turns as he sleeps into a stand-in for Diderot himself – or at least a proponent of the same philosophy. All opposition to Diderot's theories disappears from the text as d'Alembert, going to bed, undergoes a full-fledged conversion to materialism, an experience that affects not only his dreaming mind, but, almost as though parodying some conversion manual, his heart as well: the new philosophy will add extra zest to d'Alembert's sexual activity, quite graphically described by Mlle de Lespinasse. She too will find herself a convert to materialism, though the process is more erratic and drawn out than for d'Alembert. And whereas d'Alembert's original opposition to Diderot came from metaphysical differ-ences, hers was simply a lack of the philosophical experience needed to draw together the bits and pieces of d'Alembert's dream that she overhears and form a coherent view, so that she could see the wisdom of his folly. Eventually her adeptness at the new materialism will bring perceptions that break fresh ground and lead the discussion towards new dimensions. Her progress is by no means regular, however, and particularly in the early stages she seems ever ready to revert to giddy incomprehension; even later on in the trilogy (p.180, p.202), she will be reproached for indulging in an intellectual timidity and lack of rigour typical of her sex.

The person to make that charge is Bordeu, and he – taking over from

1. Text with introduction and notes by Jean Varloot in DPV, xvii.91-209 (page numbers in the text refer to this edition); the introduction and notes to the edition by Paul Vernière in Diderot, *Œuvres philosophiques* (Paris 1964), p.249-385 have also been extensively used in my discussion, as has the introduction by Jacques Roger to his edition (Paris 1965), p.19-32. On various literary and philosophical works that may have inspired Diderot's creation, see Jean Varloot, 'Le projet "antique" du *Rêve de d'Alembert* de Diderot: légendes antiques et matérialisme au XVIIIe siècle', *Beiträge zur romanischen Philologie* 2 (1963), p.49-61.

2. See the witty discussion by Roger Lewinter, *Diderot ou les mots de l'absence* (Paris 1976), p.159f.

6. 'Le Rêve de d'Alembert': Deus sive materia?

Diderot after the short opening dialogue – is the character who remains consistent, at least during the main dialogue, the 'Rêve' proper. As supposedly the most experienced materialist of the three, and a doctor into the bargain, Bordeu plays the Socrates of these conversations, always asking the pertinent leading questions, and guiding the discussion towards truth. On the other hand, despite some obvious and intriguing parallels, these dialogues do not really fit the traditional 'Socratic' mould, if only because, however well Bordeu–Socrates–Diderot may know the answers, and d'Alembert–Diderot may suggest the questions, the indispensable mover of the action remains Mlle de Lespinasse,[3] and nothing in Plato remotely resembles the part she plays. She runs the show sexually, simply because, a night-time presence by d'Alembert's bedside, she is a woman among men, and also, on a slightly more intellectual plane, because her lack of comprehension of d'Alembert's bits and pieces, or of Bordeu's pronouncements, naturally brings the males into action, animating them to set things right. Furthermore, although Bordeu's role may have been inspired by Socrates, a far greater factor to be reckoned with in this text is Lucretius, and not only because of the well-known influence on Diderot of his anti-superstitious materialism,[4] but above all for the sexuality that informs his universe: Lucretius' entire philosophy was placed under the sign of Venus. Diderot tacitly used the same sign – which is why he made Mlle de Lespinasse the centre of attraction in every sense.[5] And since amid her questions, reversals, surprises and poutings she not only relays the substance of d'Alembert's dream but elicits the multitude of ideas and relationships that spin out the web of Diderot's materialism, the resulting philosophical discussion is in every way tinged with her presence and sexuality – one of the important reasons why Diderot's text is throughout so lively and interesting, whereas the same ideas coming from d'Holbach shrivel in their tedium.[6] For the rest, it need hardly be mentioned that one of the main poetical-philosophical climaxes of the work – d'Alembert's ejaculation – comes about amid thoughts of her, and that, far from being confined to the limits of a doctor–patient rapport, the Bordeu–Lespinasse relationship too is imbued with sexuality and seduction.[7]

3. See the remarks of Christie McDonald in 'Denis Diderot writes *Le Rêve de d'Alembert*', in *A new history of French literature*, ed. Denis Hollier (Cambridge, Mass. 1989), p.507.
4. See Jacques Roger, *Les Sciences de la vie dans la pensée française du XVIIIe siècle* (Paris 1964), p.665-66.
5. Her role seems to me rather more important than it does in the analysis of Aram Vartanian, 'Diderot and the phenomenology of the dream', *Diderot studies* 8 (1966), p.239.
6. For a comparison of the doctrines of the two philosophers see Roger, *Les Sciences de la vie*, p.678-82.
7. This relationship is explored in Rosalina de la Carrera, *Success in circuit lies: Diderot's communicational practice* (Stanford, Calif. 1991), p.156-60.

All the traits discussed so far – shifts of perspective, volatility of character, materialism and sexuality – can also be found in one or more of the other major works by Diderot considered in this study. But there is one trait characterising the present text which makes it unique, perhaps puzzlingly so, namely, the quasi-total *absence* of contrariety in the movement of ideas. Although fictional in its form, and full of fantasy, humour and philosophical speculation, nevertheless the trilogy of *Le Rêve de d'Alembert*, at least in respect to ideas, is entirely free of the backwards gestures, reversals and capsizing into opposites which, in various degrees, characterise Diderot's thought processes in the works previously examined. For once, the strong enunciation of a position is not the sign of an approaching contradiction, nor does Diderot's thinking proceed by denying itself. His thought moves positively as he explains his points, one argument always eventually fitting in with another, in a thoroughly didactic manner. For once, Diderot actually keeps track of his ideas; nor does he change his mind. In fact the power of this work derives very much from its logic, from arguments which impose themselves because they are proven, bolstered by examples, and resolve issues by their own weight. Nor can the cause of this phenomenon in the text be ascribed simply to the consistent materialistic principles which underlie the ideas, for, to give just one example, Diderot's materialism in the *Lettre sur les sourds et muets* did not prevent him from changing his mind on major issues every two or three pages. The point is that in this trilogy the whole configuration of Diderot's thought process straightens out explicitly to form the elements of a system – presented, to be sure, in an order that is more associative than logical. In short, according to all appearances this work is, uniquely among the major creations considered thus far, not contrapuntal, and not contradictory.

For other self-respecting philosophers – Condillac, d'Alembert, even d'Holbach – such an absence of inconsistency would go without saying; it would be a requirement. It may seem a paradox that one needs to point out the rarity, in a self-respecting philosopher such as Diderot, of his refraining from radical contradictions on major issues. But the fact is that even in the first dialogue of the *Rêve* he claims that a person's true opinion is not a conviction from which he or she has never deviated, but simply the one to which he or she returns most frequently, thus opening the possibility of the usual irregularities and changes of assumptions in the rest of the text – an expectation, to be sure, that is completely belied as the work proceeds. The steady course one finds here seems positively 'contre-nature'.

There is a special reason for arguments so exceptionally unvarying, namely that the main counterpoint of this work is situated outside the work proper – somewhat the way Diderot's stern letter to Angélique operated in respect to the *Supplément au Voyage de Bougainville*. But in this case the action of the counterpoint was so awesomely powerful it drew everything in the dialogues into position against it. Only the notion of the Divinity could have had such a compelling effect on Diderot's thinking, which is to say that God is the divine counterpoint against which the action of the dialogues is played. Perhaps 'atheism' or 'materialism' may seem obvious and ready-made terms to describe such a lack of belief. They give no hint, however, of the dynamics of the process that the dialogues enact, a dynamics which comes about because – such is my contention – Diderot's atheism derives backwards (so to speak) from theism[8] as a contrariety, that is, the former is a denial of, and replacement for, the latter.

'L'Entretien entre Diderot et d'Alembert'

God, in the traditional sense, is not spoken of directly in the dialogues. Yet by implication, the traditional concept of the Divinity does make a brief appearance right in the opening words of the text. As the first dialogue begins, d'Alembert is in the middle of a comically inadequate attempt to characterise the nature of a purely spiritual soul so that it be imagined to exist in a purely material body.[9] The dilemma had been a long-standing one for orthodox partisans of the soul, and one whose problematics had sharply increased with the Cartesian definition of matter as extension. If the soul was so pure and so spiritual, just where was it located when it 'united' with the material body? Perhaps it should be thought of as everywhere at once? Or perhaps as having a single location that somehow was not exactly material? Diderot had amused himself by reviewing some of the more absurd explanations (including those of Descartes) in his highly subversive, but heavily camouflaged, addition to the article 'Ame' of the *Encyclopédie* (i.340B):

Ceux d'entre les physiciens qui croient pouvoir admettre la spiritualité de l'*âme* & lui accorder en même temps de l'étendue, qualité qu'ils ne peuvent plus regarder comme la différence spécifique de la matière, ne lui fixent aucun siège particulier: ils disent qu'elle est dans toutes les parties du corps; [...] ils ajoutent qu'elle existe toute entière sous chaque partie de son étendue [...] Les autres philosophes pensent [que l'*âme*] n'est point étendue, que pourtant il y a dans le corps, un lieu particulier où elle réside.

We find d'Alembert struggling to defend these concepts, plus a few others, in the opening words of the 'Entretien' (p.91):

8. I use the term in the most general sense to include Christians as well as others who recognise a Divinity.
9. As will be suggested later on, these difficulties would also apply more generally to the relationship between the Divinity and matter.

J'avoue qu'un être qui existe quelque part et qui ne correspond à aucun point de l'espace; un être qui est inétendu et qui occupe de l'étendue; qui est tout entier sous chaque partie de cette étendue; qui diffère essentiellement de la matière et qui lui est uni; qui la suit et qui la meut sans se mouvoir; qui agit sur elle et qui en subit toutes les vicissitudes; un être dont je n'ai pas la moindre idée, un être d'une nature aussi contradictoire est difficile à admettre. Mais d'autres obscurités attendent celui qui le rejette; car enfin cette sensibilité que vous lui substituez, si c'est une qualité générale de la matière, il faut que la pierre sente.

Whereas Diderot in his article 'Ame' had kept the various theories distinct, the character called d'Alembert jumbles them together, making an almost clownish parody of a defence. Like the Philosophy Master's syllogisms in Molière's *Le Bourgeois gentilhomme*, in d'Alembert's account the explanations of the soul's relations to the body seem to self-destruct through the sheer force of their implausibility, leaving d'Alembert in the absurd situation of defending 'un être dont je n'ai pas la moindre idée'. To be sure, if the character called d'Alembert was so willing to concede the absurdity of his own arguments, he was still presumed to hold a trump card sure to win, namely, the even more obvious absurdity of his opponent's claim that all matter, even stone, was capable of feeling. But of course Diderot has set up d'Alembert as a straw man to be easily toppled, and the witty arguments of Diderot's rebuttal, coming after the tangles of d'Alembert's intellectual disarray, appear all the more intriguing, and they lead triumphantly to the conclusion, contrary to d'Alembert, that stone itself, already inertly 'sensible', may easily come to possess 'sensibilité active'.

Having lost the argument so completely, and being left with barely a leg to stand on – only his prejudices – d'Alembert appears ready to totter on the way to his conversion to materialism. Before leaving him to that fate, however, perhaps one might pause to examine what actually was at stake in his badly argued position, for the comic absurdities prevent the reader from seeing any serious dimension in his side of the argument. At stake was, first of all, the nature of the soul, and, needless to say, in Diderot's time the concept implied far more than simply the divinely given part of humanity which, possibly, went to heaven – the concept still current today. Because the concept has lost so much of its semantic richness over the years, it may be useful to recall some of the ways in which, according to Diderot's contemporaries, the soul was essential to everyone's personality and behavior: in fact it was the thinking and willing part of human beings; it was the heart, mind and even consciousness, the part of them that registered feelings, perceived, understood, had thoughts, imagined things, remembered, reasoned, made judgements; it was also the part that willed, desired and held beliefs. The soul had to be purely spiritual, they claimed, because matter was inherently incapable of such functions;

traditionalists also believed the soul was immortal, just as they do today. Diderot would have been aware, if only through his theological studies at the University of Paris, that no other doctrine spoke more eloquently of the Divinity's power in human life and of His presence in the world of His creation.

If the traditional notion of the soul is laughed off the stage at the opening of the first dialogue, so is the concept of the Divinity, for indeed they both belong inseparably together. Jean Varloot points out that in Diderot's vocabulary beings such as God and the soul are classified as one of two 'substances', both representing in fact false spiritual 'substance' – the other 'substance', the only true one, being of course matter (p.89, n.1). In the collapse of d'Alembert's opening arguments, false spiritual substance, exemplified in God and the soul, makes a rather ungraceful exit, and will remain an object of derision or sarcastic hostility throughout the text. But, as Diderot understood in a way few others have, the moment one denies the existence of God or any spiritual 'substance' in the universe, countless swarms of metaphysical questions arise as to how matter on its own (along with movement) can perform all God's former offices.[10] Despite Diderot's ingenuity, even for him the problems were endless, and the whole of Le Rêve de d'Alembert would be devoted to supplying answers to them. At the same time Diderot's intent certainly went beyond the merely utilitarian, and in addition to giving proof that matter and movement were sufficient to account for everything that existed, he proposed to demonstrate that in fact to rid the universe of the Divinity, allowing matter free play, is to comprehend for the first time the nature of things. In sum, it would not be much of an exaggeration to claim that this text is as God-centred as any theological treatise, provided one stipulates that the centring is negative, that Diderot's concern with the Divinity takes the form of denying and replacing Him. Although the Deity may seem to make a rather ungraceful exit in d'Alembert's defeat, His appearance right at the start of this work is emblematic, and in reality His presence as the opposite pole of a contrariety will remain the major factor for Diderot to reckon with, and argue against, throughout the dialogues. The Deity's role is by no means finished.

In Diderot's mind, and indeed according to traditional theology, God was associated with categories that were immutable. Just as the Book of Genesis had declared, the world and everything in it was created once and for ever: the trees and plants, the birds, the animals, man and woman. Since Jehovah had willed them into being at the start, there was no reason for any of them

10. See de la Carrera, Success in circuit lies, p.128.

ever to change essential form. This was one of the main assumptions behind the widespread acceptance in late seventeeth- and eighteenth-century philosophical circles of 'germes préexistants', the theory that all the species of nature existed already, at least *en germe*, in the original creation.[11] For Diderot, on the other hand, the immutability of forms and categories (just like the God who allegedly created them) is a prime target for attack. Naturally the theory of 'germes préexistants' is singled out for disparagement, as d'Alembert–Diderot congratulates Diderot–Diderot for not believing in it (p.97).

D'Alembert

Vous ne croyez donc pas aux germes préexistants?

Diderot

Non.

D'Alembert

Ah! que vous me faites plaisir!

Diderot's metaphysics creates a world in which – a deliberate contrariety with the fixedness permeating the theistic view – everything is seen as flux and transformation, real or potential. Since the Divinity's world has been stabilised forever at the creation, therefore, in Diderot's everything is inconstant: stability is latent instability; every object is potentially something else; boundary lines are everywhere being crossed or dissolving. Individual entities are grouping, or even bonding together to make up whole bodies, the way Diderot's bee-swarm is imagined to do. Other entities are entering into dissolution. Diderot's text too, setting off on the ruins of d'Alembert's immutable spiritualities, is continually evolving onward, creating new contexts in which to find new ideas.

Diderot's procedure has an aesthetic dimension as well as a theological one. In Diderot's art criticism too one often feels an impulse to break through the fixedness that was inherent in art, particularly in painting: a yearning to set the scene free of the single moment which binds it for ever.[12] Sometimes Diderot imagines he can move the scene beyond the frame and beyond the instant the painter has chosen, fantasies which sometimes give the uncanny impression of anticipating modern media such as film. Just such a release is enacted in the opening 'Entretien' of these dialogues when the world, formerly imprisoned in fixed and eternal categories of being, is almost deliriously

11. On this discussion I am indebted to Roger, *Les Sciences de la vie*, p.325f. On the theological resonances of the theory see esp. p.326 and p.331.

12. See the discussion by Pierre Saint-Amand, *Diderot: le labyrinthe de la relation* (Paris 1984), p.89-92.

released from its theological confines. Diderot later uses the word 'fou' to characterise his dialogues. In fact there is a certain madness, as well as excitement, in this new vision which sets everything in flux, in which even the stillness of motionless objects is interpreted as a kind of blocked movement.

Diderot states this latter view at the start, and orchestrates it with an explosion: an enormous imaginary tree-trunk flies into a thousand bits when he supposes that the atmospheric pressure surrounding it has been suppressed – indeed a forceful demonstration of the potential energy released when a *force morte* becomes one that is *vive*. Diderot adds that, under the same conditions, the human body would behave no differently. The explosive example, and its personal application, set off a new train of thought for d'Alembert, who now begins to see a meaningful parallel between the passage from *force morte* to *force vive* on the one hand, and one that might go from 'sensibilité inerte' to 'sensibilité active' on the other. Diderot brings the parallel to life by supposing that he is grinding up a marble statue of Pygmalion (the sculptor whose own marble statue came to life supernaturally),[13] then mixing the resultant pieces with earth, watering and letting the mixture putrefy, planting edible plants and vegetables in the humus eventually produced, and finally eating and absorbing this *latus* into his own body, thus indeed rendering the marble 'activement sensible'.[14]

This kind of 'sensibilité' is the goal of this witty demonstration; furthermore 'feeling' is associated with one of the functions of the soul, as Diderot, quoting his own daughter, makes clear (p.95). Thus the reader has learned that, contrary to d'Alembert's initial position, not only can stone be characterised as inertly sentient, but that the soul itself has a purely material origin.

Already brought into play in this demonstration – perhaps another consequence of the opening explosion – is the notion of the life cycle, which will be endlessly repeated or assumed during the course of the dialogues. The production of 'sensibilité active' from marble brought in only half of the cycle; Diderot's next illustration traces the whole progression during which d'Alembert was conceived out of matter, was born, grew, grew old, grew

13. The relationship between this myth and Diderot's materialism, originally identified by Jean Varloot, has been further explored by Suzanne Pucci, *Diderot and a poetics of science* (New York 1986), p.133-46.

14. P.39-95. See the astute comments of Aram Vartanian, 'Diderot and Maupertuis', *Revue internationale de philosophie* 38 (1984), p.66: 'The wider humanistic context of such a philosophical attitude was, it would seem, the irrepressible will somehow – even, if need be, through the affirmation of atheistic materialism – to survive death. Diderot's is a universe that proclaims the imperishability of life – a universe in which "dead matter" is but "living matter" blocked for a time and waiting to be born or reborn.' Proust seems to have felt similarly about memory.

decrepit, died and returned to earth, thus filling in the other half.[15] It is tempting to interpret the poise and perfection of Diderot's prose in this enunciation as a reflection of his own acceptance of the life-and-death process. One senses this particularly at the conclusion: 'des agents matériels dont les effets successifs seraient un être sentant, un être pensant, un être résolvant le problème de la précession des équinoxes, un être sublime, un être merveilleux, un être vieillissant, dépérissant, mourant, dissous et rendu à la terre végétale' (p.96).

Although complete, Diderot's cycle is typically lopsided: far more space is devoted to the production of life than to the death-producing side of the cycle. In the passages preceding the previous quotation, for example, the discussion of the process through which matter, originally scattered in d'Alembert's father and mother, journeyed towards coalescence and formed the germ which then developed into the foetus, which then was born, etc., etc. is far more explicit and anatomically detailed, far more carefully described than is the process of dying and returning to earth. Even Diderot's rhythm catches something of this preference for life. For example, in the quoted passage, the repetition of the words 'un être' before naming each stage in the life side of the cycle ('un être sentant, un être pensant, un être résolvant') slows the pulse of the rhythm and makes it more deliberate; the omission of these repetitions the moment one reaches the death side of the cycle brings a change of pace, actually making the tempo hasten, with a feeling of inexorability, slipping down the slope on its way to the end: 'un être vieillissant, dépérissant, mourant, dissous et rendu à la terre végétale'.

This particular lopsidedness, favouring the vital over the mortal, is typical of the eighteenth century, an era in which life was perceived as so much more interesting than death. (The nineteenth century would push the lopsidedness in the opposite direction.) But also to be stirred into the mixture was the fact that, for any materialistic philosopher, to produce life from matter, with no assistance from a Divinity, provided one of the greatest of all intellectual challenges. Death was not only less interesting, but easy by comparison. Naturally, nothing involves Diderot more in this part of the text than demon-

15. I am pleased to note that my interpretation, independently conceived, agrees on a number of points with the analysis of this passage by Jean Starobinski, 'Le philosophe, le géomètre, l'hybride', *Poétique* 21 (1975), p.8-23; the discrepancies are mainly due to general differences in approach. Among the precursors of Diderot's cyclical point of view, Heraclitus, Epicurus and Lucretius have often been cited. Ovid is also a strong possibility, as in the passage from the *Metamorphoses* (XV.215-27) in which the poet traces the course of life from the seed in the mother's womb to birth, infancy, youth, middle age, etc. with something of the same poetical sense of evolvement that one finds in Diderot.

strating how life and 'sensibilité active' spring from matter itself. Naturally, too, as he responds to the challenge, Diderot lingers almost complacently over the physiology that produces d'Alembert *en germe* in the Fallopian tubes of his mother. In one especially bravura moment (p.98), he imagines the sun turned off and all life on earth extinct, in order to light the sun again, and observe what occurs when life is renewed. Will the same life forms return as before? He finds that there is good reason to question whether they will: everything in the world being related, web-like, to everything else, and each individual part belonging inherently to the whole, it is not at all certain that, after the obliteration, the same combination of elements will be exactly repeated so as to reproduce the original forms and relationships. Thus in Diderot's mind the renewal of life in such an imaginary situation would go without saying, but contrary to the Book of Genesis and providentialist theories of the universe, its forms remain an open question.

Later on in the text (p.103-104), he and d'Alembert will watch with fascination, moment by moment, as the inert matter inside an imaginary egg turns into a chick which breaks out of its shell[16] and instantly displays unmistakable marks of 'sensibilité active', a whole range of feelings in fact, going from irritation and self-pity to desire and sexual satisfaction – implying an act of copulation and the start of another half-cycle. Acting as if his demonstration were airtight, Diderot seizes the occasion (p.105) to heap scorn on anyone (especially d'Alembert) who would postulate the existence of a spiritual soul or 'germes préexistants' in such a process, a postulation which, according to Diderot, only makes for confusion and unintelligibility, whereas (he forcefully argues) the simple concepts of matter, organisation of matter, heat and movement can explain everything.

After the production of life and 'sensibilité', the greatest challenge for a materialistic philosopher was of course the production of a thinking being, a being in which matter alone took over the activities of the soul in its highest function, thus again replacing the Divinity in one of His most imposing roles. In a densely composed argument (p.100), Diderot finds the theoretical solution to the problem by imagining sentient beings to be so organised that they have memory, thanks to which they also gain a sense of the past, of having existed

16. Jean-Pierre Seguin, *Diderot: le discours et les choses* (Paris 1978), p.301-302, claims a passage from Colonna as the main inspiration for this part of the text. Aram Vartanian, 'La Mettrie and Diderot revisited: an intertextual encounter', *Diderot studies* 21 (1983), p.179-80, sees the source as La Mettrie. According to Jack Undank, it was Lucretius: see 'Diderot's egg: life, death, and other things in pieces', *Fragments; N.Y. literary forum* 8-9 (1981), p.85-97. For that matter the hatching may come from Pliny, x.liii. (See Holland's translation given in *OED*, art. 'chick': 'By the twentie daie ye shall heare the chick to peepe within the verie shell.')

in time, and hence, of identity. This last element, the sense of being oneself through memory, is the crucial one, which carries with it the power to affirm or deny, to reach conclusions, in other words, to think. Diderot's dialectic is admirably precise, and his argument is brilliantly convincing. As a metaphor to illustrate the actual process by which the soul is brought into action, Diderot invokes his celebrated image of resonating harpsichord strings,[17] an analogy that almost magically conveys a process which is, for all intents and purposes, indescribable. Psychologically, it is an inspired device; nor could one conceive of any literal description so apposite as this.

Although the point is not always recognised, the harpsichord resonances illustrate two different kinds of thinking. The one presented first is rational: even as a string when plucked continues to resound afterwards on its own, so too in the mind, the subject[18] of a proposition-to-be automatically maintains its presence, while the mind makes judgements and reaches conclusions about it[19] – thus forming a true proposition, even though, Diderot claims, only 'thinking' of one thing at a time.

This judgemental or reasoning function will now disappear, replaced by a completely different modality of thinking – so different indeed it might almost be operating as a contrariety – introduced by the disjunctive 'Mais'. The new modality is expressed metaphorically as sympathetic vibration, thereby implying a process that is essentially unconscious and associative, in contrast to the deliberate, reasoned, active movement of ideas described above. Of course Diderot's analogy with musical vibration is one of his most creative insights, and, as if sensing his genial originality, Diderot articulates his concept with a special intensity: even as other parts of the text conjured up the boundless world of the potentialities of matter, here these shimmering resonances evoke the infinite possibilities of thought, ideas being linked, not by logical derivatives, but creatively by natural accord. Diderot points out that the harpsichord resonances sometimes make astounding leaps, setting in vibration some har-

---

17. In *Monstrous imagination* (Cambridge, Mass. 1993), p.67-68 Marie-Hélène Huet makes a convincing case for the source of this passage being Isaac Bellet, *Lettres sur le pouvoir de l'imagination des femmes enceintes* (1745); see also Jacques Chouillet, *Diderot, poète de l'énergie* (Paris 1984), p.245-78.

18. I use the modern terminology; the text says 'objet'. See the *Encyclopédie* article 'Objet', xi.302A: 'OBJET, s.m. (*Logique*) signifie la *matière* d'un art, d'une science, ou le *sujet* sur lequel on s'exerce.'

19. In the *Encyclopédie* article 'Proposition', xiii.471B-72A, Beauzée also stresses the dual nature of the simple proposition, normally composed of a subject (in Diderot's terminology, 'l'objet') and an 'attribut'. Beauzée notes too that the enunciation of the 'attribut' implies a judgement being made relative to the subject: 'une *Proposition* est l'expression total d'un jugement' (emphasis mine). One of his examples is 'God is just', the word 'just' obviously requiring the mind to reach a conclusion concerning the qualities befitting the Divinity.

monic at an interval incomprehensibly distant from the main tone, even as (the reader supplies) some unexpected idea spontaneously crops up in a seemingly unrelated train of thought. Finally Diderot brings the point home, asking d'Alembert to agree that if such sympathetic vibrations occur between strings of inert matter placed at some distance from one another, the phenomenon is even more likely to happen in human beings between points that are alive and joined together ('liés'), between fibres that are continuous and have feeling.

D'Alembert replies (p.102) with the French equivalent of 'Se non è vero', a doubting reaction that is not unexpected. For, in so far as Diderot's fictional d'Alembert can be imagined to bear even the slightest resemblance to the real mathematician,[20] nothing could be further from the manner of thinking of Diderot's former collaborator on the *Encyclopédie* than the one proposed by Diderot in this text. As scholars have noted in connection with the 'Discours préliminaire' of the *Encyclopédie*, d'Alembert gloried not only in mathematics – dreaming of the day when the entire universe would be expressed in a single formula – but generally in rational thinking in fixed categories. Diderot's thinking goes in just the opposite direction:[21] his approach – following the main thrust of this dream-work – tends to dissolve established categories and predetermined movements. At the end of the harpsichord passage, the individual pitches of the strings and the fixed differences between them are imagined to be dissolving as the instrument becomes a living being. This thought process has no regular boundaries anywhere; it opens widely onto experience, and seems to glory in the unexpected and the unknown – contrary to the mathematical preferences and generally deductive thinking modes of the real d'Alembert.

Still not convinced, the imaginary d'Alembert objects that the harpsichord image, supposedly designed to do away with spiritual substance, actually perpetuates it by postulating the existence of a judgemental activity – something like a musician who plays the instrument – distinct from the instrument itself. Naturally Diderot – with a slight tinge of sarcasm as if blaming d'Alembert for not paying more careful attention to the terms of the argument – denies

20. The 'reality' of d'Alembert and the other dialogists has been explored by Yvon Belaval, 'Les protagonistes du *Rêve de d'Alembert*', *Diderot studies* 3 (1961), p.27-53.

21. On the character of Diderot's conception of the *Encyclopédie*, see the classic article by Jean Starobinski, 'Remarques sur l'*Encyclopédie*', *Revue de métaphysique et de morale* 75 (1970), p.284-91. On the differences between the modes of thinking of Diderot and d'Alembert with respect to the *Encyclopédie*, see John Pappas, 'Diderot, d'Alembert et l'*Encyclopédie*', *Diderot studies* 4 (1963), p.195f., and 'L'esprit de finesse contre l'esprit de géométrie: un débat entre Diderot et d'Alembert', *Studies on Voltaire* 89 (1972), p.1241-43. See also, among more recent analyses, Saint-Amand, *Diderot: le labyrinthe de la relation*, p.69-77.

the dualism: his harpsichord is not played by a separate musical intelligence; the instrument is its own musician; it plays itself.[22] He also takes the occasion to spell out the epistemology implied in the harpsichord image, schematising and making explicit each stage in the process, which goes from an initial impression from without or within the instrument, to a following sensation, to the next impression, to a second sensation and finally to vocal sounds. The point of this fastidious analysis is to demonstrate the hermetic nature of this interlocking process, which step by step eliminates any breathing space for spiritual or pre-existing entities that are not material. Here, too, the Divinity has been shut out by the functioning of matter.

Such is the context for the previously mentioned egg-hatching episode, *ab ovo*, which explicitly matches the production of a living, feeling chick out of a purely material egg against all of theology and all the religions of the world, and declares the egg the winner: 'Voyez-vous cet œuf? C'est avec cela qu'on renverse toutes les écoles de théologie et tous les temples de la terre' (p.103-104).

After such powerful claims for the potentiality of matter to become actively 'sensible' – not to mention Diderot's heated diatribe (p.105) against the foolish absurdity of denying a truth so clear and so intellectually satisfying – one might expect d'Alembert gracefully to admit defeat. He obstinately refuses to capitulate, however, and the author is pleased to imagine him being so foolhardy as to reopen the debate on a more abstract plane: what if the quality of 'sensibilité' is essentially incompatible with the nature of matter? – thus providing Diderot with an occasion to breezily dismiss the argument as gibberish, and furnishing an opportunity for him to argue that since everything in the universe is material, the difference between objects is purely one of organisation (p.106-107).

The rest – communication between harpsichords, syllogisms and analogy (p.108-13) – is easy, especially since Diderot is primed with ready answers to all of d'Alembert's obliging questions. Meanwhile, the great mathematician is losing arguments everywhere, and running out of steam. Even his last stand – the announcement that as a sceptic he refuses on principle to take sides – is promptly overwhelmed by Diderot's audacious proposal that in reality there is no such thing as scepticism, that one is always for or against, however frequently one changes viewpoint. Thus at his departure d'Alembert is left

---

22. Cf. the remarkable analysis of this passage in Jacques Proust, *L'Objet et le texte: pour une poétique de la prose française du XVIIIe siècle* (Geneva 1980), p.181. For the rest, Diderot's sarcasms and impatience in this particular dialogue should always be regarded with suspicion: in every case they are a cover-up for weakness of argument.

with no argument at all to rely on, and, still ringing in his imaginary ears, the biblical admonition, quoted by Diderot as favouring his own cyclical materialism, that, since we come from dust, we will return to dust as well.

Earlier (p.111) Diderot had half-predicted that d'Alembert would, that very night, dream of this conversation and suggested that in his dream his ideas might take on what he terms 'de la consistence', thus announcing the grandiose elaboration of ideas to follow, after d'Alembert converts to Diderot's philosophy. Certainly, it is clear that a kind of insemination process is implied in the relationship between the two philosophers: Diderot has sprinkled the peas and beans of his materialism in d'Alembert's brain and these have only to sprout and be absorbed for the mathematician's conversion to take place. But d'Alembert's transformation has another psychological dimension, for it hints as well that the fundamental materiality of the universe so permeates every human being that recognition of that materiality is bound to emerge into consciousness eventually, as a truth we all know in the depths of our being, in dreams.[23] This attitude inverts the one usually implied in religious conversions, where it is assumed that, since something of God is in all of us, *that* fact would inevitably emerge, if only we did not prevent it from doing so. In any case, Diderot's assumption of the permeating verity of materialism will also apply to Mlle de Lespinasse, who, piecing together the fragments of d'Alembert's dream, is easily brought to see them as knowledge of her own self and life.

Throughout the opening 'Entretien', the objections raised by d'Alembert all relate to the dualism of body and soul, a dualism the mathematician claims to be indispensable since matter on its own could never organise itself so as to feel, procreate and otherwise create life, enunciate propositions, have consciousness, produce ideas, communicate, reason, syllogise, and so on. One cannot generally determine how much of the 'real' d'Alembert – as Diderot saw him – is present in this 'Entretien'. Furthermore, there is excellent reason to assume that the good-humoured, self-depreciating 'bonhomie' Diderot is pleased to attribute to him is actually more characteristic of the role Diderot liked to imagine himself playing than it was of the famous mathematician. But, however that may be, one can at least ascertain that d'Alembert's dualism in the 'Entretien' faithfully reproduces a major point of the philosophy d'Alembert had publicly claimed as his own in the 'Discours préliminaire' of the *Encyclopédie*, a text one may, for powerful reasons, be sure was graven for ever in Diderot's consciousness. D'Alembert's 'Discours' had argued for dualism,

23. A similar view is argued in Vartanian, 'Diderot and the phenomenology of the dream', p.250-51.

asserting as an obvious fact that matter, by its very nature, cannot will and conceive, in other words, that matter cannot perform the functions of the soul. The conclusion that d'Alembert drew was that in human beings the 'substance' that wills and conceives must be immaterial:

nous sommes naturellement amenés à examiner quel est en nous le principe qui agit, ou, ce qui est la même chose, la substance qui veut et qui conçoit. Il ne faut pas approfondir beaucoup la nature de notre corps et l'idée que nous en avons, pour reconnaître qu'il ne saurait être cette substance, puisque les propriétés que nous observons dans la matière n'ont rien de commun avec la faculté de vouloir et de penser[24]

Nor was the idea of the Divinity far off, along the Cartesian-influenced chain[25] of d'Alembert's reasoning:

d'où il résulte que cet être appelé *Nous* est formé de deux principes de différente nature, tellement unis, qu'il règne entre les mouvements de l'un et les affections de l'autre une correspondance que nous ne saurions ni suspendre ni altérer, et qui les tient dans un assujetissement réciproque. Cet esclavage si indépendant de nous, joint aux réflexions que nous sommes forcés de faire sur la nature des deux principes et sur leur imperfection nous élève à la contemplation d'une Intelligence toute-puissante[26]

Obviously the more Cartesian d'Alembert of the 'Discours' had given priority to 'pensée', whereas in the 'Entretien' the character named d'Alembert, following Diderot's own orientation, centres his debate on matter's capacity to produce 'sensibilité active', thought coming as the next step. But, allowing for such differences, d'Alembert's dualism distinctly comes through in both texts, particularly in the stress on the inherent impossibility that the soul be material, because of the limitations of matter. The 'Discours' also makes explicit the link between the dual nature of human beings and the existence of the Divinity. The similarities are sufficient to conclude that Diderot's stand against d'Alembert in the 'Entretien' is not entirely fiction, but relates to a real disagreement with the publicly stated opinion of a real person. On the level of philosophy at least, the debate in the 'Entretien' has a quasi-objective status.

'Le Rêve de d'Alembert'

The foregoing quotation from d'Alembert's 'Discours préliminaire' usefully exemplifies the great geometer's official style: in length, and in the number of

24. *Encyclopédie*, i.iii.
25. See the translation of the 'Discours préliminaire' by Richard N. Schwab (Indianapolis 1963), p.14, n.22.
26. *Encyclopédie*, i.iii-iv.

subclauses, the sentences tend towards the Ciceronian; the didactic tone is elevated and somewhat oratorical, making this 'Discours' sound rather like a public address; though the thought is dense, the vocabulary remains crisply clear and precise; an edifying abstraction reigns, and in all domains, from religion to style, one finds a scrupulous concern for decency: 'les bienséances'.

How Diderot must have enjoyed, in his imaginary dream, dumping the soul-theory of such a publicly prim and proper author, someone whose tone was so lofty and well-behaved, into the sludge of the very material world he had, at the head of Diderot's own *Encyclopédie*, explicitly disavowed! At the start of the 'Rêve' proper there is a feeble attempt at the fiction that d'Alembert is only repeating Diderot's words, as if he were not responsible for inventing them;[27] but soon d'Alembert begins to enunciate Diderot's philosophy as his own, while the persona of Diderot as mentor gradually fades into the background, even as the two thoughts have melded into one. Meanwhile, to be sure, d'Alembert–Diderot's ideas turn out to be essentially the same as Bordeu's, so that everyone is having the same thought, and can literally complete each other's sentences. This melding of various people's ideas into one occurs even while d'Alembert and Bordeu are describing, to a startled Mlle de Lespinasse, how individual living entities such as cells or even organs can be conceived of as melded into a continuity that forms a single living animal – almost as if the literary form, in the sliding together of the various individualities, were aping the biological process the text describes.

While the 'Entretien' had challenged the Deity by creating life, feeling and thought out of pure matter, the 'Rêve' is centred as well on the problem of animal unity mentioned above. The bee-swarm (p.122-23) is the most picturesque of Diderot's inventions to represent the way in which an individual living entity might become a functioning part of a whole, but the theme was destined to return frequently in various guises, and, as the reader soon finds out, Diderot was particularly fascinated with the conception in its cosmic framework, in which all individualities in the universe lose their private identities, becoming parts of one infinite totality.[28]

In the 'Entretien', animal reproduction was explained mainly in the conventional way, as the result of copulation between the sexes, and of course Diderot several times described the entire progression from germ to birth. But in the 'Rêve' there emerge two other processes of reproduction, only hinted

27. Later on in the dialogue, after d'Alembert awakens, there are other similarly feeble attempts to suggest the fiction that he had not known (so to speak) what he had been dreaming about. His words provide no positive evidence, however, for a relapse into dualism.
28. See C. J. Betts, 'Analogy in *Le Rêve de d'Alembert*', *Studies on Voltaire* 185 (1980), p.267-81.

at in the 'Entretien', which do not follow the usual route, indeed they avoid entirely the required preliminaries leading to normal births: one is polyp reproduction,[29] implying that one has only to cut off a part of the main animal for the severed part to develop into a complete animal on its own. The second is spontaneous generation,[30] implying the possibility that matter on its own can produce living beings. Because both types supposedly bypass the necessity of gestation, in Diderot's mind both types represented liberations from the encumbrances of real life, and hence easily lent themselves to fantasy.

In the first bizarre vision of d'Alembert's dream, polyp generation seems to explode and run riot, thanks to the fantastic ease of this manner of reproduction. D'Alembert dreams of a whole planet on which the population reproduces polypwise, males breaking into other males, females into other females. It is as if Diderot were parodying *Micromégas*, but with an emphasis on reproduction unthinkable for the Patriarch, a fantasy in which all parts of the body are seen as potentially reproductive. Mlle de Lespinasse is delicately selective in her account; meanwhile d'Alembert–Diderot amuses himself by inventing a warm hatchery in which rows of containers have labels to designate the eventual social class of the contents. Who could have imagined that at such a moment of pure fantasy and science fiction current politics would stridently enter the text? But the labels read: warriors, magistrates, philosophers, poets; containers for courtiers, for whores, for kings (p.124-27).

Climax

Diderot's daring juxtaposition of prostitutes and royalty (unthinkable for an awake d'Alembert) brings the polyp fantasy to a close, as though this bold stroke, stretching the fantasy to its limit, had snapped it. The way now opens for other grandiose visions which form an especially dense and poetical moment, visions based not on polyps, but on spontaneous generation. No doubt determined to avoid the least hint of Pascalian anguish in the contemplation of the infinitely small and the infinitely great, d'Alembert–Diderot peers into an imaginary microscope and, fascinated even as he had been when observing the chick hatching from the egg, discovers a multitude of animalcules appearing in bits of macerated meat and grain, produced spontaneously and without miracles, from matter itself.

While polyp reproductions – a relatively rare earthly occurrence – had been

---

29. The impact of this discovery on the European philosophical community has been magisterially investigated by Virginia P. Dawson, *Nature's enigma: the problem of the polyp in the letters of Bonnet, Trembley and Réaumur* (Philadelphia 1987).

30. See Roger, *Les Sciences de la vie*, p.494-520.

situated, in d'Alembert's dream-fantasy, on Jupiter or Saturn, spontaneous generation was thought to happen in innumerable parts of the real world. Yet for Diderot the creative implications of the sight he beheld in the imaginary microscope were wonder-inspiring, almost as if he were in the presence of a miracle, or the secret of life. This is why, in a breathtaking comparison, he likens the drop of liquid under the microscope with its infinite numbers of teeming generations, to the entire universe. Meanwhile Mlle Lespinasse formulates one of Diderot's most resounding phrases: 'Il voyait dans une goutte d'eau l'histoire du monde' (p.128).

In the liquid under the microscope, the generating process occurs extremely rapidly, in the blink of an eye, far more quickly than in the normal world, where, d'Alembert–Diderot admits, the process takes somewhat longer. Yet Diderot professes he is unimpressed by the difference. As if rethinking ideas from Fontenelle or Voltaire, he makes it clear that in a perspective of relativity, and in the perspective of eternity, such discrepancies are of virtually no consequence. Responding to the demands of the enormous dimensions entailed, he rises rhetorically to a grandly metaphysical verbal posture: in fact the tone he uses takes on a distinctly religious character – even mystical in the sense of the awe it conveys. Exactly as if he were a Pascal or some other visionary metaphysician, he launches into a series of observations – most of them comparisons – deliberately designed to force the mind beyond its powers of comprehension, to boggle the intelligence. Thus he contrasts the brief space of human life (a concept comfortably within our grasp) with all of time – which of course is incomprehensible. Or again, the drop of water is compared to all of space (another mind-boggler); he compares the multitude of animalcules coming from the atom of the drop to the endless series in the other atom called Earth. Such perspectives represent the ultimate stage in the boundary-dissolving tendencies that were first set in motion at the opening of the work: all set patterns are disappearing; all separations stretched beyond meaning. Having cut loose from the stable values that habitually make up the known world, the text invites the reader to float in limitless time and space, as Diderot wonders – with no answers seeming possible – what races of animals preceded the ones we know, and which races will follow after. Finally Diderot ascends to the culminating metaphysical statement in which all individualities lose themselves in the whole: 'Tout change, tout passe, il n'y a que le tout qui reste' (p.128).[31] Having elevated himself in thought to this pinnacle, Diderot

31. Again, *mutatis mutandis*, Ovid may be counted among the precursors of this metaphysics. See the *Metamorphoses* (xv.252-58) 'Nec species sua cuique manet, rerumque novatrix / ex aliis alias reparat natura figuras: / nec perit in toto quicquam, mihi credite, mundo, / sed variat faciemque novat, nascique vocatur / incipere esse aliud, quam quod fuit ante, morique / desinere

allows his text to linger on, as if floating far above mortal contingencies in some limitless imaginary realm, calmly observing how opposites unite in a universe where everything is simultaneously birth and ending.[32] Indeed – another vast observation – in the endless flux of the ocean of matter, no molecule exactly resembles any other, nor even itself for so much as an instant. As a sort of consecration of this metaphysical vision, Diderot quotes (inexactly)[33] one of the most historically famous lines from Virgil: 'Rerum novus nascitur ordo', calling it an 'eternel inscription' for the 'immense ocean of matter' which is the universe. Even as this moment forms a climax for Diderot's materialism, it is also a lyrical high point, and the quotation confirms what the reader already knew, that this densely metaphysical part of the text in particular is, in the spirit of Lucretius or Virgil, a poem.

Obviously Diderot was very much in tune with the dramatic import of Virgil's statement, which he adapts as an emblem for his own materialistic metaphysics. Apparently some evidence suggests that Diderot saw the line as Virgil's homage to Lucretius.[34] But, particularly in view of the religious overtones of the passage, it would be intriguing to know whether Diderot was aware, as well, of the centuries-old exegetical tradition which held that, in this line, Virgil had predicted the coming of Christ. Dante had paraphrased it in Statius's discourse to Virgil, in the *Divine comedy* (*Purg.* XXII.67f.), for that very reason. And if Diderot knew of the powerful spiritual load the line traditionally carried, his adaptation would give it an added dimension (not, to be sure, that the achievement of his prose needed one): the quotation would become a deliberate demystification of the allusion to the divine Saviour, who

---

illud idem. Cum sint huc forsitan illa, / haec translata illuc, summa tamen omnia constant.' In the Loeb Classical Library translation: 'Nothing retains its own form; but Nature, the great renewer, ever makes up form from other forms. Be sure there's nothing perishes in the whole universe; it does but vary and renew its form. What we call birth is but a beginning to be other than what one was before; and death is but a cessation of a former state. Although, perchance, things may shift from there to here and here to there, still do all things in their sum total remain unchanged' (p.383).

32. If Diderot's conception of 'le tout' suggests the possible influence of dom Deschamps (see the Vernière edition, p.300, n.1), at the same time other aspects of the text, especially the imagined stasis above the infinite flowings of a universe where opposites endlessly unite, bizarrely evokes the ambiance of Diderot's *Encyclopédie* article 'Bramines', ii.393B-94A: 'Ils prétendent que la chaîne des êtres est émanée du sein de Dieu et y remonte continuellement, comme le fil sort du ventre de l'araignée et y rentre. [...] Les mondes périssent et renaissent. Notre terre [...] finira par le feu; il s'en reformera de ses cendres une autre.' In both cases, there is a suggestion of arriving at a state of ataraxy, and the similarities also suggest that in Diderot's case this ultimate state is being conveyed in poetical terms that are also quasi-religious – which of course suits well the role of the Divinity which he has taken on.

33. See DPV, xvii.128, n.125.

34. Such is the interpretation of Jean Varloot in DPV, xvii.128, n.124.

now, through that telling line from Virgil, is subsumed by the only reality, which is matter.

Exactly as if following a religious pattern, this almost mystical meditation on the countless and eternal cycles of birth and degeneration in the infinite spaces of the universe leads to a mood of humility as the author perceives the vanity, the poverty and the insignificance of human accomplishments by comparison. A sighing, almost prayerful tone invades the text: 'Puis il ajoutait en soupirant: O vanité de nos pensées! ô pauvreté de la gloire et de nos travaux! ô misère de nos vues!' (p.129).

Pascal's 'Qu'est-ce que l'homme dans la nature?' would make a perfect conclusion to this meditation, for just as in the *Pensées*, the enormity of the universe has inspired the deepest awareness of the vanity of human values and accomplishments. Even Pascal's most expressive term, 'misère', turns up in the passage. In any other writer the ambience would seem positively penitential.

Yet, just when it appears that d'Alembert–Diderot might be engulfed permanently in these feelings of unworthiness, the coin turns over to the other side and a new mood swings into the text as d'Alembert realises he can still enjoy the pleasures that remain: 'Boire, manger, vivre, aimer et dormir.' Immediately putting the thought into action, he first ascertains that indeed Mlle de Lespinasse is still present, and then proceeds to produce, apparently by masturbation, a climax of his own, a nocturnal emission. Sighs of sexual contentment replace the earlier metaphysical sigh of humility. Mlle de Lespinasse, unable to comprehend what has happened beneath the bedclothes, finds herself nevertheless strangely moved – 'émue' – as she ambiguously describes her reaction, with her heart pounding, even though she recognises it was not from fear. Meanwhile d'Alembert sleeps, and eventually dreams again, smiling while he fantasises that on some planet where people multiply as fish do, his emission might still be used to procreate. Clearly the philosophical side of d'Alembert is re-emerging as he expresses regret that something potentially useful has been lost, and asks Mlle de Lespinasse to see whether the residue might not be enclosed in a bottle and taken first thing in the morning to the great Needham, 'discoverer' of spontaneous generation.[35]

The change of emotional register between the metaphysically brooding contemplator of the whole universe and the contentedly smiling, sexually gratified one could hardly be more contrastive and one might be tempted to assume that the two mood-perspectives formed a true contrariety, as if the author had changed his mind along with d'Alembert's emotional state. And

---

35. Needless to say, male semen had been, and continued to be, an object of intense scrutiny and debate among philosophers; see d'Aumont's article 'Génération', *Encyclopédie*, vii.559B-74A.

yet, in this context, the take-over by metaphysics has been so powerfully inclusive that it subsumes all possible changes. In fact d'Alembert's ejaculation, which is supposedly performed with thoughts of sexual attraction and after-thoughts of insemination, simply obeys – in an only slightly unusual way – the impulse towards procreation that energises all the cycles of Diderot's materialistic world, that makes his world go round. In this cosmic perspective, it is as if the great All, or the nature of matter, had demanded – even foreordained – both his action and the motives behind it.

Conclusions regarding the central dialogue

At this point the analysis of the great middle dialogue of the trilogy may leave off. To be sure, d'Alembert's dream is by no means over: soon will come other grandiose Lucretian or Epicurean visions of the whole earth abounding in life-germs and possibilities for fermentation, ready to teem with new generations and unknown forms of life (p.130-32). Nor can one ignore the continuous fascination of the discussion as Mlle de Lespinasse discovers reasons for her sense of identity (p.134), and Doctor Bordeu reveals the links between the development of the various senses or parts of the body, and human needs (p.136-37). Another high point is the subsequent metaphysical dream sequence in which d'Alembert pities the poor philosophers for believing in individual beings when in reality there is only one great individual, the All (p.137-40). Again Diderot rises to new heights and contrives, in just a few lines, to define brilliantly the dynamics of various large metaphysical questions, from the nature of being ('La somme d'un certain nombre de tendances'), to that of species ('Les espèces ne sont que des tendances à un terme commun qui leur est propre'), to life ('une suite d'actions et de réactions'), and even the dynamics that make death a transitory state ('Naître, vivre et passer, c'est changer de formes').[36] In short, there will be other sublime visions and pronouncements, and much remains to be explored and revealed for the participants of the dialogues. For the reader as well, some of the finest moments – including Mlle de Lespinasse's spider-web image (p.140-41), her imaginary long beam which one wishes could vibrate with sounds from outer space (p.142), and her astonishing intuition that man is the monster of woman (p.152-54), and vice versa – lie ahead.

And yet, for present purposes, i.e. the study of contrariety as a dynamic principle in this work, the essentials are already implicit: as if proceeding from d'Alembert's ejaculation, the seeds of the future discussions of this dialogue

---

36. Again see Ovid, *Metamorphoses*, XV.252-58, quoted above, n.31.

have now been sown. Not only has the reader understood that each pheno-menon is part of a great web in which the change of any single part affects the whole (as was learned in the opening 'Entretien'), but having risen to the mountain-top of the great All and surveyed the entire cosmos, the reader knows too of the constant generation–degeneration process in a world that is nothing but flux. Furthermore, Diderot's materialism being systematic, each part theoretically implies the whole.[37] Thus, as Bordeu states, Mlle de Les-pinasse's spider-web was already inherent, *en germe*, in the beehive (p.141); so was the closely allied discussion of the organs of the body and their relation to the whole, another connection suggested earlier by Bordeu (p.122). In the opening 'Entretien' the inner workings of the mind were marvellously de-lineated by the harpsichord image. The brain had not yet been shown in its more outward role as – via the network, or web, of nerve filaments – it controlled, or was controlled by, the rest of the body, a dynamics which Diderot brilliantly conveys when he avoids the term 'cerveau', replacing it instead with 'l'origine du réseau' (for example, p.155). But in sum, such discussions – numerous and historically significant though they be (not to mention how obvious their appeal for Diderot) – represent essentially a biological working-out of the details of his major hypothesis, whose outlines had already been articulated: the hypothesis that an aggressively non-spiritual substance, namely, matter on its own, can – operating via a principle of opposition or contrariety – usurp all the functions formerly attributed to the Divinity and/or the immaterial soul, and thus effectively eliminate spiritual substance everywhere in the universe.

Long ago Etienne Gilson defined the crucial but often ignored differences between Descartes's two famous criteria for being certain an idea is true, namely, knowing its truth 'clearly and distinctly', *clarē et distinctē*.[38] Gilson pointed out that the latter term, *distinctē*, concerned the content of an idea, which defined its identity and set it apart from others. *Clarē* on the other hand concerned the 'brightness' with which an idea is present in the mind, and it distinguished the Cartesian mode of thought from other philosophical modes – from Scholasticism, for example – which allowed one to think via ready-formed memories of ideas and word formulae. Descartes rejected the use of such already-givens and -knowns, requiring the perception of the truth of an idea to be a process that goes on immediately and intensely in the mind then

37. Diderot had suggested that the second part of the trilogy, the 'Rêve' proper, had originally been conceived as an 'éclaircissement' of the first part: see Vartanian, 'Diderot and the phenomenology of the dream', p.219.
38. See his edition of Descartes, *Discours de la méthode* (Paris 1947), p.200-203.

and there – a major reason for the enduring vitality of Descartes's own writings, of course.

In one sense at least, no one in the eighteenth century pushed the Cartesian criterion of *clarē* so far as Diderot, particularly in the trilogy under consideration. If only on account of the alleged ignorance of Mlle de Lespinasse, little or nothing could be taken for granted in the theories proposed by the other participants trained in philosophy, and almost perforce in the dialogues ideas are continually coming into being and imposing their truths, not at all as ready-made arguments, but as revelations or events taking place: the whole text was conceived as a 'brightening', in a way that might seem not too far removed from Descartes. On the other hand, ideas in Descartes always convey a Classical sense of equilibrium; they always follow their rightful, necessary course, as indeed they must in a philosophy modelled upon the discourse of geometry. In Diderot one finds less equilibrium, or regularity; still less geometry. However brightly the truth of an idea may be perceived, aesthetically speaking – i.e. according to appearances – ideas are not being presented as predestined,[39] at least not in the Cartesian sense: according to aesthetic appearances, they might lead anywhere, as if the 'experience' of an idea had a built-in component of 'experiment'.

Even though in *Le Rêve de d'Alembert* we are aware of a system of philosophy taking shape, curiously, the experience of reading the work (at least for the present writer) is that of a rather precarious conquest of ideas. Traversing the dialogues is a slightly unsettling reading-encounter that we eagerly undertake again and again, as if to wonder anew whether this time the chick will actually emerge from the egg so that, fulfilling Diderot's prophecy, all those temples and theologies can be overthrown, or to confirm that the unpredictable Mlle de Lespinasse will once again be convinced, rather than raising some unheard-of obstacle that throws everything out of kilter, or to make sure that d'Alembert was dreaming all the fantasies Diderot apparently wanted him to dream, instead of reverting to those earlier subversive arguments which Diderot so glibly dismissed without a proper hearing. Even Bordeu's approving reaction to the beehive image looks weak enough at the seams[40] to make one wonder whether everything will still be holding together on the next run-through.

The impression of instability is accentuated as well by the unsettling

---

39. I recognise of course that for a materialist such as Diderot, everything is ultimately predetermined. Aesthetically speaking, however, Diderot's philosophical behaviour often implies that, rather like *Jacques le fataliste*, he has forgotten that fact, as though his ideas, and their effects, were free.

40. The textual confusions are pointed out by Jean Varloot in DPV, xvii.123, n.105-106; see also Betts, 'Analogy in *Le Rêve de d'Alembert*', p.277, n.13.

phenomenon of verbal ventriloquism: at one time or another, each personage speaks words that would more properly belong to someone else. D'Alembert can sound a little like Mlle de Lespinasse (with the left side of the brain out of commission): 'Vrai ou faux, j'aime ce passage du marbre à l'humus, de l'humus au règne végétal', or, even while still wide awake, can mimic the 'désinvolture' of Diderot: '(Mais cela va nous écarter de notre première discussion.) Qu'est-ce que cela fait? Nous y reviendrons ou nous n'y reviendrons pas.' As was suggested earlier, everyone can sound like Bordeu. For example, d'Alembert, awake: 'Vous disiez donc à mademoiselle que la matrice n'est autre chose qu'un scrotum retourné de dehors en dedans, mouvement dans lequel les testicules ont été jetés hors de la bourse qui les renfermait, et dispersés.' Mlle de Lespinasse, too, can give a passable imitation: 'Je conçois que cette expansion ne saurait se mesurer, et je conçois encore que cette insensibilité, cette apathie, cette inertie de l'extrêmité des brins, cet engourdissement, après avoir fait un certain progrès, peut se fixer, s'arrêter.' This ventriloquism is by no means a constant phenomenon in the dialogues: on the contrary, there are other parts in which characters speak in a way exactly appropriate for themselves. There can be no doubt at least that the following anecdote could come from no one but the character named Diderot; it has unmistakably his energetic comic style as he proceeds by questions and exclamations, his incomparable irony and psychological insight, his rhythm, and most brilliantly, the extraordinary compression of his verbal economy – no one else could wittily convey so much in so few words (p.166):

Je me souviens que, dans un exercice public, un pédant de collège, tout gonflé de son savoir, fut mis ce qu'ils appellent au sac, par un capucin qu'il avait méprisé. Lui, mis au sac! Et par qui? par un capucin! et sur quelle question? Sur le futur contingent! sur la science moyenne qu'il a méditée toute sa vie! Et en quelle circonstance? devant une assemblée nombreuse! devant ses élèves!

No doubt it is only fair to admit that this anecdote so unmistakably Diderotian is actually spoken by d'Alembert in the text. In short, the sense of textual stability is not increased by such personality exchanges.

As for Diderot's arguments themselves, specialists seem to agree that Diderot was in touch with some of the most advanced philosophical knowledge of the time;[41] moreover Diderot's willingness to challenge all traditions and rethink everything afresh imbues the ideas of the text with such a powerful excitement and sense of discovery that one is glad to assume, clarē if not distinctē, that they must be true. Nor has even modern science seriously challenged Diderot's biological and sexual emphasis, or his basic conceptions

41. For example, Roger, Les Sciences de la vie, p.654-78; Vernière, Jean Varloot.

of change, life cycles and the origin of life in matter. Such reassuring factors may tend to obscure the degree to which Diderot's system, precisely because of his willingness to start from scratch, *ab ovo*, is an act of courage far more than it is a declaration of wisdom.[42] One grants, to be sure, that one cannot hold against Diderot the fact that the 'spontaneous generation' of Needham's experiments actually must have been produced by 'contaminated' material, since that fact was discovered only later on. But even in Diderot's own time, Needham's theories were energetically contested, and not merely by the upholders of Christianity: as Diderot was aware, the great Voltaire sarcastically dismissed them as pure superstition, no more credible than the old wives' tale of rats being born out of the mud of the Nile. In such an ambience of contestation Diderot's support for Needham's side of the argument takes on at least something of the character of a postulation, if not of an act of faith.

A similar pattern might apply to the chick-hatching episode. Thanks to later scientific discoveries, it is now clear that Diderot could not have understood the complexities of a chick being formed out of the matter of an egg. Even aside from the later revelations of science, however, Diderot himself, in a passage composed a few years after the trilogy, probably around 1773-1774, admitted that he did not understand all parts of the crucial process through which egg-matter was supposed to become actively 'sensible',[43] so that his grandiose assertion about overthrowing all religion with the hatching of a bird is not merely a picturesque exaggeration: it may, incipiently at least, contain elements of philosophical bluster besides. But – and for this part of the discussion I am using the evidence and the interpretation proposed by Jacques Roger – the most problematic part of Diderot's system is the argument he raises right at the start of the first dialogue: his claim that some sort of 'sensibilité' belongs universally to matter. Even his straw-man opponent d'Alembert tried to protest that Diderot's doctrine was unlikely on the face of it. Today, one would be tempted to declare his notion that all matter – presumably including metal and volcanic rock – has lurking in it some sort of incipient 'sensibilité' to be frankly preposterous;[44] indeed it looks very much like a *pis-aller*, the only

42. See Scherer, *Le Cardinal et l'orang-outang*, p.215.

43. 'Je vois clairement dans le développement de l'œuf et quelques autres opérations de la nature, la matière inerte en apparence, mais organisée, passer par des agents purement physiques, de l'état d'inertie à l'état de sensibilité et de vie, mais la liaison nécessaire de ce passage m'échappe' (from Diderot, *Réfutation suivie de l'ouvrage d'Helvétius intitulé l'Homme*, quoted in Roger, *Les Sciences de la vie*, p.670).

44. Cf. Vartanian, 'Diderot and the phenomenology of the dream', p.219: 'Diderot's supposition that there is no fundamental distinction between living and non-living things – of *sensibilité* as a universal property, either actual or potential, of matter – is an abstraction that is not only without the support of experience, but plainly contradicted by it.' One notes to be sure what may look like Diderot's partial equivocation pointed out by Jean Varloot, 'La sensibilité, propriété générale

argument Diderot could devise to explain how 'sensibilité active' could occur in matter without allowing for the possibility that some outside agent, like the Divinity, might have put it there. Diderot himself would come to recognise the shakiness of the concept and confess that it was only a 'supposition', whose strength lay entirely in the difficulties it overcame – not a philosophically satisfactory position, as Diderot recognised as well.[45] D'Alembert's objections were far more telling than Diderot had allowed them to appear. In retrospect one realises that it has taken, first, the sheer excitement of Diderot's dynamic conception of a world in which everything has been biologically wound up and set in movement, either going forward in metamorphosis or spinning round in cycles, and then, second, all of Diderot's charm, as he cheerfully grinds up a marble Pygmalion and eats the peas and beans which he planted in the residue, to cover over its implausibility. In the context of such difficulties, the celebrated remark of Diderot's friend, the abbé Galiani, concerning one of the most notorious atheistical works of the day, d'Holbach's *Système de la nature*, which actually comes from rather the same 'boutique', might seem wisely apropos: 'Au fond nous ne connaissons pas assez la nature pour en former le système.'[46]

If, despite such an array of pitfalls, Diderot so eagerly attempted a materialistic system, it seems clear that one reason was his absolute certainty of the falseness of the doctrines he was rejecting: he at least knew through all the experiences of his life, with every fibre in him, that there was no transcendent Being, no divine plan, no Providence, no spiritual substance, no origin of species in the Garden on Eden, and no miracles[47] – all of which seemed to indicate that matter itself must have created everything. Diderot's dialogues being an effort to demonstrate systematically how this non-miracle could have occurred, the result is necessarily semi-fiction: real persons engaged in fictional dialogues to start with, and then, given the incompleteness (not to say inadequacy) of the proofs and theories at Diderot's disposal, the elaboration of a philosophical

de la matière ou produit de l'organisation' (DPV, xvii.45). See, however, the elucidation of this point in Vartanian, 'Diderot and Maupertuis', p.64-65.

45. 'Il faut en convenir, l'organisation ou la coordination de parties inertes ne mène point du tout à la sensibilité, et la sensibilité générale des molécules de la matière n'est qu'une supposition, qui tire toute sa force des difficultés dont elle débarrasse, ce qui ne suffit pas en bonne philosophie' (quoted in Roger, *Les Sciences de la vie*, p.670).

46. *Correspondance avec madame d'Epinay*, ed. Daniel Magetti, i.196 (30 juin 1770). See the similar historical comments by Vernière in Diderot, *Œuvres philosophiques*, p.559, concerning Diderot's discussion of Helvétius.

47. Cf. Dieckmann's remark concerning the *Supplément au Voyage de Bougainville*: 'La pensée de Diderot dans le *Supplément* est une pensée 'contre' et beaucoup de ses idées doivent être replacées dans cette perspective si on veut les comprendre' (Introduction, p.xlvii-xlviii).

system that is to a significant extent a creative act, the postulation of a material world belonging as much to poetry as to 'science'.

This inherently fictional component of the 'Le Rêve de d'Alembert' leads to a final irony, namely, that Diderot, who performed such prodigies of argument so as to keep the Divinity out of the eggshell, out of the copulation of d'Alembert's parents, out of d'Alembert's ejaculation, out of the functioning of the mind or any organ one might mention, out of the growth of cells, out of the development of worms and elephants, not to mention plants and humans, ended by taking over himself the creative functions of the Divinity he excluded, playing himself the role of God.[48] It is a commonplace truth that authors of fictions usually do play this role, though some more self-consciously than others. But since Diderot's fiction involved the creation of everything in the universe, and since philosophy could not provide him with enough solid data to eliminate all elements of wishful thinking, this role for him was quasi-inescapable. Such was the unspoken motive behind the religious overtones of the 'Rerum novus nascitur ordo' passage, whose poetry indeed celebrates the new order, but an order which was actually the conception of Diderot's fictional philosophy, an order conceived in the text we read. And when, from the contemplation of the history of the world in the animalcules of a single drop of liquid, he ascends the heights to the sublime contemplation of the great All, he is – in significant ways – engaged in a creative act that invents his cosmos, his 'immense ocean' of supposedly *sentient* matter, as surely as Jehovah ever was in the Book of Genesis.

For the reader, the fictional component of this 'dream' is adroitly masked by a number of decoys, chief among them being Mlle de Lespinasse, with help from Bordeu to be sure. Each time she declares herself incapable of making sense of the gibberish of her notes, she handily deflects the reader's attention away from the central issue, which ought to be the plausibility or implausibility of Diderot's arguments, and makes the main question 'Will she be able to understand?' When she finally *does* comprehend the message, more than half the battle is won, since in dispelling her confusions we have the impression of a major accomplishment, as though making sense with respect to her was the same as making sense, *tout court*; Bordeu has only to declare that d'Alembert's words contain pearls of truth for the reader eagerly to join in the chorus of approval. Another masking device is Bordeu's alleged power to reproduce d'Alembert's ideas word for word, even though he has not heard d'Alembert

48. Although the elements of my argument are different, I entirely agree with the conclusions of Pucci, *Diderot and the poetics of science*, p.146.

speak, a presumably telepathic or philosophic accomplishment so amazing both Mlle de Lespinasse and the reader forget to ask (for example) about the serious textual confusions in the final explanations of the bee-swarm image; instead, Bordeu's ability to share d'Alembert's thoughts as if they were the only wisdom confers on them an almost supernatural authority.

One final point before concluding these remarks on the main dialogue of the 'Le Rêve de d'Alembert': Bordeu–Diderot's usual methodology in this section repeats a backwards procedure which had become something of a trade-mark for Diderot. As Jacques Scherer has pointed out,[49] in order to study the properties of sight Diderot had looked to persons without sight, the blind; for language communication, he had looked to the deaf and dumb.[50] In the present work, in order to prove the materiality of some organ and to study its functioning he imagines (or in some cases actually observes) that the nerves[51] which control the organ have been put out of commission; after studying the result, he usually restores the nerves and brings the organ back to life (for example, p.49-51, 55-56, 60-62). In their diversity these biological discussions have something of the flavour of the traditional literary genre called the Anatomy. The peculiarity of this particular Anatomy, however, is that the author often prefers to study the various organs through their absence or deprivation, rather than through their functioning presence.

Towards the end of this dialogue, Mlle de Lespinasse stops the discussion ('Un moment, docteur', p.188), which had been gliding from one topic to another. (Most recently ethics had been pithily dispatched in just a few dense pages, with 'imagination' being next on the agenda.) Announcing that she is about to give a summary ('Récapitulons'), she proceeds to claim that, following Bordeu's principles and using a sequence of purely mechanical procedures, she could reduce the greatest genius on earth to a mere mass of unorganised flesh, capable only of momentary 'sensibilité', and then, by another set of procedures, restore him to his first state. She uses Isaac Newton for her imaginary demonstration, fancying first that she destroys the use of both of his auditory nerves, so he cannot hear, then his olfactory nerves, so he cannot smell, then his optical nerves, so he has no more colour sensations, and so on, until finally all that remains of Newton is a formless mass and 'sensibilité'. In the other half of her summary she imagines that she is restoring, one by one,

---

49. *Le Cardinal et l'orang-outang*, p.217-18.

50. Dieckmann had interpreted aspects of the *Supplément au Voyage de Bougainville* in a similar fashion: 'Philosophiquement parlant, la réponse à la question de ce qu'est la morale naturelle va être fournie par des exemples de ce qu'elle n'est pas' (Introduction, p.liii).

51. My translation uses the simplest, most general term. For the particularities of Diderot's 'nerve' vocabulary, see DPV, xvii.38-39 and 70, n.34.

the nerves of all the body parts that she has just suppressed, until she finally recovers her lost man of genius with all his former senses renewed and intact, at which point she discloses what was presumably the main object of her demonstration – 'et cela sans l'entremise d'aucun agent hétérogène et inintelligible' – code words signifying that Newton's 'soul' had nothing spiritual about it, nor was some Divinity responsible for the production of his genius. Bordeu chimes in approvingly: 'A merveille: tenez-vous-en là; le reste n'est que du galimatias.' After this remark, the discussion rather briefly resumes its gliding course from topic to topic ('imagination' being first in line), until Bordeu picks up his cane and his hat and supposedly sets off for a midday appointment in the Marais, bringing the dialogue to an end.

Thus the backwards Anatomy is the only summary the author provides for the 'Rêve' proper, and it conveniently exemplifies the main point of the present analysis, namely, that Diderot's materialism, whether strictly anatomical or more generally biological, is never unmindful of the Divinity, indeed is deliberately elaborated as challenge and counter-creation. Naturally Mlle de Lespinasse's summary has an almost aggressive forcefulness – as she puts Newton's eyes out of commission, annihilates his intelligence, and so on – and furthermore she is performing the very acts which are usually the Divinity's prerogative: taking away someone's humanity (virtually his life), and then re-creating it, out of mere sentient matter. In short, the summary can be taken as further confirmation that the stimulus which inspired and sustained these dialogues emanates not from internal pressures, but from an outer contrariety with God himself. Nor was Diderot's inspiration simply a desire to create a natural system of ideas, as it had been for d'Holbach, for example; Diderot's inspiration was his determination to challenge the Divinity, whose creations are being systematically negated and replaced by a kind of matter invented significantly by Diderot himself, imbued with Diderot's own 'sensibilité', and obedient to Diderot's laws.

The final dialogue

In the 'Suite de l'entretien précédent' one finds for the first time an authentic internal contrariety, that is, the emergence of an argument which deliberately stands against the primary flow of the dialectic. Most curiously, the source of the contrary position is the usually steady and reliable Doctor Bordeu. My contention is, however, that this extraordinary event, which does indeed constitute an exception to the general rules of the text, still exemplifies the contrariety characteristic of the whole, a point which will be clarified further on.

The rapid movement from topic to topic characterising the end of the 'Rêve' proper suggests an effort towards completeness on Diderot's part, as if this *encyclopédiste* felt the need, before Bordeu takes his temporary departure, to cover all the major activities traditionally attributed to the soul, and demonstrate that each activity could be explained by matter on its own. This feeling of having already answered all the significant questions leaves Mlle de Lespinasse free, when Bordeu returns from his consultation (allowing the 'Suite de l'entretien précédent' to begin), to raise a question that was not theoretically of prime importance, but a sort of 'hors d'œuvre', a question usually classified as prurient curiosity, and which, the text claims, she has never dared to ask anyone before: what about sex between various species, especially humans and animals? (She phrases the question more delicately, but Bordeu immediately sees the point.)

The previous open discussions of unmentionable parts of the anatomy, and Bordeu's later dismissal of 'l'estime de soi', 'la honte', 'le remords' as 'puérilité fondée sur l'ignorance et la vanité' (p.186-87), lead one to expect an appropriately low-key, unprudish, and purely 'scientific' treatment of human–animal miscegenation – which in fact does occur, but only after an extraordinary number of precautions to reassure the reader, and the dialogists, about the circumstances and import of the discussion: it is made plain that no one is listening and that Bordeu's willingness to discuss such a topic does not imply any lack of respect for Mlle de Lespinasse. Nor does it reflect upon the irreproachable purity of his own morals. Mlle de Lespinasse indicates that, despite a certain nervousness, she will finally not be shocked, provided Bordeu uses a little 'gauze' (to soften the 'crudity', of course). In the same vein one notes as well the reassuringly respectable surroundings, with 'le dîner' just served and the servants sent away, while Bordeu enjoys a glass of excellent malaga, followed by his coffee, presumably provided by an unmentioned servant who instantly vanishes, leaving the two completely alone. All these fluttery precautions appear so unusual in a text normally characterised by down-to-earth straightforwardness as to suggest preparations for the introduction of a new, different perspective, which in fact will prove to be the case.

When the ceremonial allaying of apprehensions is complete and the discussion finally launched, it ranges over several sorts of unmentionables, starting with masturbation, defended at length by Bordeu as desirable in certain cases for psychological as well as physical reasons, followed by homosexual activity, declared superior to masturbation by giving pleasure to two persons rather than one. After a brief sermon to the effect that everything that is, is natural, including even chastity and voluntary continence (which in Bordeu–Diderot's eyes would be 'contre-nature' if anything could be), comes the discussion of human–animal miscegenation. Bordeu notes that little is known about it, on account of people's cowardice, their 'répugnances', their laws and their prejudices (p.203). He clearly wishes things were otherwise, indeed he has a whole agenda of unanswered questions he would like to investigate: which sorts of copulations would prove sterile, which ones would unite the 'utile' with the 'agréable', thus (he had explained earlier, p.197) providing the optimal state of sexual activity; what new kinds of species might emerge from varied and repeated experiments; whether fauns are fictional, whether the different races of hybrids might not be augmented, and whether the ones that already exist are truly sterile. Although the recent reports of experiments mating rabbits with chickens are dismissed as preposterous, he is intrigued by the possibility of working out something between humans and goats, which, producing a race of beings suitable for work, would not only provide excellent domestics, but might offer a much needed, humane remedy to the problem of colonial slavery (p.205). Mlle de Lespinasse finds the notion intriguing also because it might provide a solution to the servant problem, and urges Bordeu to get to work instantly to manufacture some of the new breed. Upon further consideration, however, she realises that the unbridled licentiousness and libido of these goat-persons would create an unmanageable threat for 'honest women'; the proliferations of the goat-men would be endless; so apparently would be their sexual demands; finally women would be left with the choice either to obey them, or 'les assommer' (p.206). Hastily changing her mind, she revokes her earlier order and urges Bordeu to abandon his plan.

Her skittish reaction of denial underscores the double nature, in fact the duplicity, of everything in the scandalous conversations of the 'Suite'. It is clear that Bordeu condemns the attitude of society which refuses to face the realities of sexuality in its laws, and stipulates his own willingness to find positive values in conduct which society judges criminal; yet the more he insists on this point, the more he insists at the same time on the spotless 'purity' of his own sexual morals, as if his own refusal to act upon the licence afforded by his theories were what rendered the discussion of them permissible. He even goes so far as to state that he can expound his ideas all the more freely *because*, as all the world knows, his conduct is beyond reproach: 'je ne m'en laisse point imposer par des mots, et je m'explique d'autant plus librement que je suis net et que la pureté connue de mes mœurs ne laisse prise d'aucun côté' (p.201-202). The ultimate stage in this trend towards social conformity in Bordeu is his statement – following an open discussion of the advantages, indeed the occasional medical necessity, for adolescents to practise masturbation (p.198-200) – that he himself would not so much as doff his hat in the street to a man suspected of implementing his own doctrine on this point, that the mere reputation of being depraved ('un infâme') would be sufficient reason for Bordeu to refuse to greet him (p.201).

Bordeu then contrasts such a public situation with the present, private one, which he says is without witnesses and without consequence. He concludes (p.201) by referring to an anecdote which Diderot had wittily used once before in the *Salon de 1767* (DPV, xvi.375): the earlier text had recounted how, as he posed naked for a portrait by Mme Therbouche, Diderot had wondered nervously whether each and every member of his body would remain as obediently under control as, for example, his arm did. As a possibly useful classical allusion with which to put Mme Therbouche at ease in case of embarrassment, Diderot was ready with a quotation from Diogenes Laertius describing how Diogenes the Cynic, naked and preparing to wrestle with a young Athenian, had explained to his opponent that he had nothing to fear, since he himself was not so wicked as 'celui-là' – the very anecdote that Bordeu repeats in the *Rêve*, presumably to calm the jittery nerves of Mlle de Lespinasse.

Modern psychology would of course disagree seriously with the last point: the 'disobedience' of the sexual member would certainly count as obedience to an unrecognised desire, and everything in the 'Suite' points to the same phenomenon in Bordeu, or rather in Bordeu–Diderot. For no matter how much Doctor Bordeu in real life may have played up the unassailable virtue of his sexual conduct, the character Diderot invented relates Diderot's own anecdote with a savoir faire that is more appropriate for someone having at least a mild penchant for libertinage, a person such as Diderot himself – who for the rest normally refrained from boasting about the unblemished condition of his sexual virtue. Bordeu–Diderot's ready-to-be-launched experiments in human–animal miscegenation also display the sort of eagerly perverse curiosity that probably owes at least as much to Diderot himself as to the real Bordeu. No doubt one should, as most scholars insist,[52] take seriously Diderot's distinction between verbal discussion (limitless freedom) and public action (total restriction), a distinction that also is operative elsewhere in Diderot, particularly in the *Supplément au Voyage de Bougainville*, both in the text proper and indirectly in Diderot's repressive letter to his daughter. Furthermore, not just the fictional Bordeu, but Diderot, too, was probably convinced that he felt freer to reveal the unorthodox sexual morality of his materialism so long as that licence was counterbalanced by some sort of continence – even if the abstention were fictional and imaginary, and attributed to someone else. Since theoretically materialism has no built-in moral boundary lines, nothing being inherently either evil or virtuous, perhaps Diderot felt the need for a distinction

52. See Jean Varloot, DPV, xvii.200, n.312, and introduction, p.49-50.

between private verbal licence and public conformity to provide an easily defined criterion (if not exactly a logical one) by which to eliminate harmfully criminal conduct. One might even concede that some part of Diderot wanted to believe in the rightness of sexual conformity of the most reactionary sort – witness his letter to Angélique. In short it is entirely possible that, in this respect at least, Diderot was a dualist: thoughts in the mind being one thing, conduct another.

But at the same time, the exposition of Diderot's philosophy in the dialogues had created something like a tidal wave going in the opposite direction. The general tendency towards moral acceptance that inherently emerges from the postulates of materialism, the tolerant implications of the doctrine that whatever is, is natural, the eager willingness to put aside prejudice, a tolerance that virtually everywhere else characterises these dialogues, all these factors would seem to be building pressures that run powerfully counter to Bordeu's prudery. In sum, Bordeu's virtue may be less helpful than Diderot might have wished in allaying one's suspicions that the subject-matter of the 'Suite' verges on pornography, or at least prurient interest. To combat such suspicions, the strongest argument would have been the seriousness of Bordeu's concerns as a doctor, an argument that is unfortunately undercut when he insists on espousing publicly the very sort of prudish prejudices which his private principles proved false and even harmful. Nor, in view of the intended hypocrisy of his behaviour, should one forget Bordeu's edifying message, preached earlier to Mlle de Lespinasse (p.187), condemning lying or falsehood ('le mensonge') on the basis that its 'benefits' are short term, whereas truth is for ever.

So many implicit contradictions and non sequiturs in the context of Bordeu's self-righteous position are sure signs that the prudish, puritanical Bordeu forms a true contrariety with the materialistic, free thinking one, as if his prudery were created in answer to his licence, a circumstance which Bordeu came very close to admitting in so many words, as was previously observed.[53] But for present purposes the most interesting point about the puritanical side of the contrariety is that to conform one's conduct to the sexual prejudices of society implies conformity to prejudices ultimately stemming from religion: to shun someone (as Bordeu intends to do) whom one knows to be innocent but whom society considers depraved implies outward acceptance of a moral code that comes straight from the Christian idea of sin. This is conduct based on fear, as though not only the eye of the neighbour or the police were upon

53. See the passage from p.201-202 quoted above, p.193.

one, but, through their ethics, the eye of the Divinity as well.[54] In other words, this contrariety between the two sides of Bordeu's character again makes visible and explicit the dominant contrariety informing the entire work, between a God-centred set of values and materialism. Although Bordeu's lessons of conduct entirely reverse the moral implications of the whole, the elements of the contrariety are the familiar ones.

Meanwhile, even as d'Alembert–Diderot had taken over God's role in order to reinvent the cosmos, so too Bordeu and Mlle de Lespinasse, setting about to invent new races, have, in their own rather frivolous way, taken over something of the Divinity's function as creator.[55] It might even be tempting to interpret the projected goat-men's fatal defect, namely their lasciviousness, as a counterpart to Christianity's original sin, noting that in this instance Mlle de Lespinasse's 'prévision' enables her to stop the disorder in time before it corrupts future generations, in contrast to the Christian Divinity, who, despite far greater 'prévision', nevertheless let Adam's sin get completely out of control. But, however that may be, and no matter how puritanically Bordeu is pleased to think of his own social conduct, there is a strong possibility that divinely sponsored morality may lose out one final time in the concluding words of the dialogue, namely, Bordeu's flippant, precipitous and not really disapproving suggestions as to why homosexual tastes and activities exist (p.209):

Mlle de Lespinasse

Ces goûts abominables d'où viennent-ils?

Bordeu

Partout d'une pauvreté d'organisation dans les jeunes gens, et de la corruption de la tête dans les vieillards; de l'attrait de la beauté dans Athènes, de la disette des femmes dans Rome, de la crainte de la vérole à Paris. Adieu, adieu.

Despite the partly feigned impatience to be off characteristic of Bordeu, and a slightly medical orientation in the mentioning of 'la vérole', again one might sense in the easygoing, worldly-wise humour of his *boutade* the kind of 'désinvolture' most easily associated with Diderot, or at least someone less immediately involved in the tight-lipped virtues of conduct supposedly practised by the alleged speaker.

54. Cf. Dieckmann's interpretation of morality in the *Supplément au Voyage de Bougainville*: 'Ce n'est qu'à la fin que nous trouvons l'accusation qui au début du *Supplément* primait toutes les autres: ce sont 'les institutions religieuses qui ont attaché les noms de vices et de vertus à des actions qui n'étaient susceptibles d'aucune moralité' (Introduction, p.vi).
55. Aram Vartanian's biblical quotation: *Eritis sicut Dei.* is entirely apropos: see his 'Diderot et la technologie de la vie', *Denis Diderot. Colloque international* (Paris 1985), p.78.

In any event, it makes for a most curious ending! As a stopping point Bordeu's final remarks appear completely arbitrary. Nor is there any obvious reason for his departure at that particular moment in the discussion; ostensibly he might just as well have left somewhat sooner, or later. This odd 'finale' also lacks one of the three main characters featured in both the other two dialogues: d'Alembert is nowhere in sight; Diderot has found a pretext to send him out of the picture, even though the end of the 'Rêve' proper suggested he would be present for the 'dîner'. But perhaps in this instance one needs to look beyond the dialogues themselves, and beyond the final topic of discussion. In the present state of research it is difficult to be sure about various aspects of d'Alembert's relations with Mlle de Lespinasse; but whatever they may have been, there is at least some documentary evidence suggesting conduct by d'Alembert that was homosexual.[56] And it remains an intriguing possibility that awareness of this side of d'Alembert's behaviour led Diderot to bring the famous mathematician subtly, indeed covertly and by suggestion, back into the picture for the end, to receive one last good-humoured wink of connivance from someone in the know. In that case – and needless to say the idea is the purest supposition – Bordeu's vaunted priggishness would be doubly beside the point.

56. See the prudently sceptical sifting of the evidence in John Pappas, 'Idées reçues contre évidences: problèmes pour une biographie de d'Alembert', *Jean d'Alembert, savant et philosophe: portrait à plusieurs voix*, Actes du Colloque du Centre international de Synthèse, 1983, ed. Monique Emery and Pierre Monzani (Paris 1989), p.92-96.

7. Diderot against Greuze?

LINGUISTS have long been aware of the word-phenomenon of 'verbal contrariety', that is, words which can mean either one thing or the opposite.[1] Among familiar examples they cite the Latin *altus*, which can signify either 'high', or its mirror opposite 'deep' (cf. 'high seas'); 'fast', the most rapid of movements or an immobile denial of movement ('stay fast' or 'cling fast'); 'cleave', which follows the same pattern, and a large group of words in French such as *plus*, *personne* and *ancien*. Freud was especially intrigued by the phenomenon because he thought it was connected to the language of dreams. In 'The antithetical sense of primal words' (1910) he quoted at some length the findings of Karl Abel, a philologist who had studied the verbal contradictions that informed the language of ancient Egypt. According to Abel's researches, the Egyptians communicated mainly through a vocabulary whose words had (simultaneously) two contradictory meanings, or in which one syllable directly contradicted the next. Noting that the Egyptian civilisation was among the most enlightened in antiquity, Abel concluded that this phenomenon in no sense indicated stupidity or lack of intellectual rigour on the part of the Egyptians. It derived instead from the fact that 'our conceptions arise through comparison', and 'every conception is [...] the twin of its opposite', which is to say that, linguistically speaking, contrariety is inherently part of the way in which word-ideas come into being. From Freud's discussion it becomes evident that to him part of the richness of words derived from their being in some sense saturated with their opposites.

In Diderot there are striking examples of verbal contrarieties, such as one finds in the dramatic reversal of meaning in the terms 'actor' and 'audience' referred to in Chapter 4.[2] More often the contrarieties occur in whole positions or arguments. And nowhere in his writings is the process more startling than in his *Salon* articles on Greuze: only a Freud might not have been surprised or disturbed by them. To be sure, received opinion holds that Diderot's attitude towards the art of Greuze, at least the famous paintings, was almost single-mindedly favourable in the early stages, a claim backed by generations of Diderot scholars, not to mention strong appearances in its favour.

1. See Rex, *The Attraction of the contrary*, p.230-31, n.31.
2. The numerous kinds of verbal reversals have been magisterially classified and analysed in Georges Daniel, *Le Style de Diderot: légends et structure* (Geneva 1986), ch.4, 'Le thème de la réversibilité', p.283-344.

I

In the *Salon de 1765*[3] the section on Greuze (p.177f.) starts with a burst of ideas that scatter abroad, lighting up everything along the way – a burst such as, in this period, only Diderot could have invented. Diderot's enthusiasm for Greuze was reaching its high point at this time (it would diminish later), and at the beginning of the text he specifies two reasons for it.

First, Greuze initiated in France a kind of painting and drawing that bestowed on art what Diderot calls 'des mœurs', a term which, in good eighteenth-century fashion, had a double implication: in addition to the familiar sense of morality, i.e. the virtues and vices of human conduct,[4] the word also applied to the pictorial concept of 'tableaux de mœurs', that is, a depiction of the way of life of a certain class. Both senses were on the cutting edge of Diderot's ideas, and in the case of Greuze (as distinct from genre scenes painted by certain Dutch artists) they were intertwined, which is to say that Diderot's enthusiasm for the simple life of Greuze's rustic scenes was part of a far-reaching social outlook, which included moral concerns as well.[5]

The second reason specified by Diderot for his esteem for Greuze was that the moment depicted in each of his scenes could be taken as a link in a chain of events, such as one might find in a novel. This perception not only reflects Diderot's interest in the literary dimension of painting, it fits perfectly, too, with the dynamics of Diderot's own materialism, particularly with his theory that every phenomenon should be presumed to be coming from somewhere and tending likewise. Obviously a painting by definition can depict only a single instant,[6] yet, particularly in the case of Greuze, in the compression of that moment the entire plot of the story may be present by implication. Thus each expression and gesture can be deciphered in terms of the continuum to

3. Parenthetical page numbers in this chapter refer to the text established by Annette Lorenceau, DPV, xiv.21-332; Seznec edition, ii.144-60.

4. This was the principal meaning of the term in Diderot's vocabulary, in respect to art; see the *Salon de 1763* on Greuze's *Piété filiale*: 'D'abord le genre me plaît; c'est de la peinture morale. Quoi donc! le pinceau n'a-t-il pas été assez et trop longtemps consacré à la débauche et au vice? Ne devons-nous pas être satisfait de le voir concourir enfin avec la poésie dramatique à nous toucher, à nous instruire, et à nous inviter à la vertu? Courage, mon ami Greuze, fais de la morale en peinture, et fais-en toujours comme cela!' (DPV, xiii.394; occasional punctuation and spelling from the Seznec edition, i.233). See also the *Salon de 1765* in the section on Baudouin: 'Greuze s'est fait peintre prédicateur des bonnes mœurs, Baudouin, peintre prédicateur des mauvaises; Greuze, peintre de famille et d'honnêtes gens; Baudouin, peintre de petites-maisons et de libertins' (DPV, xiv.169).

5. See the elegantly concise discussion of these issues by Jean Starobinski, 'Diderot dans l'espace des peintres', in *Diderot et l'art, de Boucher à David. Les Salons: 1759-1781* (Paris 1984), p.24A.

6. Lévi-Strauss, *Regarder écouter lire*, p.74-75.

which it belongs. One might describe this aspect of Greuze's paintings using the theatrical term 'vraisemblance',[7] for although one does not hear their words, the language of the gestures, expressions and general appearance of each figure has been devised to fit perfectly with the moment portrayed just as it would have been in the word-language of some theatrical *drame*. Some of the aesthetic implications of this concept will be considered further on.

Immediately after proclaiming Greuze's excellence as an artist, Diderot admits the existence, too (and here he starts to sound like Moi in *Le Neveu de Rameau*[8]), of the painter's personal defect, namely, his deplorable vanity; and the counterpoint between the two – the artistic excellence on the one side, and the personal blemish on the other – sparks everything in the lively discussion that ensues. Diderot understood the complexities of the human personality as forming not only a mixture of good and bad, but as a nexus in which the good qualities could not exist without the bad ones, indeed in which the good qualities sometimes actually created the bad ones. No one else had this insight in this period, at least not in France. And Diderot is perfectly convincing as he explains that Greuze's vanity comes from the intoxicating verve of his enthusiasm for his own work ('Voyez-moi cela! C'est cela qui est beau!', p.177), a verve on which his excellence totally depends, to the point that, without it, his genius would be eclipsed, its fire extinguished; modest would be all he deserved to be.

Having pointed out how intimately our good qualities (some of them at least) are inter-twined with our defects, Diderot assumes that readers will figure out for themselves the reasons for the ensuing contrasts. He states as self-evident that most women who are 'honnête' are ill-tempered, and great artists slightly cracked in the brain; ladies given to amorous affairs ('les femmes galantes', p.178) are usually generous as well; devout women, even the nice ones, do not always refrain from slander. Finally, a master who is sure of his beneficence may also be slightly despotic. Throughout these assertions Diderot expects that his observations will carry their own weight, and that everyone will recognise the same distinctions between 'good qualities' and 'defects', even though in the instance of the generosity of the 'femmes galantes' the pattern looks slightly askew.

Having made the same point so clearly and so many times (p.177-78) as Diderot rocked back and forth between the large virtue and the peccadillo that travelled in its wake, and having shored up his point with a strong final

7. See Rex, *The Attraction of the contrary*, p.75-81 and p.222, n.2.
8. DPV, xii.83, Fabre edition (Geneva 1963), p.14. This point has been made by E. M. Bukdahl in her 'Notice' on Greuze in *Diderot et l'art*, p.218B-C.

example (the benign but despotic master), the text swings into a new course: 'Je hais toutes ces petites bassesses qui ne montrent qu'une âme abjecte; mais je ne hais pas les grands crimes: premièrement, parce qu'on en fait de beaux tableaux et de belles tragédies; et puis, c'est que les grandes et sublimes actions et les grands crimes, portent le même caractère d'énergie' (p.178).

Before exploring the implications of this amazing and often-quoted statement, one might pause to wonder how this new line of thought arose in the first place.[9] No doubt the expression 'toutes ces petites bassesses' derives, by association, from the aforementioned peccadillos. As one moves into this new stage, these petty vices are no longer joined contrapuntally to good qualities, however, but are taken as things in themselves that denote a general condition of meanness and abjectness of soul. And the disgust that Diderot feels as he contemplates this petty abjection apparently inspires him, as a contrary reaction, to devise a new criterion, namely the idea of 'grandeur'. What is totally and brilliantly unexpected is that 'grandeur' should also be linked to the idea of 'crime'.[10] Indeed, nothing prepares one for this sudden appearance of 'grands crimes' on the pedestal, with Diderot not only confessing a certain liking for them ('je ne hais pas les grands crimes'), but actually comparing them to 'sublimes actions'. Even less does the preceding text lead one to anticipate Diderot's declaration that great crimes provide the substance of beautiful paintings and fine tragedies, in other words the substance of great art.

This *Salon* article began with Diderot's enthusiasm for Greuze precisely because he had bestowed morality on art. The sudden admiration for art based on great crimes takes the discussion to the opposite pole of the original position.[11] No doubt the move was made possible by Diderot's momentary abandonment of morality as the main criterion, and his substitution of mindless, amoral 'énergie' in its stead – a quality by no means restricted to the souls of

9. See the moderate analysis of Jean Starobinski, who sees Diderot's admiration for great crimes as an inherent part of his value system: 'Car la morale de l'énergie a besoin de l'opposition entre vice et vertu pour manifester qu'elle vit de leur conflit tout en le transcendant' ('Diderot dans l'espace des peintres', p.31A-32B). See also in this connection my analysis of the 'Renégat d'Avignon' episode in *Le Neveu de Rameau* in 'Two Scenes', *Diderot Studies* 20 (1981), p.259f.

10. See the broad-based discussions of this phenomenon in Diderot's correspondence and art criticism in Michel Delon, 'La beauté du crime', *Europe* 62 (1984), p.73-83, and René Démoris, 'Peinture et cruauté chez Diderot', *Denis Diderot 1713-1784: Colloque international* (Paris 1985), p.299-307.

11. Concerning the same passage from the *Salon*, Michel Delon writes, 'Il est intéressant que ces lignes effervescantes aient été justement écrites dans l'article consacré au vertueux et larmoyant Greuze. Diderot ne s'enferme pas dans un moralisme bourgeois du style Travail, Famille, Patrie' ('La beauté du crime', p.78).

the virtuous.[12] But the important point for present purposes is that Diderot's former adherence to the morality of Greuze has suddenly been replaced by a liberation from the defining boundaries of that morality, a perspective in which sublime heroism and terrible crimes are seen in exactly the same light.

Several subliminal reasons may help to explain this bizarre happening in a text supposedly centred on Greuze. One may relate to Greuze's aesthetic manipulations. For indeed, this painter's 'moral' scenes, precisely because of their relentless intensity, have an effect on the viewer which is deliberately constricting.[13] Behind the drama played out in these paintings one senses the artist's intent to eliminate systematically the viewer's freedom of choice. These scenes were designed, not to open up possibilities, but to force the viewer to assume a judgemental position either by pointing guilty fingers or sprinkling benedictions. Thus, for example, in a pair of drawings for which Diderot, later in the same *Salon* (p.196-200), would claim to feel virtually nothing but admiration, *Le Fils ingrat* (Figure 6) and *Le Mauvais fils puni* (Figure 7),[14] everything combines to enjoin, even compel, the viewer to condemn this callous, unfeeling son who abandons his family in their time of need and eventually, amid a horrendous scene of woe, is denounced as causing his own father's death. Who would be so heartless as to resist all those anguished faces – the distraught mother, the despairing elder sisters, the hapless younger children – those frenzied gestures and the spectacle of such abject want? Or, at the opposite end of the scale, who, viewing *L'Accordée de village* at the *Salon de 1761*,[15] could be so base that his heart was not warmed at the sight of that honest, worthy father with his worn countenance and white locks, as he betrothes his pretty daughter to the nice young man, surrounded by the entire family, displaying various gestures and expressions, ranging from contentment to jealousy to incomprehension, and which are all so entirely suitable for their ages and the happy event they witness? Not Diderot, in any case. On the

12. This is the central topic of Chouillet, *Diderot poète de l'énergie*, esp. p.102f.; see also Delon, 'La beauté du crime', p.75-77.

13. See the astute analysis by Scott Bryson: 'The techniques used by Greuze more than just focus the spectator's look on the canvas; they train this look, enclosing it within the frame, imposing upon it a set direction by means of figures and objects that discreetly, almost imperceptibly redirect the viewer's gaze back to the focal point. The viewer's look is "imprisoned" and submitted to a system of visual constraints that render it docile. It is more than the moralistic tenor of Greuze's family scenes that is disturbing, it is the means by which this moral message is achieved [...] The moral genre is inextricably linked to control' (*The Chastized stage*, p.30).

14. These two sketches are reproduced as Figures 6 and 7. It has not been thought necessary to provide reproductions of the other pictures referred to in the following discussion, since they have become so familiar to Diderot scholars in exhibition catalogues, critical editions and studies of eighteenth-century French art.

15. DPV, xiii.266-72; Seznec edition, i.141-44.

Figure 6. Jean–Baptiste Greuze, *Le Fils ingrat*

contrary, Diderot vibrated with Greuze at the perfect unison, and went into paroxysms of approval for some of these scenes. On the other hand, Diderot's meditation on Greuze somehow also produced – by an equally powerful contrary motion – the other passage favouring the art of great crimes, and it seems reasonable to conclude that the sudden, unprepared appearance of such a totally incongruous and inappropriate point of view represents a liberating gesture whose refreshing effect is to get rid of everything that Greuze supposedly stood for. For the moment one has the illusion that Greuze has vanished from the map of Diderot's mind.

The particular 'grands crimes' and 'grands criminels', as well as the counterbalancing virtuous actions mentioned by Diderot in this part of the text, come from antiquity or some other distant past – no doubt it is safer to express a liking for criminality when it is far away, confined to history or art, and given simply as the other side of the coin of virtue (p.178):

Si un homme n'était pas capable d'incendier une ville, un autre homme ne serait pas capable de se précipiter dans un gouffre pour la sauver. Si l'âme de César n'eût pas été possible, celle de Caton ne l'aurait pas été davantage. L'homme est né citoyen tantôt du Ténare, tantôt des cieux; c'est Castor et Pollux, un héros, un scélérat, Marc-Aurèle, Borgia, *diversis studiis ovo prognatus eodem*.

The remoteness of Caesar and Borgia, mentioned by name, almost makes one forget that much closer to home, indeed right at hand, was another truly monstrous moral criminal, someone with whom it is certain that Diderot was just then very much preoccupied: namely, the cruel, heartless, selfish son in the two drawings by Greuze which Diderot was about to analyse down to the least detail. Diderot's seemingly gratuitous expression of admiration for great criminality, an expression that comes out of the blue, with no direct link to anything that preceded, may represent a momentary, unrecognised – or at least heavily camouflaged – impulse to reject the line that Greuze demanded he toe. One has only to move Diderot's admiration for great crimes into the present to bring him perilously close to the 'wrong' side of Greuze's moral dramas, to – unthinkable thought – the side of the wayward son.

It may seem astonishing that Diderot himself was aware of this kind of negative possibility, of the impulses to reject, and even to do the opposite, that are automatically engendered by the demand that one conform to virtue: 'Donner des mœurs à un peuple, c'est augmenter son énergie pour le bien et pour le mal; c'est l'encourager, s'il est permis de parler ainsi, aux grands crimes et aux grandes vertus.'[16]

16. 'A Sophie Volland' (au Grandval, 14-15 octobre 1760), *Correspondance*, ed. Georges Roth, iii.141.

Diderot had originally praised Greuze for being the first to 'donner des mœurs à l'art'. Following the precepts of the present quotation, it is no wonder that Greuze's 'morality' produced, as one result, Diderot's admiration for great crimes, perhaps – one is free to imagine – even for those depicted by Greuze himself.

There may be a still more curious overtone in the appearance of such a contrariety in the text of the *Salon*. For it is just possible that the inexplicable switch to the theme of great crime was also brought on by some subliminal awareness of the element of cruelty, indeed the sadistic violence, of some of these creations by Greuze, which makes them intolerable to the present era:[17] no doubt the sketch of *Le Mauvais fils puni* – which leaves so much to the imagination – has some of the merits Diderot thought it did; if one tries, however, to give serious consideration to the painted version, which spells out all the contorted facial expressions and frantic gestures in detail, it seems clear that the artist has overplayed his hand, and that such exaggerated postures are not marks of tragedy, but signs of a particularly painful sort of melodrama.[18]

In sum, I have been proposing two hypotheses that form opposite sides of the same coin. First, that Diderot's admission – in the middle of an article praising Greuze specifically for his morality – of an attraction to great crimes represents an impulse to escape from, and even rebel against, Greuze's moral manipulations. And then, second, the hypothesis that at the same time the appearance of this unprepared topic may also indicate, subliminally, an awareness of the cruelty inherent in Greuze's allegedly moral scenes. Diderot sometimes uncannily anticipates twentieth-century attitudes – no doubt this is why he could not be widely appreciated before the present era. Both the gratuitousness and the ambiguous implications of this passage of his text suggest how well Diderot sensed what we see today as the darker, inhuman side of Greuze's contrivances.

II

The *pièce de résistance* of the articles on Greuze in the *Salon de 1765* is 'La Jeune fille qui pleure son oiseau mort' (p.179-82).[19] No text better reveals the

17. See Bryson, *The Chastised stage*, p.33.

18. Reproduction in Seznec, ii, plate 60.

19. On the background of this painting see E. M. Bukdahl, 'Notice', p.240-41. Other reproductions appear in the exhibition catalogue *Jean-Baptiste Greuze* (Hartford, Conn. 1976), p.105; Anita Brookner, *Greuze: the rise and fall of an eighteenth-century phenomenon* (Greenwich, Conn. 1972), colour plate III; Michael Fried, *Absorption and theatricality: painting and the beholder in the age of Diderot* (Berkeley, Calif. 1980), p.58.

uncanny accord between this painter's and Diderot's own sensibilities. For the rest, this delicately attentive and perspicacious account is the kind of review of which any artist would dream. By describing his own reactions to each aspect of the picture Diderot manages to conjure up the painting, so that, even unseen, it somehow becomes a presence for the reader. And then one is drawn into the account because behind the image of the young girl allegedly grieving for the loss of her bird the narrator claims to discover an archetypical allegory of seduction in which the lost bird symbolises lost virginity, a tale which he recounts in classic fashion: enticement, fall and aftermath. Only in a single sentence at the very end will the author tip his hand, revealing the true character of his own motives.

Among the strategies enlivening the account is the narrator's pretence that he can actually speak to the girl in the picture, divining what has happened to her almost as though she had told him herself; coaxing her into confirming the 'truth' which the narrator had guessed, namely, that her sorrow concerns a loss far more significant than that of a bird; coaxing her too into letting him recount her own story for her; coaxing her finally into bringing her mother into the picture and, above all, confessing her worries about the (un)faithfulness of the young man who seduced her. Meanwhile he depicts himself as sympathising with her pain, offering consolation and reassurance, and so on, until the entire story and everything about the emotions of the girl stand revealed.

A well-established iconographical tradition connects caged birds with women's sexual (in)continence, and if in addition one is aware of other iconographies in paintings by Greuze connected to this same topic – *Le Miroir cassé*, which Diderot mentions (p.182-83), or the even more obvious *La Cruche cassée* – Diderot's sexual interpretation seems entirely justified, indeed unquestionable, for Greuze was much given to this titillating sort of quasi-allegory. The narrator's role, as he pretends to read her mind, sympathise with her, and excuse her yielding to the charms of her seducer – not to mention giving in to her own desires – and then at the end telling her exactly what she wanted to hear about the young man's fidelity (while winking in connivance at the reader), has something of the pimp or go-between about it. One might even recall the cynical scene of the procurer in *Le Neveu de Rameau*,[20] where the Nephew persuades a young girl to surmount her scruples and become the mistress of a wealthy young man. The Nephew reads the girl's mind, just as the narrator of the painting does, and then plays on her vanity and greed. 'Et maman qui me recommande tant d'être honnête fille?', the girl of *Le Neveu de Rameau* weakly protests, and the Nephew easily allays her not very serious

20. DPV, xii.93-94; Fabre edition, p.22-23.

worries and pangs of conscience. Curiously, the girl in the painting, as if borrowing from the Nephew's account, asks almost exactly the same question of the narrator, even though the question does not really fit the context: 'Et ma mère?' (p.181). Indeed the narrator's role in the *Salon* article on Greuze is only slightly less cynical than the Nephew's: he imagines himself toying with her feelings, manipulating her responses; towards the end, there is even a suggestion of laughing at her being such easy prey. It is almost as though the narrator were seducing her himself – which, he confesses in his final statement at the end, is exactly what he would like to do: 'qu'elle est belle! qu'elle est intéressante! Je n'aime point à affliger, malgré cela, il ne me déplairait pas trop d'être la cause de sa peine' (p.182).

Here at last Diderot puts his finger on the element of sadism inherent in the appeal of the painting and which is probably one of the reasons why this picture – and Greuze did a number of versions of it – strikes our own gender-conscious era as distasteful. No one today likes this scene. No doubt the sexism of Diderot's attitude is reprehensible as well. On the other hand, because of his unique awareness of the presence in the painting of powerfully implicit sexuality,[21] Diderot has understood this work as no one else in his time could have done. If Diderot's attitude towards the girl and her seduction contains recognisable elements of cynicism and male sadism, this is a perspicacious and entirely truthful revelation of the only slightly more covert cynicism of the painting itself.

III

As he describes the famous betrothal scene, *L'Accordée de village* (DPV, xiii.266-72), Diderot is pleased to linger over each facial expression, each body posture, even the clothes worn, in order to point out their appropriateness to the occasion and to the particular moment chosen for depiction. Except for the identity and the dress of the elder sister, about which Diderot had some rather odd second thoughts, in each case he found everything about the

21. E. M. Bukdahl, 'Notice', p.240, points out that no critic other than Diderot understood the sexual implications of the picture. See also, in a letter to Sophie Volland, Diderot's similarly ambiguous, but more guarded, reaction to the young woman, whose youthful charm he had already remarked upon as she played the harpsichord *chez* Mme d'Epinay: 'Je la regardois, et je pensois au fond de mon cœur que c'étoit un ange et qu'il faudroit être plus méchant que Satan pour en approcher avec une pensée déshonnête. Je disois à Mr. de Villeneuve: "Qui est-ce qui oseroit changer quelque chose à cet ouvrage là? Il est si bien." Mais nous n'avons pas, Mr. de Villeneuve et moi, les mêmes principes. S'il rencontroit des innocentes, lui, il aimeroit assez à les instruire' (15 octobre 1760, *Correspondance*, iii.68).

personage and its relation to the others to be perfectly suitable. According to eighteenth-century theatrical conventions, the achievement of this sort of suitability, or *vraisemblance*, implied that the spectator would have no choice but to believe in the reality of these personages: in effect they became real.[22] Likewise in Greuze, the perfection of the figures is supposed to force the viewer to believe in them. The other side of this coin is that, because they all fitted so perfectly into their context, theoretically at least, they could not have been any other way: the continuum in which each lived and which brought them together for the betrothal ceremony would not have allowed anything to be different. To Diderot the drama was so all-involving that he claimed that even the artist had been personally affected by the characters he depicted: 'Lorsqu'il travaille, il est tout à son ouvrage; il s'affecte profondément: il porte dans le monde le caractère du sujet qu'il traite dans son atelier, triste ou gai, folâtre ou sérieux, galant ou réservé, selon la chose qui a occupé le matin son pinceau et son imagination' (*Salon de 1761*, DPV, xiii.260; Seznec edition i.135).

In sum, Greuze's drawings and paintings represented for Diderot the extreme of one sort of art in which the creation itself is thought of as dominating the artist, rather than the other way round: the figures are presented as being so completely enmeshed in chains of causality – like the ones which govern the real world, or for that matter the theatrical world of *Le Fils naturel* and the *Entretiens* – that they tend to take on a life of their own, as though they had been created as much by their situation, and the external causes behind it, as by the artist's genius. Gratuitousness has theoretically been banished from this representation, and, in his respect for the laws regulating the way things are, the artist is seen less as an improviser or inventor than as a registrar of true facts or events. Perhaps this is the reason why the broad presence of the *tabellion* (notary) in *L'Accordée de village*, seen from the back, bulks so large – almost obtrusively – in the painting (and also in Diderot's description): the notary's legal function was first of all to legitimise this betrothal and certify that it did in fact take place. By extension, the *tabellion* supposedly certifies that the viewer too is witnessing not a staged event with actors or models, but reality itself.[23]

The official title of *L'Accordée de village* was *Un Mariage, et l'instant où le père de l'accordée délivre la dot à son gendre*. In keeping with this emphasis (as critics have already pointed out) Greuze makes sure that one cannot miss the

22. See Rex, *The Attraction of the contrary*, p.73f.
23. On the broader context of Diderot's 'realism' see the introduction and *commentaires* by Roland Desné in Diderot, *Textes choisis*, iv, 'Les Salons' (Paris 1970).

pouch containing the dowry money, clutched in the groom's hand and placed just at the centre of the canvas. Its conspicuous position, a counterpart to the venerable father's open mouth (another purse), makes its significance apparent even without the full title, and informs the viewer that, in this little society, money is not being thought of as either sordid or even as a symbol of power and rank (as it might have been in other social milieux in France at this time), but as a benign agent that facilitated those crucial bonds which made society flourish. In this respect Greuze very much resembles his playwright contemporary, Sedaine, who also was pleased to look on money as benign. Though we cannot hear the wise father's words we may be sure that they have to do with honest work, marital duties, faithfulness and so on, in other words with virtue, and the proximity of the purse, along with its conspicuous visibility, suggests not only that its contents have been honourably earned, but that money is being thought of as belonging inherently to the particular kind of virtue that this picture celebrates.

Although dramatised in a very different way, money plays just as central a role in the sketches of *Le Fils ingrat* and *Le Mauvais fils puni*, which Diderot reviewed in the *Salon de 1765* (DPV, xiv.196-200). If in *L'Accordée de village* money allegedly fosters happiness and honest virtue, here absence of money acts negatively as the agent of catastrophe. Diderot pointed to the poverty implied in the furnishings of the first sketch, *Le Fils ingrat*. And in fact the financial implication of this setting provides an indispensable key to the anger of the father in the sketch: one can see the violence of his emotions in the contorted fury of his face, the outstretched arms, the gesture as if trying to rise from his seat and thrust himself forward. This outburst of indignation, the viewer becomes aware, is due to the announcement that his eldest son, the only wage-earner in the family, the sole support on whom they all depend, has decided to go off and enlist in the army. The barren meagreness of the furnishings of this poor dwelling reveal to the viewer as well that in their dire financial straits this departure will mean ruin for them all; they literally cannot survive without him.

In the second sketch, *Le Mauvais fils puni*, the poverty of the scene also has special significance: as Diderot noted, the simple but carefully made-up bedding of the first scene has disappeared, because the family could no longer afford to keep a mattress on the bed on which the worthy father has just expired; what Diderot termed the 'indigence' of the first scene has now given way to abject poverty ('la misère'). The mother's eloquent gesture spells out for the wayward son the unmistakable lesson, that their plight after his departure has led to the father's death. To make doubly sure the son has not

Figure 7. Jean-Baptiste Greuze, *Le Mauvais fils puni*

missed the point, Diderot also puts words in the mother's mouth: 'Tiens, vois, regarde: voilà l'état où tu l'as mis!'

The only values that Diderot recognises as sacred in these sketches are family virtues; indeed the sufferings of the family are given centre stage in both the sketches and in Diderot's account. But there is also a larger social dimension – one that would have been particularly appealing to Diderot – and which involves another part of the 'story' of the first sketch: the wayward son, Diderot relates, has been enrolled in the army by an old soldier and this 'vieux soldat' has accompanied the son to his parents' house. In the first sketch Diderot describes this soldier as turning his back to the scene behind him and heading towards the door, with head bowed and his sabre under his arm. (Grimm found this figure the most masterful touch in the sketch[24]). But the visibility of his weapon may serve in addition as a reminder of the obvious, though unmentioned, fact that the wayward son has yielded to the temptation of going off to play the traditional sport of the 'noblesse d'épée', and to participate in their aristocratic game of glory.[25] These sketches are intended to bear witness to the disastrous consequences of these games on the poor. And whereas in the army desertion was held to be the most heinous of all offences, Greuze deliberately overturns these values: the crime here is not desertion of the army, but desertion of the family; the army does not matter; nor does military glory. When the wayward son returns in the second sketch, he has a missing leg and a crippled arm; yet the viewer is not supposed to feel any pity upon seeing him, much less admiration for his battle wounds. As Diderot points out, with that very leg (now denatured indeed), this 'enfant dénaturé' attempted to push aside his distraught mother when she tried to restrain him; that arm had been raised in menace against his father. In Diderot's view, this unnatural son entirely deserved his denaturing.

How could Diderot have resisted such a painter? Just as in Sedaine, everything was the way he himself claimed he would have wanted it: the concern for the humble (even, presumably, at the expense of aristocrats) for family virtue; the emotional depiction of the characters in their moments of crisis; the careful structuring of the composition so that every gesture and facial expression, everything down to the smallest rosary or barking dog, contributed directly to the increase of the viewer's feelings of pity and horror – no wonder Diderot began his account by declaring (to Grimm) 'Voici votre peintre et le mien', and naturally too at the end of his account of *Le Mauvais*

24. Seznec edition, ii.157.
25. Cf. the interpretation of J. Erhard in *Diderot et Greuze*, Actes du Colloque de Clermont-Ferrand (Clermont-Ferrand 1986), p.122.

fils puni (the one he preferred), he added (p.199): 'Je ne sais quel effet cette courte et simple description d'une esquisse de tableau fera sur les autres; pour moi, j'avoue que je ne l'ai point faite sans émotion. Cela est beau, très beau, sublime, tout, tout.' This does not prevent Diderot (*au contraire*) from suggesting an improvement in the mother's gesture to make her action 'vraie', and a change in a detail of the religious part of the décor to make it authentic.

IV

Given the power of Greuze's moral scenes, and the intensity of Diderot's favourable reactions to them, it may seem incredible that there could also be, on Diderot's part, a negative side to the story. And yet, even at the beginning of the article on Greuze one may detect hints (as I have suggested) that some other portion of Diderot's soul yearned to be free of these constrictions – perhaps even feeling some perverse urge to take the other side. Elsewhere in the *Salon de 1765*, one finds – such is my contention – still another declaration of freedom from Greuze. This second act of emancipation occurs through Diderot's fascination with a painter of a very different stamp, one who was indeed, on crucial aesthetic and moral matters, as far from Greuze as any artist could be: Vernet. My claim is that Diderot's infatuation with the art of Vernet is, while he was caught up in it, a major infidelity to Greuze.[26]

The opening of the article on Vernet in the *Salon de 1765* is a virtuoso display (p.133-36). Contrary to the tactics deemed appropriate for Greuze, Diderot generally avoids lingering over details. Even when one scene in particular takes centrestage, his account seldom remains still for long. The heavier, almost plodding pace – so appropriate for Greuze's turgid dramas – is replaced by a rapidity that might seem breathless, were it not so perfectly poised: 'Quels effets incroyables de lumière! Les beaux ciels! Quelles eaux! Quelle ordonnance! Quelle prodigieuse variété de scènes!' (p.133).

Magically Diderot evokes, usually in just a phrase or two, the essence of each picture or figure; they almost seem to float in the air, and then dissolve at his command. Near the beginning of the account he compares Vernet to

26. Diderot's articles followed the hierarchical order of painters given in the official 'Explication' that accompanied the exhibit at the Louvre, i.e. according to the rank and seniority of each artist in the Académie royale. Since Vernet was a full-fledged 'académicien', whereas Greuze was only 'agréé', Vernet was naturally listed first in the 'Explication', and hence precedes Greuze in Diderot's account of the *Salon*. Thus Diderot's order is not necessarily an indication of the priorities of his thinking. For such matters of documentation, the Seznec edition remains indispensable (see ii.17-56, esp. p.28f. and p.34f).

God the Creator for the celerity of his productions. Diderot too plays this role, calling image after image into being, obedient to the potent words that make them flash into the reader's imagination. Immediately after the preceding exclamations, with no break, violent images wrench the reader into the main scene, the disaster of a shipwreck. Contrary to the methodical presentation of Greuze, here the account rushes from one dire situation to the next, leaving no time to wonder about personal identities; no time either to doubt that they exist: 'Ici, un enfant échappé du naufrage est porté sur les épaules de son père; là, une femme étendue morte sur le rivage, et son époux qui se désole' (p.134).

The drama's immediacy is created by the instantly recognisable quality of each element described – the innocence and vulnerability of the child, the devoted father's saving gesture, the husband grieving by the body of the woman he loved and lost – which automatically awakens response and recognition. As the description proceeds Diderot plays on the sound effects which Vernet's images evoke, choosing syllables that onomatopoeically make the sea bellow, the wind whistle and the thunder growl.[27] Lighting effects are also brought into action, even as they would have been at a theatrical performance: 'La mer mugit, les vents sifflent, le tonnerre gronde, la lueur sombre et pâle des éclairs perce la nue, montre et dérobe la scène' (p.134).

Following these flashes of light, the scene widens and one can now see more than isolated individuals caught in the catastrophe. The shipwreck itself surges into view in a cracking of timber as the hull splits open, the ship's masts tilt downwards, its sails torn; some of those on the bridge raise their arms to heaven, others have hurled themselves into the water. Along with a widening of the spatial dimension which spreads out from the ship, the violence of the images will now increase, turning finally into a broad maelstrom of bodies: those who jumped into the sea are borne towards rocks where their blood mixes with the whitening foam; the narrator sees some who are still floating, others about to vanish into the deep; and still others who hasten to reach the shore against which they will be smashed.[28]

27. It is not far fetched to recall the shipwrecks which were a frequent and popular scenic effect at the Paris Opéra: in *Le Neveu de Rameau* part of the Nephew's grand operatic pantomime involved an imitation shipwreck, which Diderot describes in terms closely resembling his *Salon* texts on Vernet. See Rex, *The Attraction of the contrary*, p.117-19, and also Michel Delon, 'Joseph Vernet et Diderot dans la tempête', *Recherches sur Diderot et l'Encyclopédie* 15 (1993), p.31-39, an article which, while coinciding with my own reflections on a number of points, generally takes a different line of argument in order to stress the ways in which Vernet's shipwreck illustrates Diderot's idea of the sublime.

28. 'On entend le bruit des flancs d'un vaisseau qui s'entrouvre, ses mâts sont inclinés, ses voiles déchirées; les uns, sur le pont, ont les bras levés vers le ciel, d'autres se sont élancés dans les eaux. Ils sont portés par les flots contre des rochers voisins où leur sang se mêle à l'écume qui les blanchit; j'en vois qui flottent, j'en vois qui sont prêts à disparaître dans le gouffre, j'en vois qui se hâtent d'atteindre le rivage contre lequel ils seront brisés' (p.134).

Strangely, the increasing violence of the catastrophes does not intensify the viewer's own sense of emotional participation in these events. On the contrary, the more the cadavers proliferate the more the action becomes a distant spectacle – impressive, certainly, but not seriously involving one's sympathy. Even the introduction of the narrator's own pronoun ('je'), instead of rendering the disaster more personal or emotional, makes the distancing still more pronounced: Diderot's eye is coolly observant rather than empathetic. And in fact, just as it was doing for the reader, the scene proceeds to turn into a spectacle even for some of the participants watching the disaster from diverse viewpoints, and who then themselves become the reader's spectacle.[29] Diderot continues to insist on the fecund variety of incidents that the artist has imagined, yet after such steady aloofness on the part of the author, his extremely brief expression of sympathy at the end – as he hopes, with rather facile piety, that the expiring woman by the fire will recover after all – appears almost flippant: 'il y en a qui ont allumé du feu sous une roche; ils s'occupent à ranimer une femme expirante, et j'espère qu'ils y réussiront' (p.134).

But meanwhile, the time has come to turn to other things. Instantly the account dissolves to a scene of totally contrasting tonality: to calm seas whose serenity is evoked with such magical delicacy, and gaiety as well, that, even though no soft breezes blow, for just a few phrases it is like hearing some divine strain by Mozart (p.134):

Tournez vos yeux sur une autre mer, et vous verrez le calme avec tous ses charmes; les eaux tranquilles, aplanies et riantes, s'étendent, en perdant insensiblement de leur transparence et s'éclairant insensiblement à leur surface, depuis le rivage jusqu'où l'horizon confine avec le ciel; les vaisseaux sont immobiles, les matelots, les passagers sont à tous les amusements qui peuvent tromper leur impatience.

Diderot's exquisite delicacy reminds one not only of Vernet, but of eighteenth-century musical evocations of country landscapes and the times of day. Diderot plays these moods against one another with magical success (p.134):

Si c'est le matin, quelles vapeurs légères s'élèvent! comme ces vapeurs éparses sur les objets de la nature les ont rafraîchis et vivifiés! Si c'est le soir, comme la cime de ces montagnes se dore! De quelles nuances les cieux sont colorés! Comme les nuages marchent, se meuvent et viennent déposer dans les eaux la teinte de leurs couleurs!

As a grand finale Diderot stages a fireworks display to outdo everything that precedes (p.135-36).[30] Taking off from a text by Lucian, he likens Vernet to

29. This point has also been made by Michel Delon in his analysis of the same passage, 'Joseph Vernet et Diderot dans la tempête', p.33.
30. Preceding the finale are some rather extensive praises of Vernet as an imitator of nature (p.134-35).

Jupiter, who, wearied with mankind's grievances, gets up from the table and sends forth punishments to every part of the earth, a train of disasters in succession: hail, plague, volcano, war and famine. But Diderot's text mimics Jupiter–Vernet's acts of creation so that the moment an abstract noun such as 'volcan' is pronounced, the abstraction instantly breaks up into its constituent parts, turning into the multitude of tangibles which had given the abstraction the power to exist in the first place and that are in effect its body and substance.[31] The jump from the abstraction to the tangibles is so swift, and the resultant landscapes so compelling, that one after another, as Jupiter–Vernet–Diderot throws them down, each word in turn – 'grêle', 'peste', 'volcan', 'guerre' and 'disette' – explodes irresistibly into imaginary painting:

C'est le Jupiter de Lucien qui las d'entendre les cris lamentables des humains, se lève de table et dit: De la grêle en Thrace ... et l'on voit aussitôt les arbres dépouillés, les moissons hachées et le chaume des cabanes dispersé: la peste en Asie ... et l'on voit les portes des maisons fermées, les rues désertes, et les hommes se fuyant: ici, un volcan ... et la terre s'ébranle sous les pieds, les édifices tombent, les animaux s'effarouchent et les habitants des villes gagnent les campagnes: une guerre là ... et les nations courent aux armes et s'entr'égorgent: en cet endroit une disette ... et le vieux laboureur expire de faim sur sa porte. Jupiter appelle cela gouverner le monde, et il a tort. Vernet appelle cela faire des tableaux, et il a raison.[32]

Only Vernet's tempests and shipwrecks could have inspired these vengeances and disasters; they cannot have come from his serene landscapes and seascapes. But again Diderot's attitude is completely detached, coolly observant and careful to avoid any sort of involvement in the plight of those whose damage he so accurately describes. He rises above all mortal contingencies, above good and evil, to an admiration that is purely artistic.

In *L'Accordée de village* by Greuze the painter's creation supposedly came after the fact: the implied chains of causality joining the participants together for their scene seemed so predetermined and so convincing that one might have supposed that the event would have taken place anyway, even without the artist's presence. In Diderot's idea of Jupiter–Vernet's creations, on the other hand, an opposite species of causality emerges: the artist's creative act imposes everything *ex nihilo*; it comes *before* the fact. All antecedent chains of causality have been dispensed with, and though the artist – whether he be Diderot, Vernet or Jupiter – may devise new torments for the population of his universe, nothing can exist outside his own creation. Such an artist has no moral

31. See my discussion of the opening of Diderot's *Lettre sur les sourds et muets* in chapter 2.
32. P.135-36, with occasional punctuation from the Seznec edition, ii.121.

principles whatsoever and since he himself, entirely gratuitously, has willed whatever occurs, sympathy with sufferers is quite out of the question. Art is its own justification and the painter creates in order to create, even as Jupiter inflicts punishments on mankind out of wanton lassitude.

Diderot's final gesture in this passage ('Jupiter appelle cela gouverner le monde, et il a tort; Vernet appelle cela faire des tableaux, et il a raison') has a superb 'désinvolture': it is not exactly that Diderot has forgotten ethics, for the good-humoured allusion to Jupiter's miserable governance suggests they still might have been on his mind. But then, nevertheless, raising Vernet's art unassailably high on the pedestal, Diderot just gives a last shove that pushes morality – Greuze's speciality – completely out of his ken.

V

Returning to the original question of this discussion, 'Diderot versus Greuze?', the least one can say is that Diderot's reactions to Greuze cover a wide spectrum. Admiration holds pride of place among them, just as tradition has always maintained: Diderot and Greuze were made for one another, and significant correspondences exist between Diderot's own moral and social outlook, his sense of drama, and the sort of scenes that Greuze did so well. Needless to say, these correspondences have been well charted and Diderot's positive reactions are well known. At the same time – such is my claim – the intense moralism of Greuze and his relentless demand for sympathetic responses automatically engendered the desire to be free from, and find alternatives to, the very qualities that Diderot, in another compartment of his soul, was admiring. Such contrary impulses were behind Diderot's otherwise inexplicable expression, right in the middle of his enthusiasms for Greuze, of a hankering for both the art and the reality of great crimes, a subversive reaction that not only suggests a subliminal yearning to be free of Greuze's demands, but perhaps – momentarily – even pushes him towards the 'wrong' side of Greuze's punishments. But even though Diderot never recognised it as such, the ultimate declaration of independence from Greuze may have occurred in Diderot's admiration for Vernet, who, in effect, desecrated all the values that Greuze allegedly stood for: as if fulfilling Diderot's own half-spoken wish – 'Je ne hais pas les grands crimes' – Vernet made great art out of a gratuitous act of the imagination that Diderot recognised as, so to speak, criminal. In sum, if the texture of Diderot's enthusiasm for Greuze is densely and enthrallingly rich, perhaps part of the reason is its saturation with contrariety.

Certainly this *Salon* belongs intentionally to the category of art criticism. Yet, seeing the force of the contrary undertows that surge into the text in the wake of his adulation of Greuze and Vernet, and the unstable continuum of Diderot's own materialistic values, the issues seem destined to widen into even larger philosophical territories. Of course Diderot finds no answers to the urgent questions of art versus morality that he raises here, none at all. These themes are built in to his mode of thinking as problematics, and they will continue to send out sharply discordant resonances – along with some consonant ones – returning often to haunt the *Salons* and other writings on art. Nor is it surprising that they attain their most perfect expression in the dialogue whose shadow has, more than once, been sensed as an unspoken presence in this discussion, *Le Neveu de Rameau*, a truly sublime creation, whose impossible moral and aesthetic perplexities Diderot never solves either.

8. Stages of contrariety in *Jacques le fataliste*

I

DESPITE a curious reticence on the part of a few scholars,[1] there can be no doubt that Diderot's main inspiration for *Jacques le fataliste et son maître*,[2] his longest novel, was Sterne's *Tristram Shandy*.[3] 'Les amours de Jacques' is launched through a passage stolen from Sterne in which Diderot tells how his hero was taken from the battlefield and brought to the village with a wound in his knee.[4] This same knee with its wound is destined to reappear, via another passage borrowed from Sterne,[5] at the very end of the novel to provide the sexual climax (or a reasonable facsimile thereof) of the same story-line, just before the wedding of Jacques and Denise brings the work to its (non-) conclusion – assuming that the manuscript relating the event is authentic, of course. In short, in so far as the inner workings of the novel have a conventional structure, borrowings from Sterne provide the two main elements,[6] the beginning and the end.

Sterne's novel also tacitly provides the key to Le Maître's witty rejoinder,

1. The two most frequently used critical editions of this work, the DPV edition, xxiii.3-291, edited by Jacques Proust, and the edition by Simone Lecointre and Jean Le Galliot (Paris and Geneva 1976), do not attempt to do justice to this topic. See also the brief and one-dimensional discussion by Elisabeth de Fontenay, *Diderot, ou le matérialisme enchanté*, p.51.

2. The most useful critical assessment of scholarly work on this novel remains that by Maurice Roelens, '*Jacques le fataliste* et la critique contemporaine', *Dix-huitième siècle* 5 (1973), p.119-37, to which one may add, for later texts, the perceptive evaluations of Daniel Brewer, *The Discourse of enlightenment in eighteenth-century France*, p.227f. The only study of which I am aware that in important ways parallels my own approach, is that by Robert Mauzi, 'La parodie romanesque dans *Jacques le fataliste*', *Diderot studies* 6 (1964), p.89-132. The question of 'fatalism' will not be the main issue in the ensuing discussion if only because the theme has already had sufficient airing; whole monographs have been written about it, and such masterful treatments as Jean Starobinski, 'Chaque balle à son billet', *Nouvelle revue de psychanalyse* 30 (1984), p.17-38, leave little to say. Other reasons will be proposed further on.

3. Though by now badly out of date, the most complete study remains Alice Green Fredman, *Diderot and Sterne* (New York 1955).

4. Laurence Sterne, *The Life and opinions of Tristram Shandy, gentleman*, ed. Melvyn New *et al.* (Gainesville, Fl. 1978-1984), ii.695-97 (vol.viii, ch.19 of original edition). Also quoted in Paul Vernière's edition of *Jacques le fataliste* (Paris 1978), p.373-74, n.7.

5. *Tristram Shandy*, ii.702-704 (vol.viii, ch.22 of original edition). In Sterne, the second scene takes place only a matter of weeks, and about a dozen pages, after the first. The second borrowing has been wittily analysed by Robert Alter, *Partial magic: the novel as a self-conscious genre* (Berkeley, Calif. 1975), p.58-62.

6. As noted by John Hope Mason, *The Irresistible Diderot*, p.159.

near the beginning (p.25),[7] when Jacques claims that no wound is so painful as one in the knee: 'Allons donc, Jacques, tu te moques.' Jacques must be joking because everyone knows where the most painful wound for men is: not in the knee, but in the groin – which was where Uncle Toby received his wound according to Sterne, while giving one in the knee to the man who waits on him, Corporal Trim.

There is no part of the body, an' please your honour, where a wound occasions more intolerable anguish than upon the knee –
Except the groin; said my uncle Toby. An'please your honour, replied the corporal, the knee, in my opinion, must certainly be the most acute, there being so many tendons and what-d'ye-call'ems all about it.
It is for that reason, quoth my uncle Toby, that the groin is infinitely more sensible.[8]

Thus in Sterne the pair 'knee' and 'groin' is spelled out by the master and servant who were two of the main 'inspirations' for the roughly equivalent pair in Diderot's novel. In *Jacques le fataliste* the alternative to the knee remains unspoken;[9] the knee must pull its own weight and speak for itself. And so, to bolster Jacques's claim that knee wounds are the most painful, Diderot invents a surgeon who conveniently rides up on a horse (p.25), and says in so many words, 'Monsieur a raison.' Unfortunately, that device comes a cropper when no one is sure to whom the words are addressed, and the surgeon's assistant interrupts the proceedings by falling off the horse (p.26) head downwards and exposing her 'cul' (a judgement, perhaps, on the question at hand, or perhaps simply a salutary introduction of a note of sensuality into a discussion that was otherwise beginning to sound unsexual). In any case, undeterred, and resolved to make his point at all cost, Diderot has Le Maître himself fall off his horse and bump his knee to find out the truth first hand (p.38). All these comically cumbersome devices to certify the painfulness of knee wounds are pure Diderot, of course. So is the irony of the structural use of Jacques's wound near the end of the novel in the other passage borrowed from Sterne: as Denise's rubbing fingers slowly work their way up Jacques's leg (p.289-90), starting below the wound, going to the knee, over and beyond – to love and, after a huge interruption, marriage, one realises that the whole story of 'les

7. Page numbers refer to the DPV edition; see n.1 above.
8. *Tristram Shandy*, ii.695 (vol.viii, ch.19 of original edition). Cf. the text of the translation of the second paragraph used by Diderot: 'Non, pardieu, Monsieur, je ne moque pas. Il y a là je ne sais combien d'os, de tendons, et d'autres choses qu'ils appellent je ne sais comment' (DPV, xxiii.25).
9. The closest Diderot comes to specifying the alternative is this wily statement: 'Une autre chose, Lecteur, que je voudrais bien que vous me dissiez, c'est si son maître n'eût pas mieux aimé être blessé même un peu grièvement, ailleurs qu'au genou, ou s'il ne fut plus sensible à la honte qu'à la douleur' (p.38).

amours de Jacques', with its enormous clutter of incidents, delays, digressions, disturbances and sub-plots, really only happened in the space between the knee and the groin, the space marked out by implication at the start ('chaque balle a son adresse'),[10] and now finally closed thanks to Denise's rubbings – a selective localising unheard of in the English novelist, and which neatly insinuates a parody of a thoroughly French unity of place.[11]

Although Rabelais or Cervantes often hover in the background of both Sterne and Diderot, it was above all from Sterne that Diderot borrowed his imaginary reader whom the author addresses as though he were not only alive but present, someone to be made impatient, to be cajoled, toyed with, tricked, insulted, or given in to, according to the author's whim.[12] Sterne had carried this device to greater lengths than Diderot would by imagining a whole string of different readers during the course of the novel, who change without warning – change rank, change sex, change character or humour, and are addressed accordingly as 'Sir', 'Madam', 'My Lord', 'your worship', 'your reverences', 'my dear girl', or whatever. Diderot's imaginary reader remains the same, being throughout 'Lecteur', that is, male and apparently middle-class. Although the reader is only intermittently addressed in person in Diderot's text, one may assume that he is present elsewhere by implication, and thus acquires a status which his counterparts in Sterne do not have, for in effect Diderot's reader becomes a rather querulous, restive and sometimes demanding companion for the author,[13] in much the way that Jacques is for his own master, a character whose relationship to the author in fact creates the makings of a story-line. Sterne's imaginary readers, being diverse, do not have this simpler function.

When, at the opening of Sterne's novel,[14] in the middle (truly *in medias res*) of the copulation between Tristram's parents – the very act that would conceive the hero and alleged author of the work at hand – Mrs Shandy interrupts by popping her famous question to her husband: 'Pray, my dear, have you not forgot to wind up the clock?', she is obviously establishing a paradigm for everything that follows and indicating the sign under which the work is written, a sign equal in importance, though perhaps less visibly so, to 'le grand

10. My 'quotation' is adapted from two passages, p.23-24.

11. Cf. the remark by Paul Vernière, originally written in 1959: '*Jacques le fataliste*, dans l'incohérence pittoresque de ses anecdotes, s'insère entre deux séries épisodiques qui lui confère une certaine unité' (*Lumières ou clair-obscur? Trente essais sur Diderot et quelques autres*, Paris 1987, p.51).

12. On the various tones and attitudes employed, see the subtle analysis by Robert Mauzi, 'La parodie romanesque', p.121-23.

13. Mauzi, p.126.

14. *Tristram Shandy*, i.2.

rouleau' in Diderot's novel. Naturally, following Sterne's idea of this original conception, the story which Tristram tells will be nothing but interruptions, usually couched as digressions, and multiplied so prodigiously that the main plot all but vanishes behind the clutter of delays with which the imaginary reader must put up as best he or she can, sometimes after considerable cajoling by the narrator. The author proudly – in fact a little too proudly – boasts at one point that the merit of these digressions is that they serendipitously serve to keep the plot moving forward.[15] No doubt in Sterne's very large tomes they occasionally do just that, but, as a vastly more weighty counterpoise, dozens of other passages show up the narrator's argument as a slyly transparent bit of sophistry: in effect the digressions generally impede forward motion, and sometimes they are so numerous that everything just drifts backwards. Meanwhile, for the reader, when he thinks of how long it has taken the narrator merely to get himself born (approximately seventy chapters), the image of an unwound clock running down, or stopped entirely, assumes suitably symbolic proportions.

Like Sterne, Diderot revelled in creating delays, in part so that he could imagine the reader's impatience with them, and since, in Sterne, there are so many, and so many different kinds of delays – unexpected, expected, merely curious, useful, gratuitous, anecdotal deflections, backtrackings, sideways parallels, etc., etc., etc., enough to form a veritable encyclopaedia of delays – it seems safe to conclude that Diderot did not find it necessary to invent any new species on his own.

Yet, despite the borrowings by the handful of narrative strategies and even character traits from Sterne,[16] the texture of Diderot's narration turns out to be markedly different. Although both texts are full of breaks and pauses, their prime function in Sterne, as his narrator is the first to testify, is to fill in – down to the least detail, and with all the side issues that can occur to the author – the whole background of the action. If one turns to *Jacques le fataliste* on the other hand, it is clear that, despite numerous overlappings with Sterne, most (though by no means all) of the delays come as interruptions which add another story-line on top of the story-lines already in progress. This is to say that in Diderot the delays and interruptions serve less to fill in the background

---

15. *Tristram Shandy*, i.22.

16. *Inter alia*, Diderot also borrowed from Sterne the device of suddenly describing a scene which until then had consisted only of dialogue and was not visually accessible to the reader, thus dramatically lighting a scene that, one realises, had until then been totally dark. Both authors use the device to remind readers of how dependent they were on the author for everything they saw or heard. In other words, the device is part of the ongoing authorial manipulation of the reader. For other borrowings see Fredman, *Diderot and Sterne*, p.90-147.

(though sometimes they do have that function) than to create contrapuntal story-lines in a texture that is already contrapuntal. Because of the frequent conjunction of these story-lines, *Jacques le fataliste* becomes positively polyphonic,[17] more so than any other fiction by Diderot.

Wherever one chooses to tune in to Diderot's story, the lines of narrative in progress number at least two; often there are as many as five, and occasionally one finds even six vibrating in the text (so to speak) quasi-simultaneously either as tangible presences or as recent memories. For example, if one observes the story-lines that are interwoven in just four pages, on p.58-62, one finds that (1) Jacques and Le Maître are journeying together as usual (they are buying a new horse). (2) The narrator has called out to the reader to attribute to him thoughts he undoubtedly has never had. (3) Jacques had been telling the story of his love life. (4) As a side issue, the necessity of explaining how Jacques possessed enough money to pay the surgeon evoked the story of his brother, frère Jean, an ambitious, wily and lusty monk who had had to leave town suddenly on account of the scandals of his intra- and extra-claustral affairs, and gave his brother the money as he did so. (5) Meanwhile apparently the mere pronunciation of the name 'Jean' had, through the principle of contrariety, called forth the phonetical reverse of his name, 'Ange', and whom the text embodied as another ambitious and wily member of the clergy, père Ange,[18] who on account of monachal jealousies over his popularity with females was forced to leave town at the same moment as frère Jean. (6) The new horse, too, turns out to have its own story agenda which is put into action by bolting towards the nearest gibbet.[19]

Diderot obviously delighted in letting all these disparate stories resound together, interrupting one another, jostling for position as the prime story-line of the moment: as a result the whole text is essentially resonance, to the point that one might even be tempted to invoke in this connection a comparison

17. Pierre Weisz sees this phenomenon as relating essentially to dialogue: see 'Le réel et son double dans *Jacques le fataliste*', *Diderot studies* 19 (1978), p.185: 'La structure complexe de *Jacques le fataliste* est plus intelligible si on considère que Diderot traite l'intrigue de la même façon que les personnages: il institue un dialogue à plusieurs voix – son moyen d'expression favori – entre les différentes entités narratives de son discours.'

18. See Jean-Pierre Vidal, 'L'infratexte, mode du génotexte ou fantasme de lecture', *La Nouvelle barre du jour* 103 (May 1981), p.46. The DPV edition, p.60, n.58, invokes as a source of Diderot's personage a certain frère Ange, whom Diderot had known. See also Blake T. Hanna, 'Le frère Ange, Carme déchaussé, et Denis Diderot', *Revue d'histoire littéraire de la France* 84 (1984), p.373-89. The *rapprochement* is not entirely convincing; it is possible, however, that the order of the phonetic generation via the names is the reverse of the one I have proposed: it is entirely possible that 'Ange' generated 'Jean'.

19. For other 'sondages' of the text bringing out the number and variety of the strands one finds at any given moment, see Mauzi, 'La parodie romanesque', p.111-13.

with the great Rameau's doctrine of *le corps sonore*.[20] To be sure, given the jarringly diverse character of the tales in progress and their decidedly individual autonomy, it is rare that these various story-lines create anything like harmony as they combine.[21] Characteristically the resonances are, in varying degrees, discordant, and most of the time the pleasure of the novel lies in the enjoyment of these ill-assorted janglings, clanging away together, creating a cacophony, a ruckus of a sort that would never be tolerated in the euphonious ambiance of well-bred novels, not to mention an opera by Rameau. In effect, the counterpoints created by the story-lines of Diderot's novel are parodies of the counterpoints that were normally considered socially or musically acceptable.

In the course of their aimless wanderings the relationship between Le Maître and Jacques forms in itself the basic counterpoint against which all the others come to play. Since Diderot will perversely take pleasure in muddying the theoretical clarity of this relationship, it may be well to remember at the start that naming one principal character Le Maître, while calling the other Jacques, is at least making gestures towards the classic master–servant paradigm, already the subject of countless theatrical comedies in France, not to mention its symbolic importance as the basic feature of society in the *ancien régime*. Fortunately the present context does not require sounding the depths of Hegel's celebrated discussion of 'lordship and bondage' in the *Phenomenology of spirit*.[22] It will suffice to point out that, at least in its eighteenth-century French context, the master–servant relationship is a contrariety of the symbiotic species, in that each of the two personages, theoretically, provides all the services or qualities the other lacks or requires. Since by definition the term servant implies a master, and vice versa, unless somehow the paradigm is disrupted, the two are literally made for one another, even as two halves form a whole. In musical terms one might think of some sonorously concordant interval, like the perfect fifth.

Of course this paradigm takes no account of the hostility entailed as one species of person asserts dominance over another, who in turn is constrained by necessity to sacrifice his own immediate desires and place another's in their stead. (Hegel, taking a broadly historical view of the matter, postulated that in a stage of consciousness preceding the 'lordship and bondage' one, each of the two individuals of the paradigm would actually have sought the death of the

20. See Thomas Christensen, *Rameau and musical thought in the Enlightenment* (Cambridge 1993), esp. ch.6, p.133f.
21. The few semi-complete narrative harmonies that do occur usually come about because everyone goes to sleep.
22. Trans., A. V. Miller (Oxford 1977), p.115f.

other.[23]) In *Jacques le fataliste* the inherent hostility of the situation is vented in Jacques's seemingly endless jibes, insults, outspoken reluctance or refusal to do as he is bid, or otherwise make Le Maître pay a price for his obedience. The preservation of his own individuality depends on a defiance of the supposedly smoothly running archetype, and on his insistence that his relationship with Le Maître regularly or irregularly resound with dissonance – in varying degrees, to be sure, and also within limits; for Jacques's fundamental loyalty to his master is never in question.

It will be recalled that in La Fontaine's familiar Fables featuring opposing pairs of animals not everything was contrary, indeed the contrariety seemed to require that the Lamb and the Wolf share at least one bond in common, namely a basic animality that implied the need to eat and drink. In Diderot's novel the bond in common between Jacques and Le Maître is given as the humanity which supposedly unites the two despite their contrary social attributes. This common bond has been enormously expanded by Diderot to serve as an alleged counterweight working against all the hostility generated by subservience and social difference. In fact there are numerous moments when the human elements uniting the two seem more prominent than the class-related elements that disjoin them, so that the novel takes on the air of a lesson in equality, with the pair offering the possibility of a paradigm for mankind in general. In this light one usually sees them as just two riders going along together, or sleeping in the same room, or swapping stories and making remarks about females, a territory where their instincts and experiences share so much in common that one of them can – up to a point – stand in for the other. Normally the Master would be the one to take pleasure in impressing others, perhaps even his inferiors, with boasts of his sexual conquests. Diderot has Jacques replace him in this function, and imagine that this Master takes pleasure vicariously in hearing of Jacques's exploits, instead of vaunting his own.

But as usual in Diderot, the issues are built into the structure as tensions whose resolutions, when they occur, are momentary: though Le Maître may desire above all else to hear the story of Jacques's love life and Jacques above all else the pleasure of recounting it (which theoretically would imply consonance), Jacques obviously takes equal pleasure in frustrating his master's desires and denying his pleasure, which he does on almost every possible occasion. Such frustrations are typical of everything they do, and so inevitably the resultant counterpoint between the two – the story of Jacques and Le

23. *Phenomenology of spirit*, p.113-14.

Maître – alternates variously from blatant dissonance to almost harmonious concord.

To schematise the analysis thus far, three stages in the relationship may be distinguished: first, the archetypal level of the master–servant partnership with its symbiotic satisfactions, which seems to suggest concord. Second, the other side of the coin: the impositions of will and the sacrifices of immediate desires entailed by the subservience in the 'partnership', which imply hostility and dissonance. These make themselves heard, on the Master's side, in his impatience with Jacques and also, later on, in his anger when Jacques's love life encroaches on his own territory. Of course, the main dissonance is manifest on the other side, in the improprieties and disobedience of Jacques. Third, these last elements are in turn intermittently counterbalanced by the feelings of humanity that link the pair together, the Master's solicitude (p.87) for Jacques's well-being when he gets knocked on the head, the sharing of experiences and enjoyment of each other's foibles. The interplay of these often disparate elements forms the texture of this counterpoint, the story of Jacques and Le Maître.

Following as a shadow of this basic association is the reader–narrator relationship, well studied by scholars.[24] Authors such as Diderot and Sterne liked to pretend that in traditional novels the reader played the Master's role: as the reader was assured in the preface, the author was simply the reader's slave, his most obedient servant. Such traditional proprieties were for Diderot an irresistible occasion to play the role of Jacques, and treat the reader to an endless series of frustrations, delays and interruptions in the supposed process of getting on with the story. Meanwhile Diderot indulges himself by imagining, and actually staging in the text, the reader's indignant protests, even as the author gloats over the occasions that cause them.

These two counterpoints – Jacques and Le Maître, the narrator and the reader – are marked by irregularities of all sorts: one can never tell when the indignant reader will appear in, or disappear from, the text; when the story will jolt to a halt, or gallop ahead at full speed; whether Le Maître and Jacques will be agreeing or falling out; above all, one can never predict when some interruption will send the narrative off the course it might otherwise have held, and so on. In fact the 'frame' situation in its formless, directionless, irregular, meandering *disponibilité* might almost seem like an ambling invitation to disruption. Furthermore, through the perverseness of Diderot's disposition, when the 'frame' does give way to the stories which various characters tell,

---

24. See Fredman, *Diderot and Sterne*, p.13. By far the most perceptive and entertaining analysis is in Mauzi, 'La parodie romanesque', p.121-25.

these tales are – generally speaking – firmly structured, marked by a strong sense of form and direction,[25] going straight toward their appointed outcome[26] with an excellent sense of timing and scarcely a wasted word.[27] Were they themselves not interrupted so often by other tales or incidents, which the author takes pleasure in multiplying at will, a number of them – like the tales of Scheherazade – might strike one as 'classic', as perfectly narrated, with no improvements conceivable.[28]

This is to say that, formally and aesthetically, the stories that Diderot's characters tell are – or at least try to be, despite the interruptions – everything that the 'frame' situation is not. The two are related through contrariety. Perhaps it may seem that this generalisation does not apply to the story of

25. The opening sentence of Le Maître's story (p.235) is exemplary in this sense (despite the narrator's disclaimer): 'C'était la veille de sa fête, et je n'avais point d'argent.' It deftly cues the reader into the evolving situation, and actually contains (as any good materialistic discourse should) all the rest *en germe*. Though the more complex psychological situation of Mme de La Pommeraye's tale demands considerably more words to be launched completely (p.122), the opening sentences still have this same exemplary quality. See also the beginning of Bigre's story (p.210), which also contains all the rest *en germe*. The tale of Richard and Hudson is in three parts, beginning with the *préambule* on the melancholy which drives adolescents to convents (p.192), then the main tale (p.193-201), and finally the dividend-sequel whose whole point is the 'boutade' at the end (p.202), when père Hudson drops his mask with an obscenity. Though the beginning forms really a contrast with the main part (the adolescents' sensitivities playing against the harsh and calculating realities of convents), the middle part forms a whole that in itself is more obviously structured, beginning with the detailed portrait of père Hudson, p.193-94 ('Il y avait alors à la tête d'une des maisons de l'ordre un supérieur d'un caractère extraordinaire'), whose traits are described so as to foretell all the rest.

26. More exactly, and following the main ideas presented by Peter Brooks in his elucidation of Freud's *Beyond the pleasure principle*, one would say that these stories proceed via a sequence of plot elements (sometimes intricate, and often symmetrically enunciated) which the reader perceives from the start as designed to facilitate the outcome of his desire, i.e. the end of the story: see Brooks, *Reading for the plot: design and intention in narrative* (New York 1984), esp. ch.4, 'Freud's masterplot: a model for narrative', p.93-94, p.99-103, p.108-109. For present purposes, considerable adaptation of these ideas is required because, however pertinent for Rousseau and nineteenth- and twentieth-century authors (as well as for Freud himself), the traditional Freudian emphasis on the death instinct may be, it is inappropriate for Diderot's materialism.

27. Although one could establish this point by analysing the stories and showing in detail the extraordinary economy of expression and structuring of each, an easier pragmatic proof lies readily at hand in the facility with which the reader remembers each tale, to the point that the author can interrupt them as often and for as long as he wishes without the reader forgetting the preceding part. Such automatic remembrance is possible only because each fragment fits flawlessly in a story-line whose direction and progress is perfectly clear, and because each detail is a necessary part of that progress. Since everything is pertinent, nothing can be forgotten. In Freudian terms, one would point to the relationship of coincidence between the structured progress of the tale and the reader's desires: see Brooks, *Reading for the plot*, p.93-109.

28. Once again Diderot's narrative strategies are in contrast to Sterne's, whose interrupting stories are typically just as formlessly sprawling as the rambles of the main story line.

Jacques's life after he leaves home, or at least strains the rule to the limit by taking an endlessly zigzag course – from battlefield to peasant's house, to Doctor's house, to nearby village, to Doctor's house, to château[29] – towards the target. But even so, with all the zigzags, this part of Jacques's life conveys more of a sense of direction and cohesion than the meanderings of the 'frame', and one that enormously gathers impetus the moment the tale is within sight of the woman Jacques comes to love.

Love or sex – conceived strictly from the male point of view – of course provides the key explaining why the stories (as distinct from the 'frame') display such a pronounced sense of direction: as if following the impetus of love itself, or the hastening rhythms of the sexual experience,[30] these tales, related usually by men, head instinctively towards their goal. Naturally, sex and seduction are the most frequent themes,[31] varied according to rather familiar patterns: sometimes the male is completely successful and rewarded by getting off scot-free, as Bigre and Jacques are; sometimes he is caught in flagrante delicto like Le Maître and the 'pâtissier', or is almost, but not quite, caught (père Hudson), or escapes, but with graver consequences than expected (frère Jean), and so on. Furthermore, just as in the opening chapter of Sterne, there is often a sense of *coitus interruptus* when some unexpected break suspends the story in mid-sentence, sometimes literally at the critical sexual moment. But even in the tales in which sex does not explicitly play a part, it seems clear, if only because of Diderot's natural propensities, that the built-in sense

29. See Per Nykrog, 'Les étapes des amours de Jacques', *Etudes romanes dédiées à Andreas Blinkenberg* (Copenhagen 1963), p.113-26, and also Vernière's edition of *Jacques le fataliste*, p.25.
30. This is exactly the point suggested by Brooks, *Reading for the plot*, p.93-109. In more aesthetic terms, the classic study of sexual rhythms in Diderot's narrative is Leo Spitzer, 'The style of Diderot', *Linguistics and literary history* (Princeton, N.J. 1948), p.135-91.
31. The other frequent theme is duelling, which is also presented as a passion that tries to run its course to some sort of conclusion, and is often along the way structured by repeated patterns: the alternance of friendship and duelling in the story of the 'capitaine' and his fellow officer (p.78f.), the compulsively repeated duels of 'le camarade de mon capitaine' (or M. de Guerchy) with the pinioned man ('le cloué') leading to an unexpectedly theatrical climax, the regular diminutions of the plaster with the duels of Desglands, and so on. Generosity is the theme of three tales: one of the Gousse stories tells of his incredible generosity which was not prompted by principle; the counterpoint to the story is the tale of M. Le Pelletier of Orléans (p.74-75), whose generosity, equally incredible, was totally informed by principle. In between comes the story of 'L'Hôte' and 'le Compère' in which the hotelkeeper's generosity requires a preceding stage of stinginess in order to be activated as a denial (p.114-17). Finally, the passion of the 'poète de Pondichery' (p.56-58) is obviously based not on sex, or generosity, or duelling, but on a compulsion to write poetry. On the functioning of the main tales in the structure of the novel see Marian Hobson, 'Jacques le fataliste: l'art du probable', *Diderot: les dernières années (1770-84)*, ed. Peter France and Anthony Strugnell (Edinburgh 1985), 182-89.

of direction and the creation of tensions towards the climax are modelled on the paradigm of sexuality, in the masculine sense.[32]

Later on, some of the larger implications of these sexual rhythms for the structure of the work will be proposed. For present purposes the significant point is to record how perfectly these direction-laden structures set off by contrast the element in which they occur: how perfectly the economy of their course towards the goal makes one feel the jolt of the disruptions and other irregularities that impede their course and the chaotic-seeming disjointedness of the 'frame' in which they are set. In other words, I am claiming that, if the relationship between Jacques and Le Maître forms one basic contrapuntal element of the story, the contrary relationship between their erratic and loosely evolving situation – what I term the 'frame' situation – and the narratives themselves forms the other. If Jacques and Le Maître in their contrary social functions were made for one another, so too, by contrary motion, was the 'frame', and the stories it so loosely encloses.

II

Of all the tales, the one told by Mme de La Pommeraye is not only the longest but also the most perfect: somewhat like a comedy by Marivaux, this story works on a mechanism that is wound up at the beginning, and then (not exactly like Marivaux) is supposed and intended to unwind seamlessly, inexorably with no hitches or even much change of tempo, like weights that pull of their own accord towards the appointed end, an end that the reader supposedly sees in advance and is convinced until the very last moment is a foregone conclusion. No doubt the novels and stories of Crébillon fils are to some extent in the background of this part of the text, at least in the moments of conversational banter and mundane flirtation. But the subject of the tale being passion and revenge, and furthermore the motivations being psychological in the grand Classical tradition, inevitably one also recalls authors such as Mme de Lafayette, perhaps even Racine. As in a tragedy, the characters are few in number, and not only are Mme de La Pommeraye and her former lover highly born, but the high style of their story suggests aristocracy as well.

Naturally, given the perversities of Diderot's creative processes, all this – not only the seamless inevitability, but the seriousness of the high style, too –

---

32. Because of its essentially masculine orientation, the rhythms of this text are markedly different from those of *La Religieuse*, based supposedly on feminine patterns. In fact, except for the grandly theatrical scene when Suzanne rejects her vows, and which follows a sort of crescendo towards a climax, the two texts are, in this respect, opposites.

demanded a frame setting that thrusts low comedy into the airtight narration at inappropriate moments, a setting that features unprepared, jarring interruptions and loud, bawling voices that irregularly drown out the carefully modulated, even whispered concerns of the main narrative, and bring everything and everyone down to the very level that the tale excluded: the low or classless level of drinking, eating and bodily functions. According to Diderot's conception, an inn was nothing but irregularity and disruption, and nothing but a place for the alleviation of bodily needs, all of which created moment by moment its identity. Thus, on the simplest level at least, the setting forms a perfect contrariety to the tale. Though Sterne would certainly have been bold enough, no other French novelist of Diderot's time dared to create a background such as this one, an environment that was not only completely inappropriate for the story being told, but actively, aggressively hostile to it, working might and main to undo the very qualities that the story so powerfully embodied. Its effect is so perverse that one might even be tempted to imagine that it had been devised to bring down the elegant psychological structure the tale had been created to erect and uphold.

Such is not the case, however, for the incongruous relationship between the two elements turns out to be not destructive, but benign. Perhaps the musical conception of counterpoint can suggest by analogy why these two opposites do not work to destroy one another. For even as in certain pieces of baroque counterpoint the widely disparate character of the two main voices may not set each at war with the other, but rather strengthen and enhance each voice through contrast, so likewise in *Jacques le fataliste* the invasive vulgarity of the comic interruptions sets off and makes even more superbly expressive the high drama of private revenge enacted by Mme de La Pommeraye. Moreover, in terms of aesthetic effect it will seem (for some) that the lofty, beautifully crafted, flawlessly composed, attention-demanding style of the tale actually makes one thankful for the intermissions, and all the more grateful for being brought back down to earth by the cork-popping Hostess, shouting orders to the staff and pouring generous drinks for her sloshed male companions diversely sprawled on their seats nearby. In short, in respect to the reader it may seem that Diderot intended the second side of the contrariety to operate as a welcome social and comic relief.[33]

33. To be sure, the details of the text suggest more of a mixture than this schematic presentation does: it is pointedly hinted that the freewheeling, liberty-loving Hostess comes from a class high above her present station. If she is a perfectly qualified narrator of her tale, she partakes somewhat of Mme de La Pommeraye's world. Meanwhile, the highly born Mme de La Pommeraye enlists a prostitute as the agent of her revenge, thus undermining the moral elevation supposedly inherent in her class and bringing her somewhat nearer to the Hostess.

Of course Diderot presents Mme de La Pommeraye's personality ambiguously, as a person of great energy and determination, but whose action of revenge may either be admired or condemned. In so far as she has a heroic side, it arises from her determination to punish as he deserved a man whom society would absolve. Naturally, control[34] is the essence of her every action – combined with her acute understanding of the male libido. Thus she herself creates the illusions that her victim believes in, reads his mind and manipulates his feelings at will. Seeing this domineering *metteuse en scène* exerting her command so completely through strict observance of the rules of *vraisemblance*, success seems a foregone conclusion, so that the fascination of the story lies apparently in seeing the inevitable occur, and following down to the least detail her laying the trap and watching it spring. As with accomplished seducers, or master criminals, each precise gesture guarantees the outcome, and the mounting tension and suspense are built into the structure of the tale itself.

The key to Mme de La Pommeraye's manipulations of her victim's sexual desires is her perception of the basic verity about the eighteenth-century male literary libido, a truth that was supposedly brought home during her liaison with the unfaithful Marquis: that requited love, and even the sex act itself, quickly palls and become tiresome to the male once he has obtained satisfaction and possession. The text hints that Mme de La Pommeraye may have learned this bitter truth in her previous marriage, and one assumes that this concern was one of the reasons why she had refused to marry the Marquis and resisted him so long: given the inherent egotism of the male, she rightly feared that, by yielding to his will, requiting his love and allowing him to possess her, she risked losing him. For the rest this concept of the male libido is visible virtually everywhere, at least in upper-class eighteenth-century French literature of love or seduction.[35] Need one mention that awareness of this truth about the male libido exactly defines the Countess's dilemma at the opening of Act II of *Le Mariage de Figaro*?[36] In Act V, scene vii, her husband, believing he is speaking to the maid Suzanne, himself enunciates the same truth so that there is no mistaking it:

---

34. Curiously, one might say something similar about the interruptions that impede the forward movement of the Hostess's story, for they function also to allow her to maintain control over the world in which she presides, to tend to her inn and the desires of her customers.

35. My viewpoint on this question differs fundamentally from the brilliantly argued theories of seduction proposed by Pierre Saint-Amand in *Séduire, ou la passion des lumières* (Paris 1987), p.97f.

36. 'La Comtesse: [...] Ah! je l'ai trop aimé; je l'ai lassé de mes tendresses et fatiqué de mon amour; voilà mon seul tort avec lui' (II.i).

Le Comte

[...] Nos femmes croient tout accomplir en nous aimant: cela dit une fois, elle nous aiment, nous aiment! (quand elles nous aiment) et sont si complaisantes et si constamment obligeantes, et toujours et sans relâche, qu'on est tout surpris un beau soir de trouver la satiété où l'on recherchait le bonheur.

La Comtesse, *à part*

Ah! quelle leçon.

In another key, even the archetypical Marivaux play, *Le Jeu de l'amour et du hasard*, revolves round the same largely unspoken psychological verity: why else would the heroine have invented so many trials and testings to assure in advance the sincerity of the man she loved? So long as the curtain is up, we are charmed into believing that these testings, oaths and assurances really can be efficacious: that they can change and pin down permanently a gender whose nature was, having once achieved fulfilment after the final curtain, to wander.[37] Given the eighteenth-century context, given above all the harsh truths disclosed in Marivaux's own *Paysan parvenu*, even the enchanting ending of the play probably contains hidden ironies.

As one might expect, *Les Liaisons dangereuses* displays the quintessential paradigm of this concept of male sexual psychology, along with its equally important corollary: if yielding and passionate response to his advances was the inevitable route to boredom and fickleness, the way to augmented passion was through resistance, withholding, and obstacles which make for 'irritation', the technical term for this method of arousal.[38] When Mme de Merteuil wanted to retain a lover, she denied him a second rendezvous, thus creating an obstacle to his desire; when she decided to get rid of the lover, she gave him all the sensual pleasure he thought he craved.[39] By the same token, the pleadings to desist and denials of La Présidente, wittingly or unwittingly, acted as so many irritations assuring that Valmont would press on to overcome her 'virtue', and, one assumes, would inevitably have done so even if he had not loved her. Everywhere the pattern of seduction in this novel operates on these assumptions. Perhaps it might be objected that the most famous novel

37. For Silvia, the main weapons of seduction are the obstacles she places in the path of the suitor, and which are used both 'unwittingly', before she has admitted to herself that she loves him, and, at the end, by pure calculation. In fact, her worst fears about the sexual unscrupulousness of the male were destined to be incarnated in Jacob of *Le Paysan parvenu*.

38. As the *Encyclopédie* declares, art. 'Irriter', viii.910A: 'la contrainte *irrite* le désir'.

39. See the end of letter x, and also letter CXIII, where she announces her strategy to get rid of her lover: 'Je l'amène à la campagne [...] Là, je le surchargerai à tel point, d'amour et de caresses, nous y vivrons si bien l'un pour l'autre uniquement, que je parie bien qu'il désirera plus que moi la fin de ce voyage, dont il se fait un si grand bonheur.'

of the century, *Manon Lescaut*, is an exception to this rule in that the Chevalier Des Grieux was alleged never to wander, and instead to be singlemindedly faithful to his mistress, despite her yielding to his passion. On the other hand one notes that, according to Prévost's account, the Chevalier never understood Manon well enough to possess her completely; part of her always escaped him. And then, being a prostitute with plural loves, and addicted to pleasure, she could never, until the end when she died, completely requite the single-mindedness of his affection. Manon always remained partly unattainable, and so the hero desired her for ever.

Mme de La Pommeraye, as though anticipating the successful strategies of Mme de Merteuil, plays on her realisation that the way to create desire in the Marquis is to raise obstacles to its satisfaction: no doubt Mlle Duquênoi is pretty, but above all she is presented from the start as virtuous, and therefore inaccessible. The formula is perfect: given the libido of this active male, her allegedly pristine virtue is in itself an irritation, an obstacle-challenge that calls for violation, even as her inaccessibility demands access. Once set in movement, the process of augmentation is unstoppable and automatic, one thing leading infallibly to another. Thanks to Mme de La Pommeraye's strict rules of discipline, which reduce to an absolute minimum the tantalisingly insufficient doses of 'satisfaction' he will be allotted, the more the Marquis deploys his efforts to break through the obstacles, the higher the obstacles appear, and the more desperate his attempts to overcome them. Perhaps one is supposed to assume that the attraction of virtue, an allegedly redeeming factor, also plays a role in his ever-increasing attacks. On the other hand, when one learns (p.158) that he is supposedly willing, in effect, to starve the mother and daughter into submission to his will ('les amener à ses vues par la misère'), it becomes clear that the Marquis's motives are being shown as ruthlessly egotistical, despite his earlier claims. Above all, how can one believe that he is supposed to be guided by anything like love – as opposed to raw passion – when the text makes it so clear that he does not even know the woman he pursues so relentlessly?

There is of course a superb double-layered irony in Mme de La Pommeraye's success. First, she perfectly achieves her goal, raising the barriers between the pair to such a height that she finally gets the Marquis to marry the woman he desired with such ardour, but did not know. And then – the second layer – instead of being the cause of scandal, disgrace and despair, the woman whom Mme de La Pommeraye herself chose for her revenge turns out to be the perfect wife, the one person perhaps who could have given the pair marital bliss for ever, just the relationship that Mme de La Pommeraye would have desired for herself.

The turnabout comes in two powerful confrontations (p.166-68) that owe much to the dramatic tableau which Diderot wrote about earlier. In the first, the new wife is prostrate on the floor, fainting, unable to speak, the distraught husband seated on a chair, leaning sideways against the foot of the bedstead, groaning, bellowing his distress. In the second, she is dragging herself on her knees, rather incoherently proposing ways in which he might punish her for her deeds, while simultaneously intimating that her past actions were done against her will and that her heart remained pure. Taken together these scenes function almost literally like a sacrament: first the descent in humility to a recognition of one's abject unworthiness; second the willingness to do whatever is required to make amends – a process suspiciously reminiscent of the Christian sacrament of penance.[40] Furthermore, and also similar to the Christian view, because her repentance for her sins is allegedly sincere and complete she can be pardoned and retain her marital status. Meanwhile, her husband claims that, despite his anger, he had never ceased to respect her as his wife (p.168), an assertion that may or may not be borne out by all the particulars of the text (p.166).

One can only speculate as to why this match is alleged to be such perfection: no doubt their almost sacramental experience together of this moment of humility is supposed to bind their feelings for one another. Perhaps one imagines that the Marquis has had time to reflect on his own previous sexual conduct and to realise that it was scarcely better than hers, so that, through a perverse sort of double homeopathy, they at once deserved each other and cured each other of infidelity – an idea which may or may not be supported by the narrator's comment in the last sentence of the story: 'l'homme commun aux femmes communes' (p.173). One might also speculate that, as in *Manon Lescaut*, the condition of former prostitute created in this woman an element of inaccessibility – she had already become the sexual property of so many others – a quality that one can imagine as continually inspiring the Marquis's desire for her, exactly the kind of enduring passion which Mme de La Pommeraye had failed to incite.

Everywhere in this story ethics present problems, whether or not the author chooses to face them. As a sop to conventional morality, Diderot loads all the stigma of prostitution onto the mother, Mme Duquênoi, whom he imagines

---

40. The unsigned article 'Pénitence' in the *Encyclopédie*, xii.303A, defines its 'vertu' as being 'une détestation sincère des péchés qu'on a commis, jointe à une ferme résolution de n'y plus retomber, & de les expier par des œuvres pénibles & humiliantes'. The article further states that such dispositions are absolutely required of all who wish to return to God's grace. The article adds that according to most theologians, the term 'sacrement' applies to the three acts required of the penitent before absolution can be granted: contrition, confession and satisfaction.

the Marquis, in a fit of righteous indignation after the wedding, to have packed off to a convent where she conveniently expires in a matter of days (in *La Religieuse* the lesbian Mother Superior had suffered a similar, though longer, fate for similar reasons). Viewing these matters philosophically according to Diderot's own materialistic principles, there is no reason to consider prostitution, *ipso facto*, a crime in the first place, and certainly no reason to place all the blame on the mother in the second. Also disturbing is a strange incident occurring early in the story, in which the mother disapprovingly tells of her daughter's infatuation with a priest ('elle s'était entêtée d'un petit abbé de qualité') who was not only antiphilosophical but dishonestly ambitious, in fact trying to slander his way to a bishopric, traits that so scandalised the daughter when she found out about them that she finally broke off their relationship (p.139). Like the mother, one wonders what is supposed to have attracted her to him in the first place.[41] Later on, one wonders whether her insinuations of purity of heart to her husband tell the whole story about the character Diderot invented, or whether this one, like so many others, is actually a mixture of contraries.

But of course the main problem which the author himself presents for the reader to resolve concerns the judgement one is supposed to make of the actions of Mme de La Pommeraye. Nor is the answer a simple one. In fact there are several stages of answers. The first comes just after the tale gets under way and it is becoming clear that Mme de La Pommeraye is not about to forgive the Marquis for breaking his oath of faithfulness. An anonymous voice, supposedly disembodied in space, but sounding suspiciously like Diderot in the *Supplément au Voyage de Bougainville*, or in his article 'Indissoluble' in the *Encyclopédie*,[42] points out (p.128) the folly of swearing oaths of fidelity amid a nature that is everywhere in flux. Almost immediately after this (p.129-30), Jacques tells the fable of the quarrel of the Sheath and the Knife, whose moral points more crudely and anatomically to the foolishness of demanding faithfulness when it is contrary to the sexual nature of human beings.[43] Scholars have long recognised that these views are variants of those that Diderot

---

41. Later (p.141), Jacques proposes a mocking toast to 'l'abbé de Mademoiselle d'Aisnon', his reason (or actually, the reason for his former 'capitaine') being, explains Le Maître, that the abbé belongs to a species that, dishonouring themselves by the conduct of their lives, also bring dishonour on the religion ('la cause') they serve so poorly.

42. As the editor of the DPV edition mentions, p.128, n.144.

43. See the comment by Weisz: 'Le réel et son double', p.185: 'La fable de la Gaîne et du Coutelet, insignifiante par elle-même, acquiert la valeur d'un commentaire satirique si on décèle sa fonction contrapuntique à l'histoire de Mme de La Pommeraye.'

espouses elsewhere.[44] In other words, Mme de La Pommeraye's story of revenge against her lover's unfaithfulness is launched under a cloud of disapproval emanating from the author himself.

Jacques becomes spokesman for this point of view as the story proceeds, and when, part-way through the tale (p.135), the Hostess finally manages to put an end to the interruptions by the hotel staff, Jacques's criticisms of Mme de La Pommeraye replace the interruptions as the negative element against which the story is played. After concluding the tale (p.169-73), the Hostess tries to defend Mme de La Pommeraye against Jacques's criticisms. But the last word is left to the narrator, who takes up the defence of Mme de La Pommeraye, upholding her intelligence, her strength of character and her alleged disinterestedness. He even finds reasons to pardon her lies and deceits, declaring her anger to be justified and her exemplary revenge giving the Marquis exactly what he, and all others like him, deserved.

Need one point out that this final perspective forms a perfect contrariety with the initial one? That both the fable of the Sheath and the Knife and the author's own vision of a universe in flux make for disapproval, rather than approval, of Mme de La Pommeraye and her requirement of permanent fidelity? The contradiction is inescapable. Yet, even so, it is unlikely that the author intended these two opposing perspectives to cancel each other out. The same phenomenon occurred in the *Supplément au Voyage de Bougainville* where 'la loi de la nature', given in the singular and indicating a specific rule of conduct that ought to be followed, was set alongside a willingness to accept plural possibilities, since anything that occurred in nature was by definition natural: 'vices et vertus, tout est également dans la nature'. In the present text 'la loi de la nature' means that nature intended people not to be restricted to monogamy and to be permitted to have plural sexual partners. Thus Mme de La Pommeraye's requirement of fidelity was wrong because it went counter to this law of nature, and she deserved her unhappiness. Meanwhile, however, the other perspective, 'tout est également dans la nature', implies that, since everything that exists is not only natural but necessary, one should interpret her actions in their own context, as relating to certain social and specifically feminine values within which her desire to punish the male for his wandering lust was justified, and her doomed attempt may even have a heroic quality. The two perspectives only create a muddle when taken logically. Viewed more broadly in terms of experience, each side of the contrariety is perfectly comprehensible and essential to Diderot's conception of truth. One only wishes

44. See the DPV edition, p.128, n.144, and Paul Vernière's edition in Diderot, *Œuvres romanesques* (Paris 1981), p.911, n.80.

that he had not killed off the mother before the pertinent questions could be raised.

III

Everyone recalls the incident that follows shortly after Mme de La Pommeraye's story, the grand shouting match between Jacques and Le Maître: 'Descendez là-bas.' 'Je ne descendrai pas là-bas' (p.180-81). Even so, it is not always remembered[45] that the quarrel is created by an unexpected turn in the story of Jacques's love life, which suddenly veers from its usual safely distant course and threatens to encroach on the territory of Le Maître: the virtuous young woman, whom Le Maître long before tried, and failed, to seduce (p.177), now seems, as the story unfolds, on the verge of being seduced by Jacques. Faced with a 'quiproquo' in which his servant replaces him with a sexual success he has been denied, Le Maître turns hostile, and reminds Jacques of his inherent inferiority as 'un Jacques', an inferiority the valet indignantly refuses to accept. Suddenly, with the emergence of this sexual context, all the supposedly benign interlockings which had created the harmony between the Master and Servant become abrasive and discordant, while the deprecations and resentments implicit in their relationship reach the surface with a violence that may seem irreparable.

As usual in this text, the argument proceeds via stages. The first, given in the quotations above, centres on the power of obedience: does the Master have the authority to force Jacques to descend, despite his unwillingness? Obviously this stage freezes into a deadlock, with no agreement possible. In the second stage, the Hostess, called in to adjudicate, seems to arrange a compromise: she terms the normal, pre-quarrel relationship between them 'l'égalité qui s'est établie entre eux' (p.183), and urges Jacques – just for the moment – to show obedience to Le Maître despite his feelings, but with the assurance that his gesture is purely temporary and pro forma, and that Jacques will immediately regain all his customary rights and the relationship resume its regular course. On the other hand, it is also made clear that whatever 'égalité' is re-established, the new relationship does not change the basic functions of each as Master and Servant: 'Voulons que l'un ordonne et que l'autre obéisse, chacun de son mieux' (p.183). I interpret this to mean that the pro forma interlude – pushing

45. Particularly by those who interpret the passage as an allegory of the struggles between the Paris Parlement and the Crown. See the notes to the edition by Lecointre and Le Galliot, p.436-37. The origin of the quarrel is likewise irrelevant to the textual interpretation of Daniel Brewer, *The Discourse of enlightenment*, p.230f.

the sexual question aside, and allowing other bonds of humanity to re-emerge – has simply removed the implicit hostility from the situation, so that the normal interlockings can re-occur without abrasiveness. Although ample space has been created for friendship and mutual enjoyment of one another, a space that may indeed be thought to create equality on a purely personal plane, and furthermore though this development seems a large step forward from the days when le duc de Saint-Simon made such a scandal in his *Mémoires* about finding a titled person privately playing chess with his valet, nevertheless this stage serves to confirm the basic inequalities of society. Despite the concessions to personal feelings, the fundamental message implies the preservation of class difference.

A third stage (p.184) brings with it still another perspective: Jacques points out to his master that since his authority is entirely dependent on Jacques's willingness to obey (a point dramatised by the initial deadlock), clearly the power of obedience resides in him, Jacques, and the Master's mastery is subservient to that power. Jacques's point of view may be taken as antithetical to the previous postulation, implying a shift that is authentically 'dialectical', in the sense attributed to Hegel. In any case it is clear that, in respect to the power of obedience, the third stage forms an authentic contrariety with the previous argument of the Hostess, which assumed that this power resided in the Master. Jacques denies that assumption, even going so far as to declare 'Jacques mène son Maître', as though he were the person *de facto* in charge, and as though the reality of the situation were 'que vous vous appelleriez mon maître et que c'est moi qui serais le vôtre' (p.185).[46] The implication of both these statements is that a radical shift has taken place in respect to the power of obedience, which, in terms of real authority, has now travelled from the Master to the Servant.

There can be no mistaking the intensity of this scene: Diderot presents this third stage as a paradigm, perhaps even a lesson for the ages. Nor is there any doubt that Jacques–Diderot's realisation of the power residing incipiently in those who, by necessity or tradition, are bound to obey has historical significance of major proportions. I would agree entirely with those who consider

---

46. Earlier, during one mind-boggling instant (p.183), Le Maître seemed to agree. Overcome with delight at being reconciled with Jacques, he exclaimed: 'Il est écrit là-haut que je ne me déferai jamais de cette original-là, et que tant que je vivrai il sera mon maître et que je serai son serviteur.' Needless to say, however, the disgruntlement of Le Maître during the ensuing recital of Jacques's 'rights' ('Cela me semble dur, très dur', p.185), and his later, rather witty irony to the Marquis des Arcis about Jacques's cleverness ('Un serviteur! vous avez bien de la bonté, c'est moi qui suis le sien, et peu s'en est fallu que ce matin, pas plus tard, il ne me l'ait prouvé en forme', p.188) imply that the statement is supposed to represent at most a temporary emotional impulse, and not a dialectical shift of perspective.

this moment as recording one of those intuitions by Diderot that looks ahead not only to the Revolution, but to the whole modern era.[47] Yet at the same time it is also clear that this thought is by no means the only, or even the final, answer to the problems raised. Given Diderot's curious intellectual propensities, it is virtually certain that such an intuition only became possible through contrariety, that is, by working against other stages of thought that it allegedly denied, but which as presences in the text must be accorded their enduring share of importance.

Seen in the cold light of its context, Jacques's radical declaration represents only a momentary perception, the ultimate push of a tendency, and one that in the long run turns partly into a mirage. Jacques himself never achieves the status of Master, nor can he live without having someone else in charge. Even the stipulations of Jacques's declaration of rights (p.184) do not break the traditional master–servant mould; they do not replace it with a redefinition. No doubt Jacques's right of insolence constitutes a suitably humiliating lesson that will remind Le Maître of his dependence on Jacques's obedience. Yet at the same time such a right of insolence obviously implies the acceptance of a 'Maître', if only as someone to be insolent to. Naturally, also, when Le Maître suggests (sarcastically) that he and Jacques might as well change places, Jacques is instantly against the move, protesting that the change would not work: 'Vous y perdriez le titre et vous n'auriez pas la chose. Restons comme nous sommes' (p.185). In fine, despite the appearances of daring dialectical shifts, the basic relationship of the pair is binding, and the traditional symbiotic archetype will remain indefinitely as the situation against which contrary impulses can exert themselves.[48]

47. See the text by E. Koehler quoted in Jacques Proust, *Lectures de Diderot* (Paris 1974), p.190-92; also Hope Mason, *The Irrestible Diderot*, p.165.

48. Thus, as if by a principle of contrariety, the implication of Jacques's next paradigm (p.187) takes back, and even denies, the alleged transfer of real power from Le Maître to himself. He notes that everyone, even the poorest of the poor, needed something like a dog to give orders to: 'tout homme voulait commander à un autre'. After going up and down the social scale to show the relevance of this perception to all classes, he even accepts his own role as someone else's 'dog' as part of the scheme. Nor is there any suggestion this time that, in his relationship with Le Maître, the real power resides in Jacques; on the contrary, he now sees himself as the weak one: 'Lorsque mon maître me fait parler quand je voudrais me taire, ce qui à la vérité m'arrive rarement, continua Jacques, lorsqu'il me demande l'histoire de mes amours et que j'aimerais mieux causer d'autre chose; lorsque j'ai commencé l'histoire de mes amours et qu'il l'interrompt, que suis-je autre chose que son chien. Les hommes faibles sont les chiens des hommes fermes.' The paradigm fits better with either the Hostess's arrangement or with the views of Le Maître than with Jacques's 'revolt', and the least one may conclude from the arrival of this new perspective is that Jacques's earlier position is part of an evolving process, and in no sense represents a final answer.

IV

All this is not to deny, however, that in other ways – leaving aside the dialectical manœuvrings – the character of Jacques takes on exceptionally large dimensions in this text, far greater than those attributed to Le Maître: not only does he talk more, but the stories of his past which he relates in such intimate detail delineate his personality and secure his identity for the reader in ways never matched by Le Maître. In view of this disparity, the humbleness of Jacques's social background, that is, his typically peasant origins, and the fact that he apparently had almost no formal education, give the bias of this presentation a slightly paradoxical slant, something of a cutting edge that not only reminds one of the picaresque tradition, but brings it in line with texts by Sedaine and Mercier, not to mention Rousseau,[49] which celebrated the humble and sometimes even the illiterate by making them centre-stage heroes and heroines. In this connection Diderot cheats a little by creating Jacques as the purest peasant imaginable – far more authentic than the *opéra comique* sort of peasantry of the other playwrights just mentioned – but then having him absorb the sophisticated materialistic philosophy of his former employer, the famous 'capitaine', who had allegedly learned Spinoza by heart (p.190). Thanks to this device Jacques can remain at bottom a peasant, but formulate the most sophisticated materialistic doctrines (just like Diderot), whenever the author desires.

This strategy invites ironies which the author clearly enjoys exploiting, and which allow him, as usual, to have his cake and eat it too: the text can exude materialism, and yet, the doctrines coming from a country bumpkin who is actually embarrassed at his failure to command the right vocabulary, they acquire a quaintly comical air at the same time. No doubt Diderot was pleased to put the basic doctrines of materialism in the mouth of such a 'basic' individual, the very salt of the earth; yet at the same time, the inherent incongruity of the situation inevitably begets comedy, as though Diderot were also suggesting a sense in which these doctrines – so earnestly expounded in *Le Rêve de d'Alembert* – did not have to be taken quite so seriously after all. When, in this context, it turns out (p.178) that Jacques's famous 'fatalism', inherited from his 'capitaine', has no practical application in terms of reality, that it neither changes his behaviour nor resigns him to the present, nor consoles him for the pains of the past – in fact, that this key piece in his philosophy is of no earthly use – one is tempted to conclude, here too, in favour of comedy. For indeed, in a work in which parody and 'mystification'

49. See Rex, *The Attraction of the contrary*, p.165.

play such prominent roles, it is not only possible, but likely, that the famous 'fatalism' is, at least on one level, part of the game, and that any reader who fails to see the spoof is being hoodwinked – at least for the duration of the novel.

This element of philosophical parody, along with its ambiguities, reaches a bizarre climax (p.90-91), when Diderot – apparently deliberately – overplays his hand and attempts an 'apothéose de Jacques': since he had already contrived to make Jacques a mini-materialist, one understands his urge, given his long-standing penchants, to go the final step and imagine Jacques playing the role that he himself coveted, that of the greatest philosopher of antiquity, Socrates.[50] At the same time, of course, Diderot was aware of an element of preposterousness inherent in the idea – if only because of Jacques's alleged lack of schooling in philosophical argument. And as usual, Diderot contrives to have the best of both worlds: to indulge his not-so-secret desire to imagine his character playing Socrates, and simultaneously to satirise the idea, as though he were only joking. Putting this ambivalence into action, Le Maître claims to detect a parallel between Jacques and the great philosopher, and, in this light, launches into a mini-oration in praise of 'la race des philosophes'. The passage is clearly intended as a 'morceau d'éloquence', and, despite a certain exaggeration in the long phrases of the high-style presentation, there can be no doubt that it touches on social issues of major importance to Diderot as a *philosophe* (p.91):

Je sais bien que c'est une race d'hommes odieuse aux Grands, devant lesquels il ne fléchissent pas le genou; aux magistrats, protecteurs par état des préjugés qu'ils poursuivent; aux prêtres qui les voient rarement aux pieds de leurs autels; aux poètes, gens sans principes et qui regardent sottement la philosophie comme la cognée des beaux-arts, sans compter que ceux même d'entre eux qui se sont exercés dans le genre odieux de la satire n'ont été que des flatteurs; aux peuples, de tout temps les esclaves des tyrans qui les oppriment, des fripons qui les trompent et des bouffons qui les amusent.

No matter how perfectly suited to Diderot's vision of his own role as 'nouveau Socrate', this attempt to apply these traits to Jacques, and even get Jacques to agree to the parallel, is obviously ludicrous. The disparities[51] are almost as glaring as those of Le Maître's mock lamentation on the occasion of the 'capitaine's' (possibly authentic) funeral train. Equally absurd was the proposed starting point of the parallel between Jacques and Socrates, which

50. See the DPV edition, p.90, n.93.
51. Just to dot the 'i's and cross the 't's on this point: nothing in Jacques's behaviour with upper-class persons such as one sees it in the novel suggests that he is 'odieux aux Grands', as the passage implies that any *philosophe* (like Jacques) would be. As for the hatred of magistrates, Jacques had recently spent the night in the house of a judge who had treated him honestly and well; nor does anything in the novel suggest that his intellectual views or the state of his soul are supposed to be of any concern to the priests, poets or lower classes mentioned in the passage.

had been the pretext for the oration, namely, their politeness to their execu-tioners – if only because Jacques, for the moment, is not being executed. Nor does Le Maître help matters when he tries to bridge that gap by prophesying that, Jacques being at bottom a *philosophe*, his eventual execution is inevitable – a point which Jacques stubbornly refuses to concede, even when Le Maître promises to keep his secret identity a secret. In short, however earnest the eloquence of the mini-oration, and however forceful its radical thrusts appear as a social statement,[52] its context, applying the lesson to Jacques, distinctly invites mockery, and the best conclusion one can reach about it is just that it is, and is not, to be taken seriously.[53]

If Jacques's role is deliberately enlarged, Le Maître, by contrast, despite the authority of his title, bears the burden of the author's persistent denigrations and diminutions. Almost everywhere the author seems bent on bringing Le Maître down to the level of Jacques, showing the pair on an equal footing, or even, at the expense of Le Maître, giving the lead to Jacques and making him the brave, the sexy, or the wise one. In Diderot's only verbal portrait of Le Maître, a densely composed, devastatingly negative assessment, he is mocked for the tediousness of his personality and his lack of intelligence and origi-nality.[54] The best thing about him seems to be his admiration and even friendship for Jacques and his willingness to listen to the stories of Jacques's life, rather (one assumes) than boring the reader by telling his own. One sometimes has the impression that if Le Maître is so drawn to Jacques, it must be because his own personality is so empty. Meanwhile, he plays the role of *automate* (the word is Diderot's), repeating the same watch-consulting, snuff-

---

52. Amidst the uneasiness of the political ambiance following the Terror, for which at least some individuals held *philosophes* like Diderot responsible, the editor of the first extensive review of *Jacques le fataliste* to appear in print (1796) took Diderot to task for this passage, bitterly excoriating him for the attitude he believed the words implied: 'A force d'en vouloir trop faire l'éloge [i.e. des *philosophes*], j'ai peur que Diderot n'en ait fait ici la plus amère censure. Cet éloge, au reste, nous rappelle celui que nous entendons faire tous les jours d'une poignée de factieux, qui se croient exclusivement appellés à réformer le genre humain, et qui, fussent-ils réduits à quinze scélerats, ne s'en prétendroient pas moins les héros ou les martyrs du patriotisme' (from *Le Censeur des journaux* 18, 9 October 1796, quoted in *Jacques le fataliste et La Religieuse devant la critique révolutionnaire (1796-1800)*, ed. Jean de Booy and Alan J. Freer, Studies on Voltaire 33, 1965, p.95).

53. Cf. the rather different interpretation of Mauzi, 'La parodie romanesque', p.121.

54. Diderot's description, once it starts building up negative steam, goes far: 'si vous prenez parti de faire compagnie à son maître, vous serez poli, mais très ennuyé; vous ne connaissez pas encore cette espèce-là. Il a peu d'idées dans la tête; s'il lui arrive de dire quelque chose de sensé, c'est de réminiscence ou d'inspiration. Il a des yeux comme vous et moi, mais on ne sait la plupart du temps s'il regarde. Il ne dort pas, il ne veille pas non plus; il se laisse exister, c'est sa fonction habituelle. L'automate allait devant lui, se retournant de temps en temps pour voir si Jacques ne revenait pas' (p.45).

taking gestures, and formulating the same sort of predictable questions or comments. In stressing such traits, Diderot clearly wants him to seem a caricature.

Imagining Le Maître – following Diderot's indications (p.45-46, p.49) – sitting on the ground by the side of the road while waiting for Jacques to return, with nothing to do and no thoughts in his mind, finally out of sheer lassitude and boredom falling asleep and being robbed of his horse for his pains – it is difficult to conceive that such a nondescript person is also allegedly someone of high social station, who has just spent the night in the house of a judge (p.48, n.46; p.51), and whose friends are apparently persons of quality with titles and châteaux, someone with money and family connections,[55] and someone who, if he knows a good horse when he sees one, was formerly an officer in command in the cavalry (p.58), in short, someone whose background is supposedly *noblesse d'épée*. Diderot deliberately deprives the reader of indications of manners, dress or other accessories that would give a visual dimension to this aspect of Le Maître, insisting instead on the similarities with Jacques.[56] Most of the time one assumes that the only difference between them is that Jacques is smarter.

On the other hand, for anyone keeping track of the situation, there are so many exceptions to Diderot's initial denigrating description of Le Maître and to his insistent presentation of him as an automaton as to make one wonder whether Diderot did not set into motion these negative expectations for the fun of undermining them as he goes along. Le Maître's little discourse on 'la race des philosophes' during the aforementioned 'apothéose de Jacques' (p.91) is a good example: it attributes to Le Maître critical attitudes towards 'les Grands' and 'les magistrats' which, though perfectly suited to an embattled *encyclopédiste* such as Diderot, are most unlikely in the mouth of this speaker. It is as though Le Maître, while the author was studiously looking the other way, suddenly stopped being an automaton and turned into a pseudo-Diderot (stylistically taking the eloquence just a bit over the edge, to be sure).

By the same token, one cannot tell whose funeral lamentation Le Maître recites (p.67-68) when the (perhaps fake) funeral train of Jacques's 'capitaine' passes through the landscape, yet the startling effect of this 'morceau d'éloquence' is not only to stop cold – just before it has time to get up steam –

55. These facts are brought out especially when Le Maître explains why he does not want to marry Agathe: 'J'aime et beaucoup, mais j'ai des parents, un nom, un état, des prétentions, et je ne me résoudrai jamais à enfouir tous ces avantages dans le magasin d'une petite bourgoise' (p.247).

56. The only exception to this rule which I recall is the mention that Le Maître and Le Marquis Des Arcis have dined separately from Jacques and the Marquis's travelling companion, Richard (p.188).

Jacques's own bathetic outburst of distress, but its intensity and unexpected-ness – sliding in slantwise to distort, parody and eventually smother Jacques's efforts at grief – create one of the most splendidly comic moments of the entire novel. At the very least, it is a brilliant improvisation, not only funny, but creatively intelligent as well. The same might be said of Le Maître's ironic comments on Jacques's radical ideas: they are masterfully to the point and, in the finest Diderot tradition, exactly lay the finger on whatever in his own theories is vulnerable to ridicule.[57] But the crowning surprise from this supposedly dull-witted automaton comes when he reveals his talent as a story-teller (p.235f.): the lively *entrain*, verve and economy of his narrative, his superb sense of timing, the exactness of his vocabulary, even the subtle hint of the self-depreciating irony that tinges the story, bespeak a master of the genre. Perhaps all this may be considered the other side of the coin: the denigrations and disparagements of Le Maître may, through the impulse of contrariety, have inspired Diderot to create a story-telling vindication which, seconded by Jacques's sore throat, more and more replaces the other pejorat-ive view.

Despite whatever idea of 'fatalism' might be inscribed in the title, all these contradictions certainly register Diderot's determination to declare his freedom from the constraints – one of them being consistency – that normally tie novelists down and prevent them from changing the characters they create, at least in mid-novel. Though Diderot is reliable enough to make sure that everyone in his cast remains recognisable, he also takes pleasure in breaking the rules by endowing them with new, and hitherto unheard-of, psychological dimensions, new foibles or fixations, new costumes. Sometimes he works on the sly,[58] but many times the operation is done with a brazen bad faith that the indulgent reader is expected to absorb anyway just because he or she is enjoying the story, and the bad faith is part of the fun. The flagrant example is Jacques's 'gourde', which the narrator claims (p.231) has always been part of Jacques's accoutrements but which the author just 'forgot' to mention before the novel was more than three-quarters of the way through – an explanation that, given the importance which this object will henceforth acquire in the text, stretches beyond decent limits the credulity of even the best-disposed

57. See, for example, his drolly satirical application of Jacques's theory that someone else's pain is only comprehensible through one's own experiences of suffering (p.39).

58. For example, Diderot goes out of his way to present the literal-mindedness of Gousse as something surprising and *rarissime* in nature – certainly, one assumes (since such fuss is made about it), never before encountered in this novel (p.82), when actually Jacques has frequently exhibited exactly the same characteristic, and above all the narrator's opening 'D'où venaient-ils? Du lieu le plus prochain' (p.23) represents emblematically the same mentality.

reader. One suspects that Jacques's extraordinary, enormous hat, which Diderot so unexpectedly makes up for him (p.271), and which he sketches so masterfully for the reader's and presumably the author's delectation, is another such inspired improvisation. In any case, once created and placed on Jacques's head, the hat (contrary to the 'gourde') is never heard of again.

Another suspicious item is the narrator's sudden revelation (p.132) of Jacques's 'aversion' to repeating himself, an allegedly indelible trait inherited from his grandfather. Though the idea fits wonderfully with the family circle of the 'baillon' episode, it is hardly a doctrine one would expect from a character who talks generally in refrains (his former 'capitaine', 'le grand rouleau', 'ce qui est écrit là-haut'). But even if one assumes that the refrains are not supposed to count, Jacques himself had early on proposed to Le Maître that, in view of all the interruptions, he might just as well begin the story of his love life all over again ('que je ferais tout aussi bien de recommencer', p.35). So much for his indelible aversion to 'redites'. The same questionable pattern appears in Jacques's totally unprepared loathing for literary portraits (p.262-65): however arresting, indeed fascinating, the theoretical implications of his arguments against portraits, he has never complained about them before; in fact he himself had earlier practised the genre with considerable success. For the rest, there is nothing wrong with the particular literary portrait by Le Maître that occasioned his loud complaints in the passage in question (p.262). In fact this portrait is brilliantly realised,[59] and one suspects that Jacques's complaints are mainly a pretext for his own (i.e. Diderot's) even more brilliant ideas on the topic, and whose appropriateness probably occurred to Diderot on the spot. Who can take seriously Jacques's alleged authorship of a treatise on divination when Jacques himself later claims that he can no longer remember a word he had written of it (p.280)?

From a materialist, who saw the universe as working through laws of cause and effect, one might logically expect that his fictional universe do the same, i.e. be required to obey the same laws in order to be believable as corresponding to reality. It is equally clear, however, that in this work, this particular materialist took special pleasure in openly breaking the rules he himself created, and that the target is not merely the novel as conventionally conceived but the

---

59. My own judgement of this passage coincides with the opinion expressed in the review in *Le Censeur des journaux*. The anonymous author particularly recommended this 'portrait de femme [...] où l'on reconnoîtra la touche du grand maître, l'écrivain philosophe, le pinceau de Diderot' (quoted in Booy and Freer (ed.), *Jacques le fataliste et La Religieuse devant la critique révolutionnaire*, p.97). To be sure, this is the passage where Diderot, probably inadvertently, called the woman a 'veuve' and then touchingly claimed that the only husband she had had regretted her long after her death.

'fatalism' his own philosophy would seem to imply. Robert Mauzi has well defined this far-reaching aspect of the novel:

un univers déconcertant, rempli de signes trompeurs et d'inexplicables lacunes, où l'on ne dispose jamais de rien, où la nature des êtres et des choses n'est jamais claire, où nul ne sait jamais ce qu'il veut, ce qu'il fait, où il va. Les impertinences de l'auteur envers son lecteur apparaissent comme la contrepartie symbolique de la désinvolture du destin envers les hommes, et le destin mène le monde avec ce même mélange de liberté, d'indifférence et de malice dont s'inspire le conteur pour conduire, ou plutôt pour brouiller les fils multiples de son récit.[60]

Yet, even granting the acuteness of these observations, one of the curiosities of this novel is, as Mauzi himself suggests, that the reader is never supposed to detach himself from the experience of it sufficiently to attain the philosphical serenity, or cynicism, necessary to accept fully the implications of such a consequential diagnosis. On the contrary, like Jacques in his inability to react like a true fatalist (p.178), Diderot's supposition is that the reader never abandons his traditional expectations, which the author counts on (at least as fiction) in order to flout them. For the novel to have its effect, there must be an illusion of delicate sensibilities, belief in decent values, in rules of fair play and consistency, plus some reasonable demands that the novelistic universe make sense, and which the author can offend. Thus despite the wise lessons of Mauzi's characterisation, it is entirely legitimate, even required, that the reader, viewing the floutings and transgressions, also understand the reasons why they might have made one indignant. He must at least perceive, as the author wants him to, the outlandishness of this conduct, which is so often due simply to the author's flippant urge to undo, or redo, what he has just done so as to make it different, or to make up for some gap that he has inadvertently created. Deists such as Voltaire were always complaining that the God of the Old Testament was not to be believed because He constantly changed His mind, or revealed unseemly motives in Himself, or behaved capriciously. It is as if Diderot, over the reader's fancied protests, were carrying into his fiction this idea of God's role, for the sheer enjoyment of imagining himself in a state of lawless omnipotence, complete with the benefits that accrue when one acquires the attributes of divinity.

V

Just as in Racine's witty comedy, *Les Plaideurs*, in which the whole cast feels uncontrollable urges to take every situation that arises to court, in the world

---

60. 'La parodie romanesque', p.90.

of Diderot's novel all the main characters (the ones supposedly present in the 'frame' at least) partake of the compulsion to tell stories: it seems that past experience only has value when used as grist for this mill, perhaps somewhat like the way in which, for opera composers, plain speech may be thought of as incipiently possessing the makings of song. And even as story-telling brings out unexpected qualities of intelligence in Le Maître, and gives the Hostess so much of an aristocratic flair the author feels bound to invent for her hints of an aristocratic past to satisfy the rules of *vraisemblance* (p.128, p.144), for all the main narrators the story is a privileged event demanding special efforts and qualities, an opportune space in which to create wonderful dimensions that are always alleged to be mere copies of reality, but which everyone recognises at the same time as being somehow importantly superior to it – for reasons which are never defined, except in terms of sheer enjoyment.[61] Such built-in urges doubtless account for everyone's boundless determination to tell their tales, or to hear them, despite or because of all the frustrations and impediments perversely put in their path by the author. Such abrasions make it even clearer that these characters belong by their essences to the category of tellers of tales. However varied their alleged past experiences, they were created with a single vocation, apart from which one imagines them – like Tiberge and the Chevalier before the appearance of Manon, or like Le Maître and Jacques on their undetermined journey – aimlessly situated amid life's banalities.

It may seem a paradox that a work so resolutely planted in the real world, so full of the clanks and rattles of reality,[62] should at the same time be so determinedly literary:[63] but in fact one of the special enjoyments of this novel is the sense it gives of the author's own pleasure in literature, not only in the ebullient enthusiasm for telling stories, but in the recollection of other works of fiction and in creating his own tale in their remembrance.[64] Cervantes is the

---

61. Le Maître claims at one point (p.170) that the value of 'contes' is not merely amusement, but instruction. Later on, however (p.217), when challenged to define 'le but moral' of the story of Bigre, his arguments are easily overturned by Jacques as superficial or false.

62. On Diderot's 'realism' see the perceptive, and usefully documented, remarks in the introduction by Paul Vernière to his edition of *Jacques le fataliste*, p.32-34.

63. I use the term loosely to imply a text that is put forward as a consciously 'artistic' creation. I recognise that, whereas etymologically 'littérature' implies letters which are meant for the eye (and hence for the brain), Diderot's text is above all intended for the ear, the letters on the page being simply the means to that end.

64. Diderot's references to various authors are conveniently listed in Edouard Guitton, 'La mention du livre dans *Jacques le fataliste*', *Interférences* 11 (1980), p.57-71; see also Eric Walter, *Jacques le fataliste de Diderot* (Paris 1975), p.25, who suggests that other authors who inspire his text but are not mentioned by name, or only mentioned insufficiently; on the theatricality of Diderot's text, and the playwrights who inspired it, see p.50-53. Further literary 'sources'

prime example, not only because various incidents from *Don Quixote* may create echoes in Diderot's text, but because the ironies of the relationship between the knight and his squire obviously suggested the possibility of other ironic relationships, which were realised in Diderot's pair of travellers – even as they had earlier, and differently, been realised in Sterne's Uncle Toby and Corporal Trim, who likewise made their mark on Diderot's text, as has been noted. Though the social outlook may be quite different, one might assume that memories of Le Sage's *Gil Blas* and, through him, of the picaresque tradition may also tinge the adventures of Jacques and Le Maître as they wend their way through the nondescript landscape.[65]

Particularly after the Marquise and Marquis Des Arcis have left the scene, one discovers, sandwiched around the accounts of Jacques's various 'dépucela-ges', a series of famous authors ready to inspire the text and no doubt to restore a certain respectability to the narrative, just in case any deficiency has occurred. Dante comes first (p.205), not only in the reminiscences of the infernal punishments depicted in his *Commedia*, but in a story of a man refusing the sacraments on his deathbed despite the machinations of his family, a story inspired – negatively – by Dante, as a counterpoise to fears of the afterlife. Next, after the earthy entertainments of the lengthy Bigre episode and its sequels,[66] comes Montaigne, who is quoted and misquoted somewhat more than the author admits (p.230-31) in his justification for expressing sexual impurities in words.[67] If Jacques's 'gourde' is invented so late in the novel (p.232) the reason is probably its function as a transition to the theme of the oracular 'trinch' and the 'dive Bouteille' as in Rabelais, who is invoked with suitably intoxicating exuberance and given centre stage in the text as the inspirer of a whole school of practitioners.

Among them Diderot lists Molière, who enters as a subtext (p.235f.), a main inspirer of Le Maître's long tale of his near-undoing at the hands of Agathe and Le Chevalier de Saint-Ouin. As if mixing and refashioning the elements he had most enjoyed in *Le Bourgeois gentilhomme*, *L'Avare* and *Les Fourberies de Scapin*, Diderot creates a new, and rather more sordid, concoction from

(notably Sorel and Scarron) are proposed by Paul Vernière, 'Diderot et l'invention littéraire', *Lumières ou clair-obscur?*, p.52 (article originally published in 1959).

65. See for example the suggestion in the edition by Lecointre and Le Galliot, p.385, n.16.

66. Except for its sexual elements, the scene of the dwarf, the tiny vicar, paraded around the barn, bellowing and gesticulating on the end of a pitchfork (p.228), might easily have been inspired by Scarron's *Roman comique*.

67. I do not claim that Montaigne actually inspired the preceding tales of Bigre, and Jacques's various losses of virginity, but simply that the daringly pornographic explicitness of these tales – as distinct from the deliberately inexplicit eroticism of the story of Mme de La Pommeraye – brought the issue to the fore.

some of Molière's time-tested recipes: the gullible young man's search for cash or gifts to soften the heart of an unattainable lady, with the gifts going, right under his nose, to profit the other man's love affair, may suggest both *Le Bourgeois gentilhomme*[68] and *Scapin*. (To be sure, when the chips are down, the lady in question will turn out to be unfaithful, money-grasping, pregnant and bent on marriage at all costs, quite unlike her counterpart in Molière.[69]) The items of bric-a-brac, so meticulously described by Le Maître to show their disparate uselessness and dubious value (p.235-36), and which the picturesquely dishonest 'fripiers' – a brilliantly evoked world unto themselves with their crooked finances and exquisite politeness – are ready to unload on unwary customers (p.236-42), may have been originally inspired by the useless and damaged goods Molière so economically, and masterfully, created for Act II of *L'Avare*. The inventive mystifications of the Chevalier de Saint-Ouin, whose extravagant lies (p.253-60) are so transparent for Jacques and the alert reader, and so opaque to the love-blind Le Maître, are probably modelled on *Scapin*, although translated to a more sordid level. No doubt the sexual explicitness relates to other authors (including Regnard and Le Sage, both offshoots of the Molière tradition), but much of the time, especially as one is caught up in the brio and *entrain* of the narration, one is pleased to feel the influence of the master author of comedy inspiring Diderot's own creativity.

For sheer audacity nothing beats Diderot's final literary borrowing in which the sexual climax of the entire work (p.289-90) – Jacques's big scene with Denise – is condensed word for word from Sterne's novel – as the narrator takes pains to explain to the reader. Nor is the irregularity of the situation attenuated by the obvious bad faith of the ensuing argument between the narrator and the reader as to whether the implications of the last phrase, 'et la baisa', are merely sensual or distinctly sexual. The truth of Diderot's text has often before been brought into question, and, often before, the evident bad faith of the narrator's assurances to the reader that the text is a true account would have mightily undermined the reader's belief in the novel, assuming that it ever existed.[70] But the borrowing from Sterne of a climax which is supposed to be happening in Diderot's novel, not in Sterne's, surely certifies, if anything could, the untruth of the whole enterprise: the narrator is essentially

68. Particularly in the elegant Count's strategy to hoodwink M. Jourdain into providing the extravant gifts for the Count's courtship of the Marquise, while believing they are furthering his own cause. Obviously, the Chevalier de Saint-Ouin cheats Le Maître for similar purposes.

69. Such 'realism' recalling Regnard or Le Sage.

70. The transparent bad faith of Diderot's assurances in this connection has been wittily examined in Mauzi, 'La parodie romanesque', p.101-107.

telling the reader that he should not believe a word he reads.[71] For the rest, this incident is but the culmination of a sequence in which the veracity of the text has almost literally been shredding to pieces: even the manuscript is said to exist only in bits, of various degrees of doubtful authenticity. Meanwhile, just before the end, the author invents for Jacques the most implausible incident in the entire work (p.290-91), separating him from Le Maître and turning him into a member of a famous band of robbers in an incident identical to the kind Diderot earlier declared to be fit only for novels, and promised, nay sworn, would never occur in a true account such as this.[72] In short, at the end the author seems to be taking perverse pleasure in rubbing the readers' noses in the fakery of his invention and causing all the illusions of the novel to self-destruct.

Such are the powerfully perverse marvels of contrariety, however, which are built into the story of Jacques that paradoxically the more the author certifies the falseness of his text – sometimes even offering to the allegedly dissatisfied reader the chance to rewrite the script for himself[73] – the more the reader is determined not to believe him.[74] Just as in a comedy by Molière, no matter how many layers of unlikelihoods the audience has to swallow, the happy ending is a foregone conclusion, a necessity, from the start. With Jacques, the urgency that he find his way to Denise has been getting keener not only with the impatience of Le Maître (model of the reader's own), but as each interruption of the story causes a flare-up of the reader's 'irritation'. Even as, in the tale of Mme de La Pommeraye, the obstacles in the Marquis's path intensifies his determination to surmount them, so too, everywhere in this novel, the energy of the reader's determination to reach the satisfactions of the happy end have actually been strengthened each time the author invents some interruption. It is as though the basic pattern of seduction were being translated into the encumbrances strewing the structure of the novel, to make sure that the reader, just like the Marquis, or for that matter like Valmont, will never let go until he finally achieves his desires.

For the rest, once Denise enters the text, identified as the woman whom Jacques loves, the momentum, the grand undertow towards the conclusion,

71. I assume that the reader is intended to see through the narrator's insinuation (p.289) that perhaps Sterne had been the one to plagiarise Diderot's text.

72. See for example p.35, and the whole discussion of this topic in Mauzi, 'La parodie romanesque', p.101f.

73. In the last five pages of the text, this opportunity is offered to the reader twice (p.287 and 290), before the final envoi.

74. Mauzi, 'La parodie romanesque', p.130-32, gives a different slant to this argument, and adduces other reasons, but his point is essentially the same as my own.

becomes unstoppable, especially after Denise's touching jealousy over Jacques's garters has shown how much she loves him (her willingness being, titillatingly, just what the reader wanted to hear, while the presence of her mother creates an excitingly irritating impediment). Meanwhile, all along, dozens of tales, following what I have termed the sexual paradigm, that is, following the contours of their necessary paths – no matter how many interruptions intervene – towards some sort of fulfilment, have been schooling the reader to predict that Jacques at the end will be 'heureux' in every sense, and also that – for reasons of symbiotic necessity – if any separation occurs between Jacques and Le Maître, that pair will be reunited as well. The valences of the elements have been so clearly defined that they cannot avoid the combining that awaits them. It really does not matter whether the manuscript is tattered, corrupt, or disappears entirely; the final scene – 'C'est toi, mon ami! – C'est vous, mon cher maître! [...] – C'est vous, Denise? – C'est vous, Monsieur Jacques? Combien vous m'avez fait pleurer!...' – was given from the moment when Jacques told Le Maître how he had received his knee wound. The whole plot from knee to groin existed from the start, from all eternity, or at least from the moment when Diderot discovered the beginning and the end in Sterne. Despite all his blustery pretence of being above his own laws, once the author of this 'grand rouleau' had cranked it into operation he could not possibly have prevented the scene of the happy conclusion from taking place.[75]

Of course the scene, like everything else in the novel, arises purely from Diderot's sounds on the page and takes place solely in the reader's imagination. And now the syllables are about to cease, an event that, for any other writer concluding a story with a happy ending, would pose no problem. In Diderot's case, however, by the core and essence of his philosophy – and contrary to the form of all the sexually modelled tales within the 'frame' – events can never be finally terminal; they are always transitional, even in novels. Virtually by definition Diderot's end must be a non-conclusion, in effect a beginning of another plot. And so, having married Denise to Jacques and established him as 'intendant' in the château, Diderot puts his hero to sleep, thus bringing down the curtain on all the action, and silencing all the counterpoints; but as he does so, he gives him new worries about Denise's fidelity, along with several eager seducers in the offing, enough to put Jacques's fatalistic philosophy sorely to the test, and enough, too, for an entire *Mariage de Figaro*, had Diderot

75. Such, in my opinion, is the implication of the narrator's statement to the reader, referring to Jacques's behaviour in the final incident of the knee: 'Si vous n'êtes pas satisfait de ce que je vous révèle des amours de Jacques, Lecteur, faites mieux j'y consens. De quelque manière que vous vous y preniez, je suis sûr que vous finirez comme moi' (p.290).

not decided to put down his pen. And then, leaving no room for comments or protests, Diderot creates by implication the final gesture, his envoi, and, with silently ironic artistry, bequeaths to the reader alone the pleasure of dreaming up the rest.

9. The dialectical dynamics of
Le Neveu de Rameau

They that endeavour to abolish vice destroy also vertue,
for contraries, though they destroy one another, are
yet the life of one another.

(Sir Thomas Browne, *Religio medici*)

I

IN Voltaire's *Candide* the stream of adventures conjures up a host of countries
that characters were born in, landed in, traversed or remembered, a variety
also reflected in the character types met with in the course of the story. Such
a quantity of cultures and nationalities adds up to an international ambience
designed by the author to insinuate a message that is global: almost from the
start the reader is aware that the whole world is implicated in Voltaire's
enterprise. Diderot's *Satire seconde*, otherwise known as *Le Neveu de Rameau*,
conveys a similarly universal dimension, but its global impact is achieved by
different means, from a different angle and for very different purposes.[1] In
contrast to Voltaire, who built his story with characters and events perceived
as fictional, and in which allusions to actual events such as the Lisbon
earthquake, the Seven Years War or the Jesuits in Paraguay seem like rarities,
Diderot's satire is supposed to be perceived throughout as reality. The only
'fiction' in it takes the form of art. Whereas Voltaire's wandering narrative
travelled the globe and presumably took years to complete, Diderot's dialogue –
rivalling the compression of a Parisian stage play – goes in the opposite
direction by never leaving the same Parisian spot and crowding all the action
into part of a single afternoon.

1. Although my own view of the genesis and meaning of the work is distinctly closer to that
of Henri Coulet in his edition (DPV, xii.31-196), the references given henceforth in the text are
to the Jean Fabre edition (Geneva 1963), on account of its long-standing and widespread
currency, the accuracy of its text and the abundance of its documentation. I am also particularly
mindful of the erudition and brilliant insights of Jean-Claude Bonnet's introduction to his edition
(Paris 1983), and, of course, of the article by Leo Spitzer, 'The style of Diderot', *Linguistics and
literary history* (Princeton 1948), p.135-91. I trust that my own approach to this dialogue, through
contrariety, will be generally original. Given the sheer size of the literature that has grown up
around *Le Neveu de Rameau* in recent years, however, I cannot hope to acknowledge every
precursor for each of my ideas. As a general rule I will be content to cite the authors who were
helpful to me in formulating this interpretation.

At the same time, contrary to this tendency to concentrate and unify, *Le Neveu de Rameau* is the most allusive of Diderot's fictional works; it constantly turns to events and persons lying beyond its theoretical confines, at moments even taking on an air of 'pièces rapportées', a conglomerate or pastiche of persons, voices, scenes, ideas and, above all, music brought in from the outside. Though the rules of the unities may fix the dialogue to a single location, the miracles of the Nephew's mimicry in gesture, powerfully augmented by his verbal articulations and musical performances, cause the literal setting in the café regularly, or irregularly, to disappear, melting away, while the imaginary 'stage' of the action becomes as crowded with characters and music as if it were an opera or a scene from a play.

In so far as the Nephew is seen to take charge of the dialogue, it becomes his variety show in which talk – idle, serious and everything in between – predominates, but into which from time to time entertainments, mimed or musical, are interjected for an assortment of reasons: to lighten the mixture, to demonstrate the musical superiority of the Italians, to counteract Diderot's feeling of disgust (or perhaps, on the contrary, to reinforce it), to act as compensation for arguments or situations won or lost, as a ploy to gain Diderot's admiration, and so on. No doubt the Horatian example is to be reckoned with almost everywhere in this miscellaneous satire which so often reinterprets Horatian themes or makes gestures towards a Horatian manner.[2] Some scholars, notably Dieckmann and H. R. Jauss, have invoked the Menippean satire as a prime literary ancestor.[3] But in respect to matters of form the precedent of Villon is also not to be overlooked, for the Great Testament plays off ballades and various set poems against the more narrative *huitains* with a cynicism and/or calculated emotionality that sometimes uncannily foreshadows the way in which the Nephew's entertainments function in Diderot's context.

The result of Diderot's outward-turning, allusive strategy is a dialogue in which proper names, and people in general, are more copious than in any other of his fictional works. Furthermore, the vocabulary is enormous – as the 'lexique' of the Fabre edition attests.[4] Again this feature is unique among Diderot's creations, in fact, Diderot's verbal abundance in this work is simply phenomenal; none of the other great authors of the time shows anything like his command of vocabulary on all levels – from the most sublime abstractions at one end, to excrement and the sex act at the other. As I have argued

2. See the usefully documented discussion by Coulet, DPV, xii.40-42.
3. See H. R. Jauss, '"Le Neveu de Rameau", dialogique et dialectique (ou: Diderot lecteur de Socrate et Hegel lecteur de Diderot)', *Revue de métaphysique et de morale* 89 (1984), p.148-49.
4. P.255-86. The concordance of the vocabulary of the text is in *Entretiens sur le Neveu de Rameau*, ed. Michèle Duchet and Michel Launay (Paris 1967), p.291-405.

elsewhere, this is the only great fictional work of the century (a category designed to exclude any potentially exceptional pornographers and playwrights of the *foire*) in which one hears absolutely authentic spoken language – as opposed to the various literary styles employed universally (even in their dialogues) in the fictions of Voltaire, Rousseau, Crébillon fils, Montesquieu and all the other famous authors.[5] Various factors contributed to this lexical increase, including the author's borrowings from his encyclopaedic knowledge of technical terms,[6] and his own or the Nephew's specialised background in various technical aspects of music. The Nephew's lack of propriety also contributes to the exceptional size of this lexicon, for his kind of explicitness implies more words. By comparison, the relatively prim vocabulary spoken by Moi as he addresses Lui is smaller, and conforms more to proper literary usage, a compliance which one assumes to be reinforced negatively by the uncomfortable presence of the Nephew, whose words might wander anywhere, whether genially enunciating musical theories with exquisite taste and sensibility, or uncannily articulating and bringing into the open just the thoughts and behaviour Diderot would never have articulated for himself and on his own.

In so far as the Nephew and Diderot ostensibly function as opposites in the dialogue (and of course opposition is by no means their only mode of relationship), they form a contrariety of rare perfection, exploited with a creative richness and subtlety seldom seen since Molière. Furthermore, the author makes the reader aware of the fundamental conflict in moral values that each allegedly represents so that at least in the domain of ethics the contrariety is a conscious part of the aesthetic, just as it had been for La Fontaine. There may even be moments when Diderot wants the reader to see the Nephew as belonging to a pack of wolves, while he himself remains spotless as a lamb. The dynamic contrast between the moral values of the two speakers is announced already in the prologue by Diderot's declaration that, though others may think and behave otherwise towards such 'originals', he himself does not consider the Nephew worthy of his friendship or even prolonged acquaintance, a disapproval that will, after many vagaries, corruptions and evolutions, be found again intact at the end. Just as in the contrarieties of Classicism, finally no compromise is possible. The Nephew's farewell question and Diderot's rejoinder – 'Adieu, Mr le philosophe. N'est-il pas vrai que je suis toujours le même?' 'Hélas! oui, malheureusement' – might be taken as reviving the tacit implication of the end of *Le Misanthrope*, that at least according to outward appearances nothing has changed.

5. Laclos is perhaps an exception to my rule.
6. See the remarks of Michèle Duchet in *Entretiens sur le Neveu de Rameau*, p.179.

Meanwhile Moi, Diderot,[7] 'Monsieur le philosophe', whose devotion to truth and virtue is so abundantly displayed and eloquently argued, is the perfect foil for the ne'er-do-well Nephew, and vice versa: if the two were drawn together, they were made for one another, just as magnetically as the Lamb and the Wolf had ever been. And even as, in La Fontaine, class differences were often part of the contrariety, so too in this dialogue the persona said to be Diderot is being put forward as favouring – despite those momentary waverings that are doubtless supposed to make him more human – the solid virtues of the middle class, a point no doubt too obviously emphasised in the text to warrant lengthy discussion. To be sure, the moral concept of 'bourgeois' traditionally had several possible meanings, and it is clear from Diderot's personality in the dialogue that his persona is far more diversified, intellectual, sympathetic and engaging than the narrow, hoarding, unpitying, bourgeois 'Fourmi' played off so astutely against the 'Cigale' in La Fontaine's fable. If Diderot represents the middle class, it is in the Enlightened sense, and the only hoarding in which Diderot claims to be engaged is that of storing and fostering useful ideas, along with good principles and high ideals for his daughter and humankind.

The Nephew's class association, less obvious, is worth more attentive consideration. He has most often been listed in an unofficial class, that of 'bohemian',[8] or simply 'rogue',[9] and sometimes his patrons, Bertin and his mistress, along with their flatterers, have also been seen as forming a bohemian society, or at least a disreputable sort of *demi-monde*.[10] Hegel's interpretation

7. According to the fiction of the dialogue, the persona called 'Moi' has the same identity as the historical person we call 'Diderot'. For the purposes of this chapter there is no need to distinguish them, and I indifferently use the two appellations 'Moi' and 'Diderot' (as I do with 'Lui' and 'the Nephew'). More generally, I presume that the 'real' person we are pleased to call Diderot – identifying him from his other works, from the correspondence, or from other documents concerning him – is just as much of a persona as the Moi we encounter here, even as the personality of Diderot one meets in the correspondence with Sophie Volland is different from the one he creates in the letters to Grimm, which again is not the same personality one finds in the letters to Damilaville – however much each persona is intended to represent the same individual, whom I designate by various names. I recognise that, conceived within their functions in the dialogue, the semantic relations between the various personal pronouns may become extremely complex: see Marian Hobson, 'Déictique, dialectique dans *Le Neveu de Rameau*', *Cahiers textuel* 11 (1992), p.11-19.

8. Norman Rudich places Rameau among 'tous les gueux de la bohème parisienne' to whom Bertin's table is open: see *Entretiens sur Le Neveu de Rameau*, p.261.

9. See A. R. Strugnell, 'Diderot's *Neveu de Rameau*: portrait of a rogue in the French Enlightenment', *Knaves and swindlers: essays on the picaresque novel in Europe*, ed. C. J. Whitbourn (Oxford 1974), p.93-111.

10. This idea is classically conveyed in Eric Walter, 'Les intellectuels du ruisseau', *Cahiers textuel* 11 (1992), p.46: 'A la table de Bertin, comme à celle de Margot la ravaudeuse, se bousculent des ratés en tous les arts: poètes, musiciens, acteurs, peintres.'

in the *Phenomenology of spirit* remains the most challenging and controversial one on this, and many other, points.[11] Certainly it was pure genius on Hegel's part to choose this work by Diderot to exemplify a major phase of the French Enlightenment and its dilemmas. Hegel did not take seriously the bourgeois moral values spoken for by Moi, and he stipulated that the Nephew embodied a distinct dialectical stage, that of the 'self-alienated spirit', 'der sich entfremdete Geist' ('la conscience déchirée'), that is, someone whose importance in the advancement of the Spirit lay in having fully realised, and proclaimed he realised, the vacuous pretentiousness and falseness of all the values supposedly honoured by society, and in which, lacking a viable alternative, he knowingly was obliged to participate. This interpretation, embedded in the awesome enormity of Hegel's dialectical system, and sustained also by the depth of the insight into the character of the Nephew which it reveals, will always remain a landmark for understanding Diderot's text. It may seem ungrateful, if not impious, to undertake nevertheless to rethink the surroundings of Hegel's insight on different bases. For in fact no necessity compels one to endorse the great German philosopher's devaluation of the bourgeois values espoused by Moi: it was Hegel's privilege to consider them dialectically inconsequential. At least from a literary point of view, however, there are valid reasons to rehabilitate the importance which Diderot himself attributed to them, if only because they form the indispensable polarity against which the Nephew's role is played:

Moi

[...] Que fait alors ce cadet qui, traité durement par ses parents, étoit allé tenter la fortune au loin? Il leur envoie des secours; il se hâte d'arranger ses affaires. Il revient opulent. Il ramène son père et sa mère dans leur domicile. Il marie ses sœurs. Ah, mon cher Rameau, cet homme regardoit cet intervalle, comme le plus heureux de sa vie. C'est les larmes aux yeux qu'il m'en parloit; et moi, je sens, en vous faisant ce récit, mon cœur se troubler de joie, et le plaisir me couper la parole.

Lui

Vous êtes des êtres bien singuliers![12]

---

11. My interpretation is especially indebted to the commentary on the *Phenomenology* by Jean Hyppolite, *Genèse et structure de la Phénoménologie de l'esprit de Hegel* (Paris [1946]), p.387, p.398-401; Roland Mortier's still indispensable *Diderot en Allemagne* (Paris 1954), p.281-88; Lionel Trilling, *Sincerity and authenticity* (Cambridge, Mass. 1972), p.27-47, and H. R. Jauss, '*Le Neveu de Rameau*', *Revue de métaphysique et de morale* 89 (1984), p.143-81. One may also consult James Hulbert, 'Diderot in the text of Hegel: a question of intertextuality', *Studies in romanticism* 22 (1983), p.267-91.

12. P.43. Though generally I have maintained Diderot's original punctuation, here and elsewhere for practical reasons I have taken the liberty of silently and discreetly modernising it.

It need hardly be mentioned that in this passage the words of Moi combine three factors – (1) a stress on family values (especially filial duties); (2) sentimentality; and (3) concern for money as a beneficial social element – which together are hallmarks of the bourgeois aesthetic, and, naturally, are found not only in other texts by Diderot, but in painting (particularly Greuze), and in the theatre as well, notably in Sedaine. The point is that, though Diderot allegedly gives voice to very personal emotions here, his words also have a class resonance, and all the forcefulness of a class attitude.

Hegel's commentary on this passage – or at least on this kind of event in the text of *Le Neveu de Rameau* – is densely enthralling.[13] His view excludes all the aspects of this passage that are important for the present context: Hegel loftily ignores the bourgeois resonances of the words of Moi, seeing such a position as emanating instead from what he terms 'the simple consciousness'. Furthermore, he sees this kind of isolated anecdote (e.g. the one Diderot relates) as set, in its singularity, against 'the whole of the real world', and hence inherently in a situation of disparagement; even its dialectical alternative would lead to demands on the individual which would be illogical and wrong. In sum, Hegel sees the position of Moi as inherently doomed to be overpassed, dialectically losing out in favour of the stage of 'the consciousness that is aware of its disruption and openly declares it, derides existence and the universal confusion, and derides its own self as well',[14] in other words, in favour of the Nephew. This interpretation, given its situation in the *Phenomenology*, naturally represents the long view, the historical one.

But in the mean time, contenting oneself with the shorter run and limiting one's scope to more immediate historical and aesthetic actualities, the outlook appears very different: despite all Lui's disparagements, the sentimental anecdote recounted so feelingly by Moi not only implies the fervent adherence of the speaker, but also rides the current of middle-class ethics then surging powerfully everywhere in the arts, a widespread movement whose values even

13. See A. V. Miller's translation of the *Phenomenology of spirit* (Oxford 1977): 'If the simple consciousness compensates for this dull, uninspired *thought* by the *actuality* of the excellent, by adducing an *example* of the latter, either in the form of a fictitious case or a true story, thus showing that it is no empty name but actually exists, the *universal* actuality of the perverted action stands opposed to the whole of the real world in which the said example constitutes something quite single and separate, an *espèce*, a mere 'sort' of thing; and to represent the existence of the good and noble as an isolated anecdote, whether fictitious or true, is the most disparaging thing that can be said about it. Finally, should the plain mind demand the dissolution of this whole world of perversion, it cannot demand of the *individual* that he remove himself from it, for even Diogenes in his tub is conditioned by it, and to make this demand of the individual is just what is reckoned to be bad, viz., to care for *himself qua* individual' (p.319).

14. *Phenomenology of spirit*, p.319.

the Nephew's sneers cannot do away with. The point is that no matter how strenuously Diderot's moral philosophy will be put to the test by the ensuing debates, in terms of both its immediate historical context and its contrariety with the Nephew this morality was created to endure, and will still be cheerfully alive and, presumably, well at the end of the dialogue, even while the striking of the bell signals the start of the opera and thus the resumption of life and art – which will go on just exactly as before. At least in the perspective of the dialogue itself, contrary to Hegel's grandly historical view, the final result is a draw, each side maintaining its original moral outlook, and neither side providing implicitly the makings of a winner. The last words of the Nephew confirm this point: the Nephew declares that only time, in the sense of life or death, will award the prize to one or the other of them.

But to which social class does the Nephew's chosen role in society belong? He himself suggests the best definition of it, and, usefully for these purposes, he first pushes aside the virtuous morality of the role Diderot would have chosen for him, before revealing his own preference, which I italicise in the text (p.40):

Moi

Avoir un état dans la société et en remplir les devoirs?

Lui

Vanité. Qu'importe qu'on ait un état, ou non; pouvu qu'on soit riche; puisqu'on ne prend un état que pour le devenir. Remplir ses devoirs, à quoi cela mène-t-il? A la jalousie, au trouble, à la persécution. Est-ce ainsi qu'on s'avance? *Faire sa cour, morbleu; faire sa cour; voir les grands; étudier leurs goûts; se prêter à leurs fantaisies; servir leurs vices; approuver leurs injustices. Voilà le secret.*

Here is made explicit what is elsewhere implicit in the words he speaks: that the Nephew's role will be the most traditional one of all for buffoons, jesters, *musicians* and their like – procurers as well: to serve and amuse the great, to flatter their vanity, and especially to gratify their appetite for pleasure. Obviously such a role, the role of entertainer in the broadest sense, was originally and archetypally the province of the Court, a genesis still visible in the Nephew's choice of idiom. So long as he sees himself this way,[15] a member of the serving class, his own genealogy and inheritance, even his

15. Given that everything is in flux in this dialogue, it turns out, naturally, that the Nephew does not always choose to see himself in a servile role, and would have to be classified under various categories, according to context. Among other instances, there is the famous occasion when he chooses to stand on his dignity rather than grovel, his own family's respectability weighing upon him almost as a reproach (p.21). See also the surprising importance that suddenly accrues to the notion of his 'dignité' (p.46-47).

individuality, are theoretically of no consequence: his patrons' social station, above all their wealth, has become the only entity of significance. I presume that Hegel would not have agreed with my point about Diderot's bourgeois moral philosophy and its importance in the text, nor would he have approved of my classification of the Nephew's social affiliation: for everything the Nephew states in the foregoing quotation puts his role specifically on the *aristocratic* side of the social equation, and his statement to Moi indicates his ambition to exploit the desires for pleasure associated first of all with that part of the social order. In sum the confrontation, Moi versus Lui, is a mutation of the classic one between bourgeois values and aristocratic ones. If Diderot is playing the role of Enlightened Ant, 'la Fourmi', the Nephew is doing his best to sing with, or for, the Grasshoppers, 'les Cigales', the rich ones at least.

Nor is my classification intended to deny the supreme position occupied by money in the Nephew's scheme of things: of course money is important; in fact, in a practical sense, it is far more so than rank, a disposition of values reflecting not only the Nephew's own not very enlightened self-interest, but the general trend of the day.[16] Yet his vocabulary, which might have been taken from La Bruyère – 'Faire sa cour'; 'voir les grands'; 'servir leurs vices' – suggests someone who, in thinking about his role, still automatically divides society, not according to new trends or even immediately according to his true interests, but almost archaically in the traditional way: the Nephew automatically says '[la] cour' and 'les grands'; he does not say 'les riches'. Later on he claims that his role is directly related to the illustrious one of the king's fool, the ultimate archetype. He makes this point during a moment of self-justification in the middle of his famous description of the *ménagerie* Bertin, just before embarking on the account of his fall from grace. He gives his argument a dialectical twist that is purest genius (p.61):

Il n'y a point de meilleur rôle auprès des grands que celui de fou. Longtemps il y a eu le fou du roi en titre, en aucun, il n'y a eu en titre le sage du Roi. Moi je suis le fou de Bertin et de beaucoup d'autres, le vôtre peut-être dans ce moment; ou peut-être vous le mien. Celui qui seroit sage n'auroit point de fou. Celui donc qui a un fou n'est pas sage; s'il n'est pas sage il est fou; et peut-être, fût-il roi, le fou de son fou.

No doubt parts of Hegel's interpretation were formulated with this particular passage in mind, one of the most perfect examples of a thesis–antithesis relationship to be found anywhere, as, smoothly, inevitably, virtually by

16. The most salient example is the Nephew's account of his exertions to instil in his son a disposition to worship gold above all else (p.92), an educational programme which plays masterfully – by contrariety – against Diderot's plans for his daughter, centred of course on 'la morale', and which plays in turn against the kind of 'education' that the Nephew would have wanted for her.

definition, the fool changes places with, and wins out over, the great lords he was supposedly catering to. But whatever general social truth the argument may contain, in this context it is also self-serving: it is the Nephew's way of getting on top of those he has to put up with, and at least in theory becoming their superior, exactly as he does through his pitiless satire of his patrons, recounted by Diderot, which supposedly shows them up for what they are worth. One would hardly suspect from his description of the *ménagerie* Bertin, this hungry jungle of devouring, treacherous flatters, paying their insincere homage to the (allegedly) terrible actress who is their divinity, and falsely playing up to the scowling 'pagode' who is their patron, that the gentleman in question has a name, Bertin de Blagny, whose noble particle bespeaks aristocracy, that he is treasurer of one of the king's personal funds, and related to one of the truly great and significant figures of the age, Bertin d'Antilly.[17] Despite the jungle-like ambience created by the text, the situation is exactly the one in which the Nephew claimed he was most anxious to operate: 'servir les grands'.

As for the dialectical sleight of hand by which he would allegedly slip into his patron's place as easily as the fool makes a fool of the king, the results are not so sure. The opening statement of the passage quoted above, 'Il n'y a point de meilleur rôle auprès des grands que celui de fou', seems a rather glib simplification of the picture, if one considers the Nephew's own account of the contortions and agonies he must endure in the vain hope of gaining just some sign of approval from his unmovable and unsympathetic patron (p.47). Nor can one overlook his humiliations at the theatre, finding himself clapping alone amid the jeers as the sole member of Mlle Hus's claque (p.66), the domestic duties such as tending her scratchy cats, not to mention putting up with the *chaise percée* (p.67). Indeed, there are two sides to the question, and, as the details come to light, it looks very much as though the Patron serenely maintains his appointed role of doing whatever he pleases, while the Nephew wears himself out playing the fool for someone patently incapable of appreciating his talent. It is also clear that finally, when the Nephew greets a newly arrived guest of honour with an insult, the Patron just throws him out.[18] One might wonder whether, with respect to this particular situation, the Nephew's dialectic works the way he declared it would: even recognition of

17. This according to the researches of Jean Fabre (p.168-69, n.115).
18. I have discussed the episode of the Nephew's fall from grace *chez* Bertin at length elsewhere: see Rex, 'Two scenes from *Le Neveu de Rameau*', *Diderot studies* 20 (1981), p.246-57; see also the witty and perceptive article by Jean Starobinski, 'Le dîner chez Bertin', *Das Komische*, ed. Wolfgang Preisendanz and Rainer Warning (Munich 1976), p.191-204.

his textual revenge over Bertin will not come for years, posthumously, a cold triumph only for the eyes of posterity.

And yet, at least in one way, the evolution of events in this instance is entirely typical, for repeatedly in the dialogue a pattern emerges by which theoretical principles (here the Nephew's dialectical scheme for replacing the man on top) are fated to lose out to realities, as if one had been devised to form eventually a destructive contrariety with the other. In this particular case the Nephew is the hardest hit; far more frequently, however, it is the pious moralities of Moi that are doomed to succumb, especially when his principles have been enunciated with fervour.

The dynamics of the basic paradigm

One of the classic examples appears early, in a part of the text (p.9-13) doubtless familiar for other reasons: Moi has been defending the value to humankind of geniuses, against the Nephew's disparagements.[19] Nor has the defence always been as plain sailing as one might have assumed. Not only has the 'cher oncle' taken a drubbing, but even when Moi has cited a clear-cut historical example such as the greatness of Socrates, there has been some heavy water (p.11):

Moi

[...] De Socrate, ou du magistrat qui lui fit boire la cigüe, quel est aujourd'hui le déshonoré?

Lui

Le voilà bien avancé! en a-t-il été moins condamné? en a-t-il moins été mis à mort? en a-t-il moins été un citoyen turbulent?

And so on. No doubt it is partly to restore control that Moi reduces the discussion to his famous dichotomy, asking Lui to choose between Racine, nasty but a genius for the ages, and some middle-class shopkeeper, dutiful and pleasant but of no account for mankind or the future. In the ensuing discussion Moi supposedly encounters two surprises: first, that the Nephew chooses the shopkeeper over the genius, and second, that the choice has nothing to do with the shopkeeper's humble virtues (Diderot's stock in trade), but with his money, which the Nephew imagines him lavishly spending on entertainments that naturally would include himself, because the Nephew made the shopkeeper laugh, and provided him with some nice young girl to relieve the boredom of his marital cohabitation.

19. On Diderot's idea of the role of geniuses see Jean-Claude Bonnet, 'Diderot et la postérité', *Cahiers textuel* 11 (1992), p.129.

One assumes that Moi would disapprove, but in this case the intensity of his anger as his rhetoric works up momentum is quite unexpected. In a counter-fantasy that deliberately pricks all the Nephew's extravagant balloons, Moi imagines the shopkeeper practising honest decorum and, naturally, emptying his house of all the gamblers, parasites and flatterers that Lui had assembled there. Finally, Diderot's tone reaches something like rage as he stages a fictional *bastonnade* whose violence might recall the famous one which sent Voltaire into exile in England, but this time with the Nephew as its victim: 'et qu'il eût fait assommer à coups de bâtons, par ses garçons de boutique, l'homme officieux qui soulage, par la variété, les maris, du dégoût d'une cohabitation habituelle avec leurs femmes' (p.13).

What an astonishing reaction! Given Diderot's own marital infidelities, his repeated condemnations of marriage vows because they did not allow for the change inherent in nature,[20] and in view of his later statements in this dialogue about the pleasure he takes in seeing a pretty woman, feeling her breasts and having intercourse with her – not to mention his willingness to engage in a good 'partie de débauche' among friends (p.42) – his anger would seem distinctly overblown. One might surmise that, contrary to appearances, the Nephew has come too close for comfort to Diderot's own conduct and beliefs. The result is to make Diderot retrench, and reinforce his middle-class moralism, now defended as absolute, and with an anger that in fantasy threatens the Nephew's person.

Dialectically, this is the critical moment, the moment of reversal. And, using Diderot's anger as a handle, the Nephew rises to the occasion with superb aplomb, neatly turning the tables: Diderot's violence makes him, rather than the Nephew, the disorderly one ('Assommer! monsieur assommer! on n'assomme personne dans une ville bien policée', p.13); the Nephew's chosen activity, procuration, is an honest estate, engaged in by all sorts of persons, even titled ones ('C'est un état honnête. Beaucoup de gens, même titrés s'en mêlent'). Finally, he plays his strongest card: he wonders what the devil money is for, if not to have a fine table, good company, good wine, beautiful women, pleasures of every colour, amusements of every description. The Nephew would as soon be poor as a beggar ('gueux') as to have a fortune and lack enjoyments such as these. Here the Nephew drops the topic and returns to Racine (p.13).

But the fundamental pattern, the basic process which will be repeated in increasingly elaborate forms throughout the dialogue, is masterfully complete. Hegel might with good reason be appealed to as authorisation for seeing this

20. The essential texts are in the Fabre edition, p.137-148, n.48.

particular passage as a dialectical movement: although originally voicing the sentiments of all right-thinking people, somehow Moi, with his angry, unnatural principles, now reduced to threats of violence, has come to seem like the odd man out, the perverse one, refusing to behave like everyone else, while the Nephew, backed by the conduct of all society, including, he subtly hints, the Court, rides the tide of enjoyment, of doing the things everyone naturally wants to do. The exception has ended as the rule. One notes as well that the Nephew's programme for the shopkeeper is composed of items whose pleasure Diderot himself would have recognised, perhaps even chosen on his own.

Since this pattern, or segments thereof, are destined to be repeated later on, the component parts may be easier to identify if they are schematised thus:

(A) provocation (by either or both parties);

(B) the original contrariety (Moi invariably speaking for right-thinkers; Lui for impulses and behaviour right-thinkers would never condone);[21]

(C) the reversal (Lui becomes everybody; Moi barely anybody);

(D) ultimate irony: actually Moi is more implicated in Lui's behaviour than he admits.

The pieces of this dialectic are susceptible to numerous realignments and combinations, as will be seen, and sometimes individual pieces may be omitted, or only implied. However (such is my contention), parts (C) and (D), the reversal and the secret admission, invariably depend on the right-thinking role of Moi (B) as an antecedent, in fact as a theoretical constant, sometimes even an inspiration, against which their opposition is perversely deployed. Thus, as was stated before, Moi in his original role was created to endure. He will never evaporate entirely, although in this particular version of the argument Lui is clearly the winner, Moi being forced to operate on a shrinking territory in reduced circumstances that, for all one can tell, may not hold out much longer.

Evolutions

Actually, when Moi takes over the argument he reveals an ample reserve of arguments in favour of geniuses. It is not clear how much Lui is impressed by them, especially by Moi's easy assertion that the incidental harm geniuses do to those around them is of no consequence compared to their lasting benefits. But the Nephew's interest perks up when Moi explains how, if one wished to suppress the defects of geniuses, a new order of the universe would be required, and that the Nephew, along with much else in the cosmos, would doubtless

21. In all cases (B) indicates that Moi is thinking of himself as the norm, and of Lui as the exception.

be abolished in the grand reshuffling. Faced with immediate perils to his person, the Nephew agrees to accept things and geniuses just as they are: 'Vous avez raison' declares Lui (p.14), and, after Moi's further explanations, Lui adds 'Il est vrai' (p.15). This is one of the rare moments of agreement between the two, and in the quieter ambience of accord Lui takes a crucial further step and uncovers another layer of argument: all he knows is that he wishes he were someone else ('un autre', p.15), perchance a man of genius, a great man.

One can never rely entirely on the Nephew's 'sincerity', of course; anything he says or does may be a trap for the gullible listener. But judging by the appearances of the text, the Nephew's reaction suggests the floodgates of his own self-discontent have been opened. Everything pours out: the intensity of his envy whenever he hears praises of other people; the pleasure he feels whenever great men are degraded in personal anecdotes; his lingering over Voltaire's political mistakes, as if these could diminish his talent as a playwright, and make it less important that he, the Nephew, is not Voltaire. His summation gives every appearance of forgoing all pretence: 'J'ai donc été, je suis donc fâché d'être médiocre. Oui, oui, je suis médiocre et fâché' (p.15).

To reinforce his point, he names, and sings, two pieces by his uncle, the overture to *Les Indes galantes* (1735), Rameau's *opéra-ballet*, and *Profonds abymes du Ténare, nuit, éternelle nuit* from the celebration of the Battle of Fontenoy, *Le Temple de la Gloire* (1745), neither of which he ever hears without finding himself painfully admitting he is incapable of ever composing their equal ('Voilà ce que tu ne feras jamais'), and wishing he could have stolen some of his uncle's harpsichord pieces from his portfolio at his death and passed them off as his own ('à rester moi, et à être lui', p.15). Thus, for the moment, the Nephew's envy has brought him to accept values elsewhere denied: the category of genius is now rescued from the ruins of the Nephew's pragmatic cynicism, and some of the great Rameau's eminently French music, a style that will later undergo devastating criticism, has also been excepted from disparagement, even paid homage to.

This dimension of the Nephew's character, the admiring one that produces pangs of jealousy and regret each time he hears the genius of Rameau's *Profonds abymes*, lies beyond the intended scope of Hegel's dialectic, tuned, in respect to the Nephew's reactions, to pick up the negatives. No doubt in the long run the psychology of the Nephew's motives is inconsequential: in historical terms, especially from the viewpoint of the history of consciousness, what counts is the Nephew's extraordinary insight into the frivolity and emptiness of the values of his society, along with the realisation of his own participation in that emptiness. But even so, in the shorter run, one finds a very different picture.

At this juncture it is Diderot's values which have triumphed:[22] he has completely turned round the anti-genius position of Lui, gaining a grudging assent to geniuses, along with a confession of the self-discontent implicit in his hostility. Whatever the Nephew's pretences, it is clear that his longings are not confined to the wish for money and adulation, and supposedly include a yearning to achieve greatness in art.[23] If only because art is such a frequent theme of this work, this admission has emblematic significance. It will also give Diderot trump cards to remind the Nephew of his own alleged superiority.

Looking back over the evolution of the text thus far, one observes two main movements. One is a dialectical process in which Moi's lofty principles are dissolving into realities, the Nephew being the winner – no doubt with Hegel's benediction. The other concerns the Nephew's longings to be a genius, and the painful recognition of his failure to become one, a confession which momentarily puts Moi in the winner's seat. Meanwhile, as Moi and the geniuses triumph, Lui is left with a more intense sense of his own mediocrity.

This point is confirmed by the witty pantomime that ensues: it is partly a musical rendering of the overture to *Les Indes galantes* and *Profonds abymes* – as though the Nephew were appropriating these two most admired pieces from his deceased uncle's portfolio – and partly gestural pantomime, whereby in imagination the Nephew achieves musical greatness, acquires wealth and lords it over his flatterers. Thus the 'show' is figmented compensation for the Nephew's lack of genius and the deprivations consequent upon that lack.

Despite all the negative forces at play in this scene (and in a sense, everything in it is negative), there is another side to this coin; for the brilliance and astuteness of the satire of these pantomimes, the 'show', also looks like genius. Such allegedly extra-verbal events, engendering a new dimension in the text, introduce compelling new values: as though by a miracle, the Nephew's failure and inauthenticity have given birth to comedy that is so witty and to the point that it redeems all moral defeats by re-creating them as objects of admiration and applause in art. Thus projected as pantomime, the Nephew's own self-dissatisfaction turns outward into social derision, especially derision of everyone he is forced to serve. And, by a paradox of rare perfection, the Nephew's

22. To my mind, it is indispensable to see Moi and Lui as two distinct and opposed personages at this stage in the argument. My view on this point is not the traditional critical one; in fact, as will be discussed later on, most critics have seen Lui's sense of failure here as reflecting Diderot's disappointments with his own literary career. At least in so far as one is concerned with the dialectics of the dialogue, I believe that the traditional view hinders more than it helps.
23. My own perception (and I presume Diderot's as well) of the genius of *Profonds abymes* has strongly influenced my conclusion that the Nephew's expression of envy is supposed to be genuine.

hollowness of character, his cynical, self-serving morality, the callous deception of his imitations, the compensatory derision of others for his own defects, all turn out to provide flawless images of the society he so acutely derides, of the merry-go-round of charades, impositions of specious values and self-serving pretences that make up the lives of virtually everyone. The Nephew's quasi-total falseness has produced a truth whose importance Hegel was the first to recognise and, needless to say, to establish with magisterial authority.

The Nephew's pantomimes are so comic and his satire strikes the mark with such aplomb that it might be tempting simply to concur with Hegel's eloquently argued version. One forgets that, however gladly the reader concedes the Nephew's talents, his artistic triumph is not yet assured; the victory is still very much in suspense. For Lui is performing his act neither for Hegel nor for M. Bertin, nor even for the reader, but for Diderot, 'Monsieur le philosophe' with all his supposedly set ideals and moral principles, and the question as to the degree to which the author will allow the Nephew to succeed in respect to this persona, if at all, will remain open, perhaps even anguished, almost until the end of the work. The wait for an answer will be a long one.

Theménagerie *Bertin*

The brilliant scenes of the Bertin household (p.18f.) give a peculiar new twist to the familiar paradigm. The situation moves directly to a later stage in the dialectic, and instead of Diderot's upright values being put forward as the accepted norm, from the start the Nephew's perverted values take over, creating a mirror-world whose comedy derives from turning received moral opinion topsy-turvy. Thus, Lui's lead-in (p.18), his portrait of himself – 'un ignorant, un sot, un fou, un impertinent, un paresseux' – inverts the personal qualities that Moi most esteems, which are normally assumed to make the world go round, in fact to be indispensable to the well-being of society. Lui blithely dispenses with the indispensables (C). Moi's prudish declaration that he thought people would normally hide such defects, if they had them (B), only paves the way, by contrary motion, for further elaborations on a world in which all Diderot's character defects are taken precisely as merits, advantages, amusements (C). The compliments the Nephew receives – and certainly intended as such – are all, normally, insults: 'Rameau le fou, l'impertinent, l'ignorant, le paresseux', and, fittingly, most of the so-called 'caresses' accompanying the epithets are given as nudges, slaps and kicks. The unspecified liberties that the Nephew takes with the guests, and they with him, presumably represent more inversions (p.18-19). Naturally, given such a mirror-world, the Nephew's fall comes – so he claims to his no doubt gullible listener –

because he once displays the qualities that Diderot most admires: 'la sottise d'avoir eu un peu de goût, un peu d'esprit, un peu de raison' (p.19).[24] To be sure, the real story of his fall, when eventually the Nephew consents to relate it (p.62-65), suggests something else: that instead of wit and good taste, there was an abusive obscenity, which deliberately risked the disaster that ensued. But the revelation of that counter-truth remains far in the offing.

Meanwhile, as a choice sample of his extraordinary talent – unrecognised by the world, as he groaningly laments – the Nephew performs the famous pantomime of the procurer (p.22-23), a pantomime so witty it leaves Moi helpless to decide between laughing at it or being indignant, and ending up doing both (B, D). This double reaction is perfectly in accord with certain of the real Diderot's sexist ambiguities, chiming in especially well with his recent description of Mlle Hus: 'blanche, jolie, jeune, douce, potelée' (p.21). In sum, the Nephew's pantomime brings out in bursts of laughter feelings which Moi would have had difficulty admitting otherwise – as if, in the eyes of this philosopher, earning a livelihood by getting honest young women debauched for profit could even momentarily be a laughing matter. For the time being the Nephew triumphs, his witty and insinuating pantomime having, to various degrees, seduced both the girl of the pantomime and his prudish listener into forgetting their principles.

The 'point mort' of the dialogue, redeemed by contrariety

After the partial disarray of his 'virtue', the mood of Moi naturally becomes sombre. For his part, Lui, falling into a melancholy vein, starts remembering, with unmistakable hints of Villon,[25] the people he knew long ago, far less talented than he, who were even then so rich they clad themselves in velvet – in contrast to his own rough cloth – and who are now great lords (p.24). Moi takes up the new mood with the bizarrely bathetic exclamation, 'Ah, malheureux, dans quel état d'abjection, vous êtes né ou tombé.' And meanwhile, in this stretch of the Nephew's discourse, an extraordinary upset is occurring

---

24. A double irony underlies this claim. First, the 'goût', 'esprit' and 'raison' turn out to be a blatant obscenity, rendered in insolent Italian. The fact that the reader or listener was expecting something respectable proves that he has been hoodwinked and the joke is on him. Second, at the same time, in the Nephew's eyes, the obscenity implies an entirely just evaluation of the Bertin *ménagerie* and reveals in effect exactly what they are worth, this second irony playing against his patron, rather than against the reader or listener. See my lengthy discussion of this episode in 'Two scenes', p.246-57. Spitzer, in 'The style of Diderot', p.157, failed to connect the Nephew's claim of having exhibited taste, wit and reason to the obscenity, thus missing the irony and, momentarily, the subtlety of the Nephew's tactic.

25. I much agree with the brief comment of Henri Coulet on this point, DPV, xii.97, n.77.

in which the great journey of life reverses itself into a journey towards death. One hardly notices the shift of direction because it moves into the text camouflaged by a picturesque reference – suggestively orchestrated by the Nephew's rhythms – to the indispensable and gratifying pleasures of relieving oneself:[26] 'Le point important c'est d'aller aisément, librement, agréablement, copieusement, tous les soirs à la garderobe. *O stercus pretiosum!* Voilà le grand résultat de la vie dans tous les états' (p.25).

Scholars disagree about the Latin exclamation and have proposed several interpretations, including one that stresses (shades of Flaubert!) the value of manures. I myself find it suspiciously resembles a parody of a Catholic hymn – perhaps one that celebrates the Eucharist: *O Corpus pretiosum!* In any case, traditional religious overtones, however blasphemous, would be most appropriate for this moment in the text: the Nephew's notion of life as a journey towards death is exactly the medieval one; furthermore the Nephew's ironies, as the text proceeds, uncannily echo the humour of Villon, blasphemies and obscenities included. Only Villon's piety is missing.

The end of life being universally the same, death is the great leveller that finally makes everyone alike, even the powerful and affluent. As though copying the common practice of medieval poetry (another trait prominent in Villon's ballades), this text takes all the time it needs to place in evidence this single theme, explaining, describing, exemplifying and deepening it, but without moving beyond its confines. Typically, in order to bolster his egalitarian message, the Nephew chooses an example that is almost comically extreme: he places Samuel Bernard, the richest man within memory,[27] on one side of the scale, and himself, Rameau, who will leave nothing, Rameau whose winding-sheet will be donated by charity, on the other side of the balance, and declares Bernard's millions in gold to be (so to speak) of no consequence. Being a musician, Lui enhances the message with the sound of singing choirs; he describes a funeral procession full of pomp and – fore and aft – a long line of blazing torches. His show-stopping line – 'le mort n'entend pas sonner les cloches' – is certainly worthy of Villon,[28] and it captures flawlessly Villon's sublime strategy of tinging pathos with irony, or perhaps the other way round.

But the most fascinating single moment of this part of the dialogue comes at a break which occurs as, with no warning and totally unexpectedly, this

26. Cf. the subtle, and very different, commentary on this passage by Hobson, 'Déitique, dialectique', p.13. The rapprochement with a text by d'Alembert, suggested by both Jean Fabre and Jean Pommier (see the Fabre edition, p.lviii-lix, n.1), is not convincing.

27. The comparable figure mentioned by Villon was Jacques Cœur.

28. I do not accept Jacques Chouillet's view that this whole passage was inspired by Lucretius. See his edition of *Le Neveu de Rameau* (Paris 1982), p.189, n.87.

theme stops, while the single word 'poignet' suddenly sends the text off in a direction exactly opposite to the original one, creating a dazzling instance of contrariety. The following quotation begins slightly before the event in question, just enough to suggest how completely the Nephew's meditation, prior to the rupture, had settled into, and become absorbed by, its single idea (p.25-26):

C'est en vain que cent prêtres s'égosillent pour lui: qu'il est précédé et suivi d'une longue file de torches ardentes; son âme ne marche pas à côté du maître des cérémonies. Pourir sous du marbre, pourir sous de la terre, s'est toujours pourir. Avoir autour de son cercueil les enfants rouges, et les enfants bleus, ou n'avoir personne, qu'est-ce que cela fait? Et puis vous voyez bien ce poignet; il étoit roide comme un diable. Ces dix doigts, c'étoient autant de bâtons fichés dans un métacarpe de bois; et ces tendons, c'étoient de vieilles cordes à boyaux plus sèches, plus roides, plus inflexibles que celles qui ont servi à la roue d'un tourneur. Mais je vous les ai tant tourmentées, tant brisées, tant rompues. Tu ne veux pas aller; et moi, mordieu, je dis que tu iras, et cela sera.

The rhythms of the Nephew's discourse had slowed almost to a halt as he came to the emptiness of the scene with all the choirboys dressed in red or blue – there might as well be no one at all – almost as though the text were about to stage the finality that it described. But meanwhile, an unspoken gesture ('qu'est-ce que cela fait'), the Nephew – about to mention both the wrist and the fingers – has been staring at the part of the body in which death is most visible, namely the hand – extension of the wrist – with its bony joints, awesome reminders, when stiff, of mortality, especially for a string-player. But these bony fingers can also become – at least when limbered up and made supple again as the Nephew proceeds to do – agents of movement and art, even, in the Nephew's case, a livelihood playing the violin. In this life-provoking moment of contrariety – suggested only by implication – the tokens of death are metamorphosed into a principle of life, the movement of the text taking on new energy and velocity as the change occurs and the Nephew readies himself to perform in imitation a violin sonata by Locatelli. For the rest, this transitional happening flawlessly exemplifies Diderot's own materialistic philosophy, which sees mortality as simply one stage in a great cycle: life of necessity springs from the matter of death, *O stercus pretiosum!*

The wit, liveliness and constantly surprising acumen of the ensuing performances on an imaginary violin and harpsichord (p.26-28) completely wash away the solemnity of this passage. Nothing that subsequently happens in the dialogue alludes to it or to the passing bleakness of its message. Even as this moment of death occurred it is now apparently gone, obliterated by the life it gave birth to.

Flux, stability and dialectical manoeuverings in favour of Lui

For the rest, impermanence is a major factor in this dialogue. Nothing stands still for more than a moment. And as the values shift, they often slide into their opposites (even as the bones of death turn into the bones of life). Sometimes even simple facts wobble out of place: the famous example is that of the Uncle, said (by the Nephew) on page 8 to be alive and well and just as disagreeable as ever, but declared (by the Nephew) on page 15 to be dead, buried and apparently to have had his inheritance divided. Another instance involves the Nephew's idea of the wife's role in marriage: at one moment the male is in charge, and the Nephew declares that he himself, thundering like Zeus, was always the one to give the orders while his wife docilely obeyed (p.29); he even congratulates himself that this wise strategy produced four years of peace in the household. A few pages later (p.41) he declares that the best policy with one's 'chère moitié' is always to let her have her own way and do whatever she pleases. In one place in the text Diderot does not know of any good music teacher for his daughter and is not sure how much he even wants her to study (p.31). Elsewhere, without quite admitting that he is speaking of himself and his daughter, Diderot recounts the anecdote of how he found an excellent teacher for her, an event that in real life did not take place until years after the first situation (p.91-92). Such changes are part of the flux that informs all this dialogue, which is a little like Heraclitus's philosophical river, into which one can never step twice and find it the same.

On the other hand, Moi insistently puts his own moral character forward as cutting across this unstable current: he prides himself on his fixed principles, which give him a long-term stability totally lacking in Lui, unprincipled, morally empty parasite that he is, whose shifting modes are at the mercy of survival (p.43-44). By contrast, Moi is supposed to have reflective qualities, *recul*; he is the observer, the one who listens and supposedly learns. In the deepest sense, the dialogue happens to him. Naturally, from his lofty philosophical perch, he chides Lui not only for the weakness (p.46) but even the unhappiness, or lack of success, supposedly inherent in vacillations (p.10). Hearing Moi go on, one might assume that he is unaware of his opponent's mastery as a tactician and of his trump card, the basic dialectical manoeuvre described earlier, which is so perfectly suited for the undoing of received morality.

When Moi makes the mistake of sarcastically criticising Lui (A) for employing 'viles ruses' to make his music pupils believe he is more sought after than he really is (p.35), the nephew's tactical machinery clicks into action so smoothly that it is as if Moi's undoing were already implicitly inscribed in the criticism itself. For the rest, nothing could seem more innocent than the Nephew's likening of the 'viles ruses' of the harpsichord lessons (p.35-36) to idioms in language, which all languages employ, even though they make exceptions to the general rules. Moi, whom the Nephew has taken care to involve in the elaboration of his theory (p.36), gullibly supplies the example of Fontenelle, who wrote excellent French though his language swarmed with idioms (B). The example is perfectly apropos for the Nephew's purposes: applying Moi's own concept to society, it immediately becomes clear that everyone from the sovereign to the voice-teacher is busily practising, not the rules, but the exceptions to them (C), the tricks of the trade,[29] which multiply all the more as institutions age or as times get hard. The tricks of the trade *are* the rule, and provide the only sure way to make money. No one bothers with anything else. Diderot's rule, the rule of conscience, has turned out to be an unwanted, irrelevant exception. In this brilliantly composed argument, the dialectical inversion is flawless: the Nephew, supported at first by the few, ends with the backing of multitudes, while Diderot's rigid rule of conscience melts into irrelevance (C).[30]

According to Karl Marx's children, when they asked Marx to name the greatest authors of literature, Shakespeare came first for poetry. For prose, first place went to Diderot,[31] and it is a likely guess that this whole development (p.37-38) was one of those that gained Marx's high esteem. The next part of the text in particular foreshadows Marx's own perceptions, one of those uncanny instances when Diderot seems at least a century ahead of his time. Following logically and naturally from the preceding dialectic, the Nephew's vision of society as a jungle still astonishes by its astuteness, and in its day, perhaps only Rousseau, from the depths of his social alienation, might have articulated a view so comprehensive and at the same time so differentiated. Naturally, Lui assumes that money is the sole object of the general scramble of society; at the same time he sees the mêlée as being divided between the haves and have-nots, an opposition within which he discovers even a third war between various classes: 'Dans la nature, toutes les espèces se dévorent; toutes les conditions se dévorent dans la société'(p.37-38).

Jansenists, such as the *moraliste* Pierre Nicole, confronted with a world full

29. I borrow Peter France's translation of 'tours du bâton', from his *Diderot* (Oxford 1983), p.78.
30. Later on (p.37), Lui will soften the appearance of his position somewhat, claiming, as if to please Moi, that in his own case he now gives his pupils an honest lesson for their money. But he also makes it clear he feels no obligation to do so, nor does he feel remorse for the early days when, in his incompetence, he essentially stole from his pupils – whose parents' money, he implies, was probably at least as ill-gotten as his own.
31. For references, see Wilson, *Diderot*, p.792, n.35.

of sin and largely devoid of true grace, postulated that in society almost everyone would strive, even pretend, to follow the good, if only to be esteemed worthy in the eyes of others.[32] Thus, though mostly lacking in grace, the society they created would give the appearance at least of obeying ethical principles. In contrast, the Nephew's world is totally empty of divinity, and hence empty of all such strivings and illusions. Contrary to Nicole, the awesome power of the Nephew's vision of society lies in his having stripped away every appearance, to the point that there are no pretences; nothing remains but the raw matter of envy and greed lying underneath. The upshot of all the devouring, in the Nephew's eyes, is a rapacious sort of justice, in which both the haves and the have-nots get exactly what they deserve, through the unwritten laws of 'restitution' (p.37). Diderot apparently has no rebuttal, no arguments in reserve. His response is simply sarcasm of the most scathing sort, which only brings the Nephew to reveal all the more energetically the strength of his position (C) (p.39):

Lui

Mais je crois que vous vous moquez de moi; monsieur le philosophe, vous ne sçavez pas à qui vous vous jouez; vous ne vous doutez pas que dans ce moment je représente la partie la plus importante de la ville et de la cour. Nos opulents dans tous les états se sont dit à eux-mêmes ou ne se sont pas dit les mêmes choses que je vous ai confiées; mais le fait est que la vie que je mènerois à leur place est exactement la leur.

As the ultimate insult, Lui proposes an ironical toast to the total desecration of Diderot's useless concept of virtue, substituting instead, in the name of philosophy (Diderot's province), the infinite pleasures of the senses. His tone is one of triumph: 'Tenez, vive la philosophie; vive la sagesse de Salomon: boire de bon vin, se gorger de mets délicats; se rouler sur de jolies femmes; se reposer dans des lits bien mollets. Excepté cela, le reste n'est que vanité' (p.40).

If only because Moi appears to be fighting with his back against the wall, this is one of the most intensely dramatic confrontations of the entire dialogue. In the ensuing back-and-forth, Moi's compact protests, thrown out one after another, represent the irreducible verities of the citizen of responsibility, the *sine qua non*s of civic virtue (B) ('Défendre sa patrie?' 'Servir ses amis?' 'Avoir un état dans la société et en remplir les devoirs?' 'Veiller à l'éducation de ses enfants?'). They call for a species of conduct – actually not too far from certain of Montesquieu's concepts[33] – in which people's immediate instincts are sacrificed in the name of values which are more long term. In contrast, Lui's

32. Such is the view elaborated in his *Essais de morale* (Paris 1693-1696), which had numerous editions in the eighteenth century.

33. They also echo the traditions of Classical moralists, as Jean Fabre has noted (p.182, n.142).

astonishing replies, whether resonating prophetically and ominously for this age of revolution ('Il n'y a plus de patrie. Je ne vois d'un pôle à l'autre que des tyrans et des esclaves'), or anticipating the harsh insights of Freud ('Est-ce qu'on a des amis? Quand on en auroit, faudroit-il en faire des ingrats?'), are entirely dominated by self-interest and the impulse towards immediate gratification. All the Nephew's answers have the quality of breaking through illusions, cracking open the pitiless truths concealed by Moi's well-meaning platitudes. Philosophically the conflict is one of *altruisme* versus *intérêt*.[34] In psychological terms the conflict is between the impatiently childish on one side and the rationally, generously, impractically adult on the other, each serving to bring out the other's defects, perhaps also their merits.[35] In the extreme position each has taken, it is as though the Ant and the Grasshopper were still bent on continuing their disagreements, but meanwhile, since their diverse positions have shifted so radically, it is harder than ever to communicate.

The charms of altruism alleged

Even while he was coping defensively, one by one, with Lui's potent rejoinders, pressures were apparently building on Moi's side to launch a counterattack that would both disprove the Nephew's false assumptions and substitute inspiring new values in their stead. Unfortunately, when at last Moi takes the

34. For Lui, it is clear that whatever benefits may happen to accrue to others from someone's wealth are incidental and of no real consequence to the aim of self-gratification. In so far as the moral views of Lui and Moi revolve around the polarity 'self' and 'other', with Moi placing at the centre of his concern a species of conduct that for Lui was inherently on the periphery, the merest by-product of the essentials, they form a perfect contrariety.

35. Diderot's four objections ('Défendre sa patrie; servir ses amis' and so on, p.40-41) are ordered according to their degree of altruism – which inverts the 'natural' order. The one that is farthest away, and requires the most altruistic imagination (defence of one's country, presumably beginning at its borders) comes first; then the circle narrows to that of one's friends (no doubt numbered among life's pleasures). The circle of one's business (presumably counted as necessity) comes next, followed by the family circle in last place. Thus the two that are ostensibly of the greatest personal concern (business and family) bring up the rear. In his discussion of established laws ('Des lois positives') Montesquieu followed a somewhat similar pattern, going from the laws that affect individuals least, namely laws between nations, to laws between the rulers and the governed, arriving at the end at laws between individual citizens (*De l'esprit des lois*, I.iii). Nor is this the only instance in this dialogue when Diderot seems to partake of the same mentality as the great theorist of the laws. In this particular part of the text Diderot puts in the highest possible relief the contrasting attitudes of the adversaries. One can be sure that no irony is intended, much less comedy, when Moi's rejoinder to the Nephew's powerfully sensuous evocations – 'se gorger de mets délicats; se rouler sur de jolies femmes; se reposer dans des lits bien mollets' – come from ideals so far away and abstract as to seem from another planet: 'Quoi, défendre sa patrie?'

floor, his proposals – though in another key – are just as transparently self-serving as those of the Nephew. For example, he disparages the so-called contentment of 'nos opulents', claiming that their surfeit of pleasures has made them so bored one would actually be doing them a favour(!) to put them out of their misery (p.42). He also attempts to appropriate for himself the Nephew's hedonism, making a great show of his own capacities for sensual enjoyment, for vibrating with exactly the impulses the Nephew described, for enjoying as much as anyone good food, the sheer pleasure of a woman's breasts and sexual intercourse (p.42). He has done it all, and knows all about it. Such an overriding of the Nephew is supposed to make irresistibly persuasive Diderot's opting, nevertheless (step three), for virtue. Who would be so base as to hold out against the dramatic 'Mais', the alleged frankness of his avowal, and the fastidiously cleansed morality of the alternatives to debauchery (p.42)?

Mais je ne vous le dissimulerai pas, il m'est infiniment plus doux encor d'avoir secouru le malheureux, d'avoir terminé une affaire épineuse, donné un conseil salutaire, fait une lecture agréable; une promenade avec un homme ou une femme chère à mon cœur; passé quelques heures instructives avec mes enfants, écrit une bonne page, rempli les devoirs de mon état; dit à celle que j'aime quelques choses tendres et douces qui amènent ses bras autour de mon col.

This exceptionally long sentence is essentially the poem of the happy altruist: it celebrates the enjoyment of doing things for, and also with, others, first of all to please them, and hence, on the rebound, to please oneself. It illustrates perfectly Diderot's idea of *bienfaisance*. Sexuality, while not denied, takes on the guise of tenderness; specific identities are pushed to the background, indeed the deliberate preference for the general ('secouru *le* malheureux', '*une* lecture') indicates how mindful Diderot was of the didactic import of his words. 'Mes enfants', coming from Diderot, who had only one child, reveals how much this is a hypothetical example, nothing more. Montesquieu's famous letter on 'le bonheur des Troglodytes', another celebration of the virtues of altruism, is scarcely more calculated and didactic in this respect.

It is a pity to stop the rhythm of the passage as I have. For this long sentence also functions in a wind-up, a grand crescendo, in which Moi confesses to his own envy of the great accomplishments of others such as Voltaire – just as the Nephew had done. But unlike the Nephew, his envy is predictably of the generous, altruistic sort, prizing Voltaire's rehabilitation of the memory of the persecuted Calas family even above his 'sublime' tragedy of *Mahomet*. But the crowning moment is Diderot's story, referred to earlier, of a younger son whose hard-hearted older brother has dissipated the family fortune and sent away the parents to fend for themselves. The conclusion of the tale – in which the younger son, having made a fortune, returns with all his wealth, brings his parents home, and marries off his sisters (p.43) – has already been quoted and discussed for its sentimental overtones of bourgeois morality.

This tearful end of the anecdote needs no further comment, except to note that its altruism comes in a double layer: the virtuous action recounted by Moi is not his own; it is someone else's generosity that so affects him he cannot speak – as if altruism, by definition implying removal from immediate, self-interested participation, could even be increased if a second degree of removal and disinterestedness were added, as Diderot has done, weeping over another man's weeping over his selfless good deed (one is free to imagine a good deal of weeping on the part of the elderly parents and sisters as well).[36] No doubt this extra dimension of disinterest is supposed to make it a perfect climax for Diderot's *morceau d'éloquence*, its doubly potent effect being counted on to soften irresistibly the Nephew as well.[37]

Counter-arguments of pure self-interest

With a philosopher whose thinking mode was as perverse as Diderot's, such an energetic and passionate enunciation of principle, especially after the spectacular build-up to the climax, constitutes almost inherently a call for the undoing of the moral doctrine so emotionally upheld. If only because of the familiar dialectical pattern, Diderot's strong positives are bound to collect negatives, or perhaps one should say that, in the cynical context of the Nephew's presence, such a *morceau d'éloquence* becomes something of a bravura gesture, as if defying the inevitable to occur. In any case, the Nephew is the agent of the counterforces that soon set to work undoing what Diderot has just done (p.44). First come arguments from morality that systematically apply contrary values: since Diderot places doing good for others at the centre of his system, the Nephew makes it doing good for oneself and never taking the other into consideration, except for reasons of self-interest; since Diderot stresses the long term, the Nephew goes for the short run, in fact the immediate; since Diderot's conduct is entirely guided by principles of right and wrong, the Nephew recognises no principle whatsoever, except expediency.

Here once again, at this stage of the contrariety between Moi and Lui it seems apropos to cite the precedent of Montesquieu, particularly the *Lettres persanes*: certainly no one before Montesquieu in the Enlightenment had

36. Admittedly Diderot's sort of sentimentality is difficult to take seriously in our own age: see the remark of Bronislaw Baczko quoted in the *compte rendu* by Alain Cernuschi of 'Diderot mis en pièces', *Recherches sur Diderot et sur l'Encyclopédie* 11 (1991), p.179.

37. As mentioned earlier, Diderot's bourgeois sentimentalism failed almost entirely to register importance with Hegel. On this point see Trilling, *Sincerity and authenticity*, p.44.

celebrated so seductively and with such influential eloquence the charms and benefits of virtue (Letter 13), that is to say, of systematic altruism. But at the same time, as the apologue of the Troglodytes makes clear (Letters 11-14), virtue is conceived of as a remedy for the destructiveness of a society governed by self-interest. In fact, beneath the theory there is an underlying assumption that, however desirable, the virtue of altruism is not natural; it is acquired, and, given mankind's tendencies towards self-interest, must struggle to win a position of dominance for itself.[38] Diderot's concept of virtue is keyed to the same kinds of values:[39] certainly he does his best in the tearful anecdote to orchestrate the benefits and pleasures of altruism, with all the dramatic force at his command. But, like Montesquieu, Diderot conceives of virtue as a stage which supposedly rises above other gratifications (his argument mentions appetite and debauched sexuality) that in their original, impulsive state are selfish pleasures, and this recognition, unsupported by Montesquieu's deism, leaves him fearfully vulnerable to attack. Why should anyone waste his time on practices that are unnatural, and which, on the deepest, original level, no one wants? The Nephew argues like an early Troglodyte, but one better attuned to current social realities and, psychologically, far more sophisticated: 'On loue la vertu [(B)]; mais on la haït [(C)]; mais on la fuit; mais elle gèle de froid, et dans ce monde, il faut avoir les piés chauds' (p.44).

With just the slightest tilt to the argument, virtue turns into hypocrisy: 'il seroit bien singulier que j'allasse me tourmenter comme une âme damnée pour me bistourner et me faire autre que je ne suis [...]. Et [si Rameau] se mettoit un jour [...] à catoniser, que seroit-il? un hippocrite. Il faut que Rameau soit ce qu'il est' (p.44, 46).

It has often been pointed out that the Nephew presents an insoluble philosophical dilemma for Moi because he exemplifies Diderot's own materialism: as the Nephew declares so articulately, his behaviour is simply dictated by what he is, and to behave 'better' (according to Diderot's lights) would amount to tampering with the truth. Not only does Diderot have no valid principles that would rebut the Nephew's arguments, but the arguments seem

38. By the same token Montesquieu recognised that virtue is only preserved by the inculcation of education; such is implicitly the function of the multitude of examples given in Letter 13 of the *Lettres persanes*. In *De l'esprit des lois*, even though the concept of 'vertu' is presented from a slightly different angle, the importance of education for the preservation of the virtuous principle of a 'gouvernement républicain' is unmistakable (bk.IV: 'De l'éducation dans le gouvernement républicain').

39. To be sure, Montesquieu's virtue is given an antique rustic setting, whereas Diderot's has a bourgeois one. It is also true that, theoretically, Montesquieu's system, being based on deistic assumptions, supposedly avoids the difficulties incurred in a materialistic context, as will be seen below.

actually to have been produced by Diderot's own doctrines. Lui's cynical views only gather strength as he embroiders on the reasons recognised by Diderot himself elsewhere[40] as to why people should never attempt to behave other than they really are: 'pourquoi voyons-nous si fréquemment les dévôts si durs, si fâcheux, si insociables? C'est qu'ils se sont imposés [*sic*] une tâche qui ne leur est pas naturelle. Ils souffrent, et quand on souffre, on fait souffrir les autres' (p.44). And it all fits flawlessly together; there is not even the smallest crack in the Nephew's logic, designed to prove, tiny step by tiny step (and decked out with 'et ..., et ...', 'or ...', 'donc ...', as if he were nailing the point down with a syllogism), that the reality of his existence – i.e. his patronage – rules out 'virtue' and demands he be exactly what he is:

La vertu se fait respecter; et le respect est incommode. La vertu se fait admirer, et l'admiration n'est pas amusante. J'ai à faire à des gens qui s'ennuyent et il faut que je les fasse rire. Or c'est le ridicule et la folie qui font rire; il faut donc que je sois ridicule et fou; et quand la nature ne m'auroit pas fait tel, le plus court seroit de le paraître. Heureusement, je n'ai pas besoin d'être hippocrite.[41]

At the conclusion, after a mocking allusion to Molière's Alceste, the Nephew congratulates himself on not feigning virtues he does not respect and on his resolve to remain a happy brigand among the opulent brigands – instead of following Diderot's principles and finding himself a beggar (p.46).

During this entire stage of the Nephew's argument, the classic pose for Moi has been disapproval, evident, *inter alia*, in his prim and sarcastic responses. It is also clear that the judgemental attitude implied in these rejoinders links Moi not only to Montesquieu, but to the grand traditions of Enlightened rationalism and, most particularly, to the fundamental conviction of his generation that humankind had both the capability and the duty to use the

---

40. The dilemma of virtue analysed by the Nephew is the same as that put forward in Diderot's own *Encyclopédie* article 'Cynique': 'D'où l'on voit que la vertu d'Antisthène était chagrine, ce qui arrivera toujours lorsqu'on s'opiniâtrera à se former un caractère artificiel et des mœurs factices. Je voudrais bien être Caton, mais je crois qu'il m'en coûterait beaucoup à moi et aux autres, avant que je le fusse devenu. Les fréquents sacrifices que je serais obligé de faire au personnage sublime que j'aurais pris pour modèle, me rempliraient d'une bile âcre et caustique, qui s'épancherait à chaque instant dehors. Et c'est là peut-être la raison pour laquelle quelques sages et certains dévôts austères sont si souvent sujets à la mauvaise humeur. Ils ressentent sans cesse la contrainte d'un rôle qu'ils se sont imposé, et pour lequel la nature ne les a point faits. Ils s'en prennent aux autres du tourment qu'ils se donnent à eux-mêmes' (quoted by Françoise Picot, 'Le Fou, le Sage, le Philosophe, le Poète', *Entretiens sur le Neveu de Rameau*, p.205).

41. P.44-45. The broad theme of hypocrisy allows the Nephew to throw in two extra dividends (p.45). He complacently contrasts the merits of his own natural behaviour, first with the false bluster of the chevalier de La Morlière, a cowardly Matamor familiar to both himself and Diderot, and, secondly, with the classic type of the false prude, another literary trope, the woman who outwardly affects chaste morals while secretly seething with sexual desire.

natural light of reason to distinguish between right and wrong in moral matters. In this sense, Diderot's position is inherently the strong one, the one to which he himself was committed as an *encyclopédiste*, and behind which lay the forces of history. On the other hand one need hardly add that the irony of this dialogue lies in observing how poorly such strong cards play out, and how easily these strengths, falling into the wrong hands, dissolve into weaknesses. No doubt Moi shows admirable tenacity in cleaving to his principles. Yet, by some unwritten law of perversity, even the most upright of motives seems to produce an underside: not only do Diderot's expressions of contempt serve as stimuli goading Lui to new inventions of depravity, but even the lofty purity implied in Moi's moral disdain may function as a *laissez-passer* giving both him and the reader licence to hear more about the despicable Lui and all the terrible people he has consorted with (D).[42]

II

One side of the ensuing drama is easily described because it repeats the dialectical pattern, the nexus of reactions, that has already become familiar (A, B, C), in which Moi's well-meaning theories are ever more seriously put to the test, sometimes apparently even overthrown, by Lui's potent arguments from reality.[43]

Two factors contribute most prominently to the Nephew's successes. The first is simply that he embodies so flawlessly and so consciously a condition that both he and Diderot (not to mention Hegel and Jean-Jacques Rousseau)[44] acknowledged as the dominant social reality of that era, the condition of dependence, which in this case derives from the simple fact that the Nephew

42. See Diderot's own astonishingly pertinent analysis of the reasons why society tolerates the company of 'libertins': '[Si les] libertins sont bienvenus dans le monde, [...] c'est qu'ils ajoutent sans cesse à notre estime, par le mépris que nous faisons d'eux; c'est qu'ils nous mettent à notre aise; c'est qu'ils nous consolent de notre vertu, par le spectacle amusant du vice; c'est qu'ils nous entretiennent de ce que nous n'osons ni parler ni faire; c'est que nous sommes toujours un peu vicieux' (à Sophie Volland, 7 octobre 1761, *Correspondance*, ed. Georges Roth, t.iii.330-31). See also the observation of Jean Starobinski, 'L'emploi du chiasme dans "Le Neveu de Rameau"', *Revue de métaphysique et de morale* 89 (1984), p.195: 'le secret d'alcôve se propage et [...] tout le monde finit par en être informé: les domestiques secourables, les commensaux bavards [...], le Neveu, puis le philosophe qui, par ses lecteurs (audience peut-être limitée, à l'origine, mais universalisable) fait à son tour office de "colporteur", sous couvert d'une désapprobation laconique.'

43. Though independently conceived, my analysis coincides on a number of these points with the elegantly concise one by Peter France, *Diderot*, esp. p.74-84.

44. Rousseau, *Discours sur l'origine de l'inégalité*, *Œuvres complètes*, t.iii, ed. Jean Starobinski (Paris 1964), p.171-74.

serves those more wealthy and powerful than he. As the final pantomimes will reveal, subservience in this sense makes the Nephew a spokesman for virtually everyone (C), a verity which even Diderot, with mixed emotions, is constrained to recognise, if not condone. But the Nephew's most powerful authority over Moi – it almost goes without saying – comes from his uncanny ability to mimic Diderot's own penchants and desires – a phenomenon of which scholars have been aware ever since Daniel Mornet's radical (not to say exaggerated and, in important ways, mistaken) proposal, in 1927, that Lui and Moi are simply two aspects of the same personality.[45]

Mornet and followers went wide of the mark, if only because of the moments in the text when Moi and Lui play off one another as separate and disjunctive, historically identified personalities. Furthermore, as the present discussion is seeking to establish, the phenomenon of Lui being an extension of Moi's own principles is not a given factor, but an event that evolves in the text, usually as the underside, or an aftermath, of preceding stages of relationship, stages that indispensably imply, as the other side of the coin, a disagreement between the two personae. Only in the context of such a dialectical continuum is it true that the Nephew may come to represent Diderot's own ideas.[46] To be sure, it is also clear that, when such events do occur, they represent exceptionally significant occasions, and the present discussion has been regularly pointing them out (D).

The most sensational and shocking instance is the anecdote (p.72-75) of the Renégat d'Avignon (a passage whose details I have scrutinised elsewhere[47]), which not only uncovers baseness of an unsuspected degree in the Nephew, but covertly implicates Diderot in its lessons as well. No doubt it would have been impossible for Moi, with all his sense of decency and virtue, not to feel horror at the cruelty of the story (B), especially at the gratuitousness of the Renégat's final gesture as he sends the kindly, trusting, generous Jew who befriended him to perish at the stake. But even so, despite the horror and the virtue, the anecdote fits so perfectly with Diderot's admitted fascination

---

45. 'La véritable signification du *Neveu de Rameau*', *Revue des deux mondes* 40 (1927), p.881-906. I trust that the present discussion will make it clear that I by no means agree with Mornet's idea that this satire is merely an inner dialogue.

46. It has long been recognised by Freudians that the Nephew functions in respect to Moi as a kind of 'id'. See Wilson, *Diderot*, p.420, and Jacques Ehrmann, '*Rameau's Nephew*: an existential psychoanalysis of Diderot by himself', *Journal of existential psychiatry* 4 (1963), p.59-68. In the present context as well, such an interpretation of the relationship between the two dialogists may seem plausible and pertinent; I would add the proviso, however, that this relationship be viewed as belonging to the general flux of the dialogue; thus it is not a permanent feature, but an intermittent one, evolving in and out of being, like everything else.

47. 'Two scenes', p.257-66.

with evil that almost inevitably one detects a nightmarish symbolism at the conclusion, as Lui, staging his song and dance of triumph to celebrate the fool of kings and the king of fools, invites Moi to join in with him for the chorus (D) (p.76).

The peculiar perfection of this anecdote becomes most clearly visible if one perceives it as deliberate counterpoint, an antidote, to the sentimental one told earlier by Moi (p.42-43), a strategic denial of the moral values that Diderot has so emotionally upheld. But whereas Diderot's sentimental story was doomed because it awakened no sympathetic resonances in the listener, Lui's anecdote of the Renégat sails in on Diderot's own admiration for the energy of great crimes, especially when, as here, they are works of art. Above all, it gains right of way through the licence implicit in Diderot's philosophy, whereby, objectively speaking, nothing is good or bad, since everything is simply necessary. For in fact, in Diderot's deterministic world, values such as 'blame', 'honour', 'vice', and 'virtue' have no objective status; even the atrocity recounted in the Nephew's anecdote would ultimately have to be absorbed by Diderot's materialistic system as part of the order of things. Such is the load which Lui's anecdote brings home and deposits on Diderot's doorstep. In only one other place in the dialogue[48] is Diderot so deeply entangled in the Nephew's behaviour, which is intentionally at its most loathsome: 'J'ai voulu que vous connussiez jusqu'où j'excellois dans mon art; vous arracher l'aveu que j'étois au moins original dans mon avilissement' (p.76).

Perhaps it was to be expected that Diderot would never face openly the devastating subliminal resonances that implicated him in this spectacle of cruelty.[49] On the other hand, backhanded evidence suggests that Moi is supposed to have come to terms with the most painful of the philosophical implications of the anecdote, bringing him at least to accept the Nephew, and even the infamous Renégat as necessary results of the causes of things.[50] But

48. That is, in the final pantomimes, as will be discussed further on.

49. Ostensibly, Diderot is unaware of the degree to which his criticisms of the Nephew might apply to himself and his own admiration for crimes as art: 'Je commençois à supporter avec peine la présence d'un homme qui discutoit une action horrible, un exécrable forfait, comme les beautés d'un ouvrage de goût; ou comme un moraliste ou un historien relève et fait éclater les circonstances d'une action héroïque. Je devins sombre, malgré moi' (p.76).

50. I infer this acceptance from the rather strange way, in the aftermath of the 'Renégat' anecdote, that Moi resumes the conversation following a silence in which (p.77) he confesses to have been as if 'tracassé de quelqu'idée fâcheuse': allegedly turning to music, he compares his ignorance of the true meaning of 'le chant' to most people's ignorance of the true meaning of terms like 'blâme, honneur, vice, vertu, pudeur, décence, honte, ridicule'. This list is unnecessarily long, nor does it really fit in a musical context. As Diderot's *Encyclopédie* article 'Laideur' (ix.176A-B) makes clear (along with *Le Rêve de d'Alembert* and other texts), these terms represent commonly accepted moral values, Diderot's point being that, contrary to the usual presumptions about them, they actually have no objective status. In other words, the list makes most sense if

even if one chooses to discount such backhanded admissions, Moi's reaction to the Nephew's fugal pantomime powerfully suggests his own involvement in terms of behaviour: just as in the pantomime of the procurer, Diderot cannot decide whether to laugh or become indignant, whether to stay or leave the scene,[51] and in this case too – presumably after weighing at least some of the reasons to withdraw – he decides to stay. Thus, for the second time in this text the Nephew is shown to have seduced Moi into feeling impulses of laughter, irrepressible impulses which threaten to override all his alleged principles and other sentiments that could not be further from mirth, and which also reveal at least something of the gravity of the predicaments implicit in Moi's philosophy, however unspeakable they might be. Meanwhile, of course, Diderot's involvement in the evil of the Renégat has stretched the moral problematics of his materialism to the limits of the endurable.

In this respect the contrast with *Le Rêve de d'Alembert* could not be more striking. In fact, in *Le Neveu de Rameau* Diderot deliberately problematises, and fills with anguish, notions that Bordeu breezily summed up in a philosophical nutshell, brushing aside, even ridiculing, any suggestion of the dilemmas that might lurk underneath. The tones and attitudes are so dissimilar that one can scarcely believe these two works came from the same pen (DPV, xvii.186-87):

Mlle de Lespinasse

Et l'estime de soi? et la honte? et le remords?

Bordeu

Puérilité fondée sur l'ignorance et la vanité d'un être qui s'impute à lui-même le mérite et le démérite d'un instant nécessaire.

The evil people do is also easily, almost mindlessly, accounted for (DPV, xvii.186):

Bordeu

[...] On est heureusement ou malheureusement né; on est irrésistiblement entraîné par le torrent général qui conduit l'un à la gloire, l'autre à l'ignominie.

Of course Diderot would have wanted to see himself on the 'gloire' side of this pair of terms, relegating both Lui and the Renégat to 'ignominie'. And, for the rest, given the general flux of *Le Neveu de Rameau*, even such direly implicating episodes as that of the Renégat d'Avignon represent simply

one considers it as a leftover from Diderot's moral ruminations after the 'Renégat d'Avignon' episode, a hint that, for reasons of materialism, he has finally accepted the non-objective status of Renégat's 'evil' as well.

51. See Rex, 'Two scenes', p.257-66, in which I discuss the two-stage mechanism of the ending in more detail.

moments in an evolution that inevitably moves on to produce fresh per-spectives. This continuousness suggests another reason why Mornet and later scholars in his wake are wide of the mark: even though one does indeed find instances, some of them powerfully dramatic, in which the Nephew is simply acting out Diderot's own thoughts and desires, the dialogue necessarily pro-gresses to other situations, so that the Nephew cannot remain always, or merely, one side of Diderot. Detachment was bound to happen, even as new moods replace old ones. At times Lui goes on to reveal experiences from his life which lie beyond Diderot's ken, and to stage pantomimes and musical performances that go beyond Diderot's talent,[52] not to mention the volume capacity of his vocal cords. The Nephew is very much a presence in his own right in the text.

Nor was Diderot alone in being dazzled by the virtuosity of this personality. André Magnan has assembled the relevant documents concerning his character and the events of his life,[53] and it is evident that several of the Nephew's acquaintances, themselves writers of distinction, bore witness to his extra-ordinary qualities, even brilliance.[54] To be sure, the Nephew's existence, from the very start, was a miserable affair: aside from a few publications of music (almost none of which has survived), a few performances of his pieces at the 'Concert spirituel' and some movingly awful autobiographical verses, he accomplished nothing, dying in conditions close to the wretchedness he had predicted in that sombre page of *Le Neveu de Rameau*. Professor Magnan, pointing out that the Nephew's only immortality lies in Diderot's dialogue, also refers to the legend – the purest hypothesis, of course – that Diderot's presence may have elicited from this *raté* his finest performances, his moment of 'gloire', and allowed him through Diderot's text to attain the greatness that everywhere else eluded him.

Despite Professor Magnan's wise and scholarly cautions,[55] the hypothesis remains a possibility. But the present discussion is proposing the other, equally undemonstrable, side of that same coin: that the presence of the Nephew in Diderot's dialogue – real and invented, and in the infinite complexity of its relationship to the author – brought Diderot to create in this text a sort of projection, or playing out, of the dynamics of the self (actions and reactions,

---

52. This statement is not intended to disparage Diderot's talents as a mime, which were apparently considerable, but simply to underscore the Nephew's superiority, to which Moi himself pays homage.

53. See *Rameau le neveu: textes et documents* (Paris 1993).

54. Magnan, *Rameau le neveu*, p.109-10 (Piron); p.221-22 (Cazotte); p.224-26 (Mercier). The main documents are also in the appendix to the Fabre edition, p.243-54.

55. *Rameau le neveu*, preface, p.14-15.

accords and disaccords) that is unique in Diderot's work; and moreover that, in terms of the realities of psychological individuality, Diderot accomplished here what seventeenth-century moralists could only achieve in terms of generality, and most often through the categories of Christianity or antiquity. Perhaps the psychology of this achievement may recall Montaigne's idea of individuality, but if so it is a Montaigne to whom has been added not only a sense of class conflict and social dynamics but also the anxieties of self that belong specifically to the modern world.

'La Querelle des bouffons'

Once the wrangles over morality get pushed aside and music becomes the main issue the antagonisms between Lui and Moi devolve into the quarrel over the French versus the Italian musical style (p.78-83). Lui, sometimes sounding a little like Jean-Jacques Rousseau, leads the attack on the French, whose greatest exponent, needless to say, was the 'cher oncle'. The virulence of his criticisms recalls 'La Querelle des bouffons' at its hottest, during the 1750s.[56] Thanks to the indispensable researches of Daniel Heartz,[57] Béatrice Didier[58] and Catherine Kintzler[59] and the proposals of Béatrice Durand-Sendrail,[60] the long-ignored musical portions of *Le Neveu de Rameau* are at last beginning to be comprehensible.

As Béatrice Didier has pointed out,[61] despite the Nephew's Italian partisan-ship, his attitude towards French opera in Diderot's text is a mixture, or at least it swings back and forth between condemnation and esteem. Already at the beginning, two compositions by the great Rameau had been cited for admiration, the overture to *Les Indes galantes* and *Profonds abymes*. Later (p.83), even after the Nephew's scathing and far-reaching criticisms of French opera, the wind will suddenly change and the Nephew's argument will veer into a warning against dismissing the accomplishments of the most famous exponents of the French style: Lully, Campra and Rameau, the latter being cited for a whole group of compositions including his violin pieces, his gavottes, the entry music of soldiers, priests and sacrificers from *Les Indes galantes*,

---

56. This point is suggested in a different context by Béatrice Durand-Sendrail, *La Musique de Diderot: essai sur l'hiéroglyphe musical* (Paris 1994), p.61.

57. 'Diderot et le théâtre lyrique: "Le nouveau stile" proposé par *Le Neveu de Rameau*', *Revue de musicologie* 54 (1978), p.229-52.

58. *La Musique des lumières: Diderot – L'Encyclopédie – Rousseau* (Paris 1985).

59. *Jean-Philippe Rameau: splendeur et naufrage de l'esthétique du plaisir à l'âge classique* (Paris 1983).

60. *La Musique de Diderot*, passim.

61. *La Musique des lumières*, p.190-92.

Téláïre's aria from *Castor et Pollux* and, once again, *Profonds abymes*, which the Nephew sings so loudly that the listeners in the café are forced to stop their ears. Despite the Nephew's scornful predictions that the ossified old French style is doomed to be replaced by the vibrant new Italian one, these old-style composers, especially the 'cher oncle', remain indelibly part of his thinking about great music.

Musical pantomimes, translating words into notes and operatic gestures, have been woven so frequently into the texture of the work, so often filling the scene with musical sounds and gestures, that their unexpectedness has become almost an expectation. The climax of these interludes is the Nephew's grand opera imitation (p.82-83), itself an apotheosis of unexpectedness, which disjointedly throws together in surrealistic outbursts snippets of every opera he can think of, he himself taking all the roles, singing all the parts and mimicking all the instruments in a breathless and partly doomed effort at simultaneity. Critics have already noted the extraordinary literary qualities of the passage,[62] which I too have elsewhere analysed at length.

During this whole display the Nephew attempts to turn himself into pure simulation, calling on every possible opera composer and every scenic effect[63] in the repertoire, as if these representations, if only multiplied, diversified and intensified enough, could provoke an imitation so powerful that no one could gainsay it. Such an astonishing and exhausting parade of mimetic virtuosity suggests how much, allegedly, is at stake in the performance for the Nephew, as though he were striving, in the aesthetic domain, to rival his own efforts in the Renégat d'Avignon episode to reach the sublime in evil. And he goes at it almost literally like a madman,[64] creating intensities that suggest a sort of poetic insanity, as though he were trying to break through the confines of artistic expression and soar into some new dimension.[65] But it is equally

62. The most famous commentary is by Spitzer, 'The style of Diderot', p.158-59, who also (p.184-85, n.34) gives a critical commentary on the then well-known one by Daniel Mornet.

63. I have discussed the role of these scenic effects in the Nephew's imitations at greater length, and with illustrations from the plates of the *Encyclopédie*, in *The Attraction of the contrary*, p.117-22.

64. The Nephew's 'madness' is the main point explored in the famous discussion of Michel Foucault, *Histoire de la folie à l'âge classique*, 2nd edition (Paris 1972), p.363-72.

65. In this connection it is instructive to compare Diderot's rhythms with those of the rather similar passage from Rousseau's *Lettre sur la musique française*, which Diderot may have been remembering. Whereas Diderot was deliberately creating an uncanny effect centred on the Nephew's performance-imitation, Rousseau was striving to reveal to the reader the dramatic intensity of the works performed. From *Le Neveu de Rameau*: 'Ici, c'est une jeune fille qui pleure et il en rend toute la minauderie; là il est prêtre, il est roi, il est tyran, il menace, il commande, il s'emporte; il est esclave, il obéit. Il s'apaise, il se désole, il se plaint, il rit' (p.83). From Rousseau's: '[Dans les opéras italiens] Tantôt c'est un père désespéré qui croit voir l'ombre d'un fils qu'il a fait mourir injustement lui reprocher sa cruauté; tantôt c'est un prince débonnaire

obvious that, however impressive the momentary effects may be,[66] the Nephew's frenetic efforts to reproduce, alone, the opera of operas stretches the practice of imitation beyond its capabilities, pushing it so far that it becomes a parody of itself, a derision that, even while staging the music which the Nephew has chosen with such exquisite taste, and whose power he knows so well, undermines the effect at the same time. No one was more skilful than Diderot in inventing and orchestrating such ambiguities: *Le Neveu de Rameau* is essentially, to its very core, a celebration of the 'arts of imitation', above all an act of homage to music, one of the most witty and movingly perceptive ever written. At the same time, in the irony of the Nephew's grand pantomime the text not only reveals the hollow precariousness of all performances, but, precisely because of the depth of understanding that informs the Nephew's display, brings art-as-imitation into question, to its foundations.

The Nephew as object of derision

It is certainly clear that in the broadest sense – not merely in the grand opera pantomime, but everywhere in the agon of the dialogue – each word the Nephew speaks, each note he sings, every gesture he makes, is calculated to win out over Moi – whether by trouncing his arguments, seducing him into laughter, or winning admiration for his musical acumen, his story-telling, his prowess at evil, his singing, or his pantomimes. The self-interest is so obvious and pervasive that any exceptions one might find, that is, any absence of self-interest on his part, might have special significance, and if it lowers his listener's opinion of him, doubly so.

Such would appear to be the Nephew's previously mentioned admissions of mediocrity, of being wanting in genius, the one essential characteristic of great persons. Nor is there any real advantage in making such confessions in terms of the ongoing jockeying for position. Though Diderot might claim that he thinks more highly of the Nephew for his honesty, on the other hand the dialogue depicts Diderot using the Nephew's mediocrity rather patronisingly

qui, forcé de donner un exemple de sévérité, demande aux dieux de lui ôter l'empire, ou de lui donner un cœur moins sensible. Ici c'est une mère tendre qui verse des larmes en retrouvant son fils qu'elle croyoit mort; là c'est le langage de l'amour' (*Ecrits sur la musique*, ed. Catherine Kintzler, Paris 1979, p.302).

66. The climax of this passage is the Nephew's performance of a 'récitatif obligé' from the Jommelli *Lamentations*, the only religious music in this part of the text. The effect is so intense that one has the momentary impression that the Nephew may finally have won Diderot's unreserved admiration – an impression only belied at the very end, by the last word of the passage. This music was rediscovered by Marita P. McClymonds and published for the first time, with detailed commentaries, in Marita P. McClymonds and Walter E. Rex, ' "Ce beau récitatif obligé": *Le Neveu de Rameau* and Jommelli', *Diderot studies* 22 (1986), p.63-77.

to lord it over him, superciliously telling him to work harder and be more disciplined, as if it were somehow up to him to overcome his defect. One would have thought that at least the sheer pathos of the Nephew's pantomime of the creative act, in which he re-enacts his vain struggles to summon the god of inspiration, and which lead only to the realisation that greatness is beyond him, would have gained a measure of sympathetic response from Moi: 'Serviteur. Bonsoir. Le dieu est absent; je m'étois persuadé que j'avois du génie; au bout de ma ligne, je lis que je suis un sot, un sot, un sot' (p.98).

One would also have imagined that his explanation for his failure – his lack of the essential fibre of greatness – would also prove convincing to someone as interested in the physical basis of psychology as Moi. But the philosopher's only response, as though he himself were totally secure in his own creative capabilities, is to urge more effort: 'A votre place, je ne me le tiendrois pas pour dit; j'essaierois' (p.99).

At which point the Nephew's words take on an extra poetical dimension, brightening in fact into a sort of surrealism – an occurrence apparently connected to Diderot's lack of sympathy and to the poignant degree of the Nephew's abjection ('Et vous croyez que je n'ai pas essayé'). A series of marvellous metaphors emerge in his discourse: the statue of Memnon vibrating sonorously in the rays of the sun, but leaving all the other statues silent (p.100), even as Voltaire stands alone in poetical genius, or as the great composers – the Nephew lists nothing but Italians, except for the Uncle – make all the rest seem like pairs of ears stuck on the ends of sticks. It would be hard to find more intense, or better, poetry anywhere in Diderot's century than in the lines that follow immediately after the ears and the sticks (p.100):

Aussi sommes-nous gueux, si gueux que c'est une bénédiction. Ah, monsieur le philosophe, la misère est une terrible chose. Je la vois accroupie, la bouche béante, pour recevoir quelques gouttes de l'eau glacée qui s'échappe du tonneau des Danaïdes.

And just as in Villon, the poignancy is immediately doused with irony: 'Je ne sçais si elle aiguise l'esprit du philosophe; mais elle refroidit diablement la tête du poète. On ne chante pas bien sous ce tonneau. Trop heureux encore, celui qui peut s'y placer' (p.100).

To the reader, the genius of this passage may make it seem that the Nephew has accomplished momentarily, and almost inadvertently, what he never could achieve when consciously striving for greatness.[67] But one is not allowed to dwell on such reflections, for meanwhile (p.101-102) the text has moved on, almost jerkily devolving into a narrative of the Nephew's picaresque adven-

---

67. See the telling remarks of Georges Benrekassa on the Nephew as combining the oracular with the surprising ('Diderot, l'absence d'œuvre', p.135).

tures, constantly seeking, and never finding, the ideal patron, knocking about from pillar to post. Occasionally a rather special tone creeps into his account – eerily anticipating Rimbaud's *Saison en enfer* – and one finds Lui speaking of his banal or absurd projects for survival as though they were magical proposals or, for some secret reason, wonders in disguise, possibilities that had emblematic significance. In the following passage Lui calls his father an apothecary, whereas in reality he was, at least primarily, an organist – no doubt, as Jean Fabre[68] and others have suggested, Diderot momentarily confused Rameau with his compatriot, Piron. But the mistake contributes oddly to the sentiment of alienation that permeates this part of the text, particularly in the fantasy that the Nephew's own misfortunes could be displayed and cried up for money at the crossroads, as itinerant showmen did with the lives of popular heroes (p.102):

Il me passa toutes sortes de projets par le tête. Un jour, je partois le lendemain pour me jeter dans une troupe de province, également bon ou mauvais pour le théâtre ou l'orchestre; le lendemain je songeois à me faire peindre un de ces tableaux attachés à une perche qu'on plante dans un carrefour, et où j'aurois crié à tue-tête: voilà la ville où il est né; le voilà qui prend congé de son père l'apothicaire; le voilà qui arrive dans la capitale, cherchant la demeure de son oncle; le voilà aux genoux de son oncle qui le chasse; le voilà avec un Juif, et caetera et caetera. Le jour suivant je me levois, bien décidé de m'associer aux chanteurs des rues; ce n'est pas ce que j'aurois fait de plus mal; nous serions allés concerter sous les fenêtres du cher oncle qui en seroit crevé de rage.

In this fantasy of setting up his life in pictures at the crossroads, the Nephew is imagining that the humiliations of his existence, in their misery, can be skimmed off, turned into entertainment, and put up for sale as a livelihood.[69] A look behind the text at the real historical Nephew confirms the poignance inherent anyway in this gesture: the documents assembled by Professor Magnan reveal that the cruelty of his real father towards him as an infant was positively pathological;[70] that his father summarily sent him away from home and disinherited him.[71] Though no document attests to his uncle's refusing to retain him despite his pleas, there is proof that his uncle got in touch with the authorities to get him exiled to the colonies;[72] nor is there any reason to disbelieve the other banishment either. In short, even allowing for factual

68. Fabre edition, p.157, n.74; p.234, n.307.
69. The Nephew also put his misfortunes up for sale in his autobiographical poetry, although there he never spoke of the cruelty of the 'cher oncle' towards him, the element that forms the central fact of this pictorial autobiography.
70. *Rameau le neveu*, documents 2-4, p.19-23.
71. *Rameau le neveu*, document 10, p.35-36.
72. *Rameau le neveu*, document 15, p.45.

discrepancies and other deceits, these imaginary pictures are densely compressed, and extremely personal, tokens of the cruelty that the Nephew has endured, stigmata, but the poignance is cut across by the irony of using them as mock-heroic entertainment for a public consisting of anybody at all.

The entertainment to which the Nephew refers, being a common form of amusement, particularly at fairs, found its way into popular iconography, and at least once was painted by a truly great artist, Watteau de Lille (nephew of the more familiar Watteau) (Figure 8). His picture fills in the details of the kind of scene the Nephew has in mind: the 'perche' which holds the picture up, the canvas divided into scenes, with the showman, a violinist just like the Nephew, pointing with his bow towards the parts of the story that he is singing about to the idly curious listeners, while his wife (not a feature of the Nephew's thinking) goes around collecting contributions. It is easy to put the Nephew into the picture.

III

Ultimate truths

The Nephew ends the account of the haphazard events of his life in a similarly haphazard fashion (p.103): his present uncertainties in the wake of the Bertin disaster seem like a turn of the Wheel of Fortune, the wheel then spinning off by association to the odd fantasy that somewhere in some mill on Montmartre there may be a miller's assistant whose only music is the clicking of the mechanism of a millstone, but who might have been capable of greatness as a composer; perhaps he himself should now go to change places with him – another extreme gesture of alienation.

Most unsympathetically, Moi proposes that whatever is, is natural: 'A quoi que ce soit que l'homme s'applique, la Nature l'y destinoit' (p.103).

This cold, distant statement marks the beginning of the final segment of the work, in which the agon between the two characters reaches its ultimate stages. Lui does not agree with Moi about Nature ('Elle fait d'étranges bévues'), but leaves such lofty generalities to the likes of the philosopher. His own starting point is the – eminently natural – desire to eat: appetite.[73] And from this basic

---

73. As various critics have pointed out, this doctrine fits perfectly with what we know of the real Jean-François Rameau, whose main dictum was quaintly described by Louis-Sébastien Mercier, to wit, that everything in life – prodigies of courage, genius, heroisms – is a result of the laws of mastication: 'Selon lui, tout cela n'avait d'autre but ni d'autre résultat que de placer quelque chose sous la dent. Il prêchait cette doctrine avec un geste expressif et un mouvement de mâchoire très pittoresque' (quoted in Magnan, *Rameau le neveu*, p.224).

Figure 8. Watteau de Lille, *Le Violoneux*

principle Lui will proceed to extrapolate a dazzling vision of all of society, one that must have set Marx's pulse positively racing with approval (p.103-104). The Nephew speaks truth not only with the wisdom of a prophet, but like a logician. First comes an indignant observation of an incontrovertible social fact: he protests against an order that leaves people hungry, an order in which some people have indecent amounts of everything, while others have nothing at all to eat ('pas de quoi mettre sous la dent'). Seamlessly the Nephew's discourse travels to the next point: the posture of constraint that such privation demands and requires; and this point again, of its own accord, ramifies into the physical movements – the hops, crawls, twistings, draggings – of 'l'homme nécessiteux'. Again the clustering together of movements brings on the next genial point, which, like the musical pantomimes, opens up a new dimension of the text: dance. The person of necessity spends his life dancing attendance, and the Nephew's last pantomimes will be performed as choreography, just like the final *divertissements* of an *opéra comique*.

It has long been a cliché of literary criticism to note that true comedy is born of distress, and, once again, Villon's 'Grand Testament' would be a pertinent example to cite in this connection. But the passage just given in résumé is among the few texts of great comedy in which one can observe that genesis spelled out in each of its particulars: the step-by-step progression that leads all the way from hunger and its necessities to the art form of comedy-dance. The roots of this process in the most elemental, lowliest experience are no doubt what make the Nephew automatically reject the philosopher's elevated outlook ('Je suis trop lourd pour m'élever si haut. J'abandonne aux grues le séjour des brouillards. Je vais terre à terre'). But even so, the Nephew is brought, willy-nilly, into a universal perspective as he goes from his brilliant demonstrations of 'pantomimes de style', the basic 'positions' of 'l'homme nécessiteux', to his observation that these 'positions' are practised by all who are flatterers, courtiers, valets and beggars – already a rather broad spectrum of society. The wit and truth of his performance elicits from the narrator one of his most approving comments,[74] an *aperçu* which has often been quoted by critics as if its meaning were self-evident. Actually, as Starobinski has demonstrated,[75] the statement is surprisingly dense (p.104):

74. One notes as well that in the extreme stylisation of the pantomimes – 'il attend un ordre, il le reçoit; il part comme un trait; il revient, il est executé; il en rend compte. Il est attentif à tout; il ramasse ce qui tombe; il place un oreiller ou un tabouret sous des piés', and so on – the Nephew has outwardly come to seem like a parody of the notion of altruism, his every breath and gesture being dedicated to the benefit of the other. Only his underlying, and invisible, motives remain determined by self-interest.

75. 'L'accent de la vérité', *Diderot et le théâtre* (Paris 1984), p.9f. Chouillet, in the introduction to his edition of *Le Neveu de Rameau*, p.21, also brings out the double nature of Diderot's idea of mask.

Les folies de cet homme, les contes de l'abbé Galiani, les extravagances de Rabelais m'ont quelquefois fait rêver profondément. Ce sont trois magasins où je me suis pourvu de masques ridicules que je place sur le visage des plus graves personnages; et je vois Pantalon dans un prélat, un satyre dans un président, un pourceau dans un cénobite, une autruche dans un ministre, une oye dans son premier commis.

In the first sentence, mentioning Rabelais, the idea of the appearance of extravagance or folly masking hidden wisdom probably looks back to Rabelais's prologue of book I; so also does the grotesque assortment of the clown, satyr, pig, ostrich and goose, for the boxes called *sileni* of the prologue likewise had ridiculous figures painted upon them. But having referred to the image in Rabelais's sense, Diderot's application then turns everything upside down and goes backwards: the idea of the ridiculous mask floats free from its original function, and instead of representing that which obscures the truth, turns into that which bespeaks the truth. The masks no longer cover over and disguise secret wisdom, they display and reveal the hidden realities which officious people try to keep out of sight. (Thus the two senses of the idea of 'mask' have the makings of a rather complicated contrariety.) In sum, the first sentence applies to the deceptively ridiculous appearance of the Nephew himself; the rest to the truth of his satire, which, as satires classically do, discloses the clownish or brutish side of 'les gens en place', their masking by Diderot amounting to their unmasking.

And now, after some haggling over whether the sovereign at least is exempt from the laws of dependency that govern everyone else, the final *entrée de ballet* begins. For once Moi and Lui – ostensibly and momentarily – are in perfect agreement, so that Moi can speak the text of the ballet, the *livret*, of which Lui performs the steps or 'positions', and which he executes to such perfection that, by sleight of hand, the text seems transfigured into dance: 'Mais tandis que je parlois, il contrefaisoit à mourir de rire, les positions des personnages que je nommois' (p.106).

The Nephew's vision of society supposedly involves everyone from beggar to king, and so, symbolically at least, the whole world now joins with him, forming a universal chorus of dancers, everyone participating in the *grand branle*. The point of this dance is exactly opposite to the famous medieval one in which all classes likewise participated, but only to be seized, one by one, and carried off by the figure of Death. On this occasion the ballet certainly represents (ostensibly at least) not death, but life in the social sense, and the Nephew's pantomime-in-dance functions as a welcome, a comic benediction addressed to all, in choreography.

Rousseau had maintained that when words were set to music as melody, not merely did melody express a variety of passions and language accents by imitating vocal inflexions, melody itself could speak ('elle n'imite pas seulement, elle parle'), and its own inarticulate language could be 'vif, ardent, passionné' a hundred times more energetically than words could.[76] Likewise, as Moi relates how Lui translates his spoken words into gestures, he attributes to the 'positions' in pantomime something of the same property, as though Lui's gestures (such as we imagine them) could be infinitely more affecting than syllables alone, so that the collaboration of Moi and Lui could generate, through the signs of the printed page, something like a new dimension.

Yet, even as Moi invents, and comments on, the *livret*, one feels a growing irony that Diderot himself is bringing about the last great dialectical reversal (C) in which the no-account *raté* becomes emblematic of the whole world, perhaps even to the inclusion of Moi. Naturally there is an ever-increasing sense of his disapproval of these 'vile' pantomimes (p.105), and although the ballet is a perfect enactment of the Nephew's philosophy of life, 'servir les grands', there is little reason to think that this tableau of universal fawning and flattery would have provoked much enthusiasm from the author of *Les Eleuthéromanes, ou les furieux de la liberté*. To be sure, Diderot's feelings of disapproval do not prevent his recognising and admiring the truth and wit of the Nephew's insight, thus in one way consecrating the dialectical reversal (C/D): 'Ma foi, ce que vous appellez la pantomime des gueux, est le grand branle de la terre. Chacun a sa petite Hus et son Bertin' (p.105).

But inevitably Diderot's disagreements re-emerge (B), nor will he himself consent to be incorporated among the fawners without a fight: he reproachfully reminds the Nephew of an important exception to his rule, namely, the philosopher, people like Diogenes[77] who, possessing nothing, need nothing and refuse to take part in the pantomime. Lui strongly protests, giving Moi a very hard time over this so-called exception (p.106-107): does not even a philosopher need clothes? – food? – good food? – sex? – a prostitute? At the end of the pursuit of Lui's questions, the philosopher ends up, supposedly like Diogenes, naked, making do without the prostitute, in a barrel.

But even when the arguments run out, Diderot has quantities of moral indignation in reserve: 'Je veux mourir si cela ne vaudroit mieux que de ramper, de s'avilir, et se prostituer' (p.107).

And when Lui replies that he himself prefers a nice bed, good food, warm clothes for winter, cool ones for summer, rest, money and lots more besides,

---

76. See Rousseau, *Essai sur l'origine des langues, où il est parlé de la mélodie et de l'imitation musicale*, ed. Charles Porset (Paris 1970), p.159.

77. The background of this personage in Diderot's dialogue has been explored in Jean Starobinski, 'Diogène dans *Le Neveu de Rameau*', *Stanford French review* 8 (1984), p.147-65.

which he prefers to acquire from someone's else's benevolence rather than from his own hard work, Moi just explodes at him: 'C'est que vous êtes un fainéant, un gourmand, un lâche, une âme de boue' (p.107).

Anyone else might have been shaken by the sheer outrage of such a righteous discharge, but not only is Lui unperturbed ('Je crois vous l'avoir dit'), but the force of the righteousness creates, by contrary motion, a display of depravity by the Nephew to outdo all his previous accomplishments, one of the most genially outrageous contrarieties ever invented. This last pantomime wittily perverts Diderot's own idea of 'philosopher' (probably including Diogenes' nakedness and sensual desires as well as his stoical courage), embroiders on the words 'se prostituer' (also helpfully supplied by Moi himself), and takes up Moi's suggestion of his being 'une âme de boue'. It is almost as though Diderot had created the *livret* of this ballet, even as he had done for the others, this time by backwards motion from Diderot's intent (p.108):

Lui

[...] Mais je vois à ce que vous me dites là que ma pauvre petite femme étoit une espèce de philosophe. Elle avoit du courage comme un lion. [...] Quand j'étois de quelque concert, je l'emmenois avec moi. Chemin faisant, je lui disois: Allons, madame, faites-vous admirer; déployez votre talent et vos charmes. Enlevez. Renversez.

Of course the wife, deploying her charms for the benefit of her penniless husband, is also a perverted image of Diderot's altruism. Naturally as well, the high-minded philosopher cannot stop himself from enjoying the Nephew's pantomime as, with swishing hips ('ah! Dieu, quelle croupe'), mincing steps and fluttering fan he shows exactly how she plied her trade in the Tuileries, the Palais Royal and the Boulevards. As usual with Diderot in this work, his amusement (D) is only permitted when accompanied by a frown, however slight, indicating his moral disapproval (B): 'c'étoit la charge de nos petites coquettes la plus plaisante et la plus *ridicule*' (p.108, emphasis mine).

Despite or because of the frowns, distancings, indignations and denunciations, Moi has been more deeply implicated with the Nephew here in the last pantomimes than anywhere else, to the point of creating the Nephew's script and writing his stage directions. Yet, at the climactic moment, just when it appears that Lui, having flooded the stage with the whole world doing his dance, having driven Moi, naked and virtually engulfed by the dialectic, into a barrel, and with the daring immorality and the sheer brilliance of his last personification – the ultimate pantomime in which 'servir les grands' literally means prostitution and gaining Moi's approval means changing sex – was on the verge of winning the day, suddenly the Nephew recalls in a despairing, bathetic outburst that his wife has died, leaving him to fend for himself without her income; then the bell strikes the half-hour, marking the end of this stage of the agon and announcing the start of the opera, so that instantly both dancer-actors return to their original 'positions'. However much Alceste has been finding himself tacitly involved in the compromises of Philinte, and however difficult for the Ant to extricate herself from the temptations of the Grasshopper, Moi has never really admitted to any identity other than his enlightened philosophical one (B), nor can the Nephew indefinitely play the role of his deceased wife, so that normal appearances are almost automatically restored for the final lines, the last of which speaks of laughter: 'Rira bien qui rira le dernier.'

IV

Le Neveu de Rameau resounds with echoes of Diderot's other creations, suggesting connections that it might be intriguing to investigate. As was mentioned earlier, the *Lettre sur les sourds et muets* looks like a seedbed, or preliminary dry run, for the dizzying language displays, tippings and border crossings between media that occur in the later satire. Gesture, enthusiastically explored but eventually dropped in the earlier work, now comes superbly into its own, taking centre stage, seeming to leave words miles behind. Music, obviously another featured topic of the *Lettre*, is given a partly ironic 'apothéose de la musique', with concert performances by all sorts of voices and instruments, eventually pushing this art to the limit of its expression, perhaps even beyond. Visual representation, another earlier concern, is less emphasised, yet it too turns up in suggestions of stage scenery and scene changes, which, in the Nephew's opera pantomime, accelerate as if going out of control. As for the language of words, verbal expression may often seem to defer to performances in other media, yet these theatrics are usually conveyed in verbal descriptions,[78] so that eventually words come out on top of everything else. Thus, the relations between the various arts so tentatively put to the test in the earlier work reach fulfilment in the later one.

There is a downside to the comparison, however, in that the superb accomplishment of the later work tends by comparison to diminish the daring of the open-ended experiments of the earlier texts, making them, unjustly, appear quaint and ill-formed, mere precursors by contrast. In fact *Le Neveu de Rameau* is generally not concerned with the basic issues which constituted

---

78. To be sure, there is an important exception to this verbal hegemony in the music mentioned in the text, whose notes are supposed to be heard in the reader's imagination – thus going beyond the confines of words.

the prime matter of the *Lettre*. Even when, exceptionally in *Le Neveu de Rameau*, the Nephew does take up the elementary task of defining 'le chant' in relation to 'la déclamation' (p.78-79) and goes on to find the origins of musical expressivity in 'le cri animal de la nature' (p.86-87), this is no experiment taking place, as would have occurred in the earlier work: the final answers are known in advance and instantly supplied for the listener, so that the discussion can move on to other things. The hot topics of the *Lettre* have cooled off enough to provide resources for exploitation, instead of being viewed as problems or questions of interest in themselves. All this is the long way round to saying simply that the same questions are no longer interesting in the same way in the two works: the early ones are not really pertinent later on. And though the *Lettre sur les sourds et muets* was indeed the original, indispensable seedbed without which *Le Neveu de Rameau* could not have occurred, time, indeed much of a lifetime, has intervened and meanwhile the author, the world and art have naturally been evolving.

The same double (positive–negative) conclusion is reached if one returns to consider *Le Rêve de d'Alembert*, which is also indispensable to *Le Neveu de Rameau*, if not as a previous stage, then certainly because it makes manifest the implicit philosophical context of everything in the latter work. The moral issues which were dispatched in just a few dense pages in *Le Rêve* come fully into their own in *Le Neveu de Rameau*, and are developed beyond expectation. That expansion is, in fact, where the downside begins, for the moral issues, embodied in Lui, turn almost uncontrollably problematic, in a way that would never have occurred while the authoritarian Bordeu was in charge, and the only objections were left in the hands of a still ignorant and slightly giddy d'Alembert, and Mlle de Lespinasse. Whereas *Le Rêve* was a rigorous, positively oriented exposition of doctrine, the other is an apparently uncontrolled exploration of the moral underside of the principles, a discussion where relevant questions cannot simply be ruled out – in the way, for example, that Mlle de Lespinasse did with the fantasy of creating new races of goat-men. In the long run the relationship between the two works – however identical their philosophical bases – turns into something that has aspects of a contrariety,[79] perhaps even a parody, the exalted, inspiring 'scientific' insights of the *Rêve* being set against the jungle of devouring species of the other, a world in which civilisation, in a decadent, artificial sense, has taken over, 'natural' family values are not allowed much play, and the only conceivable 'redemption' is given as art.

79. See Didier, *La Musique des lumières*, p.367, which discusses the spatial and literary aspects of the opposition between the two works.

In connection with comparisons, scholars have often claimed that the Nephew is the perfect realisation of the ideal actor proposed in *Le Paradoxe sur le comédien*,[80] and certainly the Nephew usually exhibits the total self-control demanded by Diderot's theory. Yet, in *Le Neveu de Rameau* the introduction of improvisation (as opposed to given dramatic texts), of moral issues and musical dimensions, puts such a different spin on the situation that *Le Neveu de Rameau*, particularly in so far as its pantomimes are deliberately derisive, brings the theory of imitation into question as often as it exemplifies its principles.[81] Certainly the *Paradoxe* belongs to the background of the latter work, but only minimally in ways that contribute to its understanding. Comparisons with the *Supplément au Voyage de Bougainville* work the same way: the similarities of their moral concerns prove conclusively that they belong to the same author's universe; the Nephew may even be a parody of the primitive values put forward in the other work. But in the last analysis, the mixtures are so different that the comparison hinders as much as it helps.

All this is to declare, paradoxically, that although *Le Neveu de Rameau* may indeed be viewed as the climax, even the summation, of Diderot's literary life, and although it is the most allusive work he ever created, at the same time it is so intensely self-contained and aesthetically self-sufficient, the causalities that bring each moment of it to life are so absolute, that these other works which certainly belong in its background seldom provide significant keys to its secrets.[82] How different from Rousseau, whose major works were sometimes actually designed to work hand in hand as complements or corollaries one to another. How different, above all, from a writer like Voltaire: no doubt *Candide* is a self-contained masterpiece just as *Le Neveu de Rameau* is; but even so, it is wonderfully revealing to read it in chronological sequence with the other *contes*, or to read it after the *Lettres philosophiques*, or alongside the *Essai sur les mœurs*. Voltaire's works constantly illuminate one another so as to make each more approachable. In respect to the privately conceived and posthumously published *Le Neveu de Rameau* at least, most other fictional works by Diderot seldom do; they get in the way as often as they are helpful, and eventually they play off one another less as sources than as denials. Considered internally, the dynamics of

---

80. Starting with Spitzer, 'The style of Diderot', p.153, which sees the Nephew as being a pendant to the theories of *Le Paradoxe*.

81. For rather different reasons, Michel Foucault also recognised a dichotomy separating the two works. See Benrekassa, 'Diderot, l'absence d'œuvre', p.133. On the Nephew as parody of the theories of *Le Paradoxe*, see Pierre Chartier, 'Le paradoxe de l'entretien', *Cahiers textuel* 11 (1992), p.110.

82. The *Salons* and the *Correspondance* would be among the non-fictional exceptions to the rule I am suggesting.

Le Neveu de Rameau never add up in terms of a conclusion; nor does this dialogue give a sense of completion to Diderot's other major fictional works.

Style

Another special feature of Diderot's writing – found nowhere else in the French Enlightenment – is his prose style. Given the language theories of the age, one might perhaps expect that mimesis would remain the central issue here. But it is also clear that the mimetic dimension of Diderot's style goes distinctly beyond this function as normally practised – even by the great writers who were his contemporaries – and that in addition to simply conveying ideas, Diderot's style is able to give words a mimetic twist making them 'participatory' in a special sense. In *Le Neveu de Rameau* and various other works of Diderot's maturity, the text becomes a perpetual onomatopœia (to use Spitzer's term).[83] Sometimes words seem to be imitating the thinking process that called them into being. Thus in Diderot's rhythms one may feel an idea coming to the surface, taking shape, gathering strength, breaking full force and then retreating – such as one does with Mme Diderot's nasty caricature of the Van Loo portrait.[84] Elsewhere, the text is not so much an imitation of the thinking process as a representation of the thing designated, as though the act of naming automatically summoned all the appropriate sounds and rhythms to project the object or experience that had been brought into words.[85] When the Nephew tells of the insouciant pleasures of relieving oneself, he naturally, automatically, does so with suitably rhythmic impulses, and naturally again, when he speaks of the essential solitude and poverty of the moment of death, the rhythms are appropriate for that topic as well.

As a parallel one might think of the way in which Bach automatically has the singer rise to a high note at the word 'hoch', or rumble down to the lower depths at the mention of hell. The point of Bach's imitations is not merely picturesque entertainment, but rather to make the sacred word reach out to involve the listener actively, rendering the text so vivid and compelling that one is constrained to pay heed. Curiously, we might say something similar about the experience of reading Diderot, whose syllabic mimesis is certainly of the active variety, reaching out, forcing the reader – for distinctly unspiritual reasons – to hear and see.

83. This point, though developed differently, is a major one in Spitzer's analysis, 'The style of Diderot'; see p.139f., p.164.

84. Spitzer stresses particularly the erotic aspect of these rhythms ('The style of Diderot', p.140).

85. Spitzer, 'The style of Diderot', p.173, n.2, writes of Diderot's 'acoustic rendering of feelings'.

One of the most virtuosic examples occurs in the middle of the grand operatic pantomime:

Avec des joues renflées et bouffies, et un son rauque et sombre, il rendoit les cors et les bassons: il prenait un son éclatant et nazillard pour les hautbois; précipitant sa voix avec une rapidité incroyable, pour les instruments à cordes dont il cherchoit les sons les plus approchés; il siffloit les petites flûtes; il recouloit les traversières, criant, chantant, se demenant comme un forcéné.[86]

Not only does the Nephew imitate, but the text itself imitates the imitation: the penetrating yet drawling sounds of the word 'nazillard', so perfectly suited to the oboe; the whistling cluster of fricatives, labials and dentals for the piccolos ('siffloit les petites flûtes'), the cooing 'recouloit' for the flutes; with a bit of imagination one can hear the bassoons and horns combining, too, in 'rauque' and 'sombre', while the syllables of 'précipitant sa voix avec une rapidité incroyable' rush by with exactly the same unbelievable haste as the notes of the strings are said to do. But all this is not simply an isolated virtuoso display, it is generally symptomatic. Diderot's prose not only imitates flutes and violins, but the thousand-and-one different intonations of the Nephew's voice (more obviously so than Diderot's): sarcasm, playful banter, impatience, indignation, irony, defensiveness, *hauteur*, hatred, good humour, bad humour, self-pity, enthusiasm, *désinvolture* and all the degrees and combinations thereof that belong to the intonation of great clowns. This performative quality makes Diderot's prose style unique among the great writers of the period, who generally indulged in syllabic onomatopoeia far less, even as they preserved the characteristics of their authorial voice far more. To be sure, the fact that Diderot can do performatively with his prose what the Nephew does with his voice and gestures is further evidence of the ideal suitability of the Nephew's character (such as the author imagines him) for Diderot's style, a conjunction that contributes not a little to the perfection of the dialogue.

The art of this satire

Even as this work is comedy, the experience of it remains, as Dieckmann stated long ago in *Cinq leçons sur Diderot*, a theatrical one. This means that it has been a privileged event which could only take place within certain confines, under special circumstances, and that however much true persons and events are present or alluded to, everything one sees and hears ultimately, as the performance ends, turns into a metaphor of truth in the way that Classical

86. P.84. Cf. the commentary by Sylvette Milliot, 'Violons et violinistes dans l'œuvre de Diderot et dans l'*Encyclopédie*', *Diderot, les beaux-arts et la musique* (Aix-en-Provence 1986), p.294.

plays do, rather than remaining reality in the raw. In some ways the text itself gives a different impression. The reader is convinced at least that he or she has been imagining real people with real emotions and attitudes regarding real things. The whole texture of the satire appears woven from actual experience, and furthermore abundant scholarly documentation has patiently ferreted out exactly what many of these experiences were. This basis in 'reality' contributes enormously to the pleasure of the dialogue: the sense it gives of hearing exactly the way people spoke, of knowing the topics they talked about and seeing their gestures, the sense of life that is recorded in every syllable we read.

It is equally evident that these 'realities' have all been transformed as they were absorbed, or imagined and restated in this satire as *comedy*. Furthermore, the special manner whereby the transformation took place, has been charted with exemplary clarity by the Nephew. I refer once again to his paradigm of the way everything in society begins with the need to eat (ultimate universal reality), a need so imperative that it creates dependence (second reality), which in turn produces the constrained posturings of the have-nots as they seek to supply their wants from the haves (p.103-104):

Mais s'il est dans la nature d'avoir appétit; car c'est toujours à l'appétit que j'en reviens, à la sensation qui m'est toujours présente, je trouve qu'il n'est pas du bon ordre de n'avoir pas toujours de quoi manger. Que diable d'oeconomie, des hommes qui regorgent de tout, tandis que d'autres qui ont un estomac importun comme eux, et pas de quoi mettre sous la dent. Le pis, c'est la posture de contrainte où nous tient le besoin. L'homme nécessiteux ne marche pas comme un autre; il saute, il rampe, il se tortille, il se traîne; il passe sa vie à prendre des positions.

Already taking on life in the enumerative rhythms of the last sentence one senses incipiently the movements of a dance: 'il saute, il rampe, il se tortille, il se traîne', postures which are given further choreographic specification in the terms of the conclusion: 'prendre des positions'.[87] Thus, the final result of this argument (as the Nephew is about to demonstrate) is the creation of art, a comic sort of dance. At the same time, however, it may also seem that the humour of this choreographic event is occurring under the most unlikely circumstances imaginable.

Obviously nothing is inherently funny about hunger, or about the demeaning necessity of, in effect, begging from others, much less the slavish sort of behaviour the Nephew proposes. Yet the Nephew's dance-pantomimes are hysterically funny, 'à mourir de rire' (p.106), to quote the frequently solemn narrator. One of the profound implications of the Nephew's analysis is that

87. On the technical meaning of these terms see the Fabre edition, p.237-38, n.316, and the Bonnet edition, p.37-38.

the mirth of these pantomimes derives from, and is a function of, the hardship underlying them. It might be tempting to recall in this context how the rictus of pain can be identical to its opposite, the grimace of laughter. The Nephew does not actually employ such an image; yet the whole point of his analysis is to reveal how distress can be made, through contrivance and art, to produce its opposite: mirth. In sum, the realities of life, and most particularly its direst needs, are what yield – through the principle of contrariety and the discipline of art – comedy, and make everything in this text satire.[88]

Throughout the dialogue, nothing except – occasionally – music is allowed to stay serious for long, nothing is sacred: Diderot's tear-jerking sentimental anecdote is immediately cut across by mockery; the climactic musical moment, the breathtaking rendering of Jommelli's *Lamentations*,[89] is finally undercut by ridiculousness. The poignance of the Nephew's failure at poetical creation becomes tinged with irony, suggesting something of the frog trying to be an ox, or at least so one assumes from Moi's icy reaction to it, and also from Lui's own pantomime of the disdainful grimaces on the face of Nature as she created such a ridiculous object as himself (p.96). Most astonishing, the horrors of the Renégat d'Avignon devolve into a pantomime-dance, one so witty that Moi cannot forestall intermittent impulses of laughter. Thus, this work is satirical and comic in the broadest and deepest sense, to its essence. If sentimentality is not allowed much scope and cuts off brusquely when it does appear, one might say that, however much it informs the general mixture, it is doomed to exclusion by the brittle necessities of the satirical texture.

Perhaps Moi's indignation may appear to stand outside the generally comic mode of the dialogue, for Moi is determined to be taken seriously: his denunciations are supposedly heartfelt and uncalculated (in contrast to the Nephew), nor are they intended to be laughable. But of course, as Spitzer suggested long ago, albeit in rather different contexts, the Nephew is ready to bring everything that Moi stands for into question and into mockery.[90] Such was at least the unconscious reason why Diderot (re-)created Lui as parody:

88. I count myself among the admirers of the conclusion of Spitzer's great essay, 'The style of Diderot', in which he inverts a line from Victor Hugo, observing that it gives the essence of Diderot's satire: 'On fait du radieux avec du ténébreux'. In the present context, however, it is important to note that Spitzer was concerned with 'le ténébreux' only in so far as it applied personally and aesthetically to Lui and Moi; he did not see the social dimensions which are the main concern of the present analysis.

89. See above, n.66.

90. In this connection, two fragments of Spitzer's comments seem especially pertinent: 'It is as if [Diderot] has created the nephew out of the doubtful material of his own artistic nature, as a gesture of rejection and condemnation' (p.156), and 'In that parody of the nephew which was a parody of himself [...]' (p.167).

so that he could flout, desecrate, deny and try to unravel the philosopher's own most sacred precepts, making them part of the comedy, too. At the same time, on a less visible level, the fact that Lui is also intimately connected with Diderot's feelings and doubts – so much so that he sometimes acts as the merest extension of Diderot's thoughts – testifies, as well, to the seriousness and difficulties of the issues dividing and uniting them, and which, naturally, can never be laid to rest, only enacted.[91]

Genesis

When all is said and done, the unforthcomingness of the dialogue about final moral answers is so absolute – 'Rira bien qui rira le dernier' – that it has tempted scholars to search outside the text for guidance. Nothing is known for certain about the genesis of this satire; its creation remains a mystery, perhaps even a secret. Given the seriousness of the questionings that form the essence of the work, it might seem logical to perceive *Le Neveu de Rameau* as reflecting a particular crisis in Diderot's life. Multitudes of scholars have done so, most often as a corollary to the famous 'revenge theory': they postulate that Diderot underwent a 'crisis in pessimism' during the early 1760s, the aftermath of the humiliations of the Palissot Affair (for which *Le Neveu de Rameau* is allegedly Diderot's reprisal), along with Diderot's disappointments in the theatre, and still amid the continuing tedium and perils of the publication of the *Encyclopédie*. Following the logic of this theory, it is sometimes argued that the pantomime of the Nephew's failed inspiration actually enacts Diderot's own self-doubts and disillusions.

The theory has been masterfully argued;[92] it has been sanctioned by generations of scholars; its main origins go back to Goethe.[93] But even so, and

---

91. Despite my enduring admiration for his essay, I disagree fundamentally with Spitzer's conclusion that the dialogue (especially through the person of the Nephew) reflects Diderot's experience of the 'self-annihilation of the self-igniting mind', and that one should be 'grateful' that his satire is a 'warning of the danger of expressivity when it severs its ties with Logos' ('The style of Diderot', p.167). Despite Spitzer's eloquence, I am not at all convinced that uncontrolled expressivity and Logos are the central issues here. But in any case, it is clear that the conclusion of Diderot's dialogue is not a warning, but a question (or questions) left open.

92. The classic interpretation is by Georges May, 'L'angoisse de l'échec et la genèse du *Neveu de Rameau*', *Diderot studies* 3 (1961), p.285-307. The evidence presented in Jean-Claude Bonnet's edition, p.19-20, tends towards the same conclusions.

93. 'Goethe isole un noyau qu'il considère comme primitif: le scandale occasionné par la comédie des *Philosophes*, cherche à définir une intention première: la polémique contre Palissot et ses pareils, puis, rend compte de tout le reste par la théorie des révisions ou des rédactions successives. Avouons franchement, qu'après un siècle et demi d'exégèse, la critique du *Neveu de Rameau* procède toujours de la même méthode et n'est guère plus avancée' (Fabre, p.xxviii). The introductions by Chouillet and Bonnet to their editions take this same tack, along with virtually every other editor of the text, except Henri Coulet.

despite its ostensible plausibility, there are compelling reasons to reject the interpretation. The evidence is all circumstantial, and many of the pertinent facts actually point towards other conclusions. However large the cluster of dates relating to 1760-1762,[94] and suggesting this period as the original time of composition, the action of the text refuses to stay within these confines, and wanders over the borderlines with complacent vicissitudes that draw one away from the 1760-1762 time-frame. As was noticed earlier, sometimes the action is situated while the great Rameau is alive, and sometimes – with no warning, and no indication that the author notices the change – after his death (in 1764). Sometimes the Nephew's son is spoken of as alive with his doting father watching over his education; at other times (the 'prologue', and during the Nephew's laments over his fall from grace, p.19) there is no son in the picture: the Nephew is portrayed as living entirely alone, as if another unprepared, back-and-forth shift in the chronology had taken place. In the 'prologue' we are told that the Nephew has gained entry to various houses where he is fed on condition that he will not speak without special permission. Later on, *chez* Bertin, at whose table the Nephew has gained entry, there is no question of any such stipulation; at table, the Nephew pointedly speaks whenever he pleases. These vicissitudes suggest a conception that deliberately forgoes a single, or even a principal, temporal centre: Diderot's centre is everywhere and nowhere.

For the rest, other dates for the original inspiration of the text are just as likely as 1760-1762: for scholars whose training is in literature it may be difficult to imagine that the 'origin' of a text might be non-literary. But actually, an even more plausible starting point for this text would be the musical discussions of 'La Querelle des bouffons'. And here, as musicologists have noted in various other contexts,[95] even though a number of allusions to concerts and musicians relate to the 1760s, another cluster of dates,[96] and above all the provocative tone of the discussions of French versus Italian music, point to an earlier period: the time of the 'Querelle' at its hottest, the early 1750s. Given the importance of the Nephew's musical background, it is at least a likely possibility that the origins of *Le Neveu de Rameau*, instead of being Diderot's alleged literary disappointments, were real conversations with a real musician, going back to the 'Querelle' at the time when everyone was

94. See the documentation in the edition by Chouillet, p.10-11, and in the Fabre edition, p.xxxiif.

95. Daniel Heartz, without reaching the same conclusion I am proposing, first pointed out this discrepancy to me. See also the discussion of the Nephew's musical anachronism in Durand-Sendrail, *La Musique de Diderot*, p.61.

96. See Durand-Sendrail, *La Musique de Diderot*, p.19.

talking about it. To be sure, the allusion to Duni's *Peintre amoureux de son modèle* (p.80) indicates 1757; the Bemetzrieder anecdote (p.91) allegedly moves the time to 1769, at the earliest. Other groups of events relate to the 1770s. The authentic title of this dialogue is *Satire seconde*, and the satire which is numbered *first*, that is, the one entitled *Satire première*, dates from no earlier than 1773, suggesting another possible year for the redaction of the dialogue, as Henri Coulet has pointed out.[97]

In sum, given the unfixed time-frame and the multiple possibilities that the dates might imply, the one conclusion which remains sure is that the presumed origin of the text cannot objectively be confined to any one period: the myriad references and allusions to specific people and events – so precise, so contradictory[98] – make it impossible to pin the text down. The author's blatant disregard for the rules of fair play, the rules by which one might conceivably reach legitimate conclusions concerning the moment(s) of origin of the text, render postulations pointless, if not counter-productive. Diderot has in fact masterfully covered his tracks – probably through inadvertence, as he attended to the vibrancy of the eternal present which makes the text so intensely compelling.[99]

The 'revenge theory' also draws on quantities of circumstantial evidence and has been accepted by virtually everyone since Goethe invented it. Diderot did in fact undergo (at a distance) the humiliation of being pilloried in Palissot's miserable comedy, *Les Philosophes* (1760), on the stage of the Comédie-Française, in performances facilitated by Mlle Hus. No doubt the play was discussed and 'edited' by Bertin and his guests, with the 'scène du colporteur' being contributed by the Nephew himself, just as Lui describes it. Even so, it is clear that the text of Diderot's satire simply does not function as a revenge: it is not a satire in that sense;[100] it does not serve transitively as a personal

97. DPV, xii.35. Professor Coulet also cites numerous other allusions in the text which do not fit the 1760-1762 time-frame.

98. Jean-Claude Bonnet writes of 'l'extraordinaire brouillage systématique des repères du temps dans *Le Neveu de Rameau*'. He sees this phenomenon – surely correctly – as showing how much this dialogue is 'adressé exclusivement à l'avenir', 'Diderot et la postérité', *Cahiers textuel* 11 (1992), p.129. Though Jean Fabre does not interpret the phenomenon in the way I do, he also has written: 'Dans sa conception même, le *Neveu de Rameau* se moque de la chronologie et de la vraisemblance toute matérielle qui en résulte' (p.xxxviii).

99. Once again in the blurring of chronology one perceives parallels with Proust. See Lévi-Strauss, *Regarder écouter lire*, p.9. The main difference is that, as Lévi-Strauss goes on to explain, in Proust dates are never given, whereas – I would add – in Diderot the chronological *points de repère* are almost always identifiable, and certainly would have been recognised by an eighteenth-century Parisian. In his edition of *Le Neveu de Rameau*, p.10, Jean-Claude Bonnet, although supporting the traditional theory of the genesis of the work, finds similar parallels with the Proustian treatment of character.

100. Jean Fabre (p.lv), even though finally yielding to the revenge theory, has masterfully

attack.[101] Diderot's mature fictions never do: obviously, *Le Supplément au Voyage de Bougainville* is not an attack on Bougainville, or even, ultimately, on civilisation; *Jacques le fataliste* is essentially intransitive; *La Religieuse*, being a 'satire des couvents' in the plural, does not aim at anyone in particular. *Le Neveu de Rameau* is a satire not of individuals, but of the morals and manners of an entire society, sublimely impersonated and caricatured by Bertin–Hus and their coterie.[102] The issues at stake point far beyond any private 'jeu de massacre'.[103] For the rest, others have suggested the unlikelihood of Diderot's placing his revenge on Palissot in the hands of someone whose morals he claims, at one stage of the dialectic (B), to repudiate, and doing so in a work he himself would never publish.[104] The later stages of the dialectic, in which the Nephew becomes the whole world (C), and Diderot secretly shares his point of view (D), make the theory still more unlikely.

But the main evidence against the theory is that the 'lesson' of Palissot in

defined the place of *Le Neveu de Rameau* in the traditions of a kind of satire that is essentially not vengeful, but a sort of 'jeu', in this case connected to the traditions of the Saturnalia, and with 'le maître fou Rameau' leading the revellers in their dance (p.xlii-xliii).

101. See Rex, 'Two scenes', p.261-62. My view is even in disagreement with the finely-researched and seductively argued one of Jean-Claude Bonnet, in the introduction to his edition of *Le Neveu de Rameau*, p.11: 'Malgré la manière dense et allusive de Diderot qui refuse l'attaque frontale et publique, une lecture attentive ne laisse rien ignorer des circonstances dans lesquelles fut écrite cette œuvre de réaction à l'expérience traumatisante de la fin des années cinquante. L'encyclopédiste règle élégamment ses comptes à part soi, sans oublier personne.'

102. In a late addition to the last work he (re)published, *Essai sur les règnes de Claude et de Néron* (1782), speaking of himself in the third person singular and looking back over his entire lifetime, Diderot declared that his works never attacked people in particular: 'Il obtient de temps en temps quelques larmes et quelques applaudissements au théâtre; le jugement qu'il porte lui-même de ses autres ouvrages, c'est qu'ils attaquent les erreurs sans attaquer les personnes, et que s'ils n'instruisent pas toujours, ils n'offensent jamais' (DPV, xxv.425). This text was brought to my attention by de Fontenay, *Diderot ou le matérialisme enchanté*, p.31.

103. Sylviane Albertan-Coppola has made this point with perfect clarity: 'la satire des anti-philosophes n'occupe pas une place centrale dans ce dialogue, plutôt tourné vers l'art, la morale, la philosophie et par-dessus tout la personnalité du Neveu' ('Les Antiphilosophes dans *Le Neveu de Rameau*', *Cahiers textuel* 11 (1991), p.33-34). One only wonders why Professor Albertan-Coppola also accepts without question the assumptions of the statement which precedes the above quotation: 'Bien que la comédie de Palissot, *Les Philosophes*, créée en 1760, ait été un facteur déterminant dans la genèse du *Neveu de Rameau*.'

104. See Coulet's edition of *Le Neveu de Rameau*, DPV, xii.35: 'le procédé d'expression qui consistait à faire juger la clique antiphilosophique par l'un de ses suppôts, *Lui*, le parasite Rameau, excluait les mesquineries venimeuses chez *Moi*, interlocuteur et narrateur. Diderot, qui refusait de polémiquer publiquement, ne s'est pas servi d'un ouvrage secret pour insulter ses ennemis.' For the rest the Nephew's derision of himself fundamentally undermines his derision of others. While agreeing with a number of Professor Coulet's interpretations, I do not, for reasons that will presently be made clear, accept his proposal (DPV, xii.35) of 1773-1774 as the date of composition: although it has the advantage of avoiding the false perspectives of the 'revenge theory', its proofs are entirely circumstantial, and in fact arbitrary, making it no more likely than a number of other dates one might have chosen.

this text goes in a direction opposite to revenge: following the precepts of Diderot's materialism, the 'lesson' lies in Diderot's effort to accept such a treacherous person as part of the natural order, as a phenomenon resulting from the necessity that informs everything, and for which ultimately no one is to blame. The Nephew's arguments on this point are so persuasive, that Moi actually agrees to accept them: Palissot is only acting according to his nature as scoundrel, rather as the Nephew is doing, in his way.[105] In short, Diderot's materialism is not a good seedbed for personal resentments and revenge: in so far as individuals are concerned, everything in it tends both psychologically and philosophically towards understanding and acceptance – however regretful and painfully problematic.

It may sound as though my argument plays down the significance for this text of Diderot's public humiliation at the hands of Palissot, or of the discouragements, difficulties and even persecutions he underwent during the early 1760s. In fact the inference is true in so far as I reject entirely the classic interpretation of this dialogue as an act of revenge on, a settling of accounts with, or even an answer to Diderot's opponents. My argument is simply that, given the lack of evidence concerning the genesis of this satire, the unsettled chronology, the breadth and significance of the moral and social issues that were Diderot's main concern, and the inherent tendencies of Diderot's philosophy towards tolerance, one cannot conclude that certain events, rather than others, made Diderot write it: one cannot assume that specific attacks, or the 'crisis in pessimism' of the 1760s,[106] and not other attacks or moments, perhaps a whole host of them, were the ones that gave the text its conception. My point is that this satire, with its temporal meanderings and references to events that are early, middle and late, brings not just some things, but almost everything, into a final focus.

In sum, I am claiming that this work is comic in almost exactly the way *Le Misanthrope* is: all the issues it raises are potentially serious, in fact they could not be more so, just as Hegel saw – although obviously for other reasons. Throughout this satire the issues brought into light are those that Diderot cared about most deeply – everything except love (another parallel with Villon),

---

105. See Rex, 'Two scenes', p.261-62. Assuming from the start that Diderot is taking revenge on Palissot through the Nephew, Jean Starobinski, 'Sur l'emplois du chiasme dans "Le Neveu de Rameau"', *Revue de métaphysique et de morale* 89 (1984), p.183-91, analyses a number of relevant passages in an appropriately transitive sense, contrary to my own. One may note, however, that the chiasmas so carefully scrutinised in this article are actually quite ambivalent as to outcome and final direction, and in fact Starobinski's analyses are just as pertinent and telling when interpreted in the intransitive sense I am proposing.

106. On this point I agree entirely with Henri Coulet: 'En aucune façon l'œuvre ne trahit cette angoisse de l'échec qu'on a voulu y voir en datant de 1761 sa première rédaction' (DPV, xii.36).

which flickers only briefly in the text, and which is otherwise substituted by the enthralment and passion of art. Certainly one would agree that the humiliations of the Palissot Affair are woven into the texture of this dialogue, as are the injustices of a social system based on birth and privilege, and so are the weaknesses and dangers of a philosophy that finally had no objective moral categories by which to condemn anything as inherently evil. Even as the Fables of La Fontaine contained all the stresses and frictions of seventeenth-century society, this dialogue contains the makings of a lifetime of discontents and disappointments. Like some mysterious pearl that grew – we know not how – to perfection, it now gives back the hard-won experience of a person, and of a time in history. And just as in Molière (however different the mixture and proportion) these issues, woven deeply into the texture, are the seriousness of this work, the things that make it so intensely moving, and wise – but especially so because everything – every word, gesture and song – has been turned, via the method of contrariety that the Nephew so exactly describes, into glorious comedy. This is the reason why the dialogue is so uproarious, an explosion of gaiety to which nothing else compares in the century, at least not before Beaumarchais. As one savours the pleasures of the satire, it is difficult to lend credence to the 'revenge on Palissot' theory: for if this work is about anything, it is about how droll life can seem, especially if one joins hands in circle with the Nephew, with Diderot and Mlle Hus, with all their friends and enemies, for the last *branle*.

Conclusions

There's a dialectic in many of [these] works that is
uniquely palpable [...] If they give joy, it is a joy
intensified by the surmounting of conflict.

David Sylvester, on Brancusi

CONTRARIETY, like the paradox, or the dialogue in which it was so often
comfortably intertwined, was one of the modes that enabled Diderot to think.
It not only fostered the conception and development of ideas, but served as a
liberating force, to free him from himself, or from others through denial. His
most enduring works (the *Salons, Jacques le fataliste, Le Neveu de Rameau, Le
Rêve de d'Alembert*, even *La Religieuse*[1]) are all, in very different ways,
prominently marked by this mode, which is to say that it was the agent of
some of his most astounding insights and conferred on these writings their
unique exuberance; in fact, in so far as contrariety formed part of an action–
reaction process, it became the life of the text. In the early *Lettre sur les sourds
et muets* one finds Diderot searching for ways to recover the energy smothered
by abstraction, the vitality lost through the civilising process. Thinking via
contrariety served a similar function by creating dynamic new alternatives to
the rationality of normal discourse. Though contrariety alone did not guarantee
success, generally speaking, when in his fictional works Diderot deliberately
tried to suppress this mode of thinking – his *drames* being the prime example –
the result was a deadening of the natural responsiveness of the thought process.
The life of the text was forced into a detour, and had to come, rather
ponderously and turgidly, through dramatic conventions and modes of sentimentality.

With Classical forms such as a château or a garden, if one sees one half the
building and grounds the principles of symmetry usually enable one to divine
the other half, even as, in a play by Racine, one can often foretell the fatal
outcome long in advance. In contrast, Diderot's major works are never
structured this way, not even *Le Rêve de d'Alembert*: reading Diderot it is often
difficult to see ahead or around the corner; there are no large symmetries to
help with predictions. The exhilaration of his work is the feeling he conveys
of an absence of such givens: the sense that the events of the past may not at

1. See Rex, *The Attraction of the contrary*, p.125-35.

all tie down the present, which in fact is – in so far as it remains stationary long enough to be defined – a space of endless potentialities, of unknowns waiting to happen. Even when there are predictables – the Master's watch and Jacques's 'gourde' in *Jacques le fataliste*, the prim responses of Moi to Lui's lack of morals in *Le Neveu de Rameau*, the punishments endured by Suzanne – they are almost always decoys in the sense that they give a false feeling of regularity in a context where drastic irregularity is apt to intervene. Naturally, contrary to the structures of French Classicism, Diderot's greatest works never reach true conclusions. Diderot's thought was created and predestined to go onward, not to stop: *La Religieuse* tries to have an ending, but becomes incomprehensible; the 'shaggy-dog' conclusion of *Jacques le fataliste* leaves the choice of a continuation up to the reader; the last words of *Le Neveu de Rameau* deliberately leave the door open; even Bordeu's blustery exit after the encyclopaedic colloquies of *Le Rêve de d'Alembert* does not preclude a return visit, with lots more conversation, the next time d'Alembert spends a restless night. Such fundamentally un-Classical modes of writing again suggest why Diderot's *drames* – with their deliberate conformity to the rules of the unities and their gestures towards Classical structures – are so much less successful than the works which go along with Diderot's 'natural' mode, one which implies the apparent absence of an outside, pre-crafted framework, and instead involves a texture that seems spontaneously to create itself from within.

But how is it possible that such an aesthetic – an aesthetic of freely evolving structures, of surprise and unexpectedness, of spontaneous liberations and *disponibilité* – can have sprung from such a determined materialist, someone whose whole philosophy called for cause-and-effect predictability and rational structurings? No doubt Diderot would have replied, as he did in the *Supplément au Voyage de Bougainville*, that 'tout est dans la nature', including his own unpredictable impulses. Yet such an answer really sidesteps the question, for even if everything that is is ultimately natural, this is no explanation of the existence in him of an illogical gap between philosophy and aesthetics, when other certified materialists, remaining truer to their principles, managed to do without one: d'Holbach and Helvétius produced writings that are in no way surprising, or freely evolving, or liberating. Indeed, their systematic productions, grimly based on the cause-and-effect principles of their philo-sophy, have virtually none of Diderot's ingratiating aesthetic qualities. For the moment, the question must remain open.

Of all French writers the one whom Diderot most resembles is Montaigne, if only because Montaigne's thought too is essentially an evolvement which cannot be fixed in time, a thought that in the deepest sense belongs to change, and in which the whole idea of 'expérience', as Jules Brody has reminded us,[2] is fundamentally underwoven by contrariety. Given such similarities – and of course there are many more, in terms of personality traits and moral outlook as well – it may appear something of an anomaly that Diderot mentions Montaigne so seldom – far less frequently than he mentions either Horace, another writer for whom he obviously felt a deep personal affinity, or Racine, whom he admired, so to speak, from afar.

Part of the explanation may lie in the fact that Montaigne took as his principal doctrine for examination, explication and justification what for Diderot had to be at least partly an unconscious, unexamined process, namely, the changeability of himself and his thoughts. Diderot's was a kind of thinking which required for its existence that he remain blind to this aspect of it. Thus while Montaigne deliberately brought into daylight the shiftings of his perceptions, Diderot endlessly wrote dialogues where he could pretend that the other side of his thought was somehow external to himself, or, as so notably in the *Salons*, that his thoughts belonged to an associative mode of discourse, one thing just sliding into another, a situation so ill-defined that it allowed veerings in opposite directions, with no necessity to acknowledge the change of tack. Whenever Diderot did take cognisance of his own changeability, the usual way was to state it as a generality (his head was like a weathervane), or as materialistic philosophy, through which he recognised himself as belonging to the eternal flux of everything. But these general moments of self-awareness do not seem to have penetrated very deeply into his writing processes: all the great reversals of his mature fictions remain unperceived.

This is simply another way of stating that Diderot, the most public and extroverted of *philosophes*, editor of the biggest of the Enlightenment's projects of popularisation, who in his literary creations could hardly conceive of the act of writing without imagining some correspondent or dialogist at the other end – as though literature required an out-loud dimension of communication in order to exist – was also the most strangely private of the *philosophes*, not only because he preferred not to print his major fictions during his lifetime, but in the sense that he remained deaf, dumb and blind to the essentials of his own thinking processes and to the nature of his own genius. Such blindness is unthinkable in the creative processes of d'Holbach and Helvétius, whose philosophies were entirely conscious productions that had no other dimension. This is the reason why Diderot has a gap where they do not. And in fact Diderot's peculiarly liberating kind of 'désinvolture', all his surprising, contradictory impulses and secret thought processes, would be difficult, pro-

---

2. *Nouvelles lectures de Montaigne* (Paris 1994), p.151, p.171.

Figure 9. Joseph Vernet, *Clair de lune*

bably impossible, to categorise as 'philosophy', even if one used Diderot's own rather freewheeling 'Système figuré des connaissances humaines' in the *Encyclopédie* as a measuring stick. At the same time – and perhaps this is the main answer to all the questions I have been posing – such dimensions are easily the marks of a poet,[3] certainly marks of an artist, and, in Diderot's case, one whose privacy and daring are particularly appealing to our own age, raised, as we have been, in the conviction that artistic genius is always out of kilter with, and seeing beyond, its own time. Particularly in so far as the counterpoints of contrariety are involved, Diderot's modes of thought are only secondarily 'philosophical'; their primary strain – Diderot's title to glory – relates to art, in the modern sense. Since Diderot preferred to think of himself essentially as a philosopher, 'Monsieur le philosophe', he was apt to feel somehow, reviewing his own accomplishments, that lasting achievement still waited around the corner, and recognition would be delayed until the judgement of posterity.

For us the suspense is over, and no doubts or hesitations seem possible as Diderot, artist and poet, casts his spell – this time a night scene out of Vernet (Figure 9), in which the moonlit calm is rendered even fuller and more intense by a faint, subliminal awareness of the potential elements of violence and fear included in the scene, but which, like the storm-clouds above or the ruddy glow of the fire below, are being held in suspension, circumscribed, made benign in the tranquillity of the setting. Their slightly disturbing, contrapuntal presence – like the unmixed colours of certain impressionist painters – powerfully deepens the calm even as it gives Diderot's prose its special feeling of tension and concentration. I always choose to conceive of these contrary elements as separate, in order to imagine more easily the free play of the dynamics. In the present instance, those who prefer unified fusions may want to apply Diderot's – and Burke's – own term, and simply call the description 'sublime':

La lune élevée sur l'horizon et à demi cachée dans des nuées épaisses et noires, un ciel tout à fait orageux et obscur, occupe le centre du tableau, et teint de sa lumière pâle et faible et le rideau qui l'offusque et la surface de la mer qu'elle domine. On voit à droite, une fabrique; proche de cette fabrique, sur un plan plus avancé sur le devant les débris d'un pilotis. Un peu plus vers la gauche et le fond, une nacelle à la proue de

3. Needless to say I am not the first to notice this quality in Diderot: see, for example, the Jean Fabre edition of *Le Neveu de Rameau*, p.lxxxi and Jacques Chouillet, *Diderot poète de l'énergie* (Paris 1984). As Diderot himself noted late in life: 'J'ai voulu être un philosophe, et la Nature m'avait destiné à être poète.' Quoted by Roland Mortier in 'Diderot au carrefour de la poésie et de la philosophie', *Le Cœur et la raison: recueil d'études sur le dix-huitième siècle* (Oxford 1990), p.166.

laquelle un marinier tient une torche allumée. Cette nacelle vogue vers le pilotis. Plus encore sur le fond et presque en plaine mer, un vaisseau à la voile et faisant route vers la fabrique; puis une étendue de mer obscure, illimitée [...]

Je ne sais ce que je louerai de préférence dans ce morceau. Est-ce le reflet de la lune sur ces eaux ondulantes? sont-ce ces nuées sombres et chargées de leur mouvement? est-ce ce vaisseau qui passe au-devant de l'astre de la nuit et qui le renvoie et l'attache à son immense éloignement? Est-ce la réflexion dans le fluide, de la petite torche que ce marin tient à l'extrémité de la nacelle? sont-ce les deux figures adossées à la fontaine? est-ce le brasier dont la lueur rougeâtre se propage sur tous les objets environnants, sans détruire l'harmonie? est-ce l'effet total de cette nuit? Est-ce cette belle masse de lumière qui colore les proéminences de cette roche, et dont la vapeur se mêle à la partie des nuages auxquels elle se réunit?

On dit de ce tableau, que c'est le plus beau de Vernet, parce que, c'est toujours le dernier ouvrage de ce grand maître qu'on appelle le plus beau. Mais encore une fois, il faut le voir. L'effet de ces deux lumières, ces lieux, ces nuées, ces ténèbres qui couvrent tout et laissent tout voir; la terreur et la vérité de cette scène auguste, tout cela se sent fortement et ne se décrit point.[4]

4. '7eme Tableau (de Vernet)', *Salon de 1767*, DPV, xvi.225-26.

Index